The Chile Pepper Bible

The Chile Pepper Bible

From Sweet to Fiery & Everything in Between

250 RECIPES

Judith Finlayson

Robert ROSE

For complete cataloguing information, see page 439.

Disclaimer
The recipes in this book have been carefully tested by our kitchen and our tasters. To the best of our knowledge, they are safe and nutritious for ordinary use and users. For those people with food or other allergies, or who have special food requirements or health issues, please read the suggested contents of each recipe carefully and determine whether or not they may create a problem for you. All recipes are used at the risk of the consumer.

We cannot be responsible for any hazards, loss or damage that may occur as a result of any recipe use.

For those with special needs, allergies, requirements or health problems, in the event of any doubt, please contact your medical adviser prior to the use of any recipe.

Design and production: Kevin Cockburn/PageWave Graphics Inc.
Editor: Tina Anson Mine
Copy editor/proofreader: Jennifer D. Foster
Recipe testers: Audrey King, Meredith Dees
Indexer: Beth Zabloski
Cover and recipe photographer: Colin Erricson
Associate photographer: Matt Johannsson
Food styling: Michael Elliott
Prop styling: Charlene Erricson

Additional photography: Parts 1, 2 and 3 openers © istockphoto.com/matthewennisphotography; Chapter openers paper background © istockphoto.com/SvetlanaK; Moreovers paper background © istockphoto.com/tomograf; Extra recipes paper background © istockphoto.com/SvetlanaK; Wood background © istockphoto.com/Juhku; page 1 © istockphoto.com/EddWestmacott; page 2 © shutterstock.com/Chen WS; page 5 © istockphoto.com/Yuri_Arcurs; page 6 © istockphoto.com/Young777; page 8 © shutterstock.com/DC_Aperture; page 10 © istockphoto.com/jpll2002; page 12 © istockphoto.com/laughingmango; page 16 © istockphoto.com/FredFroese; page 18 © istockphoto.com/kentarus; page 19 © istockphoto.com/lmjp; page 22 © istockphoto.com/holgs; page 24 © istockphoto.com/patronestaff; page 28 © istockphoto.com/hadynyah; page 31 © istockphoto.com/Sasha64; page 32 © istockphoto.com/vikif; page 34 © istockphoto.com/LanaCanada; page 36 © istockphoto.com/OscarEspinosa; page 37 Datil pepper on the plant © Dave DeWitt; page 38 © istockphoto.com/tella_db; page 39 © shutterstock.com/mircea dobre; page 40 Anaheim chile © istockphoto.com/Cabezonication; page 40 Banana peppers © istockphoto.com/yodaswaj; page 40 Bell peppers © istockphoto.com/timsa; page 40 Cayenne peppers © istockphoto.com/StillBrown; page 40 Cherry peppers © istockphoto.com/sndr; page 40 Cubanelle pepper © istockphoto.com/Photographer1773; page 40 Fresno pepper © shutterstock.com/Mike Flippo; page 40 Jalapeño pepper © istockphoto.com/eddieberman; page 40 NuMex Big Jim pod © Harald Zoschke; page 40 Pimiento pepper © istockphoto.com/fcafotodigital; page 40 Poblano pepper © istockphoto.com/Suzifoo; page 40 Serrano pepper © istockphoto.com/Suzifoo; page 41 Shepherd peppers © istockphoto.com/yoh4nn; page 41 Shishito peppers © istockphoto.com/studio-pure; page 41 Aleppo pepper © shutterstock.com/elena moiseeva; page 41 Ancho pepper © istockphoto.com/keithferrisphoto; page 41 Chile de árbol © istockphoto.com/bonchan; page 41 Chipotle peppers © istockphoto.com/keithferrisphoto; page 41 Guajillo pepper © shutterstock.com/Glenn Price; page 41 Kashmiri chile © istockphoto.com/jeehyun; page 41 Pasilla pepper © istockphoto.com/bonchan; page 41 Piment d'Espelette © istockphoto.com/VvoeVale; page 41 Takanotsume © shutterstock.com/matin; page 42 Datil pepper © istockphoto.com/Tree4Two; page 42 Habanero pepper © istockphoto.com/crazy82; page 42 Scotch bonnet peppers © istockphoto.com/wuviveka; page 42 Ají panca pepper © shutterstock.com/Only Fabrizio; page 42 African bird's-eye pepper © istockphoto.com/tongwongboot; page 42 Malagueta pepper © istockphoto.com/kaanates; page 42 Tabasco pepper © istockphoto.com/RG-vc; page 42 Thai bird's-eye peppers © istockphoto.com/MadamLead; page 42 Manzano peppers © shutterstock.com/Ildi Papp; page 42 Rocoto peppers © istockphoto.com/michelepautasso; page 49 © istockphoto.com/chill123; page 52 © istockphoto.com/BruceBlock; page 59 © istockphoto.com/DejanKolar; page 83 © istockphoto.com/153photostudio; page 88 © istockphoto.com/tbradford; page 101 © istockphoto.com/_ultraforma_; page 105 Chiles in the Bangkok wholesale market © Dave DeWitt; page 113 © istockphoto.com/traveler1116; page 118 © istockphoto.com/myrrha; page 123 © istockphoto.com/penguenstok; page 141 © istockphoto.com/DeniceBreaux; page 144 © istockphoto.com/lim_jessica; page 149 Serrano chiles in the Oaxaca market © Dave DeWitt; page 164 © istockphoto.com/DejanKolar; page 171 © istockphoto.com/justhavealook; page 179 © istockphoto.com/caitrionad; page 180 © istockphoto.com/BDphoto; page 202 © istockphoto.com/ma-no; page 215 © istockphoto.com/CollinsChin; page 217 © istockphoto.com/kkkpai; page 220 © istockphoto.com/JannHuizenga; page 231 © shutterstock.com/Sea Wave; page 236 © istockphoto.com/LauriPatterson; page 241 © istockphoto.com/wanderluster; page 253 © istockphoto.com/Nikada; page 262 © istockphoto.com/pierivb; page 272 © istockphoto.com/FooDFactory; page 273 © istockphoto.com/kickstand; page 279 © istockphoto.com/Sisoje; page 282 © istockphoto.com/shellabella; page 293 © istockphoto.com/THEPALMER; page 302 © istockphoto.com/fotoco-istock; page 315 © istockphoto.com/peeterv; page 329 © istockphoto.com/aluxum; page 332 © istockphoto.com/BruceBlock; page 347 © istockphoto.com/mateusmax; page 356 © istockphoto.com/N8tureGrl; page 380 © istockphoto.com/mariusz_prusaczyk; page 387 © istockphoto.com/nito100; page 393 © istockphoto.com/bhofack2; page 400 © shutterstock.com/JeniFoto; page 402 © istockphoto.com/Paul_Brighton; page 408 © istockphoto.com/bhofack2; page 412 © istockphoto.com/BruceBlock

The publisher gratefully acknowledges the financial support of our publishing program by the Government of Canada through the Canada Book Fund.

Published by Robert Rose Inc.
120 Eglinton Avenue East, Suite 800, Toronto, Ontario, Canada M4P 1E2
Tel: (416) 322-6552 Fax: (416) 322-6936
www.robertrose.ca

Printed and bound in Canada

1 2 3 4 5 6 7 8 9 TCP 24 23 22 21 20 19 18 17 16

To Bob and Meredith,
as always my most
appreciative audience

Contents

Preface

I CAN'T SAY for sure when I fell in love with chiles—I think it was on my first trip to Mexico, sometime in the late 1970s. I was visiting Cuernavaca, a lushly picturesque enclave in the mountains not far from Mexico City and was invited for lunch at Las Mañanitas. This gorgeous hacienda-style hotel includes a restaurant, which, at the time, was thought to be the finest in Mexico. Certainly, it was visually splendid; in fact, I had never seen anything quite like it.

The outdoor tables, where we sat, were positioned at the edge of glorious gardens teeming with flowering trees and tropical blooms. The landscaping was lavish— the entire expanse was bursting with bougainvillea, and a mesmerizing population of birds, including multihued parrots and spectacular peacocks, roamed freely around the grounds. I was enchanted by the grandeur and would probably have been content if my meal had turned out to be little more than an afterthought. Instead, it overwhelmed the occasion.

I really can't remember what I ate, other than chicken in a mole sauce and numerous other dishes flavored with chiles. What I do recall is that the meal was unlike anything I had ever experienced. The flavors were varied and complex: pungent yet fruity, tangy and sometimes sweet. It was an experience I immediately wanted to repeat.

Prior to this earth-moving event, my relationship with Mexican food was limited and dismal. With hindsight, I see it was built on the worst examples of Tex-Mex fast food: soggy enchiladas, greasy refried beans, perhaps a tasteless taco or two. In those days, that was the *gringa* experience of Mexican cuisine. Unknowingly, at breakfast the same day I ate lunch at Las Mañanitas, I'd been tossed a tantalizing clue that it didn't have

to be that way. The *huevos rancheros*, most likely made with farm-raised eggs (although I didn't understand the difference at the time), were served over freshly made, lightly fried tortillas and topped with garden-ripe tomato salsa. It immediately moved to number one on my list of best egg dishes ever—and since I knew fresh jalapeño peppers were available at my local greengrocer, it was one I could more or less duplicate when I returned home.

Since then, I have visited Mexico too often to easily recall the exact number of times and enjoyed many wonderful meals at excellent restaurants throughout the country. Based on my remarkable introduction to that country's cuisine, I have also made two trips with a culinary focus. About 10 years ago, I did a culinary tour of Yucatán, which included cooking classes and market visits with chef Rick Bayless (his Chicago restaurant Topolobampo is one of my favorite places to eat Mexican food in the United States). Prior to that, in 2003, I spent a week cooking in Michoacán under the excellent tutelage of the great Diana Kennedy. No one is more passionate about Mexican cuisine than Diana. Not only does she seem to know everything there is to know about the subject, but she is also constantly upgrading her knowledge through research and travel. It was a remarkable experience.

Of course, Mexico is not the only place I have traveled to and enjoyed chiles. In fact, I may have been primed to appreciate their potential before my experience at Las Mañanitas. In my early twenties, I traveled to equatorial Africa, where I was introduced to capsicum-laced food as an antidote to the sweltering heat. One of my fondest memories is of a dinner in Addis Ababa, Ethiopia; given my imaginative proclivities, this meal whispered of tales of

the Arabian nights. Sitting cross-legged on the floor, we were served an assortment of berbere-seasoned stews (called *wat*), which were ceremoniously ladled onto injera. This slightly bitter flatbread, made from teff, served as a plate; it lined exquisite handwoven baskets that stood in for tables.

On another enchanted evening, I recall a moonlit dinner in Mombasa, Kenya. Chile-rich Indian food was served in a temple-like open-air restaurant perched high on a cliff overlooking the ocean. And I'll never forget enjoying curry for lunch on the terrace of the Mombasa Club, a whitewashed emblem of Kenya's colonial heritage, while Arabian-style dhows in full sail languidly floated by.

It was a far cry from the basically bland British-type diet and chilly northern climate I grew up with, and these experiences struck a deep, neglected chord in my soul. Fortunately, I have been able to travel widely as an adult. Most of my trips—even those not focused entirely on food—have had a culinary component. I always make an effort to learn about indigenous ingredients, taste regional dishes and visit local markets. Obviously, because I have a special interest in chiles, I've found some locales more exciting than others.

I've traveled to places such as Thailand and India, where cooks prepare fabulous dishes seasoned with capsicums, but in my capacity as a chile lover, I've found that visiting markets in Mexico is probably my ultimate experience. There, the range and depth of the offerings is truly inspiring—even at outdoor markets in small towns, the options are abundant. Practically every kind of fresh and dried chile imaginable is on display, as are packages of prepared mole (in various colors), each intended for a specific culinary purpose. I'm always tempted to purchase extravagant quantities of everything, restrained only by customs regulations and what my suitcase will hold.

Aside from their culinary value, I suspect there is something about chile peppers that resonates with my personality. I've always had a soft spot for what might be described as upstarts—the quintessential Davids who defeat Goliaths by unconventional means. It may seem like an odd comparison, but chiles remind me of *The Little Engine That Could*, a book I loved as a child. The story stressed the positive value of giving your best effort (not to put too fine a point on it, but it is a kind of Dale Carnegie course for kids). Without delving into the story, the little engine succeeds at a Herculean task that much larger engines have passed on because they didn't think it was possible to achieve.

Viewing the spice trade from this perspective, I can see parallels between chile peppers and much more highly valued spices, such as nutmeg, cloves and black pepper, which, by the time chiles arrived in the Old World, was known as "black gold." Beginning in the mid-15th century, countries such as Spain, Portugal, England and Holland spent enormous amounts of money on exploration in the hope of finding a sea route to Asia, where they believed vast stores of wealth, including precious spices, would be found. In pursuit of this bounty, countless lives were lost. In retrospect, it's possible to see that when Columbus returned to Spain with capsicum seeds (which were then planted at a monastery in Spain), and the Portuguese navigator Vasco da Gama arrived in India

(opening the door for trade with South America), a revolution was launched. It took about 50 years for chiles to reach India, Africa, Southeast Asia, China and Japan, and the arrival of these extremely cost-effective seasonings changed the culinary landscape around the world.

Naturally, I wouldn't devote an entire book to chile peppers simply because I find their history so interesting. I also enjoy eating them. Like so many people before me, my proper introduction to chiles sparked a lifelong passion. They made my tongue tingle and awakened my taste buds to entirely new gustatory sensations. For me, the taste of appropriately used chiles was, quite simply, "love at first bite."

While I would never describe myself as a "chilehead," I love the way chiles enhance so many dishes by adding just the right degree of pungency, along with subtle flavors. In writing this book, my hope is that I can share some of the excitement and pleasure my interest in chiles has brought me over the years. Learning more about chiles and the myriad ways they are used around the world has been a fascinating experience—and it isn't over yet.

In this book, I have tried to use traditional recipes from across the globe: Korean kimchi (page 404), Hungarian goulash (page 222), Anglo-Indian mulligatawny soup (page 93) and Chinese kung pao chicken (page 200) are just a few examples of the more than 200 dishes I've included. These demonstrate how deeply capsicums have rooted themselves in disparate cultures, to our collective benefit. When you consider that none of these dishes existed until Columbus returned from the New World, that in itself is a testament to this plucky little plant.

I hope you enjoy learning more about chiles and making my recipes as much as I have enjoyed working on this book. Happy cooking.

— Judith Finlayson

Acknowledgments

ANY BOOK ON chile peppers is a work in progress. As I've noted elsewhere in these pages, nobody knows how many varieties of capsicums actually exist. As for heat levels, given divergent growing conditions, cross-pollination and other factors, the pungency of an individual pepper is often the unique experience of the person consuming it. I found establishing precise heat levels of individual peppers to be extremely challenging because sources weren't consistent.

In other words, peppers are not an easy subject to corral. That's why I owe a serious debt of gratitude to all who have tilled this fractious ground before me. Numerous people who have written about chiles broke a trail that I could follow, including the late Jean Andrews, chef Mark Miller, aficionados Dave DeWitt and Robb Walsh, and horticulturist Paul Bosland, to name just a few. Others, in the course of researching particular regions, provided invaluable information on chiles and how they are used in various cuisines. These include the incomparable Diana Kennedy, Claudia Roden and Maricel Presilla, to name just three remarkable authors, whose work I deeply respect and admire. The Chile Pepper Institute at New Mexico State University was also a valuable resource, because it added institutional scholarship to the mix. I owe a debt of gratitude to all of these sources and many others too numerous to mention. (Please see Selected Resources, page 438,

for a more comprehensive, but by no means complete, list.)

Anyone who has ever written a book knows that there is far more to the process than putting words on a page. Manuscript copy is transformed into a beautiful volume thanks to a team of designers, photographers and food stylists. I am fortunate to have worked with many of the same players for years: the design group at PageWave Graphics (Joseph Gisini, Daniella Zanchetta and, especially, Kevin Cockburn, who makes my books look smashing); photographers Colin Erricson and Matt Johannsson, whose photographs are breathtaking to behold; food stylist Michael Elliott, who makes my recipes look mouthwatering; and prop stylist Charlene Erricson, who creates the stage upon which my creations can strut their stuff.

At an earlier stage, when my work was still just "words on a page," a number of people worked quietly behind the scenes to encourage those words to sing. Audrey King and Meredith Dees diligently tested recipes and, when required, offered helpful suggestions for improvement. Tracy Bordian was a great help by taking a preliminary run at verifying chile terminology and doing early fact-checking. Copy editor Jennifer D. Foster dotted the i's and crossed the t's, and indexer Beth Zabloski organized recipes and information to make the contents easily accessible for readers. My editor, Tina Anson Mine, was a delight to work with: eagle-eyed, deeply informed, impressively multilingual and very funny.

As always, the Robert Rose team goes above and beyond to ensure that my books find a warm reception in the marketplace. Thanks to Bob Dees, Marian Jarkovich, Martine Quibell and Nina McCreath for their constant support.

PART 1

ALL ABOUT CHILES

A SHORT HISTORY OF PEPPERS

WHEN COLUMBUS RETURNED from his travels in the Americas, he brought with him some flavorful plants belonging to the *Capsicum* genus. In their wild state, these plants—which belong to the Solanaceae family and now include a wide range of fruits both cultivated and wild, from sweet bell peppers to the incendiary bhut jolokia (ghost pepper)—had helped sustain the indigenous peoples from as early as 7,000 B.C.E. Sometime after 5,000 B.C.E., people began to selectively breed these feral varieties and cultivate their hybrids, which suggests that capsicums may have been the first spice used by humans. By the time Columbus encountered them, peppers were certainly an important food throughout Central and South America, the Caribbean and Mexico.

In early August of 1492, Columbus departed Spain and set sail for India. His was an entrepreneurial voyage directed toward establishing his funders in a key role in the highly profitable spice trade. In addition to "powerful kingdoms and noble cities," he expected to find black vine pepper (*Piper nigrum*), which was known as "black gold." This so-called "king of spices" had been a valuable commodity in Europe since the Middle Ages, but when Columbus arrived in the bucolic Caribbean islands, he unearthed an entirely different species of plant from the one he was seeking—pungent capsicums.

If his discovery of chile peppers was disappointing, Columbus tried not to let it show. As he later wrote, the Americas were "found to produce much aji [one of the words the Spanish used for chile] which is the pepper of the inhabitants, and more valuable than the [black peppercorn]. They deem it wholesome and eat nothing without it."

On his return from his second voyage to the New World, Columbus was welcomed by the Spanish queen, Isabella, and her husband, Ferdinand, at a monastery in Guadalupe. Apparently, the monarchs were not impressed by what one contemporary observer described as a "pepper more pungent than that from the Caucasus." Fortunately, the monks from the monastery became interested in the exotic plants and began to cultivate them. Meanwhile, Portuguese explorers were visiting parts of Brazil and stocking their ships with new and unusual produce, including capsicums. Thanks to these world travelers, it took a mere 50 years for the chile to reach India, Africa, Southeast Asia, China and Japan.

Unlike other imports from the Americas (notably tomatoes and potatoes, both of which were initially thought to be poisonous), the chile received a relatively warm welcome, especially in tropical climes. In her book *The Pepper Trail*, Jean Andrews notes that in the warmer regions where capsicums were enthusiastically embraced, local cookery was invariably dominated by a basic starch. Depending on the locale, rice, maize, yams, barley or legumes—whatever was plentiful and indigenous to the area—would be served with a sauce. The people were accustomed to using herbs and spices to liven up their bland fare, but these foodstuffs were often expensive and relatively difficult to grow. Costly black pepper was likely the most pungent ingredient in these dishes until chiles were introduced.

Capsicums, unlike many spices, were so easy to cultivate that they could be grown in a home garden. They matured quickly, dried well and were easy to transport. All these features made them very affordable, which meant that spicy, peppery flavor was no longer a rare treat or a luxury reserved for wealthy people. Chiles, something of a gastronomic democratizer, were soon keen competitors in the culinary sweepstakes.

What's in a Name?

It is unlikely that there is any subject that is more confusing in terms of nomenclature than chiles. Despite serious attempts at standardization over the past 20 years, it is still not unusual to find different chiles with the same name. For example, a poblano is often called a pasilla, and a chile chilacate can be called just about anything from ancho to guajillo to some type of New Mexico chile.

Even experts have problems identifying what species many chiles belong to. The late Jean Andrews, a self-taught botanist who also held a doctorate in art, knew more about capsicums than most horticulturists. According to her, the only way to positively

identify the difference between the species is by examining the corolla and the flower, not the fruit. When they are in flower, chile species look very different. *Capsicum annuum* flowers are milky white, and there is just one flower (occasionally two) per node; *C. frutescens* flowers are a bit green; *C. chinense* flowers are greenish, and there are always two flowers per node; and *C. pubescens* flowers are purple with a thin white border, and the seeds are always black.

Chile Greens

The fruit isn't the only part of the capsicum plant that is suitable for consumption. In Asia, pepper leaf is often eaten. These leaves are usually from chile plants that are similar to the Thai variety, and they are always cooked, perhaps because some cultivars may be toxic. Look for them in Filipino, Korean and Vietnamese markets, where they are sometimes sold frozen and labeled "sili leaves."

In Korea, chile greens may be added to kimchi, while in Japan they may turn up in *tsukudani*, a long-simmered dish that often includes seaweed. In the Philippines, these leaves are a component of a comfort-food chicken soup known as *tinola*. And in Mexico, some types are used in a green soup from the Veracruz region called *huatape*.

A Chile Is a Chili Is a Chilli

Many aspects of the chile are extremely confusing, from its historical misnomer (pepper) to the nomenclature of its many varieties, which even horticulturalists have difficulty sorting out. So it is probably not surprising that the spelling for the word itself is somewhat problematic. Is it chili, chilli or chile? You are likely to come across all of those spellings if you are reading up on the topic.

According to horticulturist and capsicum expert Paul Bosland, the name is derived from the word *chil*, which comes from the Aztec dialect and refers to plants from the *Capsicum* genus. The "e" ending is the correct Spanish spelling. English linguists (who probably didn't know any better) changed it to an "i."

Although most people associate the word *chile* with hot peppers, in fact the word refers to capsicums in general, whether they are spicy or not. The word *chili* refers to the dish, as in chili con carne.

Where Chiles Get Their Heat

Capsaicin (and, to a lesser extent, other alkaloid components) is the active chemical compound in chile peppers—without it, a spicy jalapeño would taste more like a sweet bell pepper. Capsaicin is produced by the placenta of the chile, the white internal membrane or "core" that holds the seeds. From there, lesser amounts of it migrate into the seeds and along the inner walls of the pepper. Capsaicin was discovered in the early 1800s, and by the end of that century it was confirmed as the dominant flavor component of hot chile peppers.

Capsaicin is a member of two chemical families: alkylamides and vanilloids (the principal flavor components of vanilla). When consumed, capsaicin makes us feel warm, increases the body's metabolic rate, and stimulates blood flow and sweating. It also has antibacterial properties. When capsaicin touches sensitive areas of your body—such as the mouth, lips, throat, tongue, eyes and genitals—it creates a distinct burning sensation. It binds to nerve receptors that register heat and pain, causing those nerves to become hypersensitive and, as part of that process, to produce the same physical sensation you would get if you were actually burned. This triggers the release of pain-relieving endorphins in the brain, which produce a mild anesthetized feeling of well-being similar to that caused by opiates.

Because of this desensitizing effect, capsaicin is now used as a pain-relieving component in muscle creams and other pharmaceuticals (see The Health Benefits of Chiles, page 25).

Conditions Affect Spiciness

The concentration of capsaicin in a chile depends on variables in the plant's genetic makeup, growing conditions and the pepper's ripeness. Hot and dry growing conditions increase the plant's capsaicin production, which peaks when the green fruit starts to mature and change color.

Not All Chiles Are Hot

Contrary to accepted wisdom, a pepper does not need to make your eyes water or start a fire in your mouth to qualify as a chile. *Chile* is the common name for the fruit of plants in the *Capsicum* genus. These plants belong to the Solanaceae (nightshade) family, which includes eggplant, potatoes and tomatoes.

Capsicums include a wide variety of cultivars, which vary dramatically in terms of color, shape and flavor. They also differ in degree of pungency, from sweet bell peppers, which rate zero on the Scoville scale (a system for measuring pepper pungency; see below),

The Scoville Scale

Capsaicin content is typically measured in Scoville heat units (SHU), a system invented by Wilbur Scoville, a chemist who worked for the Parke-Davis pharmaceutical company. In 1912, he devised a test whereby an extract of pepper was diluted in sugar water until it lost its pungency. To neutralize one drop of jalapeño extract requires approximately 5,000 drops of sugar water, hence the jalapeño's rating of 5,000 SHU. Today, chemists use high-performance liquid chromatography to analyze capsaicin concentration, although they still express that concentration in terms of SHU. Sweet bell peppers measure zero on the Scoville scale, jalapeños average 5,000 and pure capsaicin clocks in at 16 million SHU. However, it should be noted that the capsaicin content varies dramatically among peppers of the same variety. Depending on the growing location and conditions (see above), the bhut jolokia pepper, which once held the title of The World's Hottest Pepper (see page 21), has a Scoville rating that can range from just shy of 500,000 to more than 1 million SHU.

Chiles: The Next Chemical Warfare Weapon?

Chile peppers have very complex chemistry, so it's not surprising that capsaicin in extremely high concentrations can be poisonous. Most people are familiar with pepper spray. In India, that country's Defence Research & Development Organisation took this idea one step further by developing bhut jolokia grenades. Made from military-grade capsaicin, which tops the Scoville scale at 5 million SHU, these weapons (and, to a lesser extent, run-of-the-mill pepper spray) have the potential to be lethal. In sensitive individuals, they are powerful enough to inflict permanent damage to the eyes and respiratory system. In rare cases, such as in people who suffer from asthma, death may result.

to the bhut jolokia, one of the world's hottest peppers, which ranks at a vigorous 1 million Scoville heat units (or so). Somewhere in between are many popular chiles, including jalapeño, serrano and poblano peppers.

And the Winner Is...

It would be hard to imagine gardening as a blood sport unless you were introduced to the group of men (and so far they are all men) who are actively competing to develop the hottest pepper in the world, as recognized by Guinness World Records. Until 2007, that record was held by a pepper known as the Red Savina, a relative of the habanero, which (depending on the source you consult) had a rating of between 250,000 and 577,000 SHU. That year, its position was usurped by an Indian pepper, the bhut jolokia, the first pepper to break the 1 million SHU barrier. At the time of this writing, it, too (along with the Infinity, Naga Viper and Trinidad Moruga Scorpion varieties), has been dethroned, and the Carolina Reaper has been declared the hottest of the hot. Likely by the time this book is published, another variety will be wearing the crown.

How you actually identify the world's hottest chile is challenging, and not only because any normal person's taste buds would likely suffer the equivalent of cardiac arrest if exposed to one of the competitors. However, it should be noted that some "gastromasochists" do taste so-called "super-hot" chiles and claim to be able to discern variations among their intense levels of heat. Also, the achievements of Anandita Dutta Tamuly should not go unrecognized. On April 9, 2009, under the watchful eye of chef Gordon Ramsay, who filmed the event for verification, this Indian woman consumed 51 bhut jolokia chiles in two minutes, then smeared the seeds of 25 of these "super-hot" chiles in her eyes, thereby setting a Guinness World Record of her own.

These chile contests are very competitive, and identifying the world's hottest pepper is not for the faint of heart. At the time of this writing, competition for the title of The World's Hottest Pepper is being waged between British and American growers. The title has been moving back and forth between England and the United States, and matters of national pride have likely upped the ante on the need to establish definitive criteria. But the chile world is populated by a cast of wild and colorful characters, who devote superhuman amounts of attention and energy to their beloved plants. Arriving at any kind of consensus will likely be challenging. And consider this: there have been rumblings that some growers may be using the horticultural equivalent of performance-enhancing drugs to bump up the heat levels of their chiles.

Many responsible growers are pressing for rigorous standards, overseen and directed by a reputable entity such as the Chile Pepper Institute. For the purposes of verifying SHU ratings, this affiliate of New Mexico State University has grown peppers in the controlled circumstances of a greenhouse and

tested their heat levels not only at the institute but also in two other independent labs.

However, there is more to this problem than identifying the spiciness of an individual chile; the heat levels for different peppers of the same variety frequently fluctuate (see page 20). Scoville testing performed on random samples of the same variety grown from as many as 150 plants identified wide differences in scores. When horticulturist Paul Bosland was testing the Trinidad Moruga Scorpion, which briefly held the title of The World's Hottest Pepper, he reported levels of between 1.2 and more than 2 million SHU. At the very least, those entering peppers in the competition should be prepared to produce samples from a large number of plants so that testing, which should be rigorously controlled, can identify a mean heat.

Survival of the Spiciest

For the chile plant, pungency is much more than a flavor. Thanks to the work of professor Joshua Tewksbury, we now know that capsaicin and its other capsaicinoid components have evolutionary value. These substances protect the plant from external threats, such as fungi or being devoured by creatures that masticate. Sadly, chewed seeds lose the ability to germinate. By making themselves unappetizing to most creatures with teeth, chiles have cleverly ensured their long-term survival.

Other than humans, birds are the only species that consumes chiles, and they are actively involved in the plant's propagation. As they digest capsicums, birds soften the seeds; when they defecate, they expel them encased in ready-made fertilizer. Once the seeds hit the ground, they are ready to germinate.

Being avid travelers, birds fly great distances in migration, transporting chile seeds to new and distant places. Chile plants appreciate this free ride. They are very adaptable, aren't particularly fussy about soil and are self-pollinating. By broadening their geographic reach, their feathered friends increase chiles' chances of survival and reproductive success, thereby supporting their evolutionary advantage.

The capsicum seeds Columbus brought to Spain were originally planted in Extremadura, a region in the central western part of the country. Two aides-de-camp facilitated the first stage of their journey across Europe: traveling monks and birds. In dispersing their seeds, they assisted in the proliferation of what we now call wild "bird" chiles. Some, such as Mexico's chile piquin, Africa's piri-piri and Thailand's bird's-eye, have been domesticated and now rely primarily on human interventions for propagation.

There are thousands of unknown varieties of wild chiles. They grow undetected in various parts of the world, their survival ensured by birds and their own self-propagation skills. Perhaps they are patiently waiting for their next big evolutionary step—the arrival of chile hunters, such as Tewksbury, a self-proclaimed "gonzo botanist." Traveling the back roads of tropical climes, he searches for undiscovered peppers (the ecological equivalent of the lost ark), which, with luck, might provide important insights into how we create and sustain life on Earth.

Cayenne Revisited

In some ways, the cayenne pepper has been a victim of identity theft, because the term *cayenne* is widely used to describe ground pungent red chile that is not necessarily sourced from cayenne peppers. In fact, many spice merchants feel the term should be discontinued and the product should be renamed something along the lines of "ground red pepper." This also raises concerns about cayenne that is used medicinally—in the past, at least, bodies such as the British Pharmacopoeia have expressed interest in standardizing the source of the peppers used

in its manufacture to ensure appropriate medicinal quantities of capsaicin.

In any case, as a seasoning, the ground red pepper known as cayenne has enjoyed broad reach for a very long time. British herbalist Nicholas Culpeper was using it in 1652. Writing in *An Herb and Spice Cookbook* published in 1963, when blandness was a distinguishing factor of American cooking, the late Craig Claiborne, food editor of *The New York Times*, described cayenne's uses as "legion." He also wrote at the time, "For centuries, it has added zest and piquancy to soups and sauces, eggs and meat and, used sparingly, it seems to accent the natural flavors of most savory foods."

Today, cayenne is just one of a number of types of dried ground red pepper a cook is likely to have on hand. There are so many options: sweet, hot and smoked paprika; Aleppo, Kashmiri and ancho chile powders; and spice blends that contain chile, such as Cajun seasoning, berbere seasoning blend and Mexican-style chili powder, to name just a few.

Chiles on the March

In North America, the popularity of hot and spicy foods has been trending for more than 50 years. When the Immigration and Nationality Act was passed in 1965, large numbers of Mexican people began to immigrate to the United States. They brought their love of a wide range of chiles with them, expanding the capsicum's reach well beyond the traditional territory of sweet bell peppers and pungent cayenne.

In his highly entertaining book *The United States of Arugula*, which documents the so-called "gourmet revolution" in America, David Kamp includes a telling fact: in 1972, Mexican food authority Diana Kennedy published her first book, *The Cuisines of Mexico*. By 1986, she felt compelled to revise it because so many ingredients that were unobtainable 14 years earlier had become "routinely available throughout the country." In 1992, this trend was officially documented: that year, statistics revealed that salsa overtook ketchup as the most popular condiment sold in North America.

Since then, interest in numerous other cuisines that make liberal use of chile peppers has grown dramatically: Thai, Vietnamese, Malaysian, Indonesian, Sichuan, Hunan, Caribbean, Senegalese and Ethiopian, to name just a few. Sriracha sauce (see page 393), the so-called "rooster" chile sauce that originated in Thailand but is now made in California by a Vietnamese immigrant, sells more than 14 million bottles a year. Sriracha has become so popular that in 2007 there was a much-publicized outcry when the company experienced a three-month production shortage in the United States. In 2012, the *Culinary Trend Mapping Report* confirmed that hot and spicy foods remained one of the sector's fastest growing segments. Every year between 1991 and 2011, the worldwide consumption of chiles increased by 2.5%. During that same period, individuals increased their intake by a whopping 130%. Today, it's hard to get through a restaurant menu that doesn't feature chiles in prominent ways, from basic pub-grub deep-fried chicken wings to hip, wine-focused, small-plate restaurants such as A.O.C. in Los Angeles, where the white beans may be seasoned with spicy merguez sausage and the burrata is finished with a dollop of pungent Middle Eastern pepper-based spread. Feel the glow—chiles are here to stay.

THE HEALTH BENEFITS OF CHILES

WHETHER THEY WERE aware of it or not, people have recognized the health benefits of chiles for centuries. Because chiles are highly antimicrobial, prior to the invention of refrigeration they reduced pathogens in food. Conventional wisdom suggests that, in the past, people used spices such as chiles primarily to disguise the taste of ingredients that may have passed their peak. However, some scientists believe that developing a taste for pungent food may have been an evolutionary advantage. People who consumed the fewest pathogens were the healthiest and they passed this robustness on to their offspring. Not surprisingly, in this age of antibiotic-resistant bacteria, food scientists are actively exploring capsaicin as a tool for reducing or eliminating a variety of foodborne pathogens.

At the most basic level, chiles are extremely healthful because they are nutrient-dense. That means they pack a powerful nutritional punch while adding few calories. One medium red bell pepper has fewer than 40 calories. It is particularly high in vitamin A (75% DV) and vitamin C (253% DV). It also provides a wide range of additional vitamins and minerals, including hard-to-obtain copper, as well as valuable phytonutrients, such as antioxidant carotenes.

Long before we understood the ins and outs of nutrition, chiles were being used for medicinal purposes. For instance, the Mayans used chiles to treat a variety of illnesses, including respiratory problems and gastrointestinal complaints. Folk wisdom has long suggested that consuming chiles is a good idea when you have a cold. Now science confirms that capsaicin really does help clear mucous membranes. In addition, the abundant quantity of vitamins A and C that peppers provide boost your struggling immune system.

Many of the health benefits associated with chiles are derived from capsaicin. This compound has been shown to reduce inflammation and promote healing in a number of painful conditions, from arthritis to psoriasis. Capsaicin also has a psychotropic component; when you eat hot peppers, the brain releases endorphins, which are natural painkillers.

Chiles have also been associated with benefits to the heart and vascular system. For instance, one laboratory study demonstrated a connection between capsaicin consumption and lower blood pressure. Population studies have linked the consumption of chiles to lower rates of cardiovascular disease, and laboratory studies indicate that capsaicin can help prevent blood clots and arrhythmias. Capsaicin, which may help prevent free radical formation, has also been shown to reduce damage to heart cells following a heart attack. Scientists are also exploring capsaicin's potential as a cancer preventive—so far, the work on prostate cancer is the most compelling. Capsaicin may also help prevent type 2 diabetes. The most popular health benefit of eating chiles may turn out to be the promise they have shown as potential fat burners: eating hot peppers raises your metabolism, so it may help you to lose weight.

And last, but certainly not least, there is evidence that increasing your consumption of chiles may help you live longer. Researchers, who published their results in *The BMJ* in August 2015, followed almost half a million people in various parts of China for several years. They concluded that people who ate spicy food once or twice a week showed a 10% reduction in total mortality. Those who ate spicy food more frequently increased those odds.

PART 2

THE TYPES OF CHILES

Capsicum annuum

The vast majority of capsicums cultivated globally belong to the *C. annuum* species, which has an extraordinary number of varieties, from sweet bell peppers to zesty cayennes. Once again, even experts can't provide a precise head count. Not only are breeders constantly creating new cultivars, but wild peppers are also hybridizing themselves, so it is impossible to say exactly how many varieties of chile peppers exist— probably thousands in this species alone.

The heat levels of the chiles in this species vary dramatically, from sweet to incendiary. However, they can also vary within specific varieties. For instance, Anaheim and Hatch are both New Mexico chiles, but the Anaheim is mild and the Hatch ranges from slightly to very hot. Heat levels can vary even within the fruit of a single cultivar (see Padrón and Shishito Peppers, page 77), resulting in unpleasant surprises. I have purchased jalapeño peppers that don't have much more heat than bell peppers and some that are extremely hot; other chile aficionados have similar stories. Many factors can affect not only the flavor but also the heat level of peppers (see Conditions Affect Spiciness, page 20).

Pimiento Peppers

Pimiento peppers are a well-known variety of C. annuum. They are small and can be heart-shaped (like the Spanish piquillo) or round and ridged. They are sweeter than bell peppers. Fresh ones are very difficult to find; most end up canned (and called pimentos) and are used to stuff olives or to make pimento cheese, a favorite in the American South (see page 54). According to pepper expert Jean Andrews, the canned pimento industry didn't develop until after 1914, when a roasting machine was invented that made peeling easier.

Increasingly, I am hearing the word *terroir* applied to chiles. This term was originally used in relation to wine; it is the basis of the designation *Appellation d'Origine Contrôlée* (AOC), which has been used in the French wine industry for decades to identify the provenance of grapes and the wine produced from them. Now terroir is being used in relation to other agricultural products, such as cheese, chocolate and coffee, to capture the unique characteristics of crops based on the environment in which they are produced. Food products with specific geographically based qualities may seek official recognition, such as the European Union's Protected Designation of Origin (PDO) or India's Geographical Indication (GI). Many regions are now seeking such status for chiles.

As noted, C. annuum is the most cultivated chile species in the world. It is grown throughout North America and Europe, and in India, Mexico, China, Korea, Oceania and Southeast Asia, among other locations. The wild chiltepín pepper, known as "the mother of all peppers" (see below), belongs to this species, as does the Pusa Jwala, one of the most popular chiles grown in India. The pimiento variety of C. annuum is the source of paprika (see page 32), which is produced in numerous locations around the world.

Various capsicums belonging to the C. annuum species appear in signature dishes of many different countries, from Hungarian goulash (see page 222), which depends on paprika for its unique flavors, to Mexican salsas (see page 359), many of which rely on serrano or jalapeño peppers for their bite. And let's not forget the famous Balkan spreads ajvar (see page 57) and *lyutenitsa*, which traditionally rely on red roga peppers (or perhaps red bell peppers) plus locally produced hot paprika for their lusciously rich taste.

Chiltepín Peppers

In their book, *Chasing Chiles*, Kurt Michael Friese, Kraig Kraft and Gary Paul Nabhan describe the chiltepín pepper as a "cultural icon" of the borderlands between Mexico and the United States. This tiny firebomb, a member of the C. annuum family, has been described as "the mother of all chiles" and has a Scoville rating in the 100,000 SHU range. It grows wild in the undergrowth beneath hackberry bushes and mesquite trees and is still harvested by hand.

Among chile lovers, the chiltepín has acquired near-mystical status. It captures "the potency of the desert," the authors write; it is "small but as fierce as the desert sun blazing on a summer day." They believe that if you've been weaned on chiltepíns, their uniquely fiery flavor weasels itself into your being. Demand is so great among Mexican-American connoisseurs that chiltepíns command exorbitant prices on both sides of the border.

While a real chiltepín pepper is unique, the authenticity of some may be questionable. Mexican culinary authority Diana Kennedy reports that, throughout Mexico, there are many tiny wild chiles that may be identified as chiltepín. She calls these *chile piquin*.

PIMENT D'ESPELETTE

PIMENT D'ESPELETTE IS a sweet, fruity and slightly hot—2,500 Scoville heat units (SHU)—chile pepper grown in 10 communes in the Basque region of France. Spice authority Ian Hemphill defines it as a type of paprika. It is an *Appellation d'Origine Contrôlée* (AOC) product; only peppers grown under strict supervision in the designated region can use the name.

The harvest begins in August and culminates on the last weekend of October with the Fête du Piment à Espelette, which attracts thousands of visitors to the area. The peppers are picked and processed by hand. Traditionally, they were strung into ristras and hung to dry on household exteriors, making for an extremely picturesque sight. Nowadays, commercial producers dehydrate the peppers using wood-fired stoves or tobacco dryers. They are subsequently ground coarsely into flakes or more finely into powder.

Although France lays claim to the actual product, piment d'Espelette has a place in the cuisine of the Basque region of Spain, where it is used in many applications, such as simple vinaigrette-type sauces to season grilled fish or in *piperada*, their version of peppers and eggs, which the French claim as *pipérade*. In France, the spice is found in a variety of prepared products, such as piment jelly, mustard and even caramels. In Paris, I have purchased *sel de Guérande* seasoned with piment d'Espelette. It makes a lovely finish for grilled meat or fish. Other classic dishes containing it include *axoa* (page 261) and *marmitako* (page 146).

Chile Savvy

A ristra is a string of chile pods. The peppers are tied to together and hung to dry, sometimes for use in cooking and sometimes as decoration.

PAPRIKA

PAPRIKA IS A powder made from different ground dried *C. annuum* varieties. The peppers it is sourced from vary widely in size and shape, from long and pointed to small and round. Each type provides a different flavor profile and level of heat.

Paprika is a popular spice in many parts of the world. Historically, it has played a significant role in the cuisines of Spain (where, thanks to Columbus, its Old World experience originated in 1492) and Hungary (where it has been made since the 16th century). Paprika has also played supporting roles in other regions, including portions of the Balkans. Today, it is used widely in the food processing industry as a flavor and color enhancer, and is a vital part of many traditional recipes, such as goulash. It is frequently sprinkled over finished dishes, such as deviled eggs or potato salad, and is a staple on the American barbecue circuit in spice rubs and sauces.

While Columbus initially brought capsicums to Spain, the varieties used to make paprika were developed in Europe, according to food historian Alan Davidson. A group of Spanish monks from the Jerónimos monastery in Guadalupe, in the western region of Extremadura, were likely the first Europeans to cultivate this tasty import. Today, paprika, or *pimentón*, grown in La Vera, not far from the original monastery, is among the best in the world. It has identifiable characteristics, based on centuries of hybridization and traditional processing methods.

Unless they are intended for smoking, the chile pods are sun-dried before being ground and sifted. Those being used to make smoked paprika are dispatched to smokehouses. There, the freshly picked fruits are gently dried over slow-burning oak before being milled. Pimentón de la Vera was granted a *Denominación de Origen Protegida* (DOP) in 2005, meaning its artisanal status is guaranteed.

Spanish paprika is also produced in the Murcia region, from the ñora pepper. This small, dark burgundy pepper has a sweet, mild flavor. Traditionally, it is left on the vine until it is very ripe. A *picante*, or hot, paprika is sometimes produced in northern Spain, in the La Rioja or Basque regions. It is made from the guindilla chile, a long red pepper (see page 329).

In Spain, there are three categories of paprika: *dulce* (sweet), *agridulce* (bittersweet) and *picante* (hot). Smoked paprika also comes in *dulce*, *agridulce* and *picante* levels.

In his culinary treatise *El Practicón*, which was published in 1894, Ángel Muro wrote that paprika had become an essential ingredient in Spanish cooking. Today, paprika plays a less significant role in Spanish cuisine, although it is still widely used in many traditional dishes, such as paella and romesco sauce.

In Hungary, as George Lang wrote in his book *George Lang's Cuisine of Hungary*, "Paprika is to the … cuisine as wit is to its conversation—not just a superficial garnish, but an integral element." Hungarian paprika captured the nation's imagination in the late 18th century, when it began to be widely used in cooking. However, paprika peppers have been cultivated in Hungary, specifically in Buda (now part of Budapest), since the 16th century. They were likely introduced during the Turkish occupation—initially they were known as "Turkish peppers." However, it's also possible they arrived by traditional trade routes, such as by way of Muslim merchants traveling from Egypt or from North Africa via Portuguese traders.

Like Spain, Hungary continues to produce paprika using traditional methods. The industry is centered near the towns of Kalocsa and Szeged, south of Budapest, in the sunniest part of Hungary. A number of different capsicums are used, but the process is standardized. After harvesting, the peppers are washed and woven into ristras (see page 31) or placed in mesh bags and hung to dry. Dehydration is often completed in large earthenware ovens. Once dried, the peppers are crushed and ground using a variety of methods.

In Hungary, unlike Spain, paprika is never smoked. However, there are six different flavor and heat classifications, ranging from *különleges* (mild and delicate) to *erős* (very hot). Hungarian paprika also varies in color. The sweet varieties are bright red. As the pungency increases, the shading turns brownish. The Hungarian government's application for Protected Designation of Origin (PDO) status for paprika grown in both the Szeged and Kalocsa areas is currently under consideration by the EU.

Paprika peppers are also grown in other parts of the world, including Serbia and the Netherlands. The United States is a fairly large producer, as well. The first pimientos arrived from Spain in 1911 and were planted in Georgia. Shortly thereafter, growers in South Carolina took up the challenge. As a side note, it's possible that Hungarian peppers are the basis for crops in other parts of the country. The Second World War interrupted the spice trade, depleting America's paprika supply. According to a story published in the *Milwaukee Journal* in 1942, a Hungarian-American businessman with roots in the paprika business accessed paprika pods from Yugoslavia and smuggled them into the country. These formed the basis for commercial plantings in Louisiana.

Although the United States has been cultivating paprika for more than a century, the American industry isn't particularly concerned about distinctions among the peppers it is sourced from. Horticulturist Paul Bosland says that, in America, paprika is simply a "sweet, dried red powder that can be made from any type of *C. annuum* that is non-pungent and has brilliant red color." Both paprika and its oleoresin, an extract of the essential oil made using a solvent, are widely used in food, cosmetic and pharmaceutical manufacturing.

Capsicum frutescens

While this species has certain similarities to both the *C. annuum* and *C. chinense* species, its uniqueness has been a subject of much debate among botanists. The consensus is that it qualifies as a separate species. Many bird chiles fall into this category.

By far, the best-known *C. frutescens* chile is the tabasco. It was originally grown in Louisiana by Edmund McIlhenny from seeds supplied by Maunsel White (see below) or perhaps by a soldier who had served in the Mexican-American War—the facts are not clear regarding its origins. The pepper itself, in either the fresh or dried form, is not used in culinary applications. Rather, it is made into hot pepper sauce.

The pepper commonly known as piri-piri (African bird's-eye) is acquiring an international reputation, thanks to the prepared sauce that bears its name. This pepper is used widely in Africa.

The malagueta pepper (not to be confused with melegueta pepper, a spice also called grains of paradise) is another well-known member of this clan. It plays a significant role in Bahian cuisine in Brazil. The malagueta is cultivated and also grows wild in parts of the country. It is often used dried or pickled for making hot sauces, and may turn up fresh in salsas.

Tabasco Sauce

Thanks to Tabasco sauce, the legendary hot sauce, the tabasco chile (a variety of the relatively rare *C. frutescens* species) is famous around the world. The sauce originated in the mid-1800s, just as Creole cooking was putting down roots, when Edmund McIlhenny began to grow these tiny firebombs on Avery Island, off the Louisiana Gulf Coast. A former banker who turned to gardening following the Civil War, he transformed his crop into the now-ubiquitous Tabasco hot sauce, which he patented in 1870. Although McIlhenny's heirs vigorously deny it, he may have "borrowed" the idea for his sauce from New Orleans public figure and plantation owner Maunsel White.

In 1850, the *New Orleans Daily Delta* reported on White's crop of "the very strongest of all peppers [the Tabasco]." According to the reporter, he boiled these pungent peppers, doused them in vinegar and turned them into a sauce, which was described as follows: "a sauce or pepper decoction … which possesses in a most concentrated form all the qualityes of the vegetable. A single drop of this sauce will flavor a whole plate of soup or other food." In terms of ingredients and preparation method, it is very similar to today's Tabasco sauce.

The source of White's inspiration—if not the actual recipe (and possibly McIlhenny's)—was likely the slaves who worked on their plantations. The enslaved ancestors of African-Americans arrived in the United States in the early 1600s. By that time, they had acquired a taste for "New World foods," such as peanuts and chile peppers, which they brought with them. (They had already experienced these foods, which had arrived in Africa via merchant traders.) On the plantations in the American South, enslaved women worked as cooks, and our knowledge of foodways suggests the recipes of these black women influenced the fare in the "Great House." In some cases, this African presence extended as far as authorship of the recipes published under the names of the white mistresses of the plantations. For instance, five black cooks were explicitly credited in *The Carolina Rice Cook Book*, which was compiled by Mrs. Samuel G. (Louisa) Stoney in 1901.

As Laura Schenone notes in her culinary history *A Thousand Years Over a Hot Stove*, "the heat of the red pepper" is one of two features of Southern cooking that can be traced directly to Africa. The other is sauces made with smoked meats.

Capsicum baccatum

This species, which is usually called ají, dominates South America. The word *baccatum* means "berry-like." These peppers have a recognizable fruity flavor, with citrus notes, but they are also hot: heat levels range between 20,000 and 50,000 SHU. This category includes many of the ají family of chiles. There are many different pod shapes and sizes, from long and pointed to short and squat. Colors range from green to yellow to red to purple. This species has not been widely cultivated beyond South America until relatively recently, when it was introduced to Central America. Large commercial growing operations are not the norm in that part of the world, which means that most peppers are grown in home or market gardens.

The ají amarillo is the most common chile belonging to this species. It is used widely in ceviches and fresh salsas and in *pibil*-type dishes, in which ingredients are wrapped in banana leaves and baked with chiles and herbs. The ají amarillo is also dried and ground into powder or made into a paste, which is bottled and provides a readily available substitute for the fresh peppers.

The criolla sella is a thin-skinned, not-too-hot (about 20,000 SHU) slender cylindrical chile that matures to a lovely shade of golden yellow. It is sometimes confused with the ají limon (also known as the Peru yellow), which is a bit smaller and somewhat hotter. This cone-shaped chile ripens from green to bright yellow. It is medium-hot and characteristically fruity, with a hint of citrus.

The chile puca-uchu is the basis for bottled hot sauces and for *salsa de ají*, a very hot fresh salsa that often appears on restaurant tables in tiny bowls alongside the fiery bottled sauces.

The ají ayucllo is a moderately hot wild chile that is sometimes cultivated; it is oval in shape and purple, ripening to orange-red. It is eaten fresh or used as an ingredient in a variety of dishes.

Capsicum chinense

The *C. chinense* species was named (or misnamed) in 1776 by a Dutch-born botanist who, at the time, was cataloguing plants for the Austrian court and mistakenly assumed it had arrived from China. This species dominates most of the Caribbean. It arrived there from the Amazon basin, thanks to Native Americans. Most of the incendiary chiles, such as habanero (see page 38), belong to this species. When naturalist Bernabé Cobo explored South America in the early 17th century, he noted at least 40 different varieties of *C. chinense*. To add a bit of local color, in Guadeloupe the species is called *le derrière de Madame Jacques*.

The pods of this species vary dramatically in size and shape, from tiny and berry-like to long and pointed. Many are lantern-shaped. Scotch bonnet peppers, which give Jamaican jerk seasoning and the island's famous Pickapeppa Sauce their distinctive flavor, have a flattened top that resembles a beret. The datil pepper (see below), grown in St. Augustine, Florida, is another unique member of this family. The bhut jolokia, which once held the record for being the hottest pepper in the world (see page 21), belongs to this species, although botanists believe it may have naturally hybridized with *C. frutescens* varieties to achieve its "super-hot" status.

Other prominent members of this species include the popular Peruvian chile called ají limo (not to be confused with the ají limon of the *C. baccatum* species). It is a small (2 to 3 inches/5 to 7.5 cm long and about 1 inch/2.5 cm wide), very hot chile that ripens to a deep red, yellow or orange. It is used fresh with seafood, especially ceviche. The ají panca is very common in Peru, where it is often used fresh. Mildly hot, it has a fruity berry-like flavor and ripens to a deep shade of burgundy. It is added to stews, sauces and fish dishes, and is also sold dried.

The fatalii is an explosively hot *C. chinense* chile that is used in central African cuisine (see page 314). Despite their pungency, they smell amazingly citrusy when fresh. Scotch bonnet peppers are often suggested as a substitute.

Datil Peppers

The datil (pictured, above right), a yellow-orange member of the *C. chinense* family that is also known as the "yellow lantern chile," is an unusual pepper because it is grown virtually exclusively in St. Augustine, Florida. It likely arrived in the state via trade with the Caribbean. Among other acknowledgments, it is the focus of an annual festival. Much of the local crop ends up in hot sauces, pepper jellies and mustards, which are sold to tourists.

HABANERO PEPPERS

THE HABANERO IS the most readily available member of the *C. chinense* group. Perhaps surprisingly, it appears to have been named after Havana, Cuba. Chile expert Jean Andrews makes a good case for its emigration from Cuba to Mexico's Yucatán Peninsula, where it now plays a significant role in that region's cuisine. Not only are Cuba and Yucatán in close proximity, but also the habanero is the only pepper cultivar in that region that has no Mayan name, which implies its status as an import.

Highly aromatic and blisteringly hot, the habanero is also noted for having many different pod types, all with unique characteristics. In the early 1600s, missionary and naturalist Bernabé Cobo commented on this diversity. "Some (are) as large as limes or large plums; others as small as pine nuts or even grains of wheat, and between the two extremes are many different sizes. No less variety is found in form and shape." The chocolate habanero is particularly interesting for its color: it matures to chocolate brown.

Capsicum pubescens

This species is the only one that has no wild form. It was domesticated 6,000 years ago and was used by the Incas. Peppers belonging to this species are also known as *rocotos* or *locotos*. According to chile gurus Paul Bosland and Dave DeWitt, they are grown extensively in household gardens and, because they prefer cooler temperatures, in mountainous areas from Mexico to Peru. These peppers have not traveled widely beyond South and Central America and, as a result, are the least-known group around the world.

When they are growing, *C. pubescens* peppers are easily identifiable because they are the only species with purple flowers. The plants have hairy leaves and stems, and dark brown seeds, which are unpleasantly firm; they need to be removed before using. The fruits have different pod shapes—some are pear-like, while others resemble apples and are almost as large. *C. pubescens* chiles are known for being particularly hot and are sometimes called *el más picante de los picantes*, or "the hottest of the hot." Bosland and DeWitt say they rate only 30,000 to 50,000 SHUs, but they have a unique collection of capsaicinoids that makes them seem hotter than they actually are. Because the pods are rather thick, the peppers don't dry well and are usually used fresh.

Rocoto peppers ripen from green to yellow, orange and red. The yellow and orange ones have migrated to Central America and Mexico. In Guatemala, the rocoto pepper is called *chile caballo*, or "horse pepper." Mexican culinary authority Diana Kennedy refers to a pepper belonging to this species as the chile manzano, although she says it has different names throughout Mexico, such as canario in Oaxaca and (God forbid!) jalapeño in parts of Chiapas. She notes two varieties that are used in the country—one produces chiles that ripen from green to yellow or orange, the other that ripens from green to deep red. In Mexico, rocoto peppers are used in pico de gallo, or roasted and peeled. In South America, they are often stuffed and baked. I have bought them frozen in Latin American markets.

Commonly Used Chile Varieties

Capsicum annuum

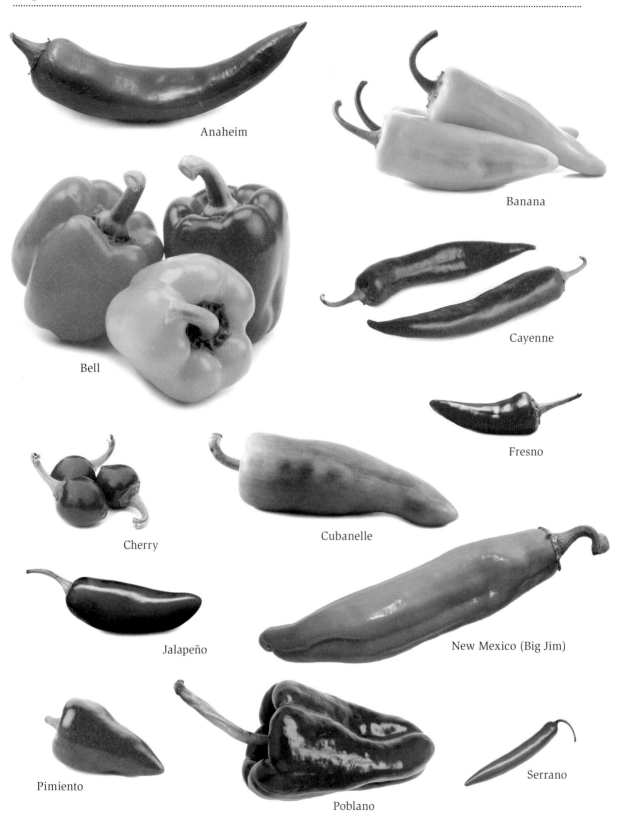

Anaheim

Banana

Bell

Cayenne

Fresno

Cherry

Cubanelle

Jalapeño

New Mexico (Big Jim)

Pimiento

Poblano

Serrano

Capsicum annuum

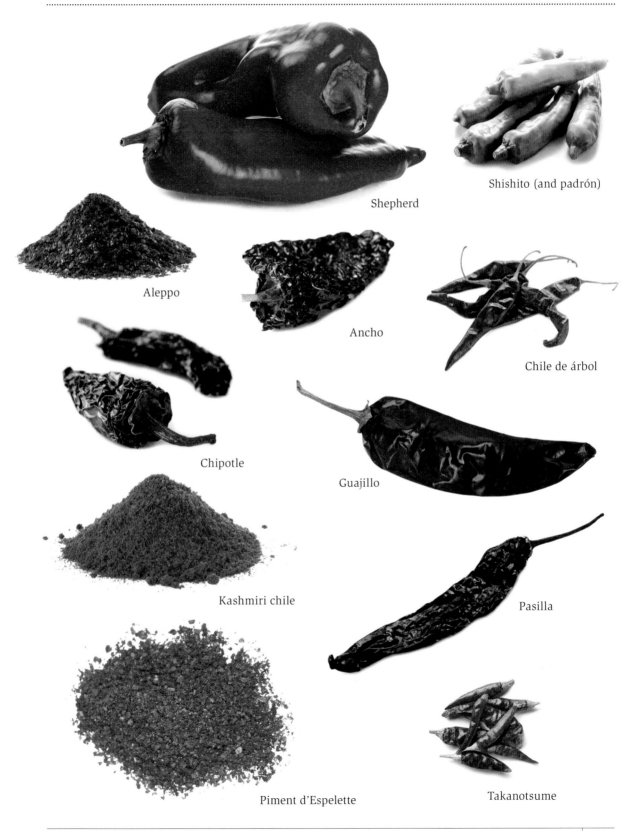

Shepherd

Shishito (and padrón)

Aleppo

Ancho

Chile de árbol

Chipotle

Guajillo

Kashmiri chile

Pasilla

Piment d'Espelette

Takanotsume

Capsicum chinense

Datil

Habanero

Scotch bonnet

Ají panca

Capsicum frutescens

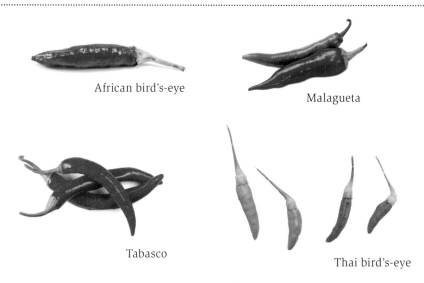

African bird's-eye

Malagueta

Tabasco

Thai bird's-eye

Capsicum pubescens

Manzano

Rocoto

Capsicum annuum

This is the most common species of cultivated chile, encompassing a wide range of varieties, from sweet mild bell peppers, which rate 0 SHU on the Scoville scale (see page 20), to wild chiltepín peppers, which can be as hot as 100,000 SHU. In addition to being the most cultivated species, *C. annuum* cross-pollinates easily, so there are likely many unidentified varieties growing around the world.

Name	Heat level	Physical description	Brief overview
FRESH VARIETIES			
Anaheim	Mild to slightly hot: 500 to 2,000 SHU	Green when unripe; red when ripe, at which point it becomes known as Colorado. Narrow and pointed; about 6 inches (15 cm) long.	Origins lie in Mexico and New Mexico. Technically a variety of New Mexico chile (see page 44), but achieved independent identity in California. May also be called California chile. Substitute poblano, banana, or a mild New Mexico chile, such as Sandia.
Banana (mild to medium hot); hot varieties may be known as Hungarian wax peppers	Mild: 500 to 1,000 SHU Medium hot: about 5,000 SHU	Yellow, sometimes green, ripening to red. Tapered and pointed; about 5 inches (12.5 cm) long.	Often pickled and used as a garnish. Good for roasted salsas. For mild varieties, substitute Anaheim, Cubanelle or bell peppers with a pinch of ground cayenne. For hot varieties, substitute a moderately hot New Mexico pepper, such as Hatch, or red bell peppers with a bit of ground cayenne.
Bell	Sweet: 0 SHU (no heat) Exception: Mexi-Bell variety, which has a trace of pungency (100 SHU)	More than 100 cultivars. Broad range of colors: green, red, orange, yellow, brown and purple. Squarish; about 4 inches (10 cm), although some cultivars are slightly tapered (about $3\frac{1}{2}$ inches/8.5 cm long by $2\frac{1}{2}$ inches/6 cm wide). The Mexi-Bell is smaller, about $2\frac{3}{4}$ inches (7 cm) long and wide.	One of the most widely used capsicums. Good raw in salads as a vegetable; often stuffed and baked, as well. A key component of *sofrito* and the Louisiana "trinity." Substitute Shepherd, NuMex Garnet or pimiento, or Cubanelle for Mexi-Bell.
Cayenne	Medium hot to hot: 10,000 to 25,000 SHU	Many different cultivars. Dark green ripening to red. Long and narrow; about 5 inches (12.5 cm) long by 1 inch (2.5 cm) wide.	The most common capsicum across a wide variety of cuisines. Named after the city Cayenne in French Guiana. Often sold dried or ground into powder. Very popular in North America, India, Africa, Asia and Mexico. Called by different names in various regions. Cayenne applies to peppers often described as finger chiles. Substitute jalapeño, serrano or a smaller quantity of habanero peppers for the fresh version, and chile de árbol for the dried version.

Name	Heat level	Physical description	Brief overview
Cherry	Sweet and mild to mildly hot: 100 to 3,500 SHU	Green ripening to red. Small and round; about 2 inches (5 cm) in diameter.	Often pickled or made into condiments. Does not dry well. Substitute Cubanelle, pimiento or piquillo peppers.
Cubanelle	Sweet and mild to slightly hot: 100 to about 2,000 SHU	A wax-type pepper, yellowish-green to bright red. Elongated; about 6 inches (15 cm) long by 2 inches (5 cm) wide.	Sweeter than the bell pepper. Used extensively in Cuba, Dominican Republic and Puerto Rico. May be Italian in origin. Substitute banana, bell, Shepherd or sweet Hungarian peppers.
Fresno	Mildy hot to medium hot: about 3,500 to 10,000 SHU	Green ripening to red. Cone-shaped; about 2 inches (5 cm) long by 1 inch (2.5 cm) wide.	Often mistaken for the jalapeño but wider at the top and slightly milder, although pungency and flavor intensify with ripening. Developed in California and named for the city of Fresno. Used widely in Californian cuisine in many applications, from garnishes to sauces to marinades. Substitute jalapeño or hot Hungarian peppers.
Jalapeño	Mildly hot to medium hot: about 3,500 to 10,000 SHU	Dark green to black, ripening to red. Usually about 3 inches (7.5 cm) long by 1 inch (2.5 cm) wide, although more mildly flavored jumbo versions are often found.	Often pickled, used raw in salsas, cooked or stuffed. One of the best-known chile peppers in North America; used widely in Tex-Mex cooking. Substitute serrano pepper, finger chile or a hot variety of New Mexico chile. Does not dry well unless smoked, in which case it is called a chipotle.
New Mexico (refers to a pod type); Hatch, Chimayo and Big Jim are well-known varieties, as is the Anaheim (see page 43)	Slightly hot to medium hot: 2,500 to 7,500 SHU	Dark green usually ripening to red but sometimes yellow, orange or brown. All taper to a sharp point but vary in length, from about 4 inches (10 cm) long to the Big Jim variety, which is about 8 inches (20 cm) long and 2 inches (5 cm) wide.	Originated in 1894 as part of the program at New Mexico State University. Widely used in Tex-Mex and Southwestern cooking, often in soups and stews. Substitute Anaheim or poblano for fresh. May be dried. Ancho or guajillo are common substitutes for dried. The pasado chile is a member of this pod type that is traditionally roasted, peeled and dried by the Pueblo Indians and used in Southwestern cuisine.
Peperoncino (catchall term for hot red Italian peppers of this species); also called Tuscan peppers; types vary regionally	Depending on the variety, most are hot to very hot: 15,000 to 30,000 SHU "Little devils" are very hot: more than 30,000 SHU	Bright red; may have wrinkly skin. Usually thin; about 4 inches (10 cm) long. The most fiery, known as "little devils," are tiny, around $\frac{1}{2}$ inch (1 cm) long.	Used fresh, sprinkled over pizza. Often pickled. Substitute cayenne, red finger chiles or jalapeños for fresh. Often sold dried as *peperoncino* (Italian hot pepper flakes). Substitute chile de árbol for dried.

Name	Heat level	Physical description	Brief overview
Pimiento (also pimento)	Mild and very sweet: 100 SHU	Bright red. Medium-large, about 3 inches (7.5 cm) long and 2½ inches (6 cm) wide. Usually pointed and heart-shaped, although various cultivars have different shapes.	Exceptionally sweet and highly aromatic. Usually pickled and bottled; used primarily for stuffing olives. Fresh peppers are delicious in salads. Substitute bell, sweet wax or Shepherd.
Poblano (often incorrectly called fresh pasilla)	Mild hot to slightly hot: 1,000 to 2,000 SHU	Bright green, with smooth skin. Large, triangular shape; about 4½ inches (11 cm) long by 2½ inches (6 cm) wide.	Originated in Puebla, Mexico, and fundamental to Mexican cuisine. Very versatile. Often stuffed and used in salsas and condiments, such as *rajas* (see page 368). Substitute Anaheim or a mild New Mexico chile, or Cubanelle or bell pepper with a pinch of ground cayenne.
Serrano	Hot: about 20,000 SHU	Medium to dark green, with smooth skin. Pointed and small; about 2 inches (5 cm) long by ½ inch (1 cm) wide.	Used extensively in Mexican cooking. Very popular for fresh or cooked sauces. Substitute jalapeño or a smaller quantity of habanero.
Shepherd	Sweet: 0 SHU	Green ripening to deep red. Tapered; about 7 inches (18 cm) long and 2 inches (5 cm) wide.	Closely related to the sweet Hungarian pepper. Can be substituted for bell peppers or sweet wax peppers.
Shishito (and padrón)	Usually mild: about 200 SHU, but some slightly hot, up to 1,000 SHU	Green, with slightly wrinkled skin. Softly pointed; 3 to 4 inches (7.5 to 10 cm) long.	Japanese. Often stir-fried or grilled (see page 77) or used in tempura. Shishito and padrón can be used interchangeably.
DRIED VARIETIES			
Aleppo (also known as *halaby* or *pul biber* in Turkey)	Medium hot: about 10,000 SHU	Green, ripening to deep burgundy. Short and sturdy; about 2 inches (5 cm) long by ½ inch (1 cm) wide.	Deep fruity flavor. Used extensively in Middle Eastern cuisine. Usually sold dried and coarsely ground. May actually be Turkish Maras peppers (see page 122). Substitute coarsely ground ancho or a smaller quantity of Italian hot pepper flakes.
Ancho (dried form of poblano)	Mild to slightly hot: 1,000 to 2,000 SHU	Purple-brown, with wrinkled skin. Stout; about 4 inches (10 cm) long by 2 inches (5 cm) wide.	Name means "wide." Sweet flavor with a bit of heat. Used extensively in Mexican and Tex-Mex cooking, in soups, stews and sauces. Sometimes ground to a powder. May be identified as mulato, pasilla or even chile Colorado, all of which may be substituted in recipes.
Chile de árbol	Hot: 15,000 to 25,000 SHU	Vivid red. Small, long and narrow; about 4 inches (10 cm) long by ¼ inch (0.5 cm) wide.	Used in Mexican cooking for table sauces. Usually sold dried but may be sold fresh, which can be green or red. Sometimes ground to a powder. Substitute ground cayenne.

Name	Heat level	Physical description	Brief overview
Chipotle	Hot: about 15,000 SHU	Pale brown. About 3 inches (7.5 cm) long by 1 inch (2.5 cm) wide.	Dried smoked ripe jalapeño. Used extensively in Mexican, Tex-Mex and Southwest cooking to flavor soups, stews and sauces. Sold whole or ground to a powder, or pickled in adobo sauce. Nothing else quite captures their unique flavor; fortunately, they are widely available.
Guajillo	Mildly hot to medium hot: about 4,000 SHU	Reddish, with tough shiny skin. Elongated and triangular; about 5 inches (12.5 cm) long by $1^1/_2$ inches (4 cm) wide.	Very common in Mexico. It has tough skin so it requires cooking. When fresh, this pepper is called mirasol, and is often confused with the dried ají mirasol, which is widely used in South America (see page 346). May also be mistakenly identified as cascabel, which is a round dried pepper that rattles when shaken. However, the cascabel may be substituted for the guajillo, as can ancho and dried New Mexico chiles.
Kashmiri chile	Hot: about 20,000 SHU	Intensely red skin. Elongated finger-type chile with pointed tip; about 4 inches (10 cm) long.	Bright red when ground. Good to use in Indian dishes calling for powdered chile. Substitute a small quantity of ground cayenne.
Pasilla (also known as chile negro; dried form of chilaca chile)	Mildly hot to medium hot: 3,500 to 6,000 SHU	Deep chocolate brown, with shiny, ridged skin. Long and narrow; about 6 inches (15 cm) long by 1 inch (2.5 cm) wide; sharply pointed.	Used extensively in Mexican cooking. Name means "little raisin." Used in moles and toasted as a condiment. Readily available. Ancho chiles are often misidentified as pasilla. Substitute guajillo.
Piment d'Espelette	Slightly hot: about 2,500 SHU	Bright red. Slightly stocky with a wide top, tapering to a point; about 4 inches (10 cm) long by 1 inch (2.5 cm) wide.	Slightly smoky, warm and fruity. The only chile used to any extent in France; it is a staple of Basque cooking (also in Spanish Basque territory). Usually sold coarsely ground. It is also used in a variety of condiments, such as mustard. Substitute sweet paprika with a tiny bit of ground cayenne.
Takanotsume (also known as hawk's claw)	Hot to very hot: 20,000 to 30,000 SHU	Green ripening to red. Small and shaped like a talon; about $1^1/_2$ to $2^1/_2$ inches (4 to 6 cm) long.	Japanese. Dried when red and ground to make the seasoning *ichimi togarashi*. Often used to flavor udon and ramen noodles. One of the essential spices in *shichimi togarashi* (seven-flavor) seasoning.

Capsicum chinense

This species was introduced to the Caribbean, where it dominates, by Native Americans. Apparently, it was introduced to Mexico's Yucatán Peninsula from Cuba. The pods vary dramatically in size and shape, from tiny and berry-like to long and sharply pointed, as well as in color, from pale yellow to deep chocolate brown. Scotch bonnet peppers have a flattened top that resembles a hat. Many of the "super-hot" chiles (see page 21) are bred from this species.

Name	Heat level	Physical description	Brief overview
FRESH VARIETIES			
Datil	Very hot: about 40,000 SHU	Yellowish-orange. Stocky; about $3\frac{1}{2}$ inches (8.5 cm) long and 1 inch (2.5 cm) wide	Cultivation originally limited to St. Augustine, Florida. A unique local pepper used to make hot sauces and condiments that are sold to tourists.
Habanero	Extremely hot: from 80,000 to more than 600,000 SHU, depending upon the variety	Wide variety of colors, from orange to red to chocolate brown, depending on the type. Some types are wrinkled. Tapered to a point; about $2\frac{1}{2}$ inches (6 cm) long and 1 inch (2.5 cm) wide.	Fruity, citrusy flavor. Used extensively in Caribbean cooking and also in Yucatán, Mexico. Substitute Scotch bonnet or other Caribbean pepper from the *C. chinense* species.
Scotch bonnet	Extremely hot: 150,000 to 325,000 SHU	Green ripening to yellow, orange or red. Short, squat and shaped like a tam-o'-shanter; about 1 inch (2.5 cm) long by $1\frac{1}{2}$ inches (4 cm) wide.	Fruity, slightly smoky flavor. Used extensively in Jamaican cooking; the basis of jerk seasoning. Has a different flavor than the habanero, but they can be used interchangeably.
DRIED VARIETIES			
Ají panca	Hot: 20,000 SHU	Deep claret red. Gently tapered; about 5 inches (12.5 cm) long by 3 inches (7.5 cm) wide.	Fruity, berry-like flavor. Very common in Peru. Used in soups, stews and sauces. May be sold fresh, but is usually sold dried outside of Peru, either whole or in ground form to use as a finishing spice.

Capsicum frutescens

Some say *C. frutescens* is the same species as *C. annuum* or even *C. chinense*. However, botanists have made a sound case for identifying it as separate. In general terms, these peppers are very hot (from about 30,000 to 70,000 SHU) and relatively similar in size (small) and pod shape (long, narrow and pointed).

Name	Heat level	Physical description	Brief overview
FRESH VARIETIES			
African bird's-eye (also known as piri-piri and occasionally pili-pili or pere-pere; *piri-piri* means "pepper pepper" in Swahili	Extremely hot: 80,000 to 200,000 SHU	Green ripening to various shades of red. Narrow and pointed; about $1\frac{3}{4}$ inches (4.5 cm) long by 1 inch (2.5 cm) wide.	Popular in Portugal and Africa, particularly Mozambique. Best known in piri-piri sauce. Also sold dried and pickled. Substitute Thai bird's-eye for fresh or dried; substitute malagueta for pickled.
Malagueta	Very hot to extremely hot: 60,000 to 100,000 SHU	Green ripening to red. Tiny and pointed, about 1 inch (2.5 cm) long by $\frac{1}{4}$ inch (0.5 cm) wide.	Popular in Brazil; often used in Bahian cooking. Some grow wild. Relatively readily available pickled. Substitute dried or pickled piri-piri peppers for the dried or pickled versions.
Tabasco	Very hot: 30,000 to 50,000 SHU	Green ripening to orange or red. Narrow and pointed; 1 to 2 inches (2.5 to 5 cm) long.	Best known of the *C. frutescens* species. Originally grown on Avery Island, Louisiana, but cultivation has moved to South and Central America. Used to make Tabasco sauce. Can be purchased dried. Substitute dried piri-piri for the dried version.
Thai bird's-eye (*prik kii nuu suan* in Thai)	Very hot to extremely hot: 50,000 to 100,000 SHU	Green or red. Tiny and pointed; about 3 inches (7.5 cm) long by $\frac{1}{2}$ inch (1 cm) wide, tapering to $\frac{1}{8}$ inch (3 mm).	There is some confusion regarding the species this chile belongs to: some say *C. annuum* but *C. frutescens* is the most likely. Used widely in Thai and Southeast Asian cooking, often in fresh dipping sauces. Can be dried and ground. Substitute serrano or finger chiles for fresh. Substitute ground cayenne for ground.

Capsicum pubescens

This species, which is commonly known as rocoto, is unique because there are no wild forms—only cultivated. It is easily identified by its unique purple flowers, dark brown seeds and hairy leaves. Its pod types resemble apples; all varieties are green ripening to red, yellow or orange. Its use was traditionally confined to South America, but in recent years, cultivation has been undertaken in Central America and Mexico.

Name	Heat level	Physical description	Brief overview
FRESH VARIETIES			
Manzano	Hot to very hot: 20,000 to 30,000 SHU	Green ripening to yellow, orange or red. Squarish; about 2 inches (5 cm) long by 1½ inches (4 cm) wide.	This is the exported version of the rocoto chile, grown in Mexico or Central America. It must be seeded before use. Citrusy flavor. Used raw for salsas, as well as pickled or stuffed. Thick walls make it unsuitable for drying.
Rocoto	Very hot: 30,000 to 50,000 SHU Although this cultivar is not as high on the Scoville scale as many others, it contains unique chemicals that intensify the sensation of pungency when consumed.	Wide range of colors: green ripening to yellow, red, orange, even brown. Looks like a small apple; about 2 inches (5 cm) long by 1½ inches (4 cm) wide.	Very fruity, citrusy flavor. Seed before use. Used in garnishes, salsas, salads and often stuffed. Thick walls make it unsuitable for drying. Available frozen in Latin American markets.

PART 3

RECIPES

Appetizers

Pimento Cheese

This recipe illustrates the chile's journey from Europe to the American Deep South. Originally, those who could afford imported Spanish pimiento peppers mixed them with cheese. In the early 20th century, when Kraft began making processed cheese, Southern farmers began to grow pimientos for popular consumption, calling them pimentos. Serve this spread with sliced baguette, crackers, cracker bread or celery sticks.

Tips

Pimientos, a member of the *Capsicum annuum* family, are used to make authentic pimento cheese, and most recipes call for canned or jarred pimentos. However, I prefer the taste of a red bell pepper if I can't find fresh pimiento peppers.

Fortunately, I have a farmer friend, who provides me with a few batches of fresh pimiento peppers every summer. If you can get them, substitute 2 or 3 fresh pimiento peppers for the red bell pepper.

If you prefer, substitute ¼ cup (60 mL) coarsely chopped sweet onion, such as Vidalia, for the green onion.

Use the type of paprika you prefer—hot, smoked or sweet—for sprinkling both the finished cheese mixture (Step 2, right) and the crostini in the Variation, right.

If you are comfortable coloring outside the lines, for a Tex-Mex spin, add grated dill pickle to taste, and use pickled jalapeño peppers.

- **Food processor**

3 cups	shredded sharp (aged) Cheddar cheese (about 8 oz/250 g)	750 mL
1	red bell pepper, roasted, peeled, seeded and chopped (see Tips, page 60, and left)	1
½ cup	mayonnaise	125 mL
3 tbsp	chopped green onion (white and green parts) or red onion (see Tips, left)	45 mL
	Hot pepper sauce, pickled peppers or cayenne pepper	
	Freshly ground black pepper	
	Paprika (optional), see Tips, left	

1. In food processor fitted with the metal blade, combine cheese, roasted red pepper, mayonnaise, green onion, and hot pepper sauce and black pepper to taste. Pulse until onion is finely chopped and mixture is blended.

2. Transfer to a small serving bowl. Cover and refrigerate for at least 2 hours or for up to 2 days. Before serving, let stand at room temperature to allow the flavors to bloom, about 20 minutes. Sprinkle to taste with paprika (if using).

Variation

Bacon-Topped Pimento Cheese Crostini: Spread Pimento Cheese on crostini. Sprinkle with crisp bacon bits and paprika (optional, see Tips, left) and bake in 400°F (200°C) oven until cheese begins to melt, about 2 minutes.

TASTY TIDBIT

Pickled peppers are a mainstay of American Lowcountry cuisine. Southern food authority John Martin Taylor says that no pantry there is without a jar of pickled peppers, hot or mild. They are often added to pimento cheese, which author James Villas calls "the most distinctive and sensual of all Southern spreads."

Greek-Style Feta and Pepper Spread (*Htipiti*)

Hot and sweet peppers are integral to the cuisine of Macedonia, which was once part of Greece. Pepper-laced feta cheese is a traditional Greek meze known as *htipiti* and is particularly popular in the area around Thessaloniki. It is often stuffed into Florina peppers (see page 59). I've been making this simplified version for decades. Served with crudités, crackers or pumpernickel rounds, it is an elegant appetizer, but it is also a flavorful addition to a mezes platter. If you have the ingredients on hand, it can be ready to serve in about 5 minutes.

**MAKES ABOUT
1¾ CUPS (425 ML)**

VEGETARIAN FRIENDLY

GLUTEN-FREE FRIENDLY

Tips

Creamy feta cheese (about 26% M.F.) is a better choice for this dip, because lower-fat versions produce drier results. If your spread seems dry, add about 1 tsp (5 mL) of extra virgin olive oil and pulse to combine. If you want to thin the spread, add up to 2 tbsp (30 mL) plain full-fat Greek-style yogurt.

Boukovo are Greek dried chile flakes, which have an interesting, smoky flavor. If you have them on hand, by all means use them in this recipe.

If you prefer, substitute 1 red finger chile, 1 to 2 serrano pepper(s) or 1 jalapeño pepper, roasted, for the hot pepper flakes.

- **Food processor**

2	red bell peppers, roasted (see Tips, page 60, or store-bought)	2
8 oz	feta cheese (see Tips, left)	250 g
	Hot pepper flakes (optional), see Tips, left	

1. Peel, seed and quarter roasted red peppers. In food processor fitted with the metal blade, combine roasted red peppers, cheese and hot pepper flakes (if using) to taste. Process until smooth, about 30 seconds, stopping and scraping down the side of the bowl as necessary.

2. Transfer to a small serving bowl or earthenware crock and serve immediately, or cover and refrigerate for up to 3 days. If refrigerated, before serving, let stand at room temperature to allow the flavors to bloom, about 20 minutes.

Persian-Style Feta and Pepper Spread

In the Middle East, a traditional appetizer or snack is nuts mixed with cheese and/or yogurt, which is seasoned with a bit of hot pepper and combined with various types of fresh greens. This herbaceous spread, with just a hint of pungency, is a refreshing take on that flavorful combination. I like to serve it with warm pita bread, cucumber slices or sliced radishes.

MAKES ABOUT 1½ CUPS (375 ML)

VEGETARIAN FRIENDLY

GLUTEN-FREE FRIENDLY

Tip

Adding the Aleppo pepper to taste allows you to adjust it according to the heat level of your finger chile and the tolerance of your taste buds. I usually find about ½ tsp (2 mL) provides a nice level of spiciness. I'd avoid adding more than 1 tsp (5 mL), because this spread is really about the nuts, herbs and cheese. The chile is there for a bit of mysterious enhancement.

• Food processor

½ cup	shelled pistachios (about 3½ oz/100 g)	125 mL
4	green onions (white and green parts), sliced	4
½ cup	packed fresh dill fronds	125 mL
½ cup	packed fresh parsley leaves	125 mL
¼ cup	packed fresh cilantro leaves	60 mL
1	red finger chile, seeded and thinly sliced	1
1	clove garlic, minced	1
7 oz	feta cheese	210 g
¼ cup	plain Greek-style yogurt	60 mL
¼ cup	extra virgin olive oil	60 mL
2 tbsp	freshly squeezed lemon juice	30 mL
	Aleppo pepper (optional), see Tip, left	
	Salt and freshly ground black pepper	

1. In food processor fitted with the metal blade, combine pistachios, green onions, dill, parsley, cilantro, finger chile and garlic. Pulse until finely chopped, about 20 times, stopping and scraping down the side of the bowl as necessary.

2. Add cheese, yogurt, oil and lemon juice and process until smooth and blended. Add Aleppo pepper (if using) to taste. Season to taste with salt and black pepper. Pulse to blend.

3. Transfer to a small serving bowl. Serve immediately or cover and refrigerate for up to 2 days.

Ajvar

Vinka Vukicevic, my Pilates coach, introduced me to ajvar. She is from Bosnia and tells me that no house in the former Yugoslavia is ever without this tasty spread. She always looked forward to arriving home after school and enjoying it as a snack, spread on bread and sprinkled with crumbled feta cheese. Once I learned how to make ajvar, it quickly became a popular appetizer at my house—I spread soft goat cheese over toast triangles or crackers and top them with a good dollop of this instant, positively ambrosial treat.

MAKES ABOUT 1½ CUPS (375 ML)

VEGAN FRIENDLY

GLUTEN-FREE FRIENDLY

Tips

Instead of all bell peppers, you can use a combination of red bell peppers and a hotter variety, such as Hungarian wax peppers (if you do, you might reduce the quantity of hot paprika). In Balkan countries, ajvar it is often made with roga peppers, a long horn-shaped pepper that resembles North American Shepherd or red bull's horn peppers. You can also use chervena chushka, a Bulgarian heirloom pepper that is very similar; its seeds are becoming easier to find for planting in North American gardens.

This is a very accommodating recipe. I'm told that, in the Balkans, every family has its own version. Add more lemon juice, salt and even eggplant, if desired.

The quantity of hot paprika in this recipe may seem small, but it does pack a punch.

I prefer my ajvar slightly chunky; you do not want the ingredients to be puréed in Step 1.

- **Food processor**

3	red bell or Shepherd peppers, roasted (see Tips, left and page 60)	3
1	small eggplant (8 oz/250 g) roasted, peeled and cut into chunks	1
4	cloves garlic, coarsely chopped	4
¼ cup	extra virgin olive oil	60 mL
½ tsp	salt	2 mL
2 tbsp	freshly squeezed lemon juice (see Tips, left)	30 mL
½ tsp	hot Hungarian paprika (see Tips, left)	2 mL
	Freshly ground black pepper	

1. Peel, seed and cut roasted red peppers into quarters. In food processor fitted with the metal blade, combine roasted red peppers, eggplant and garlic. Process until blended but still slightly chunky (see Tips, left).

2. Pour into a small saucepan. Add oil and salt, and bring to a boil. Reduce heat and simmer gently until thickened and slightly dry, about 20 minutes.

3. Remove from heat. Stir in lemon juice and paprika. Season to taste with additional salt and black pepper if necessary. Transfer to a small bowl. Cover and refrigerate for up to 5 days.

Focus on: Chiles in the Balkans

Chiles, both sweet and hot, play a lively role in Balkan gastronomy. The Balkans typically include countries such as Albania, Bosnia and Herzegovina, Bulgaria, Greece, Macedonia, Serbia and Slovenia. In culinary terms, Hungary and even Turkey are members, although technically neither country belongs to the group. However, a good case can be made that the Ottomans brought chiles to the region in the 15th century, when they conquered Hungary. The area has experienced a turbulent history and occupies a strategic geographical position between Europe and Asia. This means that it is located at a gastronomic crossroads and there is a great deal of overlap among the various cuisines.

Throughout a large chunk of the region, specifically the area often described as "the former Yugoslavia," peppers are deeply interwoven into the culinary tapestry. Farmers' markets abound with capsicums—there are varieties of sweet bell peppers, roga peppers, Hungarian wax peppers and small pointed chiles, as well as the ubiquitous paprika. I have both mild and hot varieties of paprika that were purchased in Sarajevo. The peppers were grown in Serbia, where the paprika was produced.

The Serbian government touts pepper production as a significant component of its agricultural output, noting that much of the harvest ends up in ajvar (see page 57), the pungent spread often described as "Serbian vegetable caviar." In the autumn, families prepare the following year's supply of this spicy condiment, often stirring it outdoors over an open fire. But ajvar is more than a home-preserving staple in the region; it is also produced commercially both for domestic consumption and for export.

In fact, as I write, I have an unopened jar in my pantry that was made in the Republic of Macedonia. I also have a jar of *lyutenitsa* (it, too, was made in Macedonia), a very similar spread that is often described as Bulgaria's national dish. *Ćevapčići*, small highly spiced grilled meat patties, are supposedly the national dish of Serbia—the recipes I consulted use hot paprika or a combination of sweet paprika and cayenne to spice up the meat. It is sometimes sold as street food, often wrapped in pita bread and finished, perhaps not surprisingly, with a healthy dollop of ajvar.

Throughout the Balkan region, even in Croatia, where the European (particularly Austrian) influence is more strongly felt and the taste for spicy food is less prevalent, sweet paprika and pepper-based condiments are widely used. Across the region, peppers enjoy a robust presence in various forms—as pickles, relishes and vinegars; roasted and tossed in vinaigrette; or served as salsa to accompany perennially popular meat kebabs.

Beyond being loved as fresh, seasonal vegetables, peppers don't play a major role in Greek cuisine, except in the northern part of the country and in the now-independent Republic of Macedonia, which used to be part of Greece. In those locations, cooks make liberal use of a wide variety of capsicums. As Diane Kochilas writes in *The Glorious Foods of Greece*, "Peppers are to Macedonia what corn is to Kansas—ubiquitous, a long agricultural tradition that has worked its way into every aspect of the local cookery, in the form of both vegetable and spice."

In the most northerly region of Eastern Macedonia and Thrace, sweet and hot paprika, as well as dried pepper flakes known as *boukovo*, are very popular. Little bowls of boukovo are everywhere; they are the ultimate finishing touch for the *doner kebabs* and souvlaki served in the small restaurants and food stalls that proliferate across the region. In the city of Thessaloniki, which is famous for its mezes, the ouzeries (ouzo bars) serve long hot peppers that have been poached or fried and seasoned with olive oil. They may even be stuffed with spicy whipped feta (see page 55). In that city's market, Kochilas found "mounds of deep red Florina peppers," a type of sweet pepper named for the town in which it is produced. They were awarded Protected Designation of Origin (PDO) status by the World Trade Organization in 1994.

Chileheads would probably prefer the Balkan region's spicy "goat" peppers. Called "diabolically hot" by Kochilas, they are long, thin, usually green and hornlike. They are often served fried, like padrón peppers (see page 77). Some varieties of peppers are strung into decorative ristras (see page 31) and dried for use in the winter.

Middle Eastern Walnut Dip (Muhammara)

Depending upon the source you consult, this roasted red pepper and walnut dip is Armenian, Arabian, Turkish or Syrian in origin. In any case, it is healthful, delicious and a welcome addition to any mezes platter. I like to serve it with warm pita bread or cucumber slices. If you are not meat-averse, this dip can also be used as a sauce for kebabs.

MAKES ABOUT 2 CUPS (500 ML)

VEGAN FRIENDLY

GLUTEN-FREE FRIENDLY

Tips

To roast peppers: Brush peppers lightly with oil and place them directly on a hot grill on a preheated barbecue, or arrange them on a baking sheet and place under a preheated broiler. Grill or broil, turning 2 or 3 times, until the skin on all sides is blackened, about 20 minutes. Transfer to a heatproof bowl. Cover with a plate and let stand until cool. Using a sharp knife, lift off the skin, reserving any accumulated juices. Discard skin, stems and seeds.

For the best flavor, toast and grind cumin seeds yourself.

* Food processor

2	red bell peppers, roasted (see Tips, left, or store-bought)	2
½ cup	walnut halves, toasted	125 mL
½ cup	pine nuts, lightly toasted	125 mL
4	green onions (white and a bit of the green parts), cut into chunks	4
2	cloves garlic, coarsely chopped	2
2 tbsp	freshly squeezed lemon juice	30 mL
2 tbsp	pomegranate molasses	30 mL
1 tbsp	sliced red finger chile	15 mL
2 tsp	Aleppo pepper (or ¼ tsp/1 mL cayenne pepper)	10 mL
2 tsp	ground cumin (see Tips, left)	10 mL
1 tsp	salt	5 mL
¼ cup	extra virgin olive oil	60 mL

1. Peel, seed and cut roasted red peppers into quarters. In food processor fitted with the metal blade, combine roasted red peppers, walnuts, pine nuts, green onions, garlic, lemon juice, pomegranate molasses, finger chile, Aleppo pepper, cumin and salt. Pulse until finely chopped, about 15 times, stopping and scraping down the side of the bowl as necessary.

2. Add olive oil and pulse until blended and desired consistency is achieved, about 6 times. (You want some texture to remain from the walnuts.)

3. Transfer to a small serving bowl. Serve immediately or cover and refrigerate for up to 3 days. If refrigerated, before serving, let stand at room temperature to allow the flavors to bloom, about 20 minutes.

Chile-Spiked Oyster and Bacon Dip

This rich, creamy infusion is versatile. It goes just as well with vegetables—such as blanched broccoli, cauliflower or Brussels sprouts—and crispy potato wedges as it does with potato chips. No matter what it's served with, this dip always earns rave reviews.

Tip

To make Crispy Potato Wedges: Bake the desired number of baking potatoes in a preheated 400°F (200°C) oven for 1 hour. Let cool. Thirty minutes before serving the dip, cut each potato into 8 wedges. Arrange on a baking sheet and brush with olive oil. Roast in a preheated 400°F (200°C) oven until crisp and golden.

Moreover ...

I suspect the lineage of this dip is basically British. Eliza Acton was seasoning baked oysters with cayenne in 1845, and Mrs. Leyel was wrapping them in bacon and baking them with butter and paprika a few decades later.

- Preheat oven to 425°F (220°C)
- Large ovenproof ramekin

2	slices bacon, cooked until crisp and crumbled	2
4 oz	cream cheese, softened	125 g
2 cups	shredded Cheddar cheese, preferably sharp (aged)	500 mL
1	can (5½ oz/156 g) smoked oysters, drained and cut in half	1
1	red bell pepper, roasted (see Tips, page 60), seeded and finely chopped	1
1	jalapeño pepper, seeded and finely chopped	1
2 tbsp	mayonnaise	30 mL
1 tbsp	prepared horseradish	15 mL
¼ tsp	freshly ground black pepper	1 mL
	Blanched broccoli spears or cauliflower florets (optional)	
	Brussels sprouts, cooked until slightly underdone (optional)	
	Crispy Potato Wedges (optional), see Tips, left	
	Potato chips (optional)	

1. In a medium bowl, combine bacon, cream cheese, Cheddar cheese, smoked oysters, roasted red pepper, jalapeño pepper, mayonnaise, horseradish and black pepper. Mix well, using your hands if necessary. Scrape into ramekin.

2. Bake in preheated oven until hot and bubbly, 20 to 25 minutes. Serve immediately with blanched broccoli, cauliflower, Brussels sprouts, Crispy Potato Wedges or potato chips (if using).

Variation

Chile-Spiked Clam and Bacon Dip: Substitute 1 can (5 oz/142 g) clams, drained, for the smoked oysters.

South American–Style Bean Dip

I originally wanted to make a *salsa de chocho* but had no success finding chochos, a type of lupine bean (think Italian lupini beans) that is popular in Ecuador. So I threw caution to the wind and created something new that's a pan–South American take on bean salsas. Et voilà! This pleasantly spicy, highly nutritious dip can double as a sandwich spread or a substitute for butter in sandwiches. It is also tasty with crudités or tortilla chips.

MAKES ABOUT 2 CUPS (500 ML)

VEGETARIAN FRIENDLY

GLUTEN-FREE FRIENDLY

Tip

If you can't find ají mirasol, substitute guajillo chiles. They are not identical despite what some sources might tell you (see page 46), but they do have a similar heat level.

FYI: I use the term "gluten-free friendly" whenever I include prepared ingredients in a recipe that would otherwise be gluten-free. Manufacturers often add wheat products to prepared foods, so you need to check the label to ensure these products are actually gluten-free.

• Food processor

2	dried ají mirasol (see Tip, left)	2
	Boiling water	
2 cups	drained cooked navy beans	500 mL
3 oz	feta cheese, crumbled	90 g
1/3 cup	chopped red onion	75 mL
2	cloves garlic, chopped	2
1	serrano pepper, finely chopped	1
3 tbsp	olive oil	45 mL
3 tbsp	freshly squeezed lemon juice	45 mL
2	small tomatoes (about 12 oz/375 g total), peeled and diced	2
	Salt and freshly ground black pepper	

1. Place mirasol peppers in a heatproof bowl and cover with boiling water. Let stand until softened, about 30 minutes, weighing down with a cup to ensure they stay submerged. Drain peppers. Remove and discard stems, and chop peppers coarsely.

2. In food processor fitted with the metal blade, combine soaked mirasol peppers, beans, cheese, red onion, garlic and serrano pepper. Pulse until finely chopped and blended, about 15 times, stopping and scraping down the side of the bowl as necessary. Add olive oil and lemon juice and pulse until blended. Transfer to a medium bowl.

3. Fold diced tomatoes into pepper mixture. Season to taste with salt and black pepper. Cover and refrigerate for at least 4 hours or up to 3 days.

Guacamole

Technically, guacamole is a Mexican salsa, which apparently has links to Aztec cuisine. In North America, it has become a classic dip for several reasons: it is very easy to make, loaded with nutrients and absolutely delicious. People tell me that, although it's delicious, my guacamole doesn't taste like other versions. This is, I believe, because I follow the classic Mexican approach. I've been making this guacamole since the late 1970s, based on Diana Kennedy's recipe in her book *The Cuisines of Mexico*. Serve it with tostadas or tortilla chips.

MAKES
2 CUPS (500 ML)

VEGAN FRIENDLY

GLUTEN-FREE FRIENDLY

Tips

If fresh tomatoes aren't in season, you may want to substitute cherry or grape tomatoes instead. You'll need 10 for this recipe.

If you prefer, substitute jalapeño peppers for the serranos. One makes a pleasantly mild guacamole. If you are a heat seeker, add a second jalapeño.

● Food processor

3	small avocados, such as Hass	3
1	tomato, cored and peeled (see Tips, left)	1
4	green onions (white parts only), or 1 slice (about ½ inch/2 cm thick) red onion	4
2 to 4	serrano peppers (see Tips, left), seeded and cut in half	2 to 4
½ cup	fresh cilantro leaves	125 mL
3 tbsp	freshly squeezed lime juice	45 mL
	Salt	

1. In food processor fitted with the metal blade, combine avocados, tomato, green onions, serrano peppers to taste, cilantro and lime juice. Process until desired texture is achieved. (I like mine a bit chunky.) Season to taste with salt.

2. Transfer to a serving bowl. Serve immediately. If you have leftover guacamole, cover it tightly, pressing the plastic wrap against the surface of the dip and refrigerate for up to 24 hours.

To Seed or Not to Seed

Whether you seed and remove the veins inside your peppers is a matter of preference. With the exception of bell peppers, I usually don't seed and devein because, in my opinion, it affects the taste and experience of the pepper. I like the texture the seeds add to a dish. The veins are the placental tissue inside the peppers, and they contain any spiciness, so removing them may be a good idea if you are heat-averse; you can also reduce the quantity of chile called for in a recipe or substitute a chile that ranks lower on the Scoville scale.

Egyptian Hummus (*Ful Medames*)

My version of this dish resulted from a happy accident—I wasn't paying attention and overcooked my lima beans. Instead of serving them as a vegetable, I turned them into a meze. Considered by some to be Egypt's national dish, where it is often eaten for breakfast, *ful medames* is typically presented like a stew, topped with eggs or accompanied by feta cheese, olives or yogurt. It reminds me of traditional hummus, but with a slightly different flavor profile and texture, so I serve it as a spread.

MAKES ABOUT 3½ CUPS (875 ML)

VEGAN FRIENDLY

GLUTEN-FREE FRIENDLY

Tips

In Egypt, fresh frying-type peppers go into dishes like this. If you prefer, substitute a fresh pepper such as Anaheim, banana or even jalapeño for the Aleppo pepper. If you use a jalapeño, start with half because the heat level of these peppers can vary dramatically.

Aleppo pepper is quite mild, so feel free to increase the quantity to suit your taste. I suggest adding it in small increments to ensure you don't overdo it.

In the Middle East, this dip is often accompanied by a tomato salad, such as *Ezme* (page 136).

1¼ cups	dried lima beans	300 mL
½ cup	dried red lentils, rinsed	125 mL
½ tsp	salt	2 mL
2	cloves garlic, puréed (see Tips, page 82)	2
¼ cup	freshly squeezed lemon juice	60 mL
¼ cup	extra virgin olive oil	60 mL
1 tbsp	ground cumin	15 mL
1 tsp	Aleppo pepper (see Tips, left)	5 mL
1	tomato, peeled and diced	1
4	green onions (white and a bit of the green parts), very thinly sliced	4
	Salt and freshly ground black pepper	
2 tbsp	finely chopped fresh parsley	30 mL
	Sweet paprika (optional)	
2	hard-cooked eggs (optional), cut into wedges	2
	Olives (optional)	
	Grilled pita bread wedges	
	Olive oil for drizzling (optional)	

1. In a large saucepan of water, bring lima beans to a boil. Boil rapidly for 5 minutes. Cover, turn off heat and let stand for 1 hour. Drain beans and rinse thoroughly under cold running water. Pop the beans out of their skins. Discard skins.

2. Return beans to saucepan. Add lentils, salt and 3 cups (750 mL) water and bring to a boil. Reduce heat and simmer until water is evaporated and lentils and beans are extremely soft, about 45 minutes. Remove from heat. Using a fork or potato masher, mash until mixture is the consistency of coarsely mashed potatoes.

3. Stir in garlic, lemon juice, oil, cumin, Aleppo pepper, tomato and green onions. Season to taste with salt and black pepper.

4. Transfer to a platter and sprinkle with parsley and paprika (if using). Surround with eggs and/or olives (if using) and pita wedges. Drizzle with olive oil (if using).

Middle Eastern Pepper and Tomato Jam (*Marmouma*)

This is a Middle Eastern version of a spicy tomato jam that is usually served as a meze. I've seen Moroccan and Tunisian versions, which seem to have traveled to Israel, where this dish is called *matboucha*. Most recipes cook the peppers with the tomatoes until everything is reduced. It appears to be an Algerian tweak to roast them first, which I prefer. The jam is great with pita bread or tortilla chips; for a deliciously different option, spoon it over warm bruschetta.

MAKES ABOUT 2 CUPS (500 ML)

VEGAN FRIENDLY

GLUTEN-FREE FRIENDLY

Tip

If you are making this jam for vegans, be sure to use sugar that has not been filtered through bone char.

3	red bell peppers, roasted (see Tips, page 60)	3
2 tbsp	extra virgin olive oil	30 mL
2	cloves garlic, minced	2
1 lb	very ripe tomatoes, peeled and chopped	500 g
2 tsp	Aleppo pepper	10 mL
1 tsp	sweet paprika	5 mL
½ tsp	granulated sugar	2 mL
	Salt and freshly ground black pepper	

1. Peel, seed and cut peppers into thin strips, reserving the juice. Set aside.

2. In a medium skillet, heat oil over medium heat. Add garlic and cook, stirring, just until fragrant. (Do not brown.) Add tomatoes, Aleppo pepper, paprika and sugar. Season to taste with salt and black pepper. Cook, uncovered, until thickened to a jam-like consistency, about 45 minutes.

3. Add reserved peppers with juices and stir well. Cook until flavors are melded, about 5 minutes.

4. Transfer to a small bowl. Cover and refrigerate for up to 1 week. Serve cold or at room temperature.

Black Bean Quesadillas

This classic Tex-Mex recipe (see page 141) is always a hit. Quesadillas are good on their own but are even better with a dollop of fresh salsa, crema (see Tips, left) or even plain sour cream.

(see page 141)

**MAKES
3 QUESADILLAS
(18 TO 24 PIECES)**

VEGETARIAN FRIENDLY

Tips

To make this quantity of cooked beans: Soak and cook 1 cup (250 mL) dried black beans until tender or use 1 can (14 to 19 oz/398 to 540 mL) black beans. Drain and rinse before adding to recipe.

Use a chile powder blend or a single-chile powder, such as ancho or New Mexico.

If you are making these ahead, the edges of the top tortilla may curl up. You can fix this by removing the quesadillas from the oven after they have cooked for about 5 minutes and running a spatula around the edges to turn them down. Return them to the oven to complete cooking.

To make Cumin-Spiked Crema: In a small bowl, combine ½ cup (125 mL) crème fraîche or sour cream, 2 tsp (10 mL) ground cumin and 1 tsp (5 mL) finely grated lime zest. Stir well to blend. Cover and refrigerate for 30 minutes or overnight to allow flavors to blend. Spoon over finished quesadillas.

- Preheat oven to 400°F (200°C)
- Food processor
- Large rimmed baking sheet

2 cups	drained cooked black beans	500 mL
6	green onions (white and a bit of the green parts), cut into chunks	6
½ cup	packed fresh cilantro leaves	125 mL
1 to 2	canned chipotle chile(s) in adobo sauce	1 to 2
2	cloves garlic, quartered	2
1 tbsp	each ground cumin and dried oregano	15 mL
4 oz	cream cheese, softened	125 g
	Salt and freshly ground black pepper	
6	small (6-inch/15 cm) tortillas, preferably corn	6
	Olive oil	
1 tsp	chile powder (see Tips, left)	5 mL
2 tbsp	toasted pumpkin seeds (pepitas), finely chopped (optional)	30 mL

1. In food processor fitted with the metal blade, combine black beans, green onions, cilantro, chipotle chile(s) to taste, garlic, cumin and oregano. Pulse until chopped and blended, about 10 times. Add cream cheese and pulse until blended. Season to taste with salt and black pepper.

2. Place 3 of the tortillas on baking sheet. Spread with bean mixture, leaving a ½-inch (1 cm) border. Top with remaining tortillas. Brush tops of tortillas lightly with olive oil and dust evenly with chile powder.

3. Bake in preheated oven until tops are browned, about 10 minutes. Sprinkle pepitas (if using) evenly over tops. Cut each into 6 to 8 wedges.

Variations

Fried Black Bean Quesadillas: Brush a large skillet lightly with oil and cook quesadillas in batches, turning once, until tortillas are browned.

Quesadillas with Rajas: After spreading the bean mixture over the tortillas, top with *rajas* made from 3 poblano peppers (see page 368).

Crispy Vietnamese Crêpes (Bánh Xèo)

This classic, handheld treat makes a great starter for a casual evening with friends. The crêpes should be thin and crisp, and I like them really stuffed so the filling spills out a bit and gets messy. Adding a lettuce leaf wrapper around the crêpes solves this problem and adds pleasing texture and flavor. If you're cooking for people with food sensitivities, these gems are dairy-, egg- and gluten-free.

MAKES 4 CRÊPES (12 PIECES)

GLUTEN-FREE FRIENDLY

Tips

To make this dish gluten-free, be sure to use gluten-free fish sauce.

Choose a type of lettuce that is soft and easy to fold, such as Boston or red leaf.

- 10-inch (25 cm) nonstick skillet

12	medium lettuce leaves (see Tips, left)	12

Dipping Sauce

2 tbsp	boiling water	30 mL
1 tbsp	granulated sugar	15 mL
3 tbsp	fish sauce	45 mL
2 tbsp	freshly squeezed lime juice	30 mL
2	red Thai bird's-eye chiles, minced	2
1	clove garlic, puréed (see Tips, page 82)	1

Crêpes

½ cup	white rice flour	125 mL
2 tbsp	tapioca flour	30 mL
1 tsp	curry powder	5 mL
½ tsp	granulated sugar	2 mL
¼ tsp	salt	1 mL
¾ cup	coconut milk	175 mL
¼ cup	water	60 mL
3 tbsp	oil (approx.), divided	45 mL

Filling

1 tbsp	oil	15 mL
12 oz	ground pork	375 g
2	cloves garlic, minced	2
½ cup	thinly sliced green onions (white and green parts)	125 mL
1 tbsp	packed brown sugar	15 mL
1 tbsp	fish sauce	15 mL
1½ cups	bean sprouts	375 mL
½ cup	chopped fresh cilantro (leaves and tender stems)	125 mL
	Salt and freshly ground black pepper	

1. *Dipping Sauce:* In a small bowl, stir boiling water with sugar until sugar is dissolved. Stir in fish sauce, lime juice, bird's-eye chiles and garlic. Transfer to a serving bowl or individual bowls and set aside. (Or transfer to a jar, cover tightly and refrigerate for up to 1 week.)

2. *Crêpes:* In a medium bowl, whisk together rice flour, tapioca flour, curry powder, sugar and salt. Whisk in coconut milk and water. Let stand for 15 minutes (or cover and refrigerate up to overnight).

3. *Filling:* Meanwhile, in a medium skillet, heat oil over medium-high heat. Add pork and garlic, and sauté until pork is no longer pink, about 5 minutes. Stir in green onions, brown sugar and fish sauce. Remove from heat and set aside.

4. Whisk crêpe batter. In skillet, heat about 2 tsp (10 mL) of the oil over medium heat. Ladle about one-quarter of the batter into the pan, swirling to evenly cover the surface. (Crêpe should be very thin). Cook until the edge begins to pull away from the side of the pan, about 2 minutes.

5. Spread one-quarter of the pork mixture evenly over half of the crêpe. Top with one-quarter each of the bean sprouts and cilantro. Season to taste with salt and black pepper. Reduce heat to low and cook until crêpe is crisp and browned, about 3 minutes. Using a spatula, fold unfilled portion of crêpe over filling, then slide onto a serving platter. Transfer to a warm oven and keep warm.

6. Repeat with remaining oil, batter and filling. Cut each crêpe into thirds. Wrap each piece in 1 of the lettuce leaves and return to the platter. Serve with dipping sauce.

Kimchi Pancakes

If you are looking for an appetizer that is a bit different, try these tasty bites. My version of this Korean classic differs from the norm in that I use brown rice flour (rather than wheat flour) and no meat (most versions include pork). It's a great dish to serve casually on a kitchen island: guests can break the ice while they dip the pancakes in the sauce.

Tips

If you are making these pancakes for someone who doesn't consume gluten, be sure to use gluten-free fish sauce, red pepper paste and soy sauce. If you are using prepared kimchi, check the label to make sure it is gluten-free. All these products are usually available in well-stocked Korean markets.

Use the type of kimchi that best suits your taste and your heat tolerance. I prefer a pungent kimchi, such as green onion kimchi, which produces a more intense flavor, but I have also made these pancakes with mild cabbage-based Kimchi (page 404) with delicious results.

- Small (6-inch/15 cm diameter) nonstick skillet

¾ cup	brown rice flour	175 mL
2 tbsp	cornstarch	30 mL
½ tsp	salt	2 mL
Pinch	granulated sugar	Pinch
¾ cup	cold water	175 mL
2 tbsp	each fish sauce and kimchi liquid	30 mL
1	egg, beaten	1
¾ cup	chopped drained kimchi (see Tips, left)	175 mL
⅓ cup	grapeseed oil, divided	60 mL

Korean Dipping Sauce

3 tbsp	unseasoned rice vinegar	45 mL
1 tsp	Korean red pepper paste	5 mL
¼ cup	soy sauce	60 mL
1 tbsp	finely chopped fresh cilantro	15 mL
1 tbsp	toasted sesame oil	15 mL
2 tsp	granulated sugar	10 mL

1. *Korean Dipping Sauce:* In a small serving bowl, whisk vinegar with pepper paste until paste is dissolved. Whisk in soy sauce, cilantro, sesame oil and sugar until well combined. Set aside. Whisk before serving.

2. In a bowl, whisk together flour, cornstarch, salt and sugar. Stir in water, fish sauce, kimchi liquid and egg just until the mixture is the consistency of pancake batter, adding a little more water if necessary. Stir in kimchi.

3. In skillet, heat 1 tbsp (15 mL) of the oil over medium-high heat. Drop about ¼ cup (60 mL) of the batter into skillet and cook until bubbles form on top and edges turn brown and crispy, about 2 minutes. Flip and cook for 2 minutes, flattening the top with a spatula to ensure even browning. Repeat until all of the batter is used up, transferring the cooked pancakes to a baking sheet in a warm oven as completed.

4. Cut pancakes into wedges and serve with sauce.

Indian-Style Roti

Unlike Caribbean roti, which are filled, Indian roti are simply flatbreads. Here, the dough is made with potatoes and flour seasoned with fresh chiles and curry powder. The results are remarkably tasty. Serve them plain with a sprinkle of fine sea salt or top with a dollop of your favorite chutney. For something special, serve them with a fresh chutney such as Suneeta's Cilantro Mint Chutney (page 378) or Date and Tamarind Chutney (page 379).

MAKES ABOUT 24 PIECES

VEGAN FRIENDLY

GLUTEN-FREE FRIENDLY

Tips

To make these gluten-free, substitute an equal quantity of your favorite gluten-free flour blend for the all-purpose.

An easy way to cook potatoes in their skins is to microwave them. Place the scrubbed potato in a microwave-safe dish. Add cold water to a depth of about ½ inch (1 cm), cover and microwave on High until potato is tender, about 6 minutes. Leave the lid on and let cool for at least 5 minutes before running the potato under cold water and removing the skin.

For best results, use floury potatoes, which do not contain as much water as waxy varieties. The most common are russet (Idaho) potatoes.

If you have access to jwala chiles, use them here in place of the finger chiles.

Be sure to use good sea salt, such as fleur de sel, to finish the roti. Table salt has an unpleasant acrid taste that diminishes the result.

- Large heavy skillet

1½ lbs	russet (Idaho) potato (about 1 extra large), boiled in its skin until fork-tender, cooled, peeled and shredded (see Tips, left)	750 g
2	green finger chiles, seeded and diced (see Tips, left)	2
4	green onions (white parts only), finely chopped	4
¼ cup	finely chopped fresh cilantro	60 mL
1 tsp	salt	5 mL
1 tsp	curry powder	5 mL
1 cup	all-purpose flour	250 mL
¼ cup	oil (approx.), divided	60 mL
	Salt (see Tips, left)	
	Chutney (optional)	

1. In a medium bowl, combine potato, chiles, green onions, cilantro, salt and curry powder. Mix well. Gradually stir in flour, mixing until a soft dough forms and using your hands to knead when the dough becomes too stiff to stir.

2. Pinch off a piece of dough about the size of a walnut and, on a lightly floured surface, roll into a 3-inch (7.5 cm) circle. Repeat until all the dough is used up.

3. In skillet, heat 1 tbsp (15 mL) of the oil over medium heat. Add roti, in batches and adding remaining oil as necessary, and cook, turning once, until lightly browned on both sides and slightly puffed, about 2 minutes per side. Place roti on a warm platter as they are completed and sprinkle tops lightly with salt. Serve with chutney (if using).

Parmesan Crackers

These tasty little bites are just the nibble to accompany a predinner glass of wine. This is an adaptation of a recipe that appeared in Elizabeth David's book *Spices, Salt and Aromatics in the English Kitchen*. David's take on the recipe originally appeared in *The Cookery Book of Lady Clark of Tillypronie*, which was published in 1909, nine years after Lady Clark's death. It illustrates the use of cayenne in the British kitchen, which is documented elsewhere in the latter book (see page 94).

MAKES ABOUT 24 CRACKERS

VEGETARIAN FRIENDLY

Tip

To grate the Parmesan cheese, use the small holes on a box grater or a sharp-toothed rasp grater, such as those made by Microplane.

- Preheat oven to 325°F (160°C)
- One-inch (2.5 cm) round cutter
- Baking sheets, lined with parchment paper

¾ cup	all-purpose flour	175 mL
2 oz	butter (¼ cup/60 mL, or ½ stick)	60 g
1 cup	finely grated Parmesan cheese	250 mL
2	egg yolks, beaten	2
½ tsp	salt	2 mL
½ tsp	cayenne pepper	2 mL

1. In a medium bowl, combine flour and butter. Using 2 knives, a fork or your fingers, rub butter into flour until it is the size of small peas. Stir in cheese, egg yolks, salt and cayenne pepper just until combined. Stir in just enough water to hold the dough together, about 1 tbsp (15 mL).

2. On a lightly floured surface, roll out dough to ³⁄₈-inch (9 mm) thickness. Using cutter, cut into 1-inch (2.5 cm) rounds. Arrange on prepared baking sheets.

3. Bake in preheated oven until golden, about 20 minutes. Serve warm. (Store leftovers in an airtight container for up to 1 week. Warm before serving.)

Chile Savvy

It seems that more than a century ago Lady Clark, perhaps intuitively, understood at least one principle of balancing flavors—pungent cayenne with umami-rich Parmesan.

Canary Island Wrinkled Potatoes with Mojo

This unusual recipe is a specialty of the Canary Islands, where, apparently, people often boiled their potatoes in the abundant saltwater because fresh water was at a premium. It's an example of necessity spawning a spectacular result. Both of the mojos can do double duty as salsas—the red yields about 1 cup (250 mL), and the green makes ½ cup (125 mL). They are great for dipping with just about anything and make lovely accompaniments to grilled meats or fish.

MAKES 6 SERVINGS

VEGAN FRIENDLY

GLUTEN-FREE FRIENDLY

Tip

To roast peppers: Brush peppers lightly with oil and place them directly on a hot grill on a preheated barbecue, or arrange them on a baking sheet and place under a preheated broiler. Grill or broil, turning 2 or 3 times, until the skin on all sides is blackened, about 20 minutes. Transfer to a heatproof bowl. Cover with a plate and let stand until cool. Using a sharp knife, lift off the skin, reserving any accumulated juices. Discard skin, stems and seeds.

- Food processor
- Large, preferably wide-bottomed, saucepan with lid

½ cup	coarse sea or kosher salt	125 mL
2 lbs	small waxy new potatoes (about 24), unpeeled and scrubbed	1 kg

Red Pepper Mojo

2	red bell peppers, roasted (see Tip, left) and quartered	2
1	red finger chile, chopped	1
2	cloves garlic, chopped	2
¼ cup	chopped fresh parsley	60 mL
2 tbsp	red wine vinegar	30 mL
1 tsp	sweet Spanish paprika	5 mL
1 tsp	ground cumin	5 mL
¼ cup	extra virgin olive oil	60 mL
	Salt	

Cilantro Mojo

2 cups	packed fresh cilantro (leaves and tender stems)	500 mL
2 tbsp	chopped green onion (white and green parts)	30 mL
2	cloves garlic, quartered	2
1	green finger chile or serrano pepper, quartered	1
2 tbsp	sherry vinegar	30 mL
1 tsp	dried oregano	5 mL
1 tsp	ground cumin	5 mL
¼ cup	extra virgin olive oil	60 mL

1. *Red Pepper Mojo:* In food processor fitted with the metal blade, combine roasted red peppers, finger chile, garlic, parsley, vinegar, paprika and cumin. Pulse until vegetables are chopped and blended, about 5 times, stopping and scraping down the side of the bowl as necessary. Add oil and process until smooth and blended, about 30 seconds. Season to taste with salt. Transfer to a serving bowl and let stand at room temperature for 30 minutes to allow the flavors to bloom. Serve at room temperature.

2. *Cilantro Mojo:* Meanwhile, in food processor fitted with the metal blade, combine cilantro, green onion, garlic, finger chile, vinegar, oregano and cumin. Pulse until chopped and blended, about 5 times, stopping and scraping down the side of the bowl as necessary. Add oil and process until smooth and blended, about 30 seconds. Transfer to a serving bowl and let stand at room temperature for 30 minutes to allow the flavors to bloom. Serve at room temperature.

3. Meanwhile, stir salt into a large saucepan of water. Add potatoes and, if necessary, more water to cover. Bring to a boil. Partially cover, reduce heat and simmer until potatoes are tender, about 15 minutes.

4. Drain potatoes and return to pan. Place a clean tea towel over top of pan and cover with lid. Heat over very low heat, shaking the pan several times, until potatoes are wrinkled and dusted with residual salt.

5. Transfer potatoes to a serving platter. Cut in half, if desired, for dipping. Serve warm with mojos.

Variations

Cilantro and Green Pepper Mojo: Reduce cilantro to 1 cup and add $1/2$ green bell pepper, quartered, to food processor before pulsing to chop.

Salt-Roasted Potatoes with Mojo: Although they're not authentic, these potatoes are delicious and particularly easy to make during barbecue season. Boil the potatoes in regular salted water as you would to make a side dish. Cut them in half to facilitate dipping. In a bowl large enough to accommodate all of the potatoes, combine 2 tbsp (30 mL) extra virgin olive oil and season to taste with coarse sea salt (don't be shy with the salt). Toss to coat well. Place potatoes, cut side down, on a preheated barbecue or broiler pan. Grill or broil, turning once, until potatoes are beginning to brown, about 5 minutes per side. Let cool slightly before serving with red pepper and cilantro mojos.

Jalapeño Poppers

Jalapeño poppers are a Tex-Mex treat that likely developed from the Mexican dish known as *chiles rellenos*, stuffed peppers traditionally made using poblano peppers. They are a classic because they are succulent little bites, which makes them an ideal appetizer.

Tips

I speak from experience when I say that jalapeño peppers can vary dramatically in heat—even those in the same batch. I have had some that verge on bell-pepper sweetness and others that are too hot to enjoy as casings for a filling. Be brave and taste your peppers before making this recipe. It makes sense to have a soothing dairy item, such as sliced cheese, on hand just in case you get a spicy one.

If you like, you can substitute 8 padrón peppers or 4 poblano peppers for the jalapeños.

To make these poppers gluten-free, use an all-purpose gluten-free blend and gluten-free panko. Otherwise, all-purpose flour and regular panko do the trick.

When roasting the peppers (Step 1), watch carefully to ensure they don't burn.

- Preheat broiler
- Rimmed baking sheet

8	large jalapeño peppers (see Tips, left)	8
2 tbsp	oil	30 mL
1 cup	shredded Monterey Jack cheese	250 mL
4	green onions (white and green parts), thinly sliced	4
1 tsp	each ground cumin and dried oregano	5 mL
¼ tsp	smoked sweet paprika	1 mL
¼ cup	flour (see Tips, left)	60 mL
1	egg	1
¼ cup	milk	60 mL
¼ cup	almond meal	60 mL
¼ cup	panko bread crumbs (see Tips, left)	60 mL
	Shredded lettuce (optional)	

1. Lightly brush peppers all over with oil and arrange on baking sheet. Roast under preheated broiler, turning once, until skins blacken and blister, about 5 minutes per side. Transfer to a large bowl, cover with a plate and set aside to sweat. When cool, peel off skins and discard. Set peppers aside.

2. Meanwhile, in a medium bowl, combine cheese, green onions, cumin, oregano and paprika. Toss well to combine.

3. When you are ready to cook, preheat oven to 350°F (180°C). Cut a slit along 1 side of each pepper and, using a grapefruit spoon, scrape out seeds and veins. Gently stuff pepper with about 2 tbsp (30 mL) of the filling. Repeat until all peppers are filled and filling is used up.

4. Place flour on a plate. In a bowl, beat egg with milk. On another plate, combine almond meal and panko.

5. One at a time, dredge stuffed peppers in flour, then dip into egg mixture, and then dredge in almond flour mixture, making sure coating is even at each step. Place peppers, seam side up, on baking sheet. Bake in preheated oven until cheese is melted and bubbling up over the seam, about 30 minutes. Serve immediately.

Padrón and Shishito Peppers

These little green peppers, both of which are mildly hot and belong to the *Capsicum annuum* family, are very close relatives. Exactly how they differ is a subject of much debate. There is a rule of thumb with these two varieties: most peppers in any batch will be pleasantly spicy but every tenth one will be a thrilling heat seeker. Based entirely on my own experience, I would say that padróns are more inclined to be fiery than shishitos. I've often hit two fire bombs in a row. I have also found padrón peppers to be sturdier, which makes them acceptable vessels for stuffing. For instance, you can use them instead of jalapeño peppers to make Jalapeño Poppers (opposite). In his book *Made in Spain*, the Spanish-American chef José Andrés stuffs padrón peppers with tetilla, a Galician cow's milk cheese, and fries them in oil until the cheese melts. He finishes them with a sprinkle of sea salt and a drizzle of olive oil.

Perhaps not surprisingly, shishito peppers are very popular in Japan. Throughout the summer, says Nancy Singleton Hachisu, author of the delightful book *Japanese Farm Food*, shishito peppers are grilled or sautéed across the country. She likes to sauté hers, finishing them with a little miso, sake and ginger, and a hint of dried hot chile. One my favorite ways to enjoy these peppers is to grill them: I insert 2 skewers horizontally, spearing 3 or 4 peppers per pair, and then marinate them in 4 parts soy sauce and 1 part sake. As they are grilling, I brush them with the leftover marinade. The peppers are done when they are nicely blistered. Shishito peppers also make delicious tempura.

Both padrón and shishito peppers are great on pizza. If you have leftover peppers, refrigerate them overnight, chop them finely and add them to scrambled eggs for breakfast.

In culinary terms, you can treat these peppers as identical. If you are more of a purist, keep the seasonings in the family, so to speak: Asian for shishito and Mediterranean for padrón. Though, at the charming Seattle restaurant How to Cook a Wolf, I thoroughly enjoyed a dish in which grilled shishitos were substituted for Catalonian *calçots* and served with Romesco Sauce (page 388) for dipping.

Blistered Padrón or Shishito Peppers

This is the simplest, and probably the best, way to serve these peppers.

> Oil for frying
> Padrón or shishito peppers, rinsed and patted dry
> Extra virgin olive oil
> Flaky sea salt, such as Maldon

1. Pour oil into a large skillet to a depth of about ¼ inch (0.5 cm) and heat over medium-high heat. Using a small skewer, poke a hole in the end of each pepper. (This prevents bursting.)

2. Standing well back, add peppers, in batches, without crowding. Fry, turning once or twice with tongs, until blistered and charred. Remove from oil and transfer to a paper towel–lined plate and let drain. When all the peppers have been fried, transfer to a serving platter, drizzle lightly with extra virgin olive oil and sprinkle liberally with coarse sea salt.

Stuffed Piquillo Peppers

Piquillo peppers are small triangular-shaped sweet peppers from northern Spain. You can purchase them in jars or tins, already roasted over wood and peeled. (Doing the job yourself can be very time consuming.) Piquillo peppers are delicious stuffed with a wide range of fillings, including seafood and minced veal or pork. In this recipe, I have used seasoned goat cheese, but I have seen other versions made with *labneh*, a fresh yogurt-based cheese that is popular in the Middle East.

MAKES 4 TO 6 SERVINGS

VEGETARIAN FRIENDLY

GLUTEN-FREE FRIENDLY

Tips

When you remove the piquillo peppers from the jar or can, some may break—but don't worry. Just set them aside, chop them finely and add them to the filling, which is very forgiving.

Piquillo peppers are extremely versatile and are a tasty base for easy-to-make appetizers. Keep a jar or can of them in the pantry so you are always ready for unexpected guests.

- Preheat oven to 350°F (180°C)
- Large ovenproof serving plate

8 oz	soft goat cheese	250 g
2	green onions (white and green parts), thinly sliced	2
2 tbsp	drained capers, chopped	30 mL
2 tbsp	chopped toasted pine nuts	30 mL
2 tbsp	finely chopped fresh parsley	30 mL
¼ tsp	smoked sweet or hot paprika	1 mL
12	jarred or canned piquillo peppers, drained (see Tips, left)	12
¼ cup	extra virgin olive oil	60 mL
6	cloves garlic, thinly sliced	6
	Chopped fresh parsley	
	Freshly ground black pepper	

1. In a medium bowl, stir together goat cheese, green onions, capers, pine nuts, parsley and smoked paprika. Using a 1 tsp (5 mL) measure, gently stuff filling into peppers (they are fragile and likely to tear). Arrange in a single layer on ovenproof serving plate as completed.

2. In a small skillet, heat oil over medium heat. Add garlic and cook, stirring and without allowing it to brown, just until fragrant, about 1 minute. Pour over peppers.

3. Place plate in preheated oven and bake until peppers are warm and filling is heated through, about 10 minutes.

4. Sprinkle with parsley and season to taste with black pepper. Serve immediately.

Deviled Eggs

This old-fashioned appetizer is a staple at picnics and cocktail parties. You can make it the traditional way, with cayenne and perhaps a dash of hot pepper vinegar, or you can bump up the spiciness by using pickled bird-type peppers, such as malagueta or piri-piri.

Tips

Adjust the quantity of pickled peppers to suit your taste. The amount called for produces a pleasantly pungent result.

Use whichever type of paprika you prefer. Sweet paprika is the most common deviled egg topping. However, hot paprika adds a nice jolt of heat, while smoked paprika (used judiciously) adds a uniquely pleasant smokiness.

The greatest challenge in making deviled eggs is peeling the cooked egg so it's nice and smooth. Quick cooling helps eliminate that unattractive ring around the yolk, and it facilitates removal of the shell, too. After the egg has cooled, tap the wide end on the counter to create cracks in the shell. Using your fingers, gently peel away the shell and membrane.

In the American South, where deviled eggs are a tradition, hostesses have plates with indentations made specially for serving this delicacy. If you don't have this type of plate, you can still keep the eggs from slipping around: cut a thin piece from the convex side of each cooked egg half before filling to create a flat bottom.

6	eggs	6
3 tbsp	mayonnaise	45 mL
1 tbsp	Dijon mustard	15 mL
1 tbsp	finely snipped fresh chives	15 mL
1 tbsp	minced drained capers	15 mL
½ tsp	minced drained pickled bird-type peppers (see Tips, left), or ¼ tsp (1 mL) cayenne pepper	2 mL
¼ tsp	salt	1 mL
	Hot pepper vinegar (optional), see page 215	
	Freshly ground black pepper	
	Paprika (see Tips, left)	

1. In a large saucepan, combine eggs and enough cold water to cover. Bring to a boil. Cover, remove from heat and let stand for 12 minutes. Drain well. Transfer to a bowl of ice water and let stand for 5 minutes. Carefully peel the eggs (see Tips, left) and rinse well under cold running water.

2. Cut eggs in halve lengthwise and carefully scoop out the yolks, keeping the whites intact. In a medium bowl, combine egg yolks, mayonnaise, mustard, chives, capers, pickled peppers, salt, and hot pepper vinegar (if using) and black pepper to taste. Mix well.

3. Spoon filling into whites. (For a more elegant presentation, use a pastry bag and pipe filling into whites.) Dust lightly with paprika. Arrange on a serving platter, cover and refrigerate until ready to serve.

Fresh Cucumber Kimchi

This is a version of kimchi, described as fresh or "summer" kimchi by the Korean cook who introduced me to it. I like to serve it as a warm-weather treat. Served cold from the fridge, it makes a wonderfully refreshing appetizer when cucumbers are in season. The short brining time is designed to break down the vegetable tissue, which allows the flavors of the chile and fish sauce to penetrate.

MAKES 6 SERVINGS

GLUTEN-FREE FRIENDLY

Tips

To make this dish gluten-free, be sure to use gluten-free fish sauce.

I call for English cucumbers because they are widely available. However, Japanese or Persian cucumbers work equally well. For this recipe, you'll need 1 lb (500 g) of them. If they are organic, feel free to leave the skin on; otherwise, peel them first.

I don't know if it's authentic, but my Korean mentor cuts her cucumbers into large chunks (about 1 inch/2.5 cm thick), then scores each piece deeply, outlining the shape of quartered wedges. She then layers the seasoning mix over of the chunks. I find these larger pieces too cumbersome to consume easily—I prefer my more-manageable bite-size pieces.

1	English cucumber (see Tips, left)	1
1 tbsp	coarse sea salt	15 mL
4	green onions (white and green parts), very thinly sliced	4
1	carrot, finely shredded	1
1 tbsp	fish sauce	15 mL
2 tsp	granulated sugar	10 mL
1 tsp	Korean red pepper powder	5 mL

1. Cut cucumber into $\frac{1}{2}$-inch (1 cm) chunks crosswise, then halve chunks vertically. In a medium bowl, combine cucumbers with salt, tossing to coat evenly. Set aside for about 10 minutes to sweat. When cucumbers are wet and glistening, using a slotted spoon, transfer to a colander, reserving remaining brine. Rinse cucumbers well under cold water. Pat dry and transfer to a nonreactive bowl.

2. Meanwhile, in a small bowl, combine green onions, carrot, fish sauce, sugar and red pepper powder. Mix well. Add to cucumbers along with 1 tbsp (15 mL) of the reserved brine. Toss to combine. Cover tightly and set aside at room temperature for up to 2 hours to begin the fermentation process.

3. Refrigerate overnight or for up to 2 days. Serve cold.

Fresh Radish Kimchi

This simple pickle is another refreshing summertime pleasure. I very much enjoy it cold from the fridge, when radishes are at their seasonal peak. In Korea, the radish leaves are often added; if that idea appeals to you, by all means give it a try.

**MAKES
10 SERVINGS**

VEGAN FRIENDLY

GLUTEN-FREE FRIENDLY

Tips

If you are making this recipe for vegans, be sure to use sugar that has not been filtered through bone char.

Use whatever radishes are at their peak. I've made this kimchi with regular round radishes, both white and red, as well as French Breakfast radishes. All were delicious.

To purée gingerroot or garlic quickly and easily, use a sharp-toothed rasp grater, such as those made by Microplane.

1 lb	radishes (about 2 bunches), trimmed and halved (see Tips, left)	500 g
2 tbsp	coarse sea salt	30 mL
1 tsp	granulated sugar	5 mL
1 tsp	Korean red pepper powder	5 mL
¼ tsp	puréed gingerroot (see Tips, at left)	1 mL

1. In a medium bowl, combine radishes and salt, tossing to coat evenly. Set aside for about 20 minutes to sweat. When radishes are wet and glistening, using a slotted spoon, transfer to a colander, reserving remaining brine. Rinse radishes well under cold water. Pat dry and transfer to a nonreactive bowl.

2. In a small bowl, combine sugar, red pepper powder, ginger and 1 tbsp (15 mL) of the reserved radish brine. Mix well. Add to radishes and toss to combine. Cover tightly and set aside at room temperature for up to 2 hours to begin the fermentation process.

3. Refrigerate overnight or for up to 2 days. Serve cold.

Focus on: Chiles in Korea

Chiles—the spicier the better—are a key component of Korean cuisine. They are grown extensively in the country and their use is deeply ingrained in the culture. According to author Hi Soo Shin Hepinstall, author of *Growing Up in a Korean Kitchen,* chiles are one of the three quintessential ingredients in Korean cooking (the other two are garlic and green onions). She writes that "deliciously burning hot," which captures the sense of pleasure Koreans experience when eating peppers, is the "ultimate expression of delight for Korean hot pepper aficionados." It signifies "a spiciness so explosive it can make the diner break into a sweat."

Korean recipes call for peppers in a variety of forms. Fresh peppers are usually green. Physically, the hotter ones resemble Anaheim peppers (they're about 3 inches/7.5 cm long and tapered) but are more pungent—a tad hotter than jalapeños. The milder green peppers are small (about 1½ inches/4 cm long) and wrinkled. They are often fried. Red peppers are usually dried and made into the famous Korean red pepper powders and pastes.

Hot red pepper paste, called *koch'ujang* (often romanized as *gochujang*), is one of the essential Korean sauces, along with soy sauce and fermented soybean paste. The paste is made from red pepper powder and ingredients such as glutinous rice and soybean paste, and subsequently fermented. Traditionally, families made it at home and aged it outdoors in large earthenware crocks called *jangdokdae.*

Hot red pepper powder, called *koch'ukaru* (or *gochugaru*), comes in three textures: coarse, which is used for kimchi; crushed flakes, which is used most often as a garnish; and fine, which is used for general cooking. The powder does have a unique flavor, and although you could substitute a smaller quantity of cayenne pepper for it in a recipe, I would do so only if absolutely necessary. Koreans take their chile powder seriously. I buy mine at a Korean market, in a vacuum-sealed, date-stamped bag.

Hot red pepper threads, called *sil kochu* (or *sil gochu*), are made from dried hot chiles. This shredded dried red pepper looks like long strands of saffron. The threads are very pretty, and a sprinkling makes an elegant finish to many dishes.

Pickled green and red hot peppers, or *koch'uji,* are also used widely in Korean cuisine, often as appetizers or side dishes. They may be chopped and added to noodles or fried rice, or even kimchi, or tossed with ingredients such as chopped onion and oil, and served as something resembling salsa.

Crab Farci

This version of a crab "stuffing" is a Caribbean specialty that traveled via France to islands such as Martinique and Guadeloupe, where it is usually made from freshly cooked crabs. After the meat is removed, the shells are washed and the mixture is served in the shells (or, in some cases, in plastic replications of the shells). I find it much easier to use pasteurized crabmeat. Serving this appetizer in scallop shells creates, in my opinion, a far prettier presentation.

MAKES 4 TO 10 SERVINGS

GLUTEN-FREE FRIENDLY

Tips

To make this appetizer gluten-free, use gluten-free bread crumbs.

Half of a habanero pepper produces a nicely hot result. I have served this appetizer to people who are truly heat-averse and even they were on the cusp of enjoying its spiciness. I recommend adding the optional cayenne to the bread crumb mixture only if you are a heat seeker.

- Preheat oven to 350°F (180°C)
- 8 to 10 clean scallop shells
- Rimmed baking sheet

2 cups	pasteurized crabmeat (1 lb/500 g)	500 mL
½ to 1	habanero pepper, minced	½ to 1
6	green onions (white and green parts), thinly sliced	6
½ cup	chopped fresh parsley	125 mL
¼ cup	freshly squeezed lime juice	60 mL
2 tbsp	dry sherry	30 mL
1 tbsp	mayonnaise	15 mL
1 tsp	curry powder	5 mL
½ tsp	ground allspice	2 mL
	Salt and freshly ground black pepper	
1¼ cups	dry bread crumbs, such as panko	300 mL
⅓ cup	butter, melted	75 mL
1 tbsp	finely snipped fresh chives	15 mL
2 tsp	finely chopped fresh thyme	10 mL
	Cayenne pepper (optional), see Tips, left	
	Lime wedges	
	Hot sauce	

1. In a medium bowl, combine crabmeat, habanero pepper to taste, green onions, parsley, lime juice, sherry, mayonnaise, curry powder and allspice. Mix well. Season to taste with salt and black pepper.

2. In another medium bowl, combine bread crumbs, butter, chives, thyme, and cayenne (if using) to taste. Mix well.

3. Place scallop shells on rimmed baking sheet. Spoon crab mixture into shells, dividing equally. Sprinkle bread crumb mixture evenly over top. Bake in preheated oven until bread crumbs begin to brown and crab mixture is bubbly, about 30 minutes. Transfer shells to a large serving platter. Serve with lime wedges and hot sauce.

Classic Ceviche

The first time I ate ceviche, decades ago, I had just climbed out of the Pacific Ocean and onto a raft moored off the coast of Acapulco, Mexico. Young men on the raft were keeping the marinated fish chilled in plastic buckets and ladling it into paper cups to refresh exhausted swimmers. It was heavenly! This version mimics that simple presentation and is easy to make. The fish "cooks" in the lime juice in about the time it takes to prepare the remainder of the ingredients.

MAKES ABOUT 5 CUPS (1.25 L)

GLUTEN-FREE FRIENDLY

Tips

Ceviche is traditionally made in countries with hot climates. For best results, use a firm white fish from a warm location. Because of concerns about the environmental sustainability of some fish and seafood, I recommend that you check reliable websites, such as the Monterey Bay Aquarium's Seafood Watch site (www.seafoodwatch.org) or the Environmental Defense Fund's Seafood Selector site (http://seafood.edf.org) for the latest information on fish before purchasing.

To make perfectly even paper-thin slices of onion, use the slicing blade on your food processor or a mandoline.

Ceviche is a colorful dish and is very pretty served in a clear glass or crystal bowl. You can also serve it on porcelain spoons for a party, or, as they often do in Mexico, with tostadas or tortilla chips.

1 lb	skinless fish fillets (see Tips, left), cut into ½-inch (1 cm) cubes	500 g
1 cup	freshly squeezed lime juice (about 8 limes)	250 mL
2	tomatoes, peeled, seeded and diced	2
1 to 2	jalapeño pepper(s), seeded and diced	1 to 2
1	small red onion, quartered vertically and sliced paper-thin (see Tips, left)	1
1	avocado, pitted, peeled and diced	1
¼ cup	finely chopped fresh cilantro	60 mL
2 tbsp	extra virgin olive oil	30 mL
1 tsp	salt	5 mL
	Tortilla chips (optional), see Tips, left	

1. In a serving bowl, combine fish and lime juice. Toss well to coat. Cover and refrigerate until fish becomes opaque, about 1 hour.

2. Add tomatoes, jalapeño pepper(s) to taste, red onion, avocado, cilantro, oil and salt. Toss well to combine. Serve cold with tortilla chips (if using).

Variations

Shrimp Ceviche: Substitute peeled deveined shrimp for the fish.

Ecuadoran Ceviche: Substitute ½ cup (125 mL) orange juice for half of the lime juice; swap in a fresh yellow ají amarillo or red ají colorado, if available, in place of the jalapeño(s); and stir in 2 tbsp (30 mL) ketchup. Omit the avocado.

Shrimp in Piri-Piri Butter

Piri-piri sauce, made from an African bird-type chile (see page 48), is ubiquitous in Portugal. You will recognize it as the compelling flavor underlying the Portuguese flame-grilled rotisserie chicken made famous by the popularity of *churrasqueira* restaurants such as Nando's. The piri-piri is a hot, but not super-hot, chile. I have been able to buy dried or pickled versions in North America, but never fresh. But ready-made piri-piri sauce captures the chile's flavor and makes these simple yet delicious shrimp easy to prepare. The shrimp are lovely on a platter as part of an antipasti spread. They are also excellent served with chunks of country-style bread and napkins—guests can spoon the shrimp and luscious sauce over the bread and enjoy it like an ad hoc bruschetta.

MAKES ABOUT 25 SHRIMP

GLUTEN-FREE FRIENDLY

Tips

Use a baking dish that is large enough to accommodate the shrimp in a single layer, but small enough to ensure they're surrounded by the maximum amount of butter sauce.

Look for piri-piri sauce in Portuguese markets or specialty stores. It should be gluten-free, but if you have celiac disease, be sure to check the label. If you can't find it, substitute another hot pepper sauce, being aware that it might not have the same complexity. Add the sauce in small increments and adjust the quantity in case it is hotter.

Double or triple the recipe to meet your needs, bearing in mind that the shrimp will cook more quickly and evenly if they are in a single layer.

- Preheat oven to 375°F (190°C)
- Baking dish (see Tips, left)

1 lb	jumbo shrimp (see Tips, opposite)	500 g
½ cup	clarified butter (ghee)	125 mL
3 tbsp	piri-piri sauce (see Tips, left)	45 mL
2 tsp	puréed garlic (see Tips, page 82)	10 mL
2 tbsp	freshly squeezed lemon juice	30 mL
2 tbsp	finely chopped fresh parsley	30 mL
	Salt and freshly ground black pepper	

1. Peel and devein shrimp, leaving tails on. Pat dry with a paper towel.

2. In a bowl, combine butter, piri-piri sauce and garlic. Add shrimp and toss until well coated. Transfer to baking dish, pouring any remaining butter mixture evenly over the shrimp.

3. Bake in preheated oven until shrimp are pink and curled, about 10 minutes. Drizzle with lemon juice and sprinkle with parsley. Season to taste with salt and black pepper. Serve hot.

Spicy Sizzling Shrimp

These shrimp, Spanish in inspiration, are poached in olive oil and seasoned with garlic, hot pepper and sherry vinegar. The results are succulent. Serve them on a platter and allow people to spear them with forks, wooden skewers or toothpicks.

MAKES ABOUT 25 SHRIMP

Tips

One pound (500 g) of jumbo shrimp contains between 21 and 25 shrimp.

For the most succulent results, brine the shrimp before cooking them. Dissolve 2 tbsp (30 mL) kosher salt in 1 cup (250 mL) boiling water. Add ice cubes and let stand until liquid is cool to the touch. Add prepared shrimp and more water, if necessary, to cover. Set aside at room temperature for 15 minutes. Drain and rinse thoroughly under cold running water. Pat dry. Continue with recipe.

Chile Savvy

This recipe is a classic example of using hot and sweet to balance flavors. Pungent hot pepper mitigates the bitterness of vinegar, which is flattered by the sweetness of mild paprika.

- 10-inch (25 cm) skillet

1 lb	jumbo shrimp (see Tips, left)	500 g
½ cup	extra virgin olive oil	125 mL
4	cloves garlic, thinly sliced	4
2 tsp	hot pepper flakes	10 mL
1 tbsp	sherry vinegar	15 mL
	Smoked sweet paprika	
	Flaky sea salt, such as Maldon	
	Country-style bread, cut in chunks	

1. Peel and devein shrimp. Pat dry with a paper towel.

2. In skillet, heat oil and garlic over low heat until the oil begins to shimmer and garlic is fragrant, about 4 minutes. Stir in hot pepper flakes. Add shrimp and cook, stirring and coating shrimp with the warm oil, until firm and pink, about 4 minutes.

3. Using a slotted spoon, transfer shrimp and garlic to a warm serving platter, reserving oil mixture. Drizzle shrimp with vinegar and add remaining oil mixture to taste. Season to taste with paprika and salt. Serve with bread.

Soups

Down-Home Chicken Gumbo

Gumbo is a Louisiana specialty, but its roots lie in West Africa. *Gumbo* is an African word for pectin-rich okra, one of the traditional thickeners in this soup (the other is filé powder, or ground dried sassafras leaves). African slaves brought okra to the New World, along with their love of very hot peppers. Since then the dish has become a spicy, multicultural mélange that ranges in thickness between soup and stew. In this version, I have dispensed with the typical Cajun roux, which results in a pleasantly spicy broth-based soup.

MAKES 6 TO 8 SERVINGS

GLUTEN-FREE FRIENDLY

Tips

You can substitute any mildly hot chile, such as Fresno or serrano, for the jalapeño.

The quantity of Cajun seasoning you add will depend on the amount of cayenne pepper in your blend (they vary) and your preference for heat. One teaspoon (5 mL) of the blend I have produces a very pleasantly spicy soup, so I advise erring on the side of caution. In my opinion, only true heat seekers would prefer the larger quantity. You can always supplement with cayenne pepper, and you'll be able to add hot pepper sauce at the table.

Okra is a great thickener for soups, but it becomes unpleasantly sticky when overcooked.

Andouille, a spicy smoked pork sausage used in Cajun cooking, is traditionally added to gumbo. If you can find it, use it in this soup and add the smaller quantity of Cajun seasoning.

1 tbsp	olive oil	15 mL
1	onion, finely chopped	1
4	stalks celery, diced	4
1	red bell pepper, seeded and diced	1
1	jalapeño pepper (see Tips, left), seeded and diced	1
4	cloves garlic, minced	4
1 to 2 tsp	Cajun seasoning (see Tips, left)	5 to 10 mL
1	bay leaf	1
1 tsp	salt	5 mL
½ tsp	freshly ground black pepper	2 mL
¼ cup	short-grain brown rice	60 mL
2 tbsp	tomato paste	30 mL
1	can (14 oz/398 mL) diced tomatoes, with juice	1
5 cups	chicken stock	1.25 L
8 oz	skinless boneless chicken, diced	250 g
8 oz	smoked ham, diced	250 g
2 cups	sliced okra (¼ inch/0.5 cm thick), see Tips, left	500 mL
	Finely chopped green onions	
	Hot pepper sauce (optional)	

1. In a skillet, heat oil over medium heat. Add onion, celery, bell pepper and jalapeño pepper and cook, stirring, until softened, about 5 minutes. Add garlic, Cajun seasoning to taste, bay leaf, salt and black pepper and cook, stirring, for 1 minute. Add rice and toss well to coat. Stir in tomato paste. Stir in tomatoes and juice, and stock and bring to a boil.

2. Stir in chicken and ham. Reduce heat to low, cover and simmer until rice is tender, about 25 minutes. Stir in okra. Cover and simmer just until okra is tender, about 10 minutes. Discard bay leaf.

3. Ladle into warm serving bowls and top with green onions to taste. Pass hot pepper sauce (if using) at the table.

French-Style Carrot Soup with a Twist

This is my version of *potage Crécy*, a French carrot soup thickened with rice. This version is not traditional, but the addition of piment d'Espelette adds a subtle hint of sharpness that pleasantly balances the intense sweetness of the carrots.

MAKES 4 SERVINGS

VEGETARIAN FRIENDLY

GLUTEN-FREE FRIENDLY

Tips

If you use paprika instead of the piment d'Espelette, avoid smoked paprika, which would overwhelm the soup. If you want a bit of heat but don't have piment d'Espelette, substitute ¼ tsp (1 mL) cayenne pepper and 1 tsp (5 mL) sweet paprika.

If you use white rice, the soup will need to simmer for about 15 minutes. If you use brown rice, which is more nutritious, it will need to simmer for about 40 minutes. Alternatively, you can grind the brown rice into flour using a spice grinder; this will reduce the simmering time to 15 minutes.

- Immersion blender or food processor

2 tbsp	butter or olive oil	30 mL
1	onion, chopped	1
1	clove garlic, minced	1
1 tsp	piment d'Espelette (approx.) or sweet paprika (see Tips, left)	5 mL
1 tsp	salt	5 mL
2	sprigs each fresh thyme and parsley, tied together with kitchen string	2
2 cups	sliced carrots (about 12 oz/375 g)	500 mL
2 tbsp	rice (see Tips, left)	30 mL
3 cups	chicken or vegetable stock	750 mL
	Salt and freshly ground black pepper	

1. In a large saucepan or stockpot, melt butter over medium heat. Add onion and cook, stirring, until softened, about 3 minutes. Add garlic, 1 tsp (5 mL) piment d'Espelette, salt, and thyme and parsley bundle. Cook, stirring, for 1 minute. Stir in carrots and rice. Stir in stock and bring to a boil. Reduce heat and simmer until rice is tender (see Tips, left).

2. Remove thyme and parsley bundle and discard. Using immersion blender, purée soup until smooth. (Or strain soup and process the solids in food processor with 1 cup/250 mL of the broth before stirring back into the remaining soup). Season to taste with salt and black pepper.

3. Ladle soup into warm serving bowls and season to taste with additional piment d'Espelette.

Chile-Spiced Cheddar Soup

This soup makes a rich, satisfying meal-in-a-bowl or an elegant starter to the traditional roast beef and Yorkshire pudding dinner. It is likely a traditional dish from Britain or the American South. I suspect Cheddar soups evolved from English rabbits, or cheese-and-ale recipes. These are basically melted cheese, laced with ale and pungent mustard, served over toast. The addition of a jalapeño pepper, while not conventional, adds freshness as well as a kick, but more-traditional cayenne pepper works well, too.

MAKES 4 MAIN-COURSE SERVINGS

Tips

This serves four as a light meal, but you can also serve it as a starter—it will make eight small servings.

You can substitute any mildly hot chile, such as Fresno or serrano, for the jalapeño.

It's important to use top-notch stock in this soup, so I recommend using good-quality homemade stock or enhancing prepared beef stock. To enhance stock, pour 4 cups (1 L) ready-to-use beef stock into a large saucepan. Add ½ cup (125 mL) white wine; 1 carrot, coarsely chopped; ½ tsp (2 mL) celery seed; ½ tsp (2 mL) cracked black peppercorns; ½ tsp (2 mL) dried thyme; 4 sprigs fresh parsley; and 1 bay leaf. Bring to a boil. Reduce heat, cover and simmer for 30 minutes. Strain.

To make a vegetarian version of this soup, use vegan Worcestershire sauce. Substitute vegetable broth for the beef and follow the instructions for enhancing the flavor (see Tips, above).

1 tbsp	butter	15 mL
1	onion, finely chopped	1
2	carrots, finely chopped	2
4	stalks celery, peeled and finely chopped	4
½	green bell pepper, seeded and diced	½
1	jalapeño pepper (see Tips, left), seeded and diced (or ½ tsp/2 mL cayenne pepper)	1
2 tbsp	all-purpose flour	30 mL
1 tbsp	tomato paste	15 mL
1 tsp	salt	5 mL
½ tsp	dry mustard	2 mL
1	bay leaf	1
	Freshly ground black pepper	
4 cups	beef stock (see Tips, left)	1 L
3 cups	shredded Cheddar cheese	750 mL
¼ cup	heavy or whipping (35%) cream	60 mL
1 tbsp	Worcestershire sauce	15 mL
	Hot pepper sauce (optional)	

1. In a large saucepan, melt butter over medium heat. Add onion, carrots, celery, bell pepper and jalapeño pepper and stir well. Reduce heat to low, cover and cook until vegetables are soft, about 10 minutes. Add flour, tomato paste, salt, dry mustard, bay leaf, and black pepper to taste. Cook, stirring, for 1 minute. Stir in stock and bring to a boil. Reduce heat and simmer until mixture thickens slightly, about 3 minutes.

2. Cover and continue to simmer until flavors are melded, about 20 minutes. Discard bay leaf. Purée, if desired.

3. Stir in cheese, cream and Worcestershire sauce. Cook, stirring, until cheese is melted.

4. Ladle into warm serving bowls. Pass hot pepper sauce (if using) at the table.

Mulligatawny Soup

This soup is an Anglo-Indian classic. The origins are murky, but I'll accept the version of my friend and cookbook author Raghavan Iyer, who says it developed from a Tamil lentil broth often served to the English during the colonial era. They became quite enamored of this "pepper water," as it was then known, and put their own stamp on it, calling it mulligatawny soup. This is another of those anything-goes recipes, with, as Raghavan says, "variations galore."

MAKES 6 SERVINGS

GLUTEN-FREE FRIENDLY

Tips

If you have leftover cooked chicken, feel free to substitute it for the raw chicken called for here. Cut it into shreds and add it along with the cauliflower.

Some recipes call for thickening the stock with flour or adding rice to the soup. I prefer to use shredded potato, which works just as well and adds a very pleasant flavor.

Moreover ...

Eliza Acton, the British cookbook author, documented a vegetarian version of mulligatawny soup in her book *Modern Cookery for Private Families*, which was published in 1845. She used "mild currie powder" in her recipe, so in the spirit of recreating an English recipe inspired by an Indian dish, I've continued the tradition by providing a vegetarian version.

2 tbsp	oil or clarified butter (ghee)	30 mL
1	onion, finely chopped	1
2	carrots, very thinly sliced	2
2	stalks celery, peeled and very thinly sliced	2
3	cloves garlic, minced	3
1 tbsp	curry powder	15 mL
1 tbsp	minced gingerroot	15 mL
2	dried Kashmiri chiles (or other dried red chiles), broken in half	2
8 oz	skinless boneless chicken, diced (see Tips, left)	250 g
1	small potato, peeled and shredded	1
4 cups	chicken stock	1 L
	Salt and freshly ground black pepper	
1½ cups	small cauliflower florets	375 mL
2 tbsp	freshly squeezed lemon juice	30 mL
½ cup	plain yogurt	125 mL
¼ cup	finely chopped fresh cilantro	60 mL

1. In a large saucepan, heat oil over medium heat. Add onion, carrots and celery and cook, stirring, until vegetables are softened, about 5 minutes. Add garlic, curry powder, ginger and chiles and cook, stirring, for 1 minute. Add chicken and toss until well coated with spice mixture. Stir in potato.

2. Stir in stock and bring to a boil. Season to taste with salt and black pepper. Reduce heat and simmer until vegetables are very tender, about 20 minutes.

3. Stir in cauliflower and lemon juice and simmer until cauliflower is tender, about 10 minutes. Remove from heat. Stir in yogurt and cilantro. Ladle into warm serving bowls.

Variation

Vegetarian Mulligatawny Soup: Substitute ¼ cup (60 mL) dried red lentils for the chicken, and vegetable stock for the chicken stock.

Focus on: Chiles in Great Britain

Traditional wisdom suggests that the use of chiles in British cuisine is an Anglo-Indian phenomenon. The lore is that British colonials, especially during the Victorian era, acquired a taste for spicy food while living in India and longed for its pungency after returning home. While this story is not incorrect, delving deeper into it reveals that chiles are more tightly woven into the British culinary fabric than this narrative suggests.

Chiles may have landed in Britain as early as 1501, when Catherine of Aragon arrived to marry Prince Arthur (the older brother of Henry VIII, her second husband). Catherine's parents were the Spanish monarchs Isabella and Ferdinand, who received the premier shipment of capsicums from Columbus himself.

By 1597, a popular book, the *Herball, or Generall Historie of Plantes*, included woodcuts of a plant the author, horticulturist John Gerard, identified as "ginnie peppers." (It is clear from these illustrations that Gerard is referring to some type of capsicum, not to the melegueta pepper, a spice also known as grains of paradise, which is often identified as "Ginnie pepper.") Apparently, Gerard planted peppers in his garden; he describes the fruit as extremely hot. In his 1653 *Complete Herbal*, Nicholas Culpeper identified cayenne, which he called "gunea pepper." It is clear that he, too, is writing about capsicums. Culpeper was particularly interested in therapeutic applications for chiles: among other benefits, he notes that cayenne powder can help with expelling phlegm and encouraging digestion. But he was certainly aware of the plant's culinary value, too. He points out that cayenne can be baked into bread or used as a seasoning, which he opines "gives good taste."

For some time after their arrival in England, chiles were likely, at best, part of the culinary background. A cursory review of English recipes from the 14th to the 16th centuries suggests that cloves, mace, ginger and, surprisingly, saffron (which was grown in the southern regions of the country) were the main seasonings. Black pepper, cinnamon and nutmeg appeared as special treats.

In 1600, the stage was set for a dramatic shift. That year, Queen Elizabeth I granted a royal charter to The East India Company. The company was soon doing active business throughout the Indian subcontinent, and traders arrived home with a taste for more highly seasoned foods. Indian condiments were particularly popular. Because they stored well, chutneys, pickles and pungent catsups (sauces not necessarily based on tomato, like our modern-day ketchup) filled a real need for sea travelers, who were desperate to relieve the monotony of shipboard food.

These sauces were, as famed British cookbook author Elizabeth David writes, the forerunner of today's bottled sauces, which the British soon began to manufacture themselves. One version, commercialized toward the end of the 1700s, was Harvey's Sauce; the recipe called for a gallon of vinegar and an ounce of cayenne pepper, among other ingredients. Harvey's Sauce became the basis for a popular British dish of the time called "Deviled Bones."

By the mid-1800s, many families were making their own versions of hot sauce. For instance, in 1845, Ann Miller documented a recipe for hot sauce credited to a member of the Middlesex judiciary. Judge Walesby's hot sauce, which used fresh chile as well as cayenne, was to be served over steak or added to gravy. To yield about ¾ cup (175 mL) required 1 hot chile, seeded and minced, and ¼ tsp (1 mL) of cayenne pepper in addition to other ingredients.

Britain's taste for pungent food was well established long before Queen Victoria took the throne. In the mid-1600s, coffeehouses started to spring up and, at some point, they began to serve curry. In 1810, a Bengali entrepreneur, Sake Dean Mahomed, took another step forward by opening England's first curry house in London. In her book *Food in History*, Reay Tannahill notes that throughout the 1700s, curry recipes appeared in England along with those for mulligatawny soup, different types of chutneys and some pungent catsups. Elizabeth David documented a recipe for "currey" that appeared in *The Art of Cookery Made Plain and Easy* by Hannah Glasse in 1747. By the time Eliza Acton published her groundbreaking cookbook *Modern Cookery for Private Families* in 1845, she was able to include a good selection of recipes for curries and numerous recipes that use cayenne as a seasoning.

In her "remarks on curries," Acton reveals that she has quite a sophisticated palate. She comments on "the great superiority of the oriental curries over those generally prepared in England," which she attributes to the freshness of ingredients and possibly the English proclivity to overuse turmeric and cayenne. She includes a recipe for "Mr. Arnott's Currie Powder," which she describes as "exceedingly agreeable and aromatic."

In any case, Acton's curry recipes, which are quite pungent, suggest that, by the mid-1800s, British people had acquired a serious taste for spicy foods. The much-better-known Mrs. Beeton, who published her *Book of Household Management* in 1861, also used cayenne regularly in her recipes. During that era,

in Scotland, cayenne began appearing in curries and was sometimes used to season haggis, that country's national dish made from various bits of offal, aromatics and oatmeal.

Hilda Leyel, who is best known as an herbalist, also wrote what were, for the time, cutting-edge cookbooks. She may have been a bit ahead of her time when she published *The Gentle Art of Cookery* in 1925. She included a chapter called "Dishes from The Arabian Nights" and made extensive use of capsicums in various forms, from cayenne and Hungarian paprika, to pimiento peppers. In an appendix titled "Every Kitchen Store Cupboard Should Contain," she listed, "Chilli Vinegar, Hungarian Paprika, Cayenne Pepper, Chutney, Curry Powder and Whole Chilies." Where applicable, she included information on the best types and where to purchase them.

Today, London is one of the best places in the world to enjoy pungent Indian food—the restaurant choices are extensive, and the chef may even have a Michelin star. Anglo-Indian dishes, such as kedgeree (page 159) and mulligatawny soup (page 93) are deeply woven into the culinary fabric, and the tradition of tweaking spicy dishes from abroad to suit British tastes continues. Balti, a type of curry served in an iron pot, is probably an originated-in-Birmingham product. It's likely that chicken tikka masala (chicken cooked in a mild yogurt-based curry sauce) was invented in Glasgow, Scotland. Long after Harvey's was created, British people still enjoy their food with a pungent sauce. Chips (french fries) in curry sauce is a signature Glaswegian dish. Recently, in Toronto, I was chatting with a restaurant server who grew up in Belfast, Ireland. When I asked what dish she missed most from her childhood, she didn't miss a beat: chips in curry sauce.

Cabbage Soup Espagnole

Although cabbage may not seem like a traditional Spanish ingredient, there are a number of soups that contain it—perhaps the most notable is *sopes mallorquines*, a "dry soup" from Mallorca that is usually flavored with a copious amount of paprika. That inspired me to create this soup, which is completely different from sopes mallorquines but Spanish in spirit, robustly flavored and quite delicious.

MAKES 6 SERVINGS

GLUTEN-FREE FRIENDLY

Tip

The heat in this soup comes from the chorizo, so its pungency will depend on the meat. If you buy mild chorizo but prefer a spicier result, add cayenne pepper to taste along with the paprika. Or add a diced red finger chile along with the bell pepper.

FYI: I use the term "gluten-free friendly" whenever I include prepared ingredients in a recipe that would otherwise be gluten-free. Manufacturers often add wheat products to prepared foods, so you need to check the label to ensure these products are actually gluten-free.

2 tbsp	olive oil	30 mL
2	onions, finely chopped	2
3	carrots, finely chopped	3
4	stalks celery, finely chopped	4
1	red bell pepper, seeded and diced	1
4	cloves garlic, minced	4
2 tsp	sweet paprika	10 mL
1 tsp	dried oregano	5 mL
1	can (14 oz/398 mL) diced tomatoes, with juice	1
4 cups	beef stock	1 L
1	small head cabbage, cored and thinly sliced	1
8 oz	dry-cured chorizo sausage, thinly sliced	250 g

1. In a large saucepan, heat oil over medium heat. Add onions, carrots, celery and bell pepper and stir well. Reduce heat to low, cover and cook until vegetables are softened, about 10 minutes.

2. Increase heat to medium. Add garlic, paprika and oregano and cook, stirring, until fragrant, about 2 minutes. Add tomatoes and juice, stock and cabbage and bring to a boil. Reduce heat, partially cover and simmer until cabbage is tender, about 20 minutes. Stir in chorizo and cook until heated through, about 2 minutes.

Spicy Tomato Gazpacho

This is the best-known version of gazpacho—it is the typical red, tomato-based type. However, in Spain, particularly in Andulusia, people were making gazpacho long before tomatoes and peppers arrived from the New World; their traditional creamy white version is made from almonds. Basically, gazpacho is a salad-soup; the defining ingredient is bread, which is usually pounded in a mortar-like vessel with water and other ingredients. The tomato version of this soup may have originated in Seville, and the jalapeño pepper is probably a North American touch.

MAKES 6 SERVINGS

VEGAN FRIENDLY

Tip

You can substitute any mildly hot chile, such as Fresno or serrano, for the jalapeño pepper. Or, if you have access to them, you can use a green guindilla chile or two. If your guindilla chile is pickled, you may want to slightly reduce the quantity of vinegar.

- Food processor

2 cups	crustless cubed (½-inch/1 cm) bread	500 mL
1 cup	cold water (approx.), divided	250 mL
2 lbs	tomatoes, peeled and chopped	1 kg
1	red bell pepper, seeded and minced	1
1 cup	peeled seeded cucumber	250 mL
¼ cup	chopped red onion	60 mL
3 tbsp	extra virgin olive oil	45 mL
2	cloves garlic	2
1	jalapeño pepper (see Tip, left), minced	1
1 tsp	ground cumin	5 mL
1 cup	cold water	250 mL
3 tbsp	sherry vinegar	45 mL
	Salt and freshly ground black pepper	

1. In a large bowl, combine bread with enough cold water to cover. Let stand for 10 minutes. Drain. Squeeze bread dry and return to bowl.

2. Add tomatoes, bell pepper, cucumber, red onion, oil, garlic, jalapeño pepper and cumin. Mix well. In batches if necessary, transfer to food processor fitted with the metal blade and purée. Return to bowl.

3. Stir in cold water and vinegar. Season to taste with salt and black pepper. Cover and refrigerate until chilled, about 2 hours. Serve cold.

Castilian Garlic Soup (*Sopa de Ajo*)

This traditional garlic soup from Castile may very well be what sustained Don Quixote in his windmill attacks. It is a simple soup and a type of gazpacho, in the sense that bread is used as a thickener. Spanish smoked paprika, or *pimentón de la Vera*—which comes in sweet, bittersweet or hot varieties, depending on your preference—is produced in a neighboring region and provides the distinguishing flavor to the soup.

MAKES 4 SERVINGS

Tips

Use smoked sweet, bittersweet or hot paprika to suit your taste. If your chorizo is particularly spicy, err on the side of caution and use smoked sweet paprika.

Don't worry if the eggs break when you transfer them to the bowls. They break anyway when being consumed, and are just as tasty.

- Preheat broiler
- Rimmed baking sheet

1	piece (4 inches/10 cm long) baguette	1
¼ cup	extra virgin olive oil, divided	60 mL
2 tsp	Spanish smoked paprika (see Tips, left)	10 mL
4 oz	dry-cured chorizo sausage, chopped	125 g
8	cloves garlic, minced	8
4 cups	chicken stock	1 L
	Salt and freshly ground black pepper	
4	eggs	4
¼ cup	chopped fresh parsley	60 mL

1. Cut baguette into 1-inch (2.5 cm) thick slices and cut each slice cut into quarters. In a bowl, toss bread with 1 tbsp (15 mL) of the oil. Transfer to baking sheet and broil under preheated broiler, watching closely and turning several times, until evenly browned. Remove from oven. Sprinkle with paprika and set aside.

2. In a large saucepan, heat remaining oil over low heat. Add chorizo and cook, stirring, for 3 minutes. Add garlic and cook, stirring, until fragrant, about 1 minute. (Do not brown.) Stir in stock and reserved bread. Reduce heat and simmer until bread is very swollen, about 6 minutes. Season to taste with salt and black pepper.

3. One at a time, break eggs into a ladle or a cup and slide gently into the soup. Cover and simmer until the whites are firm but the yolks are still soft, about 3 minutes.

4. Carefully ladle into warm serving bowls, including an egg in each serving. Sprinkle with parsley. Serve immediately.

Hungarian Fish Soup (*Halászlé*)

Versions of this are popular in the Balkan countries, including Bosnia, Serbia, Croatia and Macedonia, but this paprika-spiced soup is most famous in Hungary, where it is traditionally served at Christmas. Historically, fisherman made it from fresh river-caught fish, usually carp or perch, and cooked it in cast-iron pots over open fires. Nowadays, a starch, such as dumplings or even small pasta, may be added. Usually, it contains copious amounts of hot paprika, but I have toned down the heat. Feel free to ramp it up, if desired.

GLUTEN-FREE FRIENDLY

Tips

I use sustainably caught local perch in this soup. In my area, these fish are tiny; each weighs about 1 lb (500 g), which means I need 3 whole fish to make this recipe. If you are using larger fish, adjust the amounts accordingly. You will need about 1½ lbs (750 g) each of trimmings and skinless fillets.

This dish was also traditionally made with carp, and I have often seen recipes calling for catfish. Use whichever sustainable freshwater fish is available in your area.

- Fine-mesh sieve

3 lbs	whole perch, cleaned (see Tips, left)	1.5 kg

Broth

1 tbsp	oil	15 mL
1	onion, finely chopped	1
2	each stalks celery and carrots, thinly sliced	2
2	sprigs fresh parsley	2
1	bay leaf	1
½ cup	dry white wine	125 mL
6 cups	water	1.5 L
1 tsp	salt	5 mL

Soup

1 tbsp	oil	15 mL
1	onion, finely chopped	1
1	green bell pepper, seeded and diced	1
2	cloves garlic, minced	2
1 tbsp	sweet Hungarian paprika (see Tip, opposite)	15 mL
2 tbsp	tomato paste	30 mL
½ cup	sour cream	125 mL
1 tsp	hot Hungarian paprika	5 mL
¼ cup	finely chopped fresh dill	60 mL
¼ cup	minced seeded green bell pepper	60 mL

1. Trim perch and cut into fillets, reserving all trimmings, including the head(s) and tail(s). Remove skin from fillets. (You should have 1½ lbs/750 g each of trimmings and fillets). Set aside trimmings and fillets.

2. *Broth:* In a stockpot or large saucepan, heat oil over medium heat. Add onion, celery, carrots, parsley and bay leaf and stir well. Reduce heat to low, cover and cook until vegetables are very soft, about 10 minutes.

Tip

I like to use sweet paprika in the soup and finish it with a bit of the hot version. However, traditional recipes call for copious amounts of hot paprika. You can adjust this ingredient to suit your taste; for instance, you can try a mix of 2 tsp (10 mL) sweet paprika and 1 tsp (5 mL) hot paprika in the soup, or increase the amount of hot paprika you add to the sour cream.

3. Increase heat to medium-high. Add wine and bring to a boil. Add reserved perch trimmings, water and salt and return just to a boil. Reduce heat and simmer (do not boil; broth will become bitter) for 45 minutes. Strain through fine-mesh sieve into a bowl, pressing the solids to release as much liquid as possible. Discard solids. Set broth aside.

4. *Soup:* In a clean stockpot or large saucepan, heat oil. Add onion and bell pepper and cook, stirring, until softened, about 5 minutes. Add garlic and sweet paprika and cook, stirring, for 1 minute. Stir in tomato paste. Add reserved broth and bring just to a boil. Reduce heat and simmer until flavors are melded, about 25 minutes. Add reserved perch fillets and cook until fish flakes easily when tested with a knife, about 10 minutes.

5. In a small bowl, stir sour cream with hot paprika.

6. Ladle soup into warm serving bowls. Stir in sour cream mixture. Garnish soup with dill and minced bell pepper.

Turkish-Style Lentil Soup with Sizzling Butter

This is a very simple soup, amped up with a dazzling finish—a drizzle of sizzling butter seasoned with a traditional Turkish pairing of paprika and mint. This recipe is very easy to make and can serve as the centerpiece of a nutritious soup-and-salad dinner. Smaller portions make a lovely starter for an elegant meal.

MAKES 6 TO 8 SERVINGS

VEGETARIAN FRIENDLY

GLUTEN-FREE FRIENDLY

Tips

These quantities of hot paprika produce a nicely spicy soup. If you are a heat lover, by all means use more.

This soup reheats well, so you can make this large batch and keep leftovers on hand for later, topping each serving with the proportional amount of the seasoned butter. You can make the entire amount of seasoned butter and refrigerate the leftovers; they will firm up, but will melt when stirred into the hot soup. If you prefer the theatricality of pouring the sizzling butter over top, melt just enough for each portion you are serving.

2 tbsp	olive oil	30 mL
1	onion, chopped	1
2	carrots, chopped	2
2	stalks celery, finely chopped	2
1	clove garlic	1
1 tbsp	ground cumin	15 mL
2 tsp	sweet paprika	10 mL
½ tsp	hot paprika (see Tips, left)	2 mL
2 tbsp	tomato paste	30 mL
1 cup	dried red lentils, rinsed	250 mL
6 cups	chicken or vegetable stock	1.5 L
	Salt and freshly ground black pepper	
2 tbsp	freshly squeezed lemon juice	30 mL

Sizzling Butter

½ cup	butter (see Tips, left)	125 mL
1 tbsp	dried mint	15 mL
1 tsp	sweet paprika	5 mL
½ tsp	hot paprika	2 mL

1. In a large saucepan or stockpot, heat oil over medium heat. Add onion, carrots and celery and cook, stirring, until softened, about 3 minutes. Stir in garlic. Add cumin, sweet paprika and hot paprika and cook, stirring, for 1 minute. Stir in tomato paste. Add lentils and stir until coated.

2. Stir in chicken stock and bring to a boil. Season to taste with salt and black pepper. Reduce heat and simmer until lentils are tender, about 30 minutes.

3. Remove from heat and stir in lemon juice. Ladle into warm serving bowls.

4. *Sizzling Butter:* In a small skillet, melt butter over medium heat until foaming. Stir in mint, sweet paprika and hot paprika. Drizzle over hot soup, dividing equally.

Thai-Style Hot-and-Sour Chicken Soup (*Tom Yum Gai*)

In Thailand, hot-and-sour soups fall into the category of *tom yum*, which Thai food expert David Thompson says includes an extensive variety of dishes best described as "boiled" and "tossed" together. Tom yum soups are an addictive blend of chile, lime, lemongrass, galangal and fish sauce. Their main ingredients can be shrimp, chicken, pork hock, whole clams, fish paste, or grilled or smoked fish. This version is extremely easy to make.

MAKES 4 SERVINGS

GLUTEN-FREE FRIENDLY

Tips

Be sure to use gluten-free fish sauce if you are making this soup for someone who is sensitive to gluten.

Both dried and fresh lime leaves work well in this recipe. Tear into shreds before adding to the stock.

To strain the soup, place a fine-mesh sieve over a bowl and pour in stock. Press the solids to release as much liquid as possible.

When adjusting the seasoning in Step 2, bear in mind that the soup should taste equally salty, sour and hot.

5 cups	chicken stock	1.25 L
4	makrut lime leaves	4
4	slices (each about ½ inch/1 cm thick) fresh galangal or gingerroot, coarsely chopped	4
2	stalks lemongrass, trimmed and coarsely chopped	2
2	red Thai bird's-eye chiles, chopped	2
Pinch	coconut sugar	Pinch
10 oz	diced skinless boneless chicken	300 g
3 tbsp	fish sauce (approx.)	45 mL
3 tbsp	freshly squeezed lime juice (approx.)	45 mL
¼ cup	finely chopped fresh cilantro (leaves and tender stems)	60 mL
	Minced red Thai bird's-eye chile (optional)	

1. In a large saucepan, combine stock, lime leaves, galangal, lemongrass, chopped bird's-eye chiles and sugar. Bring to a boil. Reduce heat and simmer until flavors are infused, about 20 minutes. Strain and discard solids. Return liquid to saucepan.

2. Add chicken and fish sauce and simmer until chicken is no longer pink inside, about 3 minutes. Remove from heat and stir in lime juice. Adjust seasoning by adding more fish sauce or lime juice to taste.

3. Ladle into serving bowls. Garnish with cilantro and minced bird's-eye chile (if using).

Variations

Thai Hot-and-Sour Shrimp Soup: Substitute an equal quantity of diced deveined peeled raw shrimp for the chicken.

Thai Hot-and-Sour Chicken Soup with Noodles: To make a more-substantial soup, add 3 oz (90 g) cooked thin rice noodles just before adding the lime juice.

Thai Coconut Chicken Soup (Tom Kha Kai)

This dish is one of Thailand's better-known culinary exports, and there are many variations on it. I have based mine on one prepared at the Boathouse Hotel on Kata Beach in Phuket; when I stayed at this hotel many years ago, it was noted for its kitchen. The soup includes mushrooms (which are optional) and substitutes chicken stock for some of the coconut milk called for in most recipes. This not only lightens the result but also adds pleasant complexity.

MAKES 4 TO 6 SERVINGS

GLUTEN-FREE FRIENDLY

Tips

Be sure to use gluten-free fish sauce if you are making this soup for someone who is sensitive to gluten.

I use 3 bird's-eye chiles when I make this soup, and that produces a pleasantly spicy result. Use the minimum if you are heat-averse, or the maximum if you like fiery food.

When serving this soup, place small bowls on the table so you can easily discard the flavoring elements (the lemongrass, galangal and lime leaves), which are not meant to be eaten.

2 cups	chicken stock	500 mL
4	dried makrut lime leaves	4
2	stalks lemongrass, trimmed and cut into 1-inch (2.5 cm) pieces	2
1	piece (about 6 inches/15 cm long) fresh galangal or gingerroot, sliced	1
2	cans (each 14 oz/400 mL) coconut milk	2
¼ cup	freshly squeezed lime juice	60 mL
3 tbsp	fish sauce	45 mL
1 tbsp	coconut sugar	15 mL
2 to 4	red Thai bird's-eye chiles, minced	2 to 4
1 lb	skinless boneless chicken, cut into bite-size pieces	500 g
4 oz	sliced mushrooms (optional)	125 g
	Finely chopped fresh cilantro (leaves and tender stems)	

1. In a large saucepan, bring stock, lime leaves, lemongrass and galangal to a boil. Boil for 2 minutes. Add coconut milk, reduce heat and simmer until flavors are infused, about 10 minutes.

2. Stir in lime juice, fish sauce, coconut sugar, bird's-eye chiles to taste, chicken, and mushrooms (if using). Return to a boil. Reduce heat and simmer until chicken is no longer pink inside, about 10 minutes.

3. Ladle soup into warm serving bowls. Garnish to taste with chopped cilantro.

Focus on: Chiles in Thailand

The Portuguese introduced peppers to what was then Siam sometime after 1511, when they arrived in that country, writes David Thompson in his encyclopedic book, *Thai Food*. Portuguese sailors consumed chiles for the same reason that their English counterparts ate limes— their high vitamin C content helped prevent scurvy. "Soon this new, fiery ingredient was incorporated into Siamese cuisine with gusto," writes Thompson.

The word for chile in Thai is *prik*. *Capsicum annuum* and *C. frutescens* are the dominant species and are used extensively. The bird's-eye chile, which is the chile we associate most closely with Thai food in the West, is *prik kii nuu suan*. It is extremely hot with slight floral overtones. In my experience, the red version, both fresh and dried, is used most often; the green ones provide the basis for green curries and pastes, which are common. The dried red chiles are often roasted and ground into powder (see Tips, page 131).

Prik chi fa are long chiles commonly used in Thailand. I have not seen them in North America but that doesn't mean they are not here. In more and more large cites, Asian market gardeners are growing "exotic" produce to satisfy multicultural populations. These chiles are about 2 inches (5 cm) long; they are usually green or red, but you'll sometimes see yellow ones. The red chiles of this variety may be grilled and used in dishes such as salads and salsa (see page 364). In their dried form, they are most often used in red curry pastes.

Other Thai chiles include dragon-eye chiles, or *prik kii nuu sun yaew*, which are thin and a bit twisted. They are larger than bird's-eye chiles (about 1½ inches/4 cm long) but not as hot. Banana chiles, or *prik yuak*, are large, yellow-green peppers that are relatively mild.

Chiles form the basis for *nahm prik*, a blend of shrimp paste and chiles, which Thompson says is at the very heart of Thai cooking along with *lon*, which he describes as a kinder, gentler relative. While chiles are not a main ingredient in lon (a fermented food earns that role), they almost always form part of the garnish for the finished dish. Chiles are often pickled in Thailand, typically in a simple coconut vinegar–based hot sauce.

Ecuadoran Potato Soup (*Locro de Papa*)

Variations of this lusciously comforting potato soup—spiked with chiles and cheese, and topped with a little salad—show up across South America, but this dish is primarily associated with Ecuador. An addictive combination of hot (chile), salty (cheese), sour (vinaigrette) and slightly sweet (potatoes and corn), it makes a perfect light dinner or lunch. I make it with serrano peppers for convenience, but ají amarillo would produce a more authentic result (see Tip, below). If you have bottled South American hot sauce, make sure to pass it at the table to top the soup.

MAKES 6 SERVINGS

VEGETARIAN FRIENDLY

GLUTEN-FREE FRIENDLY

Tip

If you are using ají amarillo instead of the serranos, I suggest substituting 2 for the quantity of peppers called for in the ingredient list. This should produce a fairly pungent result. You can also use ají amarillo paste; about 1 tbsp (15 mL) would do the trick. Since the heat levels of chiles are so unpredictable, I recommend erring on the side of caution and adding a small amount, then adjusting accordingly. You can always pass hot sauce at the table.

- Immersion blender

1 tbsp	oil	15 mL
1	onion, finely chopped	1
2	cloves garlic, minced	2
2 to 4	serrano (or 2 jalapeño) peppers, chopped (see Tip, left)	2 to 4
1 tsp	ground cumin	5 mL
1 tsp	ground annatto seeds	5 mL
2	russet (Idaho) potatoes (about 1½ lbs/ 750 g), peeled and finely chopped	2
2 cups	chicken or vegetable stock	500 mL
2 cups	whole milk	500 mL
1 cup	cooked corn kernels	250 mL
4 oz	queso fresco or feta cheese, crumbled (or Monterey Jack cheese, shredded)	125 g
1	egg yolk	1
¼ cup	heavy or whipping (35%) cream	60 mL

Topping

1 tbsp	white wine vinegar or freshly squeezed lemon juice	15 mL
½ tsp	salt	2 mL
2 tbsp	extra virgin olive oil	30 mL
4	green onions (white and green parts), very thinly sliced	4
1	small avocado, pitted, peeled and diced	1
1	small head romaine lettuce, cored and shredded	1
	Hot sauce (optional)	

1. In a large saucepan, heat oil over medium heat. Add onion and cook, stirring, until softened, about 3 minutes. Add garlic, serrano peppers to taste, cumin and annatto and cook, stirring, for 1 minute. Stir in potatoes and stock and bring to a boil. Cover, reduce heat and simmer until potatoes begin to fall apart, about 20 minutes.

2. Using immersion blender, purée. (The mixture will resemble wet mashed potatoes.) Stir in milk and corn and return just to a simmer. Stir in cheese. In a small bowl, beat egg yolk with cream. Add to soup, stirring until slightly thickened. (Do not boil.) Remove from heat.

3. *Topping:* Meanwhile, in a medium bowl, stir vinegar with salt until salt is dissolved. Whisk in oil. Add green onions and avocado and toss to coat. Add romaine and toss well to combine.

4. Ladle soup into warm serving bowls. Top with romaine mixture, dividing equally. Pass hot sauce (if using) at the table.

To Seed or Not to Seed

Whether you seed and remove the veins inside your peppers is a matter of preference. With the exception of bell peppers, I usually don't seed and devein because, in my opinion, it affects the taste and experience of the pepper. I like the texture the seeds add to a dish. The veins are the placental tissue inside the peppers, and they contain any spiciness, so removing them may be a good idea if you are heat-averse; you can also reduce the quantity of chile called for in a recipe or substitute a chile that ranks lower on the Scoville scale.

Chinese Hot-and-Sour Mushroom Soup

In Chinese medicine, which is fundamentally based on the balancing principles of yin and yang, heating foods are those that warm the body, feeding it with energy. Balance, which includes establishing equilibrium among the five flavors (sweet, sour, salty, bitter and umami), helps the body's vital spirit, called *qi*, to flow freely and support excellent health. Need I say more? Hot, sour, salty, sweet and loaded with umami from the soy sauce and mushrooms, which are also known to strengthen the immune system, this soup has all the makings of a restorative tonic. And it tastes good, too!

MAKES 4 SERVINGS

VEGAN FRIENDLY

GLUTEN-FREE FRIENDLY

Tip

Be sure to use gluten-free soy sauce or wheat-free tamari if you are making this soup for someone who is sensitive to gluten.

Chile Savvy

Bitterness is an important flavor in this soup. The sweet red bell pepper balances that component, adding lovely complexity.

4	dried shiitake mushrooms	4
	Boiling water	
1 tbsp	oil	15 mL
1 tbsp	minced garlic	15 mL
1 tbsp	minced gingerroot	15 mL
8 oz	trimmed fresh shiitake mushrooms, sliced	250 g
1	red bell pepper, seeded and diced	1
½ to 1	red finger chile, cut into paper-thin rings	½ to 1
4 cups	mushroom or beef stock	1 L
¼ cup	soy sauce	60 mL
¼ cup	Chinese black rice vinegar	60 mL
1 tsp	toasted sesame oil	5 mL
2 tbsp	thinly sliced green onions (white and green parts)	30 mL

1. In a heatproof bowl, soak dried mushrooms in boiling water for 30 minutes, weighing down with a cup to ensure they remain submerged. Drain and discard liquid. Slice mushrooms thinly and set aside.

2. In a large saucepan or stockpot, heat oil over medium heat. Add garlic and ginger and cook, stirring, for 30 seconds. Add soaked dried mushrooms, fresh mushrooms, bell pepper, and finger chile to taste. Cook, stirring, until very fragrant, about 5 minutes. (Mushrooms shouldn't be fully cooked at this point.)

3. Add stock, soy sauce and vinegar and stir well. Reduce heat, cover and simmer for until flavors are infused, about 10 minutes. Remove from heat and stir in sesame oil.

4. Ladle into warm serving bowls. Garnish with green onions. Serve immediately.

South American–Style Shrimp Chowder (*Chupe*)

Although I've taken more than a few liberties with the concept, this hearty and delicious meal-in-a-bowl was inspired by *chupe*, a Peruvian shrimp chowder that is usually served as a main dish. (The word means "a soup with many ingredients"; chupes are eaten all over South America, but Peru is one of the places where they are distinguished by the addition of hot peppers.) I like to serve this soup with thick chunks of country-style bread and not much else—that way, I can enjoy as much of the chowder as possible.

MAKES 6 SERVINGS

GLUTEN-FREE FRIENDLY

Tips

Dried ají mirasol are available in Latin American markets. They are often misidentified as guajillo peppers. While these two peppers are different, you can substitute an equal quantity of guajillo peppers in this recipe with just as delicious results.

If you are using large shrimp, cut them into thirds after peeling. Halve smaller shrimp.

- Fine-mesh sieve

3	dried ají mirasol (see Tips, left)	3
	Boiling water	
1 lb	deveined peeled shrimp, shells reserved (see Tips, left)	500 g
2 tbsp	freshly squeezed lime juice	30 mL
1 tsp	coarse salt	5 mL
1 tsp	cracked black peppercorns	5 mL
1/8 tsp	cayenne pepper	0.5 mL
1½ cups	dry white wine	375 mL
1½ cups	water	375 mL
2 tbsp	olive oil, divided	30 mL
2	onions, finely chopped	2
2	stalks celery, diced	2
4	cloves garlic, minced	4
2 tsp	finely grated lime zest	10 mL
½ tsp	salt	2 mL
2 tbsp	tomato paste	30 mL
1	can (14 oz/398 mL) diced tomatoes, with juice	1
1	potato, peeled and shredded	1
2	red bell peppers, roasted (see Tips, opposite) and diced	2
1 cup	coconut milk	250 mL
2 cups	corn kernels, thawed if frozen	500 mL
	Finely chopped fresh cilantro (leaves and tender stems)	

Tips

To roast peppers: Brush peppers lightly with oil and place them directly on a hot grill on a preheated barbecue, or arrange them on a baking sheet and place under a preheated broiler. Grill or broil, turning 2 or 3 times, until the skin on all sides is blackened, about 20 minutes. Transfer to a heatproof bowl. Cover with a plate and let stand until cool. Using a sharp knife, lift off the skin, reserving any accumulated juices. Discard skin, stems and seeds.

This is fairly substantial chowder, but you could serve small bowls as a prelude to a special meal.

1. In a heatproof bowl, soak ají mirasol in boiling water for 30 minutes, weighing down with a cup to ensure they remain submerged. Drain and discard liquid. Remove stems and discard. Pat peppers dry and chop finely.

2. Meanwhile, in a medium bowl, combine shrimp, lime juice, salt, peppercorns and cayenne. Stir well. Cover and refrigerate until ready to use.

3. Meanwhile, make shrimp stock. In a saucepan, combine reserved shrimp shells, white wine and water. Bring to a boil. Reduce heat and simmer for 15 minutes. Strain through fine-mesh sieve into a bowl, pressing the solids to release as much liquid as possible. Measure 2 cups (500 mL) and set aside. Freeze remainder for another use.

4. In a large saucepan, heat 1 tbsp (15 mL) of the oil over medium heat. Add onions and celery and cook, stirring, until softened, about 5 minutes. Add garlic, lime zest and salt and cook, stirring, for 1 minute. Stir in tomato paste. Add tomatoes and juice, and soaked dried peppers and bring to a boil.

5. Add potato and reserved shrimp stock. Stir in roasted red peppers and coconut milk. Return to a boil. Reduce heat, cover and simmer for 15 minutes. Add corn and cook until corn is tender and flavors are melded, about 5 minutes.

6. Meanwhile, in a skillet, heat remaining oil over medium-high heat. Add shrimp, in batches if necessary, and cook, stirring, until pink and opaque. Add to saucepan and stir well to combine.

7. Ladle chowder into warm serving bowls. Garnish to taste with cilantro.

Bermudan Fish Chowder

This traditional fish chowder from Bermuda is often made with wild-caught wahoo. Grouper or kingfish makes a good substitute, and I have also made an excellent version of the soup with monkfish. The unique component is a flourish of peppered sherry, a Bermudan specialty (see box, opposite).

MAKES 4 SERVINGS

GLUTEN-FREE FRIENDLY

Tips

If you can find them, substitute 2 Bermuda or other sweet onions, such as Vidalia, for the leeks and onion.

About 1 tsp (5 mL) of the peppered sherry provides pleasant seasoning to a bowlful of the chowder. Add more if you're a heat seeker.

2 tbsp	olive oil	30 mL
2	leeks, thinly sliced	2
1	small onion, finely chopped	1
4	stalks celery, thinly sliced	4
2	carrots, diced	2
6	whole cloves	6
4	whole allspice berries	4
2	sprigs fresh thyme	2
2 tsp	sweet paprika	10 mL
1 tsp	salt	5 mL
1	green bell pepper, diced	1
2	potatoes (about 1 lb/500 g total), peeled and diced	2
1	can (28 oz/796 mL) tomatoes, with juice, chopped	1
4 cups	fish stock	1 L
1 lb	skinless firm white fish fillets, cut into 1-inch (2.5 cm) chunks	500 g
	Finely chopped fresh parsley	
	Peppered sherry (see Tips, left, and box, opposite)	

1. In a large saucepan or stockpot, heat oil over medium heat. Add leeks, onion, celery, carrots, cloves and allspice and stir well. Cover, reduce heat to low and simmer until vegetables are softened, about 10 minutes.

2. Add thyme, paprika, salt and bell pepper. Increase heat to medium and cook, stirring, until pepper is softened, about 3 minutes. Add potatoes, tomatoes and juice, and stock and bring just to a boil. Reduce heat and simmer until potatoes are just starting to become tender, about 10 minutes. Add fish and simmer until it flakes easily when tested with a knife, about 10 minutes.

3. Ladle soup into warm serving bowls. Garnish to taste with parsley. Pass peppered sherry at the table.

Peppered Sherry

This special Bermudan condiment was invented by British sailors, who used it to mask the taste of food that had passed its expiration date. They steeped wild chile peppers in barrels of sherry until the liquid was infused with their fiery flavor. It didn't take too long for settlers in Bermuda to begin growing piquin peppers to sell to the sailors for their preferred condiment. A prepared version is made by Outerbridge's. You can buy bottles of it online or in specialty shops, but it is very easy to make your own at home.

To make peppered sherry: In a small jar with a tight-fitting lid, combine ½ cup (125 mL) sweet sherry; 1 tbsp (15 mL) brandy or cognac (optional); and 2 super-hot chile peppers, such as habanero or Scotch bonnet, minced. For a more authentic version, if you have access to them, use about 10 small piquin chiles in place of the habaneros. Pierce the end of each with a skewer and add them whole instead of mincing them. Cover and let the sherry mixture steep at room temperature for at least 24 hours. If desired, strain it before using (it's not necessary, because the peppers will stay on the bottom). Refrigerate the remainder for up to 1 month.

Bahia-Style Shrimp Chowder

This recipe is an amalgam of two traditional dishes from the Brazilian state of Bahia. The first is *vatapá*, a paste made of dried shrimp, coconut milk, nuts and bread crumbs that is often used as a filling for the Brazilian equivalent of falafel. The second is *moqueca*, or seafood braise. Traditionally, both rely on palm oil for their unique flavor and lovely red color.

MAKES 4 SERVINGS

GLUTEN-FREE FRIENDLY

Tips

Malagueta peppers are the traditional choice for this recipe. They are available in Latin American markets. The ones I buy are pickled, very hot and delicious. You can substitute pickled piri-piri peppers. Failing that, I recommend removing the stems from 2 dried chiles de árbol and grinding the chiles to a powder. Or try another type of red bird-type chile, such as Thai bird's-eye, which can be used fresh or dried.

Red palm oil, derived from the fruit (not the kernel) of a type of palm tree indigenous to tropical rainforests, is loaded with beneficial nutrients. It lends pleasing flavor and color to many regional dishes. It is important to buy organic unrefined oil, not only for its superior nutritional profile but also because vast quantities of the processed oil are used in packaged foods and cosmetics, at great cost to the environment. For more information on ensuring that any product you purchase is sustainably produced, visit the World Wildlife Fund website (www.worldwildlife.org).

- Food processor

1 cup	salted roasted cashews	250 mL
2 tbsp	dried shrimp	30 mL
2 tbsp	organic unrefined red palm oil (see Tips, left)	30 mL
1 lb	raw shrimp, peeled and deveined	500 g
1	onion, thinly sliced	1
1 tbsp	minced garlic	15 mL
1 tbsp	minced gingerroot	15 mL
2	drained pickled malagueta peppers, minced (see Tips, left)	2
1	bay leaf	1
1	can (14 oz/400 mL) coconut milk	1
1	can (14 oz/398 mL) diced tomatoes, with juice	1
	Salt and freshly ground black pepper	
2 tbsp	freshly squeezed lime juice	30 mL
	Finely chopped fresh cilantro (leaves and tender stems)	

1. In food processor fitted with the metal blade, combine cashews and dried shrimp. Process until finely ground. Set aside.

2. In a large skillet, heat oil over medium-high heat. Add raw shrimp and cook, stirring, until pink, about 3 minutes. Transfer to a plate and set aside.

3. Add onion to pan and cook, stirring, until softened, about 3 minutes. Add garlic, ginger, malagueta peppers and bay leaf and cook, stirring, for 1 minute. Stir in reserved cashew mixture. Stir in coconut milk, and tomatoes and juice and bring just to a boil. Reduce heat and simmer until sauce is thickened, about 5 minutes.

4. Add reserved shrimp and cook until heated through, about 1 minute. Discard bay leaf. Season to taste with salt and black pepper. Remove from heat. Stir in lime juice and garnish to taste with cilantro.

Peppery Black Bean Soup

The first time I ever tasted a peppery black bean soup was many years ago in an Argentinean restaurant in New York. I have since learned that this kind of soup is more closely identified with Cuba. Whatever its origins, I love the combination of flavors and textures.

Tips

The quantity of chile I call for here produces a pleasant level of heat that lasts on the palate. Adjust it to suit your taste. If you prefer a less pungent soup, substitute a jalapeño pepper for the habanero. Or, if available, substitute ají cachucha, small, mildly hot chiles that are often used in Cuban dishes; use about 6 in this recipe.

To make 4 cups (1 L) of cooked black beans: Soak and cook 2 cups (500 mL) dried black beans, or use 2 cans (each 14 to 19 oz/398 to 540 mL) of black beans. Drain and rinse before using.

If you are a heat seeker, increase the quantity of chile or garnish the soup with extra-spicy salsa.

Use a potato masher to mash the beans or pulse them a few times in a food processor to the desired consistency.

To make a vegan version, omit bacon. Substitute vegetable stock for the chicken stock and vegan sour cream for the regular.

4 oz	slab bacon, diced	125 g
2	onions, finely chopped	2
2	stalks celery, diced	2
2	green bell or Cubanelle peppers, seeded and diced	2
1	habanero or Scotch bonnet pepper, seeded and minced (see Tips, left)	1
4	cloves garlic, minced	4
2 tbsp	cumin	30 mL
1 tbsp	dried oregano	15 mL
1	bay leaf	1
1 tsp	salt	5 mL
1 tsp	cracked black peppercorns	5 mL
1	can (28 oz/796 mL) diced tomatoes, with juice	1
5 cups	chicken stock	1.25 L
4 cups	cooked black beans, roughly mashed	1 L
½ cup	packed fresh cilantro leaves	125 mL
¼ cup	freshly squeezed lime juice	60 mL
	Sour cream	
	Salsa	
	Lime wedges (optional)	

1. In a large saucepan or stockpot, cook bacon over medium-high heat, stirring, until crisp, about 5 minutes. Using a slotted spoon, transfer to a paper towel–lined plate and let drain. Set aside. Drain off all but 2 tbsp (30 mL) fat from pan, if necessary. Reduce heat to medium.

2. Add onions, celery, bell peppers and habanero pepper to pan and cook, stirring, until vegetables are softened, about 5 minutes. Add garlic, cumin, oregano, bay leaf, salt and peppercorns and cook, stirring, for 1 minute. Add tomatoes and juice, stock and beans and bring to a boil. Reduce heat and simmer until vegetables are tender and flavors are melded, about 30 minutes. Discard bay leaf.

3. Remove from heat. Stir in cilantro, lime juice and bacon.

4. Ladle into warm serving bowls. Garnish to taste with sour cream and salsa. Serve with lime wedges (if using).

Corn-Spiked Tortilla Soup

This version of tortilla soup is more in keeping with a Tex-Mex rather than a traditional Mexican approach. I've added beans and corn to make it more substantial, as well as spices for oomph, and employed three kinds of chiles. (I did, however, resist the temptation to add shredded cheese as a finishing touch.) I think it's delicious and wonderfully warming—a great one-dish meal.

Tips

If you like heat, include the jalapeño (without it, the flavors are lovely but mild). This soup is a great example of how chiles can create delightful depth of flavor without adding pungency.

You can substitute any mildly hot chile, such as Fresno or serrano, for the jalapeño.

To purée the soup: Use an immersion blender directly in the saucepan or transfer the solids plus 1 cup (250 mL) of the cooking liquid to a food processor and purée. Return the mixture to the saucepan before continuing with the recipe.

2	ancho peppers	2
	Boiling water	
4	slices bacon	4
2	onions, finely chopped	2
4	cloves garlic, minced	4
1	jalapeño pepper (optional), minced (see Tips, left)	1
1 tbsp	ground cumin	15 mL
2 tsp	dried oregano	10 mL
	Salt and freshly ground black pepper	
2 cups	cooked pinto beans	500 mL
1	can (14 oz/398 mL) diced tomatoes, with juice	1
4 cups	chicken stock, divided	1 L
¼ cup	packed fresh cilantro (leaves and tender stems)	60 mL
2 cups	corn kernels, thawed if frozen	500 mL
1	can (4½ oz/127 mL) chopped green chiles, drained	1

Garnishes

	Oil for frying	
3	corn tortillas, cut into 1-inch (2.5 cm) strips	3
	Sour cream	
1	avocado, pitted, peeled and cut into ½-inch (2 cm) cubes	1
	Finely chopped red onion	
	Finely chopped fresh cilantro	

1. In a heatproof bowl, soak ancho peppers in boiling water for 30 minutes, weighing down with a cup to ensure they remain submerged. Drain and discard soaking liquid. Remove and discard stems. Chop peppers coarsely. Set aside.

Moreover ...

Probably because I first tasted tortilla soup in a small town in Texas, I had assumed it was a Tex-Mex creation. I later learned that it is a made-in-Mexico original: a traditional soup in Central Mexico and the area surrounding Mexico City, according to Mexican food guru Diana Kennedy. It is not, she notes, found elsewhere in the country. Her recipe is simple and elegant, a tomato and chicken stock broth completed with fresh epazote, crumbled fried pasilla chiles and a smattering of queso fresco.

A *Los Angeles Times* story on tortilla soup concluded that, although its history is murky, it arrived in California sometime around 1940. It is now a fixture at many Mexican restaurants in that state. As the dish traveled north from Mexico, it evolved, substituting ingredients such as mint for epazote, sour cream for queso fresco and using ground tortillas to thicken the broth. Although some of these flourishes would raise the hackles of purists, I have rarely had a bowl of tortilla soup I didn't enjoy. I'm with Mrs. Kennedy, who described it as "a sort of soul food soup."

2. Meanwhile, in a large saucepan, cook bacon over medium-high heat until crisp, about 10 minutes. Transfer to a paper towel–lined plate and let drain thoroughly. Crumble and set aside. Drain all but 1 tbsp (15 mL) fat from pan.

3. Reduce heat to medium. Add onions and cook, stirring, until softened, about 3 minutes. Add garlic, jalapeño (if using), cumin, oregano, and salt and black pepper to taste. Cook, stirring, for 1 minute. Stir in beans, tomatoes and juice, soaked ancho peppers, 1 cup (250 mL) of the stock and cilantro. Purée (see Tips, opposite).

4. Add remaining stock and bring to a boil. Reduce heat and simmer until flavors are melded, about 30 minutes. Stir in corn, chopped green chiles and reserved bacon. Cover and cook until corn is tender, about 5 minutes.

5. *Garnishes:* Meanwhile, in a large skillet, heat oil over medium-high heat. (You will need $1/4$ to $1/2$ cup/60 to 125 mL, depending on the size of your skillet.) Add tortilla strips, in batches, and fry, turning once, until browned, about 30 seconds per side. Using a slotted spoon, transfer to a paper towel–lined plate and let drain.

6. Ladle soup into warm serving bowls. Top each with a dollop of sour cream and lay tortilla strips across the surface. Garnish with avocado, and red onion and cilantro to taste.

Salads

Carrot Salad with Harissa

This traditional Middle Eastern salad is, depending on the source you consult, either Tunisian or Moroccan in origin. This recipe is wonderful in the winter, because it allows you to enjoy a salad-like dish when fresh vegetables are scarce. Harissa provides the heat here, but you can use other spices (see Tips, below) if you like. This salad can also be enhanced to serve as a main course (see Variations, below). It is a perfect dish for a buffet; just double or triple the recipe if you have a bigger crowd. Serve it at room temperature or chilled.

MAKES 4 SERVINGS

VEGAN FRIENDLY

GLUTEN-FREE FRIENDLY

Tips

If you don't have harissa paste on hand, substitute 1 tsp (5 mL) sweet paprika enhanced with about ⅛ tsp (0.5 mL) cayenne pepper or 1 tsp (5 mL) Aleppo pepper.

If you like spice and have heat seekers at the table, increase the quantity of harissa paste to taste.

I prefer the carrots sliced and tossed in the dressing, but in some versions they are mashed. The easiest way to achieve this result is to transfer the cooked carrots to a food processor fitted with the metal blade, add the dressing and pulse or process until the desired texture is achieved (I prefer it slightly chunky). If your taste leans toward a purée, cook the carrots until they are quite soft, then process them with the dressing.

3 cups	thinly sliced carrots (about ¼ inch/ 0.5 cm thick), cooked just until tender (see Tips, left)	750 mL
	Freshly ground black pepper	
	Thinly sliced black olives	
	Finely chopped fresh parsley or cilantro	

Dressing

1 tbsp	freshly squeezed lemon juice	15 mL
1 tsp	ground cumin	5 mL
1	clove garlic, puréed (see Tips, opposite)	1
½ tsp	harissa paste (see Tips, left)	2 mL
½ tsp	salt, or to taste	2 mL
3 tbsp	extra virgin olive oil	45 mL

1. *Dressing:* In a small bowl, combine lemon juice, cumin, garlic, harissa paste and salt to taste. Stir until salt is dissolved. Whisk in oil until well combined.

2. In a serving bowl, combine carrots and dressing. Toss well to coat. Season to taste with black pepper. Garnish to taste with olives and parsley. Serve at room temperature or refrigerate until chilled.

Variations

I've seen this salad bumped up to a main-course offering with the addition of oil-packed tuna and hard-cooked eggs. I've also seen it elaborated upon by including onions, fresh chiles and a variety of seasonings, including preserved lemons. Use your imagination.

Moroccan-Style Roasted Pepper and Bread Salad

Green peppers and tomatoes are a classic combination in Morocco, where salads are often part of the meal, either as an appetizer or the main course.

Tips

To roast peppers: Brush peppers lightly with oil and place them directly on a hot grill on a preheated barbecue, or arrange them on a baking sheet and place under a preheated broiler. Grill or broil, turning 2 or 3 times, until the skin on all sides is blackened, about 20 minutes. Transfer to a heatproof bowl. Cover with a plate and let stand until cool. Using a sharp knife, lift off the skin, reserving any accumulated juices. Discard skin, stems and seeds.

If you prefer, substitute naan for the pita bread.

You can also substitute 3 cups (750 mL) halved cherry tomatoes for the tomatoes.

To purée gingerroot or garlic quickly and easily, use a sharp-toothed rasp grater, such as those made by Microplane.

- Preheat broiler

4	green bell peppers, roasted (see Tips, left)	4
1 lb	tomatoes, cut into chunks (see Tips, left)	500 g
1	small red onion, thinly sliced	1
½ cup	sliced black olives, such as Kalamata	125 mL
½ cup	chopped fresh parsley	125 mL
2 tbsp	chopped fresh cilantro	30 mL
	Salt and freshly ground black pepper	

Grilled Bread

1	Greek-style (pocketless) pita bread	1
	Extra virgin olive oil	
2 tsp	sweet paprika	10 mL

Dressing

1	clove garlic, puréed (see Tips, left)	1
1½ tbsp	red wine vinegar	22 mL
1 tsp	ground cumin	5 mL
½ tsp	salt	2 mL
	Freshly ground black pepper	
¼ cup	extra virgin olive oil	60 mL

1. Peel, seed and cut roasted green peppers into strips, reserving juices. Set aside peppers and juices.

2. *Grilled Bread:* Brush pita bread on both sides with oil. Place on baking sheet, top side down, and broil under preheated broiler for 5 minutes. Flip and broil until pita begins to turn crisp and golden, about 5 minutes more. Remove from oven. Sprinkle with paprika. Let cool slightly and cut into about 2-inch (5 cm) squares.

3. *Dressing:* In a bowl, combine garlic, vinegar, cumin, salt, and black pepper to taste. Stir in reserved pepper juices. Stir until salt is dissolved. Whisk in oil.

4. In a serving bowl, combine reserved roasted green peppers, tomatoes, red onion, olives, parsley and cilantro. Add pita and dressing and toss well. Season with salt and black pepper.

Focus on: Chiles in North Africa and the Middle East

Although this area is large and diverse in terms of its culinary traditions and influences, many dishes have traveled across the region. For instance, based on my research (which is by no means comprehensive), *shakshouka*, a dish of sautéed peppers with eggs (page 326), turns up in Algeria, Tunisia, Morocco, Israel and the Palestinian territories. Some say its origins lie in the dishes of the Ottoman Empire, while others suggest the primary influence is Berber cuisine. Many dishes in these areas share these characteristics; they contain similar ingredients but preparation techniques fluctuate to accommodate local norms.

Capsicum use ebbs and flows to accommodate local traditions. However, paprika is widely used across the region. Sometimes there are differences in pepper consumption within a country. For instance, Syrian food does not make extensive use of chiles except around the city of Aleppo, which is known for its eponymous pepper. Medium-hot (about 10,000 SHU) and sweet, Aleppo pepper makes an elegant culinary point—namely, that chiles are about far more than heat. A sprinkle of this coarsely ground dried red pepper adds earthy flavor, texture and visual appeal to almost any dish.

I first purchased Aleppo pepper about 10 years ago from Philippe de Vienne at his beautiful store, Épices de cru, in Montreal. I have no doubt it was the real deal, grown near the city of Aleppo. However, it appears that the civil war in Syria has seriously jeopardized production of this culinary treasure. As I write, peppers are no longer grown in Syria for export, although you can still buy a product labeled Aleppo pepper. It will likely be Maras pepper, grown in similar soil and climatic conditions, and processed just across the border in Turkey. It is a more than reasonable facsimile of Aleppo pepper and can be similarly used.

The Maras pepper is grown in the Turkish province of Kahramanmaraş, which is not far from the Syrian border near Aleppo. Along with Antep and Adana peppers, it plays an important role in Turkish cuisine. Maras peppers are dried, preferably in the sun, the seeds are removed and the pods are crushed into flakes called *pul biber*, which have many uses. In restaurants, they often appear on the table alongside salt and black pepper to season kebabs and *pide* (Turkish pizza) or to add to olive oil for dipping. They are often added to soups, frequently as part of a sizzling butter finish (page 102). The finest crushing is called *ipek*, which means "silk."

Turkish peppers can also be made into the pepper paste *biber salçasi*, which, along with tomato paste, is ubiquitous in that country's markets. Both pastes are used liberally in soups, stews, salads and marinades. Although these pastes can be purchased in bottles, I suspect that most people buy them from local suppliers, who sell them at open-air produce markets in what I can only describe as "bulk"—large gel-like blobs, from which the desired amount is selected. When peppers are in season, people often make and home-preserve their own pepper paste for use throughout the year.

The Urfa is another pepper that is used in Turkey. It is processed differently; after being split open and sun-dried during the day, it is wrapped up to "sweat" throughout the night. During this process, it absorbs some of the moisture and flavor lost by drying. Cultivated in the Urfa area of Turkey, it has a moderate heat level and a mild, slightly smoky, fruity flavor with chocolate overtones.

In general terms, countries such as Tunisia, Morocco, Saudi Arabia and Turkey tend to share similar approaches to chiles. They are often used dried, frequently in spice blends, such as ras el hanout, or in condiments, such as harissa paste.

According to Middle Eastern food expert Arto der Haroutunian, in North Africa peppers are the most popular vegetable for pickling, second only to olives. Throughout the region, roasted sweet peppers figure prominently in mezes, such as *muhammara* (page 60) and *marmouma* (page 66), as well as in Tunisia's *salata meshwiya* (page 142) and the classic chopped salad *ezme* (page 136), which is certainly ubiquitous in Turkey. Spicy merguez sausage, usually made from lamb or goat and seasoned with harissa, is very popular in North Africa, primarily in Tunisia and Algeria, where it originated. It is often served as street food in a sandwich.

Fattoush

Fattoush is a salad whose popularity has spread widely across the Middle East, tailoring itself to suit local ingredients and tastes. I believe it is fundamentally Arab, although it is very popular in Lebanon, Syria and even Israel. Its distinguishing feature is leftover pita bread (the word *fattoush* means "moistened bread"). It is often made with purslane, but parsley makes an easy-to-find substitute. I like to cut the lettuce into small pieces to resemble the chopped salads that are popular in the region. Fattoush is lovely with simple grilled meat.

Tips

If you have access to a good supply of purslane, substitute it for up to half of the lettuce and maintain the quantity of parsley.

If you like, substitute 2 cups (500 mL) halved cherry tomatoes for the diced.

If you don't have Aleppo pepper, use sweet paprika seasoned with a pinch of cayenne pepper.

- Preheat oven to 400°F (200°C)

4 cups	chopped romaine or cos lettuce (see Tips, left)	1 L
6	radishes, halved vertically and thinly sliced	6
½	English cucumber, halved lengthwise and thinly sliced	½
2	tomatoes, diced (see Tips, left)	2
1	red bell pepper, seeded and thinly sliced	1
½	red onion, cut into paper-thin slices	½
½ cup	chopped parsley or purslane leaves	125 mL
¼ cup	finely chopped fresh mint	60 mL
2 tsp	ground sumac	10 mL

Toasted Pita

1	Greek-style (pocketless) pita bread or naan	1
	Extra virgin olive oil	
2 tsp	Aleppo pepper (see Tips, left)	10 mL

Dressing

¼ cup	freshly squeezed lemon juice	60 mL
	Salt and freshly ground pepper	
½ tsp	puréed garlic (about 1 clove), see Tips, page 121	2 mL
3 tbsp + 1 tsp	extra virgin olive oil	50 mL

1. *Toasted Pita:* Brush pita on both sides with olive oil. Place on baking sheet, top side down, and bake in preheated oven for 5 minutes. Flip and bake until pita begins to turn crisp and golden, about 5 minutes more. Remove from oven. Sprinkle with Aleppo pepper. Let cool slightly and cut into about 2-inch (5 cm) squares.

2. In a serving bowl, combine lettuce, radishes, cucumber, tomatoes, bell pepper, red onion, parsley and mint. Add toasted pita. Sprinkle with sumac and toss well to combine.

3. *Dressing:* In a small bowl, whisk lemon juice with salt and black pepper to taste. Add garlic. Gradually whisk in oil until combined. Pour over salad and toss well. Garnish if desired (see Tip, left). Serve immediately.

Chile-Spiked Watermelon and Feta Salad

Melon and feta is a marriage made in heaven, as Greek cooks well know. Here, sweet watermelon, salty feta, spicy pepper, tart lime and crunchy pine nuts combine for a truly delicious result. When you're making this perfect summer cooler, keep the ingredients very cold. Speared with cocktail toothpicks, the salad works as an appetizer as well.

MAKES 6 SERVINGS

VEGETARIAN FRIENDLY

GLUTEN-FREE FRIENDLY

Tips

If you don't have Aleppo pepper on hand, substitute 1 tsp (5 mL) sweet paprika enhanced with ⅛ tsp (0.5 mL) cayenne pepper.

Make sure your feta is well chilled; if it isn't, it will become creamy when you crumble it.

I have a bottle of Spanish olive oil flavored with vanilla, which someone gave me as a gift. A soupçon of it was perfect in this salad; if your olive oil is not top-quality, omit it.

2 lbs	chilled seedless watermelon, cut into cubes (about 1 inch/2.5 cm)	1 kg
1 tbsp	freshly squeezed lime juice	15 mL
1 tsp	Aleppo pepper (see Tips, left)	5 mL
3 oz	cold feta cheese (see Tips, left)	90 g
2 tbsp	pine nuts, toasted and chopped	30 mL
	Extra virgin olive oil (optional)	

1. Arrange watermelon on a serving plate and chill in the freezer for 15 minutes.

2. Sprinkle chilled watermelon cubes with lime juice. Sprinkle with Aleppo pepper. Crumble feta evenly over top and garnish with pine nuts. Drizzle very lightly with olive oil (if using). Serve immediately.

Fried Chickpea Salad

Bell peppers and chickpeas are a popular combination across the Middle East. I must admit I hadn't thought about frying chickpeas until I came across a recipe by Sam and Sam Clark, pioneering British chefs who have extended the popularity of Middle Eastern food at their delightful London bistro, Moro. This salad is delicious for lunch or a light dinner.

MAKES 6 TO 8 SERVINGS

VEGETARIAN FRIENDLY

GLUTEN-FREE FRIENDLY

Tips

The red onion needs to be paper-thin for this salad; use a mandoline to make perfectly even slices.

You want the oil to cover the chickpeas when they are submerged. If there isn't enough once you've placed the chickpeas in the pan, add a little more.

If you don't have Aleppo pepper, substitute sweet paprika seasoned with a pinch of cayenne pepper, if desired.

To absorb excess oil, after the fried chickpeas have cooled, cover them with an additional paper towel and press down. Or lay them on a large tea towel and gently roll.

- 10-inch (25 cm) skillet

1	small English cucumber (about 1 lb/ 500 g), diced	1
1	red bell pepper, seeded and diced	1
1	yellow or orange bell pepper, seeded and diced	1
½	red onion, cut into paper-thin slices (see Tips, left)	½
16	cherry tomatoes, halved	16
	Aleppo pepper (optional)	
2 tbsp	finely chopped fresh parsley	30 mL

Fried Chickpeas

2 cups	vegetable oil (see Tips, left)	500 mL
1½ cups	cooked chickpeas, drained, rinsed and patted dry	375 mL
	Aleppo pepper (see Tips, left)	

Dressing

¾ cup	plain yogurt	175 mL
1	clove garlic, puréed (see Tips, page 121)	1
2 tbsp	finely chopped fresh dill	30 mL
2 tbsp	freshly squeezed lemon juice	30 mL
½ tsp	harissa paste	2 mL
	Salt and freshly ground black pepper	

1. *Fried Chickpeas:* In skillet, heat oil over medium heat. Add chickpeas in a single layer and cook until golden, about 5 minutes. Using a slotted spoon, transfer to a paper towel–lined plate to drain. Let cool. Sprinkle with Aleppo pepper.

2. *Dressing:* In a bowl, whisk yogurt, garlic, dill, lemon juice and harissa paste. Season with salt and black pepper.

3. In a large bowl, combine cucumber, red and yellow bell peppers, red onion and tomatoes. Add dressing and toss well to coat. Spread on a serving platter. Scatter chickpeas over top. Season to taste with Aleppo pepper (if using). Garnish with parsley and serve immediately.

Circassian Chicken Salad

The origin of this dish differs among sources, but according to Middle Eastern food guru Claudia Roden, it is a legacy of Circassian women who were captured by Turks in war. Known for their culinary skills, as well as their beauty, these women became integrated into the Ottoman aristocracy, and this dish became a Turkish classic. Paprika is the star here, but a bit of hot pepper is often added as a finishing touch. This salad is a deliciously different dish to serve as part of a buffet.

MAKES 8 TO 10 SIDE SERVINGS

GLUTEN-FREE FRIENDLY

Tip

Many recipes use bread to thicken the sauce, but almonds are also common and they make this a delicious gluten-free dish. If you prefer, substitute 2 slices of white bread, crusts removed, for the almonds. Soak the bread in just enough water to soften it. Squeeze it dry, tear into pieces and add to the food processor along with the walnuts.

- Fine-mesh sieve
- Food processor

4	chicken breasts	4
1	onion, chopped	1
2	stalks celery, sliced	2
2	bay leaves	2
2	whole cloves	2
1	clove garlic	1
2	sprigs fresh parsley	2
6	black peppercorns	6
	Grated zest and juice of 1 lemon	
	Aleppo or Urfa pepper (optional)	
	Finely chopped fresh parsley	
	Flaky sea salt	

Walnut Sauce

2 cups	walnut pieces	500 mL
¾ cup	whole blanched almonds (see Tip, left)	175 mL
4	green onions (white and green parts), coarsely chopped	4
1 tsp	sweet paprika (see Tips, opposite)	5 mL
½ tsp	harissa paste (optional)	2 mL
	Salt and freshly ground black pepper	

Dressing

1 tbsp	freshly squeezed lemon juice	15 mL
2 tsp	sweet paprika	10 mL
2 tbsp	walnut oil (see Tips, opposite)	30 mL

Tips

Using paprika alone produces a mildly seasoned dish. If you prefer a bit of heat, add the harissa.

If you don't have walnut oil, substitute extra virgin olive oil. The flavor won't be as authentic, but it's still tasty.

Chile Savvy

Walnuts have an enticing bitterness, which is balanced by the use of sweet paprika in the sauce.

1. In a large skillet, combine chicken, onion, celery, bay leaves, cloves, garlic, parsley and peppercorns. Add lemon zest and juice, and enough water to cover. Bring to a boil. Reduce heat, cover and simmer until chicken is no longer pink inside, about 20 minutes. Remove from heat. Let chicken cool in the cooking liquid.

2. Lift cooled chicken out of the cooking liquid. Remove and discard skin and bones. Using 2 forks, pull meat apart into shreds. Strain cooking liquid through fine-mesh sieve into a bowl, discarding solids. Set chicken and cooking liquid aside separately.

3. *Walnut Sauce:* Meanwhile, preheat oven to 350°F (180°C). Arrange walnuts and almonds on a baking sheet. Toast in preheated oven, stirring several times, until fragrant and lightly browned, about 12 minutes. Transfer to food processor fitted with the metal blade and process until ground. Add green onions, paprika, harissa paste (if using) and enough of the reserved cooking liquid to make a creamy sauce. Process until creamy. Season to taste with salt and black pepper.

4. *Dressing:* In a small bowl, combine lemon juice and paprika. Stir until paprika is dissolved. Whisk in walnut oil until combined. Set aside.

5. In a bowl, combine chicken and walnut sauce and toss well to coat. Transfer to a serving platter and dust lightly with Aleppo pepper (if using). Sprinkle with parsley to taste. Drizzle dressing over top. Season to taste with salt. Cover and refrigerate until chilled, about 1 hour. Serve cold.

Southeast Asian Chicken Salad

This recipe is a bit of a hodgepodge, based on Burmese and Vietnamese recipes for chicken salad with cabbage. It makes a nice light dinner or lunch and is ideal for a potluck or buffet.

MAKES 4 SERVINGS

GLUTEN-FREE FRIENDLY

Tips

Often napa cabbage is used in recipes like this, but green cabbage, thinly sliced and chopped, works well, too. Rice may or may not be included, but I feel it helps balance the flavors.

Be sure to use gluten-free fish sauce (and gluten-free soy sauce, as well, if you are making the recipe on the opposite page) if you are making either salad for someone who is sensitive to gluten.

To make Pickled Onion: Combine ¼ cup (60 mL) unseasoned rice vinegar and ¼ tsp salt in a small bowl. Stir until salt is dissolved. Add 1 red onion and 1 finger chile, each cut into paper-thin slices (preferably on a mandoline). Set aside at room temperature for 15 minutes to "pickle." Drain well, discarding liquid.

1 tbsp	oil	15 mL
1 lb	boneless skinless chicken, cut into strips	500 g
2 cups	chopped shredded napa or green cabbage	500 mL
1 cup	cooked white rice, such as jasmine	250 mL
	Pickled Onion (see Tips, left)	
8	cherry tomatoes, halved	8
2	carrots, shredded	2
2 tbsp	finely chopped fresh cilantro or mint	30 mL
	Roasted peanuts or cashews (optional)	

Dressing

2 tbsp	unseasoned rice vinegar	30 mL
1 tsp	granulated sugar	5 mL
1	clove garlic, puréed (see Tips, page 121)	1
¼ cup	fish sauce	60 mL

1. *Dressing:* In a small bowl, combine vinegar and sugar, stirring until sugar is dissolved. Stir in garlic and fish sauce. Set aside. Whisk before using.

2. In a skillet, heat oil over medium-high heat. Add chicken and cook, stirring occasionally, until no longer pink inside, about 4 minutes. Transfer to a plate and let cool. Tear cooled chicken into thin strips.

3. Meanwhile, add cabbage to pan and cook, tossing, just until slightly wilted, about 2 minutes. Transfer to a medium bowl. Add rice to pan and cook, tossing, until heated through, about 1 minute. Add to bowl along with chicken and pickled onion. Add dressing and toss well to coat.

4. Spread chicken and rice mixture evenly over a deep serving platter. Scatter tomatoes and carrots evenly over top. Garnish with cilantro, and roasted peanuts (if using) to taste. Serve immediately.

Thai-Style Noodle Salad

Noodles are a fact of life in Thailand—and they have been for centuries. This dish of cold noodles is perfect for a hot summer day. It is also wonderful to make ahead; just add the garnishes right before serving.

GLUTEN-FREE FRIENDLY

Tips

I have made this salad using both mung bean vermicelli and rice vermicelli with delicious results.

Package instructions vary, but generally, the noodles should be tossed in boiling water until softened, then drained and tossed with the sesame oil. This takes about 3 minutes for rice vermicelli. By the time the remaining ingredients are prepared, the noodles will have cooled to room temperature, which is fine.

If you prefer, use a similar amount of English cucumber and leave the seeds intact.

To make roasted chile powder: In Thailand, noodles are often finished with a sprinkle of this seasoning. If you have dried red Thai bird's-eye chiles on hand, it is easy to make. Place the chiles in a dry skillet over medium heat and cook, stirring often, until fragrant and color deepens, about 3 minutes. Remove from heat and let cool. In a mortar with a pestle, or in a spice grinder, grind the toasted chiles to a fine powder. Store the powder in an airtight container for up to 1 year.

4 oz	Asian vermicelli (see Tips, left)	125 g
1 tsp	toasted sesame oil	5 mL
4	stalks celery, diced	4
½	field cucumber, peeled, halved lengthwise, seeded and thinly sliced (see Tips, left)	½
4	green onions (white and green parts), thinly sliced	4
2 tbsp	finely chopped fresh cilantro (leaves and tender stems)	30 mL
	Roasted chile powder (optional)	

Seasoned Peanuts

½ cup	raw peanuts	125 mL
⅛ tsp	ground dried red Thai bird's-eye chile or cayenne pepper	0.5 mL
	Sea salt	

Dressing

2 tbsp	each oil and freshly squeezed lime juice	30 mL
1 tbsp	each fish sauce and soy sauce	15 mL
½ tsp	granulated sugar	2 mL
1	red Thai bird's-eye chile, minced	1

1. Prepare noodles according to package instructions. Drain and toss with sesame oil. Set aside.

2. *Seasoned Peanuts:* In a dry skillet, cook peanuts over medium heat, stirring, until fragrant, about 5 minutes. Sprinkle with chile, and season with salt. Transfer to a cutting board and chop coarsely. Set aside.

3. *Dressing:* In a small bowl, combine oil, lime juice, fish sauce, soy sauce, sugar and bird's-eye chile. Stir well until sugar is dissolved. Set aside.

4. Arrange noodles on a serving platter or in a serving bowl. Add dressing and toss well to coat. Add celery, cucumber and green onions and toss lightly to combine. Cover and refrigerate until chilled, about 1 hour.

5. To serve, sprinkle with seasoned peanuts and cilantro. Season to taste with roasted chile powder (if using).

Thai Green Mango Salad

Green (unripe) mangos are frequently eaten in salads in Thailand. Fiery Thai bird's-eye chiles provide the heat, which is nicely balanced by sour lime juice and a hint of sugary sweetness. Salty and umami-adding dried shrimp (or, in this case, fish sauce) complete the flavor profile. This recipe is quite easy to make and impressive to serve—it's not only very pretty but also a feast for the senses.

MAKES 2 TO 4 SERVINGS

GLUTEN-FREE FRIENDLY

Tips

Be sure to use gluten-free fish sauce if you are making this salad for someone who is sensitive to gluten.

I like to slice the mango on a mandoline, then cut the slices into julienne. However, I have also made this salad by simply cutting the mango into pieces with a sharp knife and then slicing. Some people prefer the large holes of a box grater or the shredding blade of a food processor for this task. Use whatever method you prefer.

The bird's-eye chile in the dressing produces a nicely pungent result. If you are heat-averse, reduce the amount by half. If you are a heat seeker, increase the quantity to taste.

1	green mango, peeled, pitted and julienned (see Tips, left)	1
2	green onions (white and green parts), thinly sliced	2
½	red bell pepper, seeded and diced	½
1 tbsp	chopped fresh cilantro (leaves and tender stems)	15 mL
1 tbsp	chopped roasted cashews or peanuts	15 mL

Dressing

3 tbsp	freshly squeezed lime juice	45 mL
1 tsp	coconut sugar	5 mL
2 tbsp	fish sauce	30 mL
1	red or green Thai bird's-eye chile (see Tips, left), minced	1
Pinch	puréed garlic (see Tips, page 121)	Pinch

1. *Dressing:* In a small bowl, combine lime juice and coconut sugar, stirring until sugar is dissolved. Stir in fish sauce, bird's-eye chile and garlic. Set aside.

2. In a serving bowl, combine mango, green onions and bell pepper. Add dressing and toss well to coat. Garnish with cilantro and peanuts. Serve immediately.

Variation

If desired, add about 4 oz (125 g) of cooked seafood, such as diced shrimp or thinly sliced squid, or diced grilled chicken to the finished salad.

Charred Romaine Salad

If you are having a summer barbecue, this "salad" is perfect to include. It is a wonderful accompaniment to simple grilled meats. Or, if you are in the winter doldrums and have grown tired of the same meals cooked indoors, use your grill pan to char the romaine and think fondly of the warm weather to come. This recipe serves two, but you can multiply it to accommodate any number of guests.

MAKES 2 SERVINGS

GLUTEN-FREE FRIENDLY

Tip

If you do not have a barbecue, grill the romaine on a preheated grill pan over medium-high heat.

- Preheat barbecue to high (see Tip, left)

1	head romaine lettuce, leafy outer leaves discarded, halved lengthwise	1
1 tbsp	olive oil	15 mL
	Salt and freshly ground black pepper	

Chile Dressing

2 oz	sliced bacon (about 2 slices)	60 g
1 tbsp	sherry vinegar	15 mL
½ tsp	salt	2 mL
½ to 1	red finger chile, minced	½ to 1
2 tbsp	extra virgin olive oil	30 mL
	Freshly ground black pepper	

1. *Chile Dressing:* In a skillet, cook bacon over medium heat until crisp. Transfer bacon to a paper towel–lined plate and let drain. Reserve 1 tbsp (15 mL) of the bacon fat and keep warm. Crumble cooled bacon and set aside.

2. In a small bowl, combine vinegar and salt, stirring until salt is dissolved. Add finger chile to taste. Whisk in warm reserved bacon fat and oil. Season to taste with black pepper. Set aside.

3. Brush cut side of lettuce with oil and place on preheated grill. Grill until lightly charred, about 4 minutes. Flip and cook just until warmed through.

4. Transfer lettuce to a serving platter and drizzle with dressing. Season to taste with salt and black pepper. Serve immediately.

Catalonian Grilled Vegetable Salad (*Escalivada*)

This grilled vegetable salad is a specialty of Catalonia. The name *escalivada* means "to cook in ashes," so for the most authentic smoky flavor, roast the vegetables on a barbecue.

Tips

If you do not have a barbecue, grill the vegetables on a preheated grill pan over medium-high heat, in batches, or broil on an ungreased baking sheet under a preheated broiler.

The vegetables will be done at different times; watch closely and remove them as completed and set aside to cool.

Ñora is a type of pepper that is associated with Catalonia. It has a rich, sweet flavor. If you can't find it, sweet paprika (preferably Spanish) works just fine.

If you want to add a bit of smoky heat to this salad, add ⅛ tsp (0.5 mL) hot smoked paprika to the dressing.

Garnish with sliced black olives. Or substitute fresh lemon juice or sherry vinegar for the red wine vinegar.

- Preheat barbecue to high (see Tips, left)

¼ cup	olive oil	60 mL
1	eggplant (about 1½ lbs/750 g), sliced	1
2	red bell peppers	2
1	red onion, cut into ½-inch (1 cm) thick rounds	1
4	tomatoes, cut into 1-inch (2.5 cm) thick rounds	4
	Salt and freshly ground black pepper	
2 tbsp	finely chopped fresh parsley	30 mL
1	red finger chile, cut in paper-thin slices	1

Dressing

1 tbsp	red wine vinegar (see Tips, left)	15 mL
1 tsp	ground dried ñora pepper or sweet paprika (see Tips, left)	5 mL
1 tsp	salt	5 mL
1	clove garlic, puréed (see Tips, page 121)	1
¼ cup	extra virgin olive oil	60 mL

1. Brush olive oil over eggplant, bell peppers, red onion and tomatoes. Place on preheated barbecue and cook, turning occasionally, until nicely charred. When bell peppers are done, place in a bowl and cover with a plate. Set aside to sweat. When bell peppers are cool, lift off the skins, seed and cut into strips, reserving accumulated juices. When the onion is cool, cut the rounds into quarters.

2. *Dressing:* In a small bowl, combine vinegar, ñora pepper and salt, stirring until salt is dissolved. Add garlic and reserved juices from roasted peppers. Whisk in oil.

3. Arrange vegetables on a platter. Drizzle dressing over top.

4. Season to taste with salt and black pepper. Sprinkle with parsley and finger chile. Set aside at room temperature until ready to serve.

Turkish Tomato and Pepper Salad (*Ezme*)

If you have visited Turkey, you have encountered this dish. It is part of virtually every meal and frequently accompanies fast-food dishes, such as *pide* (a popular pizza-like specialty). This salad is often served as a kind of dip, accompanied by pita bread or crudités, such as cucumbers, carrots and radishes. It also appears in the form of a chopped salad, served alongside grilled meats, such as kebabs. The tomatoes may or may not be roasted, but the peppers almost always are. It is a great dish to make when tomatoes are in season.

MAKES 4 TO 6 SERVINGS

VEGAN FRIENDLY

GLUTEN-FREE FRIENDLY

Tips

Although I'm not sure it is traditional, I have, at times, made this dish using a minced green finger chile instead of the Aleppo pepper. I add it to the vegetables, along with the green onions, and it is delicious.

In the Middle East, a bit of dried mint is often added to dishes to balance any chile heat.

3	red bell peppers, roasted (see Tips, page 121), peeled, seeded and cut into thin strips	3
4	tomatoes (about 1 lb/500 g), peeled and chopped	4
4	green onions (white and a bit of the green parts), very thinly sliced	4
¼ cup	finely chopped fresh parsley	60 mL
	Dried mint (optional), see Tips, left	

Dressing

2 tbsp	extra virgin olive oil	30 mL
1 tbsp	date or pomegranate molasses	15 mL
1 tbsp	freshly squeezed lemon juice	15 mL
2	cloves garlic, puréed (see Tips, page 121)	2
½ tsp	Aleppo pepper (see Tips, left)	2 mL
	Salt and freshly ground black pepper	

1. *Dressing:* In a small bowl, combine oil, molasses, lemon juice, garlic, Aleppo pepper, and salt and black pepper to taste. Whisk until well combined. Set aside.

2. In a serving bowl, combine roasted red peppers, tomatoes, green onions and parsley. Toss to combine. Drizzle dressing over top and sprinkle with mint (if using). Toss to coat.

Peruvian Potato Salad
(Papas a la Huancaína)

This is a well-known Peruvian dish from the city of Huancayo in the Andes. It is basically a chilled cheese sauce served over potatoes. It is usually served as a salad, atop lettuce, which I have done here, but the sauce can also function as an appetizer, as a dip for crudités or boiled or grilled new potatoes. It's not unlike a South American fondue.

MAKES 4 TO 8 SERVINGS

VEGETARIAN FRIENDLY

GLUTEN-FREE FRIENDLY

Tips

This dish is traditionally made with yellow-fleshed potatoes, so use Yukon Gold or another variety if they are available. For a dramatic presentation, use purple potatoes.

You can substitute prepared ají amarillo paste for the peppers. You will need about ½ cup (125 mL).

In South America, this dish is usually made with rocoto peppers, which are not widely available elsewhere. I use pickled ají amarillo because I like the slight bite of vinegar, which balances the cheese. Plus, the skins lift off easily. If you have access to fresh ají amarillo or rocoto peppers (in some parts of the United States, these may be sold under the name chile manzano), use them. For best results, blanch them and lift off the skins before adding them to the recipe.

- Blender

2 lbs	potatoes (see Tips, left), cooked, peeled and thinly sliced	1 kg
1	head Boston lettuce, separated into leaves	1
16	black olives, pitted and sliced	16
2	hard-cooked eggs, quartered	2
	Finely chopped fresh parsley	

Sauce

1	small red onion, coarsely chopped	1
2	cloves garlic, minced	2
2 to 4	pickled ají amarillo, drained and skins removed (see Tips, left)	2 to 4
1 tbsp	extra virgin olive oil	15 mL
8 oz	queso fresco or other farmer's cheese, cut into chunks	250 g
½ cup	milk (approx.)	125 mL
	Soda crackers or gluten-free alternative (optional), crumbled	
	Salt and freshly ground black pepper	

1. *Sauce:* In blender, combine red onion, garlic, pickled peppers to taste, oil, cheese and ½ cup (125 mL) milk. Purée until smooth. If the mixture is too thick, add a little more milk to thin. (It should be the consistency of a thick, creamy salad dressing.) If the mixture is too thin, add crumbled soda crackers (if using), pulsing until desired consistency is achieved. Season to taste with salt and black pepper.

2. Arrange lettuce leaves on individual serving plates or a large serving platter. Arrange potatoes, in layers, evenly over lettuce, drizzling each layer with sauce and dividing evenly among layers. Garnish with olives, egg quarters and parsley to taste.

Not-Your-Granny's Potato Salad

In Spain, potatoes, peppers and chorizo are a typical combination. This trio turns up in tapas and stew-like dishes—so why not, I thought, in a delightfully different potato salad? When new potatoes are in season, I'm always looking for ways to savor their fresh earthy flavor, and this is a showstopping presentation for them.

MAKES 4 TO 6 SERVINGS

GLUTEN-FREE FRIENDLY

Tips

When cooking for people who eat gluten-free, always check the labels of prepared products, such as sausage and vinegar. They may contain gluten.

You can use whatever type of paprika you enjoy most on this salad.

The potatoes should be warm (but not hot) when tossed with the oil mixture. It helps them absorb the flavors.

The size of your potatoes determines how you should cut them. If they are very small, cut them in half; if they are small, cut them into quarters; and if they are about the size of regular potatoes, slice them.

I like to use a mandoline to slice the red onion. It makes the job very easy, and the thread-like slices are particularly pretty.

1½ lbs	new potatoes, scrubbed, cooked, cooled slightly, and cut or sliced (see Tips, left)	750 g
2	red bell peppers, roasted (see Tips, page 121), peeled, seeded and cut into strips	2
4 oz	dry-cured chorizo sausage, thinly sliced	125 g
1	red onion, thinly sliced	1
	Freshly ground black pepper	
4 to 6	hard-cooked eggs, quartered	4 to 6
	Paprika (see Tips, left)	
¼ cup	finely chopped fresh parsley	60 mL

Dressing

2 tbsp	sherry vinegar	30 mL
1 tsp	salt	5 mL
2	cloves garlic, puréed (see Tips, page 121)	2
⅓ cup	extra virgin olive oil	75 mL

1. *Dressing:* In a small bowl, combine vinegar with salt, stirring until salt is dissolved. Add garlic. Gradually whisk in olive oil until well combined. Set aside.

2. In a large bowl, combine potatoes, roasted red peppers, chorizo and red onion. Add dressing and toss well to coat. Season to taste with black pepper. Transfer to a deep serving platter or bowl.

3. Sprinkle paprika over cut sides of eggs to taste. Arrange, cut side up, on salad (or around the edges if using a platter). Garnish with parsley. Serve immediately.

Burmese Potato Salad

Potatoes make regular appearances in Burmese cuisine, where they are known by the Hindi word *aloo*. Apparently, English colonials introduced them to the country. This easy recipe makes a wonderful addition to a barbecue or a perfect side. It is loosely based on a salad served at the Seattle restaurant Wild Ginger, which has now been around long enough to qualify as something of an institution. (I recall eating there in the 1990s.)

MAKES 4 SERVINGS

GLUTEN-FREE FRIENDLY

Tips

If you're serving this salad to someone who can't eat gluten, make sure to use gluten-free fish sauce.

Burmese shallots tend to be drier than those in the West. To help your shallots get nice and crispy, after slicing, lay them on a large plate and sprinkle them with salt. Set aside for 20 minutes or so. Rinse them under cold running water, then roll them in a clean tea towel to dry thoroughly before frying them.

To make tamarind juice: In a small saucepan, combine ⅓ cup (75 mL) water and 2 tbsp (30 mL) chopped Thai tamarind paste. Bring to boil. Reduce heat and simmer for 5 minutes. Strain through a fine-mesh sieve into a bowl, using the back of a spoon to press the solids and remove as much liquid as possible. Measure 3 tbsp (45 mL) of the liquid and use in recipe, discarding any excess.

4 cups	cubed (1 inch/2.5 cm) cooked peeled potatoes	1 L
	Finely chopped fresh cilantro or mint	

Crispy Shallots

¼ cup	peanut oil	60 mL
2	large shallots, thinly sliced (see Tips, left)	2

Dressing

	Toasted sesame oil	
3 tbsp	tamarind juice (see Tips, left)	45 mL
3 tbsp	fish sauce	45 mL
1	red Thai bird's-eye chile, minced	1

1. *Crispy Shallots:* In a skillet, heat oil over medium-high heat. Add shallots and cook, stirring constantly, until golden and crisp, about 5 minutes. (Watch carefully to ensure they don't burn.) Using a slotted spoon, transfer shallots to a paper towel–lined plate and let drain. Reserve cooking oil and let cool.

2. *Dressing:* Pour reserved cooking oil into a glass measuring cup and add enough toasted sesame oil to make ¼ cup (60 mL). Whisk in tamarind juice, fish sauce and bird's-eye chile until blended.

3. In a medium bowl, combine potatoes with dressing. Toss well to coat. Cover and refrigerate until chilled.

4. To serve, sprinkle crispy shallots over potato mixture. Garnish to taste with cilantro.

TASTY TIDBIT

In Burma, chile oil and fried chile flakes are common condiments. The fried flakes are unusual—they are made from local chiles that are dried and flaked, then fried in vegetable oil. They are drained, often added to salt and used at the table to season food in the same way that North Americans use black pepper. The oil leftover from frying is saved and used to fry meat or vegetables when making curry.

Southwestern Bean and Barley Salad

Ingredients traditionally associated with the American Southwest, such as beans, corn and peppers, combine with hearty barley to produce this deliciously robust salad. It makes a great addition to a buffet or potluck dinner. Keep leftovers in the fridge for a nutritious lunch.

MAKES 8 SIDE SERVINGS

VEGAN FRIENDLY

Tips

Pearl barley tastes great, too, but I like to use whole (hulled) barley to maximize the nutritional benefit of this salad. Whole barley takes about an hour to cook, but it's worth the effort.

To make 2 cups (500 mL) of red kidney beans: Soak and cook 1 cup (250 mL) dried red kidney beans or use 1 can (14 to 19 oz/398 to 540 mL) red kidney beans. Drain and rinse before using.

Poblano peppers are relatively mild. If you are a heat seeker, you might want to add an extra one, or even a jalapeño pepper, roasted, seeded and minced, for some real punch. If you're heat-averse, the bell peppers are a tasty alternative.

Use ground dried New Mexico chiles for the best flavor. Red Hatch pepper powder is ideal, but you can also use Anaheim or even ancho chile powder. Adjust the quantity to suit your tastes.

3 cups	cooled cooked barley (see Tips, left)	750 mL
2 cups	drained cooked red kidney beans	500 mL
2 cups	cooked corn kernels	500 mL
2	poblano or red bell peppers, roasted (see Tips, page 121, and left), peeled, seeded and diced	2
2	whole oil-packed sun-dried tomatoes, drained and finely chopped	2
1	small red onion, diced	1
¼ cup	finely chopped fresh parsley	60 mL

Dressing

3 tbsp	red wine vinegar	45 mL
2 tsp	ground cumin	10 mL
½ tsp	salt	2 mL
¼ tsp	New Mexico chile powder (see Tips, left)	1 mL
	Freshly ground black pepper	
½	clove garlic, finely grated or pressed	½
½ cup	extra virgin olive oil	125 mL

1. *Dressing:* In a small bowl, combine vinegar, cumin, salt, chile powder, and black pepper to taste, stirring until salt is dissolved. Stir in garlic. Gradually whisk in olive oil.

2. In a bowl, combine barley, beans, corn, roasted peppers, tomatoes and onion. Add dressing and toss well. Garnish with parsley. Refrigerate until ready to serve.

TASTY TIDBIT

Sun-dried tomatoes are a Native American invention, not Italian, as is often believed. For thousands of years, long before Italians were introduced to tomatoes, indigenous Americans were drying their native foods, which included squash, corn and chiles, as well as tomatoes, to sustain themselves over the winter. A recipe for making sun-dried tomatoes is featured in the cookbook *The Carolina Housewife*, by Sarah Rutledge, which was published in 1847.

Focus on: Southwestern Cuisine

Tex-Mex, Cal-Mex (see page 214), Sonoran (which is Arizona-based) and Southwestern cuisine all share the same roots: cowboys, Native Americans, Spanish settlers and the Mexican people who inhabited the area when it was still part of Mexico. In the Southwest, the Native American influence is strongly felt: in addition to chiles, culinary staples include blue corn, dried beans, squash and pine nuts (piñons).

According to chef Mark Miller, who put Southwestern cooking on the map at the legendary Coyote Café in Santa Fe, New Mexico, smoky, earthy flavors are characteristic, likely due to the tradition of cooking over open fires or in wood-burning ovens. Dishes such as enchilada casseroles, burritos and deep-fried bits of dough known as *sopaipillas* lend locality to the restaurant's menu.

In New Mexico, the chile capital of the region, the cooking is strongly linked to the peppers grown in the state. New Mexico chiles were developed around the turn of the 20th century by Dr. Fabián García, at what is now New Mexico State University, home of the Chile Pepper Institute. Various chiles have been developed from this new pod type (long and pointed), including Anaheim (which can no longer be classified as a New Mexico chile because it is not grown in the state), NuMex Big Jim, NuMex Sandia and Hatch, which is named for a town near where it is grown.

North African Tuna Salad (Salata Meshwiya)

Claudia Roden, an authority on Middle Eastern food, describes this salad of grilled vegetables and tuna as being popular all over North Africa, but most closely associated with Tunisia, where France had a strong influence. This leads to speculation that the dish is a localized version of the beloved French *salade Niçoise*. Like that classic, this salad is extremely versatile. In many versions the tomatoes and peppers are roasted, as is a quartered red onion.

MAKES 2 TO 3 SERVINGS

GLUTEN-FREE FRIENDLY

Tips

This recipe makes a small portion, which is perfect for a weeknight dinner for two, but it can easily be doubled or tripled.

Tuna comes in a variety of can sizes. If you buy one that's slightly larger than the one called for, don't worry.

Nonpareil are the smallest type of caper. I use them here to ensure even distribution throughout the salad.

If you are not a heat seeker, you can omit the harissa in the dressing.

If you want to make this salad ahead, complete it through Step 2. Cover and refrigerate for up to 2 days. When you are ready to serve, complete the recipe.

You can serve this salad in smaller portions as a first course by turning it into a topping for bruschetta. To make bruschetta, cut country-style bread into thick slices and broil or grill, turning once, until golden. Brush the warm bread with garlic-infused olive oil and top with this salad. Yum!

2	red bell peppers, roasted (see Tips, page 121), peeled, seeded and thinly sliced	2
1	hot banana pepper, roasted (see Tips, page 121), peeled and thinly sliced	1
2	tomatoes, peeled and diced	2
6	green onions (white and a bit of the green parts), thinly sliced	6
1	can (5 oz/150 g) tuna packed in olive oil (see Tips, left), drained and broken into small pieces	1
	Salt and freshly ground black pepper	
2	hard-cooked eggs, quartered	2
8	black olives, pitted and halved	8
1 tbsp	nonpareil capers (see Tips, left)	15 mL
2 tbsp	finely chopped fresh parsley	30 mL
	Finely chopped preserved lemon rind (optional)	

Dressing

1 tbsp	freshly squeezed lemon juice	15 mL
½ tsp	salt	2 mL
¼ tsp	harissa paste or spice blend (optional)	1 mL
2 tbsp	extra virgin olive oil	30 mL

1. *Dressing:* In a small bowl, combine lemon juice, salt and harissa paste (if using), stirring until salt is dissolved. Whisk in olive oil until well combined. Set aside.

2. In a serving bowl or small deep platter, combine roasted red peppers, roasted banana pepper, tomatoes, green onions and tuna. Add dressing and toss well. Season to taste with salt and black pepper.

3. Arrange egg quarters, olives and capers over top. Garnish with parsley, and preserved lemon rind (if using) to taste. Serve immediately (see Tips, left).

Thai-Style Grilled Beef Salad

In Thai, this salad is known as *nahm dtok*. Thai food expert David Thompson says that the recipe comes from the northern part of the country and that the name is derived from the beads of meat juice that form on the top of the beef when it is grilling; the literal translation is "water falling."

Tips

Use gluten-free fish sauce, and gluten-free soy sauce or wheat-free tamari if you are making this salad for someone who is sensitive to gluten.

Weather permitting, cook your beef on the barbecue. After cooking the steak, sprinkle it with coarse sea salt (smoked if you have it) and let it rest for a couple of minutes before slicing. Save the juices and add them to the drizzle prior to using.

Traditionally, roasted chile powder would provide the heat in the drizzle. I have offered the alternative of sambal oelek because it is readily available. If you prefer to use roasted chile powder (see Tips, page 131), substitute about ⅛ tsp (0.5 mL).

Chile Savvy

In Thailand, the chiles in this type of salad would likely be longer *prik chi fa*. Red finger chiles make a good substitute.

2 cups	cubed (½ inch/1 cm) cucumber	500 mL
6	green onions (white and green parts), thinly sliced	6
4	tomatoes, diced	4
½ to 1	red finger chile, cut into paper-thin slices	½ to 1
4 cups	arugula, torn	1 L
1½ lbs	New York strip loin, hanger or skirt steak, grilled to desired degree of doneness and thinly sliced on the bias (see Tips, left)	750 g
	Salt and freshly ground black pepper	
	Finely chopped fresh cilantro	

Dressing

2 tbsp	unseasoned rice vinegar	30 mL
1 tbsp	soy sauce	15 mL
2 tbsp	extra virgin olive oil	30 mL

Drizzle

3 tbsp	freshly squeezed lime juice	45 mL
2 tbsp	fish sauce	30 mL
1 tsp	Asian chile sauce, such as sambal oelek, or roasted chile powder (see Tips, left)	5 mL

1. *Dressing:* In a small bowl, combine rice vinegar and soy sauce. Gradually whisk in olive oil until well combined. Set aside.

2. *Drizzle:* In another small bowl, whisk together lime juice, fish sauce and chile sauce. Set aside.

3. In a medium bowl, combine cucumber, green onions, tomatoes, and finger chile to taste. Add dressing and toss well to coat.

4. Line a deep serving platter with arugula. Spread cucumber mixture evenly over top. Top with an even layer of beef slices. Drizzle half of the drizzle over top. Pour remainder into a small serving bowl and pass at the table. Season salad to taste with salt and black pepper. Garnish to taste with cilantro.

Fish and Seafood

Basque-Style Tuna with Piment d'Espelette (*Marmitako*)

This classic dish is named for the pot in which it was traditionally cooked, the *marmita*. It is a fishermen's dish, often prepared shipboard, using line-caught tuna and whatever other ingredients are on hand. I've dressed this version up because fresh tuna is an expensive treat these days, but it remains a very easy to prepare dish.

MAKES 4 SERVINGS

GLUTEN-FREE FRIENDLY

Tips

The piment d'Espelette produces a very mild level of heat. If you prefer a more pungent result, add ¼ tsp (1 mL) hot paprika or a couple of pinches of cayenne pepper in Step 2.

If you don't have piment d'Espelette, substitute 2 tsp (10 mL) sweet paprika enhanced with ¼ tsp (1 mL) cayenne pepper.

Be a bit cautious if you're using fish stock to make this stew. While it will add pleasant depth to the dish, some fish stocks are very intensely flavored. If that is the case, dilute yours with water to suit your taste.

Cut the potatoes into 1-inch (2.5 cm) cubes.

I like my tuna rare, so I cooked the ¾-inch (2 cm) thick fillet I used for about 1 minute in the Dutch oven with the potato mixture. The cooking time will depend on your preference and the thickness of your fillet.

- Dutch oven

¼ cup	extra virgin olive oil, divided	60 mL
1	large onion, diced	1
1	each red and green bell pepper, diced	1
6	cloves garlic, minced	6
1	bay leaf	1
2	anchovy fillets, rinsed and minced	2
1 tsp	piment d'Espelette (approx.)	5 mL
½ cup	dry white wine	125 mL
1	can (14 oz/398 mL) tomatoes, with juice	1
2 cups	vegetable or fish stock (see Tips, left)	500 mL
2	Yukon Gold potatoes, peeled and cubed	2
½ tsp	salt	2 mL
	Salt and freshly ground black pepper	
1 lb	skinless ahi tuna fillet	500 g
	Finely chopped fresh parsley	

1. In Dutch oven, heat 2 tbsp (30 mL) of the oil over medium heat. Add onion, red and green bell peppers, garlic, bay leaf and anchovy fillets and stir well. Cover, reduce heat and cook until vegetables are very tender, about 10 minutes.

2. Increase heat to medium-high and stir in piment d'Espelette. Add wine and cook, stirring, for 2 minutes. Add tomatoes and juice, and stock and bring to a boil. Add potatoes and salt and return to a boil. Reduce heat to low and simmer until potatoes are tender and flavors are melded, about 15 minutes. Season to taste with salt and black pepper.

3. Meanwhile, in a skillet, heat remaining oil over medium-high heat. Season tuna with salt and black pepper. Add to pan and sear, about 1 minute per side. Cut into cubes (about 1 inch/2.5 cm). When potatoes are tender, add tuna and cook to desired degree of doneness (see Tips, left). Discard bay leaf. Ladle into bowls. Garnish with parsley. Pass piment d'Espelette for sprinkling.

Turkish-Style Yogurt-Baked Fish

This baked fish is based on one I enjoyed so much in Istanbul that I prepared it immediately upon returning home, using an intriguing blend called "salad spice" that I had purchased at the city's Egyptian Market. I've tried to replicate the seasoning and the flavors I remember from Turkey in this dish. Serve the fish over rice to soak up the delicious sauce.

Tip

If you don't have Aleppo pepper, substitute ¾ tsp (3 mL) sweet paprika and ¼ tsp (1 mL) cayenne pepper. You can also use Turkish Maras or Urfa pepper or even Spanish ñora pepper. Although it is sweet and milder than the other options, the ñora pepper has a lovely, deep flavor.

- Preheat oven to 350°F (180°C)
- Long shallow baking dish with lid

¾ cup	plain full-fat Greek-style yogurt	175 mL
1 tsp	ground sumac	5 mL
1 tsp	Aleppo pepper	5 mL
½ tsp	dried thyme	2 mL
1 lb	skinless firm white fish fillets, such as grouper	500 g
1 tbsp	olive oil	15 mL
1	onion, chopped	1
1	small red bell pepper, seeded and diced	1
2	cloves garlic, thinly sliced	2
1	bay leaf	1
2 tsp	tomato paste	10 mL
	Salt and freshly ground black pepper	
¼ cup	finely chopped fresh dill	60 mL

1. In baking dish, stir together yogurt, sumac, Aleppo pepper and thyme. Add fish and turn to coat completely in the spice mixture. Let stand for 15 minutes at room temperature to marinate.

2. Meanwhile, in a skillet, heat oil over medium heat. Add onion, bell pepper and garlic and cook, stirring, until pepper is softened, about 5 minutes. Add bay leaf and tomato paste. Season to taste with salt and black pepper. Spoon over fish.

3. Cover and bake in preheated oven until fish flakes easily when tested with a knife, about 30 minutes. Discard bay leaf. Sprinkle fish with dill and serve immediately.

Veracruz-Style Red Snapper (*Huachinango a la Veracruzana*)

This is one of the best-known Mexican fish dishes. As with many classic dishes, there are countless ways of preparing it. I have chosen a simplified method that mimics the presentation in restaurants where I have enjoyed it. Olives are traditionally included, which suggests that the origins of the dish are Spanish. Serve with rice or tortillas.

MAKES 4 SERVINGS

GLUTEN-FREE FRIENDLY

Tips

Make sure your snapper has been sustainably harvested. If you can't find it or there are sustainability issues with your fish supply, substitute another firm white fish that is eco-friendly.

Feel free to vary the quantity of olives, capers and jalapeños to suit your taste.

Moreover ...

The herb usually identified as Mexican oregano is not the same as Mediterranean *Origanum vulgare*. While one variety of it belongs to that family, most others are *Lippia graveolens* or *L. berlandieri*, which are part of the verbena family. In any case, Mexican oregano, which is sun-dried, provides a similar but more robust flavor than its European counterpart, with strong citrus notes.

- Preheat oven to 350°F (180°C)
- 10-cup (2.5 L) casserole dish

1 lb	skinless red snapper fillets, patted dry (see Tips, left)	500 g
1 tbsp	freshly squeezed lime juice	15 mL
2 tbsp	extra virgin olive oil, divided	30 mL
	Sea salt	
1	white onion, thinly sliced	1
4	cloves garlic, minced	4
1 to 2	jalapeño or serrano pepper(s), finely chopped	1 to 2
2	Mexican bay leaves (see Tips, page 150)	2
1 tsp	dried Mexican oregano (see left)	5 mL
1	can (28 oz/796 mL) tomatoes, with juice, coarsely chopped	1
	Salt and freshly ground black pepper	
12	pimento-stuffed green olives, thinly sliced (see Tips, left)	12
2 tbsp	drained capers	30 mL
	Finely chopped fresh parsley (optional)	

1. Brush fish on all sides with lime juice, then 1 tbsp (15 mL) of the oil. Season lightly to taste with sea salt and set aside.

2. In a skillet, heat remaining oil over medium heat. Add onion and cook, stirring, until beginning to turn golden, about 7 minutes. Add garlic, jalapeño pepper(s) to taste, bay leaves and oregano and cook, stirring, for 1 minute. Stir in tomatoes and juice, and bring to a boil. Reduce heat and simmer until flavors are melded, about 10 minutes. Season to taste with salt and black pepper. Stir in olives and capers.

3. Spread about half of the sauce evenly in casserole dish. Arrange fish in single layer over top and cover with remaining sauce. Bake in preheated oven until fish flakes easily when tested with a knife, about 20 minutes. Garnish with parsley (if using).

Focus on: Chiles in Mexico

The use of chiles in Mexican cuisine parallels how the *Mona Lisa* compares to a paint-by-numbers canvas. In her book *From My Mexican Kitchen*, esteemed culinary researcher and author Diana Kennedy devotes more than 40 pages to fresh and dried chiles, even raising the possibility that some varieties may have developed in Mexico and not in Amazonia as is commonly thought. She notes that traces of both wild and cultivated chiles have been found in parts of Mexico as far back as the seventh century B.C.E. In the course of her research, she regularly packs up her truck and camps out in remote parts of the country, where she often stumbles upon previously unidentified varieties of wild chiles.

She writes, "There is no doubt, nor room for argument, when it comes to chiles: Mexico reigns supreme." In Mexico, there are hundreds of varieties, both domesticated and wild. They range from exotic (the Xcatik, a blonde chile, or the Xigoli, a tiny red or green pepper resembling the piquin) to mundane (the jalapeño). For chile lovers, visiting a market in Mexico is a heavenly experience. It is positively thrilling to see chiles you have only read about, and taking in the range and diversity of the offerings is inspiring.

In the course of daily eating in Mexico, the fresh chiles you are most likely to come across include jalapeño, poblano, serrano and, in Yucatán, the habanero. The dried chiles used most widely are ancho, chile de árbol, cascabel and chipotle, as well as the guajillo, a medium-hot dried reddish-brown pepper, which, according to Kennedy, is the most commonly used capsicum in Mexico. (Because it is used in many cooked preparations, it is not terribly visible at the table.)

Mexican-Style Escabeche

This deliciously different recipe was inspired by Diana Kennedy's recipe for Yucatán Soused Fish. It is usually made with kingfish, but Diana says she often makes it with salmon.

Tips

In Mexico, it is common to find white onions used raw in uncooked dishes, such as fresh salsas. Cooks have various techniques for taming their bite, from running them under plenty of cold water to soaking them in hot salted water. I find sweating white onions (or red, as in this recipe) in salt, then rinsing them in cold water to be quite effective.

Mexican bay leaves belong to a different genus (*Litsea glaucescens*) than their Mediterranean counterparts (*Laurus nobilis*) and have a more delicate flavor. You can purchase them in Latin American markets. If you can't find them, substitute regular bay leaves, using half the quantity called for.

- Spice grinder, or mortar and pestle

1	green bell pepper, roasted	1
1 cup	thinly sliced red onion (see Tips, left)	250 mL
2 tsp	coarse sea salt, divided	10 mL
2 lbs	salmon or kingfish steaks	1 kg
2 tbsp	freshly squeezed lime juice	30 mL
½ tsp	each black peppercorns, coriander seeds and cumin seeds	2 mL
4	whole cloves	4
1	piece (½ inch/1 cm long) cinnamon stick	1
2	Mexican bay leaves (see Tips, left)	2
½ tsp	dried Mexican oregano	2 mL
½ cup	extra virgin olive oil	125 mL
¼ cup	white wine vinegar	60 mL
3	cloves garlic, puréed (see Tips, page 172)	3
½	habanero pepper, or 1 to 2 jalapeño pepper(s), minced	½
2 tbsp	oil	30 mL

1. Seed, peel and cut roasted green pepper into strips.

2. Place red onion in a bowl and sprinkle with 1 tsp (5 mL) of the salt. Rub onions with salt to ensure the salt is well integrated into the onions. Set aside for 20 minutes to sweat. Rinse thoroughly under cold running water and drain.

3. Place fish in a single layer in a baking dish. Sprinkle all over with lime juice and remaining salt. Let stand at room temperature for 15 minutes.

4. Meanwhile, in a small skillet over medium heat, toast peppercorns, coriander seeds, cumin seeds, cloves and cinnamon stick until fragrant, about 3 minutes. Transfer to spice grinder. Add bay leaves and oregano. Grind to a fine powder and transfer to a small saucepan.

5. Add oil, vinegar, 1/4 cup (60 mL) water and garlic and bring to a boil. Add onion, habanero and roasted pepper strips and return to a boil. Remove from heat.

6. Scrape excess salt off fish and pat dry. Heat oil in a large skillet over medium heat. Add fish and fry, turning once, until almost opaque. Transfer to a serving dish. Pour oil mixture over top. Let stand for 15 minutes before serving.

Caribbean Blaff

This dish is popular across the Caribbean, and particularly so in Martinique. Often it is made with whole red snapper, but the recipe works well with other firm white fish. There are various explanations for where the rather odd name came from—the most reasonable is that it is a mispronunciation of the word *broth*. However, some say it is meant to capture the noise the fish makes when it hits the boiling liquid.

2 lbs	skin-on firm white fish fillets	1 kg
2 cups	water (approx.)	500 mL
½ cup	freshly squeezed lime juice	125 mL
6	green onions (white and green parts), finely chopped	6
4	cloves garlic, coarsely chopped	4
2	sprigs fresh thyme	2
½ to 1	habanero or Scotch bonnet pepper, minced	½ to 1
8	whole allspice berries, crushed	8
½ tsp	salt	2 mL
	Freshly ground black pepper	
1½ cups	fish stock	375 mL
	Hot cooked rice	
	Finely chopped fresh cilantro	
	Lime wedges	

1. Remove skin from fish and cut into serving-size portions. In a large nonreactive bowl, combine 2 cups (500 mL) water, lime juice, green onions, garlic, thyme, habanero pepper to taste, allspice, salt, and black pepper to taste. Add fish and turn to coat. Add a little more water, just until fish is barely covered. Cover and refrigerate for 1 hour or up to overnight, turning occasionally.

2. Transfer liquid to a large saucepan; add fish stock and bring to a boil. Add fish. Cover, reduce heat and simmer until fish flakes easily when tested with a knife. (The cooking time will depend on the thickness of the fish.)

3. To serve, spoon rice to taste into warm soup plates. Top with fish and pour broth over top. Garnish to taste with cilantro. Season to taste with additional salt and pepper. Serve with lime wedges.

Fried Fish in Spicy Chickpea Batter

I came across a reference to seasoned chickpea batter in a Persian cookbook. It is an example of interesting foodways (the intersection of food, culture, history and traditions) because the batter was inspired by a recipe for *pekareh*, an obvious relative of the delicious Indian pakora, which is also coated in this type of batter. This fish is absolutely delicious served with *dakkous* (page 382), a spicy warm tomato sauce that is popular in the region.

MAKES 4 SERVINGS

Tips

For the best flavor, toast and grind cumin and coriander seeds yourself.

Depending on the moisture content of your flour, you may need as much as 2 cups (500 mL) of soda water to make the batter.

- Wok, deep skillet or deep fryer
- Candy/deep-fry thermometer

1 cup	all-purpose flour	250 mL
¾ cup	chickpea flour	175 mL
2 tbsp	cornstarch	30 mL
2 tsp	Aleppo pepper	10 mL
1 tsp	ground cumin (see Tips, left)	5 mL
1 tsp	ground coriander	5 mL
1 tsp	baking soda	5 mL
1 tsp	salt	5 mL
1¼ cups	cold soda water (approx.), see Tips, left	300 mL
	Oil for frying	
1½ lbs	skinless firm white fish fillets, such as halibut or cod, cut into small pieces (about 3 by 2 inches/7.5 by 5 cm)	750 g

1. In a medium bowl, whisk together all-purpose flour, chickpea flour, cornstarch, Aleppo pepper, cumin, coriander, baking soda and salt. Add 1¼ cups (300 mL) soda water and stir well. If batter is too thick, add a little more cold soda water to thin. (Batter should be thick but liquidy enough to adhere to fish.)

2. In wok, heat oil until thermometer registers 350°F (180°C). (If using a deep fryer, follow the manufacturer's instructions.) Be sure to use enough oil to immerse the fish.

3. One piece at a time, dip fish into batter, turning to coat evenly. Using metal tongs and working in batches, if necessary, add fish to hot oil, standing back to avoid spatters. Fry, turning once, until batter is crisp and browned, and fish flakes easily when tested with a knife, about 5 minutes. (The cooking time will depend on the size and thickness of the fish.)

4. As fish is done, transfer it to a paper towel–lined platter and let drain. Serve hot.

Jamaican-Style Fish Cakes

Fish cakes, often made with salt cod, are an ultra-popular dish in Jamaica. Often they are encased in batter and deep-fried, in which case they are called fritters. However they are prepared, they are usually seasoned with plenty of Scotch bonnet peppers. The addition of mashed potatoes makes this version a tad rich—I like to balance that with a generous squirt of freshly squeezed lime juice.

MAKES 6 CAKES

GLUTEN-FREE FRIENDLY

Tips

The easiest way to cook the fish for this recipe is to use your microwave. If necessary, cut the fillets into 4 equal-size pieces. Place them in a microwave-safe dish in a single layer and add ¼ cup (60 mL) water. Cover tightly with plastic wrap and microwave on High for 4 minutes. Let stand for 5 minutes. Remove the plastic wrap and set aside to cool.

You will need 1 large russet (Idaho) potato that weighs about 12 oz (375 g) to make this quantity of mashed potato.

- Food processor

1 lb	skinless fish fillets, such as haddock or cod, cooked (see Tips, left), cooled and broken into chunks	500 g
1½ cups	mashed cooked potato (see Tips, left)	375 mL
¼ cup	fresh cilantro leaves	60 mL
3	green onions (white and light green parts), chopped	3
½ to 1	Scotch bonnet or habanero pepper, chopped	½ to 1
1	clove garlic	1
1	egg, lightly beaten	1
	Finely grated zest of 1 lime	
2 tbsp	freshly squeezed lime juice	30 mL
1 tsp	salt	5 mL
	Freshly ground black pepper	
¼ cup	potato starch or cornstarch	60 mL
½ cup	panko bread crumbs	125 mL
¼ cup	oil for frying	60 mL

1. In food processor fitted with the metal blade, combine cilantro, green onions, Scotch bonnet pepper to taste, and garlic. Pulse until chopped, stopping and scraping down the side of the bowl as necessary. Add egg, lime zest, lime juice, salt, and black pepper to taste. Pulse just until blended, 2 or 3 times. Add fish and pulse just until blended, 5 or 6 times. (Do not purée.) Add mashed potato and pulse just until blended, 5 or 6 times.

2. Dust a large plate with potato starch. With greased hands, divide fish mixture into 6 patties. Shape each into a ball and roll in potato starch until coated. Flatten slightly and transfer to a baking sheet. Refrigerate for 30 minutes to firm up.

Tips

If you need to gild the lily, serve these fish cakes with homemade mayonnaise made with lime rather than lemon juice. A perfect finish is a salad of frisée, baby lettuce and cherry tomatoes; if field tomatoes are in season, just toss some with a simple vinaigrette to serve alongside.

To make these cakes gluten-free, use gluten-free panko instead of regular.

3. When you're ready to cook, spread panko evenly on a large plate. With greased hands, flatten patties and press into crumbs, turning to coat both sides.

4. In a large skillet, heat oil over medium heat. Add patties, in batches if necessary, and fry until browned and crisp, about 4 minutes per side. Serve warm.

Variation

Substitute an equal quantity of salt cod (known as saltfish in Jamaica) for the fish fillets. Soak it overnight in several changes of water and drain well before using.

To Seed or Not to Seed

Whether you seed and remove the veins inside your peppers is a matter of preference. With the exception of bell peppers, I usually don't seed and devein because, in my opinion, it affects the taste and experience of the pepper. I like the texture the seeds add to a dish. The veins are the placental tissue inside the peppers, and they contain any spiciness, so removing them may be a good idea if you are heat-averse; you can also reduce the quantity of chile called for in a recipe or substitute a chile that ranks lower on the Scoville scale.

Cornmeal-Crusted Fish with Green Salsa

I'm not sure where the idea for this recipe came from—it might have been inspired by a trip to Mexico or the Caribbean—but I've been making variations of it for years. It is nutritious, delicious and easy enough to whip up for a weeknight meal. The combination of crunchy cornmeal-crusted fish and robust salsa is very pleasing. The salsa makes about ¾ cup (175 mL) and is tasty with tortilla chips, too.

MAKES 4 SERVINGS

GLUTEN-FREE FRIENDLY

Tip

The single jalapeño makes the salsa quite spicy—certainly spicy enough for me. But if you're a dedicated heat seeker, increase the quantity to suit your taste.

• **Food processor**

½ cup	fine stone-ground cornmeal	125 mL
2 tbsp	cornstarch	30 mL
2 tbsp	freshly grated Parmesan cheese	30 mL
2	eggs	2
	Salt and freshly ground black pepper	
1½ lbs	skinless firm white fish fillets	750 g
¼ cup	oil for frying	60 mL

Green Salsa

1 cup	packed fresh cilantro leaves	250 mL
1 cup	packed fresh parsley leaves	250 mL
1	bunch (about 6) green onions (white and a bit of the green parts), cut in chunks	1
1	jalapeño pepper (see Tips, left and opposite)	1
2	cloves garlic	2
2 tbsp	olive oil	30 mL
1 tbsp	red wine vinegar	15 mL
½ tsp	salt	2 mL
	Freshly ground black pepper	

1. *Green Salsa:* In food processor fitted with the metal blade, combine cilantro, parsley, green onions, jalapeño pepper and garlic. Pulse until chopped and blended, stopping and scraping down the side of the bowl as necessary. Add oil, vinegar, salt, and black pepper to taste and pulse until blended. (Don't purée; you want the ingredients to maintain some texture.) Transfer to a serving bowl. Let stand for 30 minutes to allow the flavors to bloom.

Tip

You can substitute any mildly hot chile, such as Fresno or serrano, for the jalapeño.

2. Meanwhile, in a long shallow dish, combine cornmeal, cornstarch and cheese. In a separate long shallow dish, beat eggs with salt and black pepper to taste. One at a time, dip fish fillets into egg mixture, then dredge in cornmeal mixture, turning to coat all over.

3. In a large skillet, heat oil over medium-high heat. Add fish, in batches if necessary. Cook, turning once, until fish flakes easily when tested with a knife. (The cooking time will depend on the thickness of the fish.) Serve immediately with green salsa.

Pan-Roasted Salmon with Green Salsa

The green salsa in this recipe is a variation on the theme of South American chimichurri (see page 371). In his book *Mallmann on Fire*, Francis Mallmann, the esteemed Argentinean chef, has a recipe for salmon he catches at his country retreat and bakes in a salt crust. He serves it with a sauce of this type. I have found my green salsa works very well with simple pan-roasted salmon.

- Preheat oven to 400°F (200°C)
- Ovenproof skillet

1 tbsp	grapeseed oil	15 mL
1½ lbs	skin-on salmon fillet, patted dry	750 g

Salt and freshly ground black pepper	
Green Salsa (opposite)	

1. In skillet, heat oil over medium-high heat. Season salmon to taste with salt and black pepper. Place, skin side down, in pan and sear, pressing down on fillet, until skin becomes crisp, about 5 minutes. Flip and transfer skillet to preheated oven. Roast until fish flakes easily when tested with a knife, about 5 minutes. (Cooking time will depend on the thickness of the fish and the desired degree of doneness.)

2. Serve immediately with Green Salsa.

Malaysian-Style Barbecued Fish

This is a tasty way to barbecue a whole fish. The fat in the coconut milk helps the skin crisp up, and the chiles and aromatics add pleasant flavors. This is a very forgiving recipe: you can use larger or smaller fish, depending on what is available.

MAKES 4 SERVINGS

GLUTEN-FREE FRIENDLY

Tips

Use a firm white fish, such as flounder, sole, fluke or branzino.

If only smaller fish are available, use 2 that add up to the weight called for.

- Blender

1	whole fish, cleaned and head removed (about 1¼ lbs/625 g), see Tips, left	1
	Lemon wedges	

Marinade

1¼ cups	coconut milk	300 mL
1	onion, quartered	1
2	cloves garlic	2
3	red Thai bird's-eye chiles	3
1	piece (1 inch/2.5 cm long) gingerroot, coarsely chopped	1
1 tsp	finely grated lemon zest	5 mL

1. *Marinade:* In blender, combine coconut milk, onion, garlic, bird's-eye chiles, ginger and lemon zest. Purée until smooth.

2. Using a sharp knife, cut shallow crisscross pattern into fish skin on both sides. Place fish in a shallow dish large enough to lay fish flat and pour over marinade, coating inside and outside of fish. Cover and refrigerate for at least 2 hours or up to 4 hours, turning once or twice.

3. When you are ready to cook, preheat barbecue to high. Remove fish from marinade and drain, reserving marinade.

4. In a small saucepan, bring reserved marinade to a boil. Reduce heat and simmer for 2 minutes.

5. Grill fish, turning once, and basting with reserved marinade as required to keep skin moist, until fish flakes easily when tested with a knife, about 15 minutes. Serve with lemon wedges.

Chile Savvy

In this recipe, rich, sweet coconut milk and a hint of bitter lemon create a soothing foundation that allows the fiery Thai chiles to sparkle.

Kedgeree

Kedgeree, in my opinion, is one of the great triumphs of Anglo-Indian cuisine. Properly prepared, it is mouthwatering. In the British Isles, it is often made with leftover rice and served for breakfast. This version, made fresh, is a delicious dinner dish.

MAKES 4 SERVINGS

GLUTEN-FREE FRIENDLY

Tips

Haddock is a North Atlantic fish. The smoked version known as Finnan haddie is traditionally made from Scottish haddock that has been smoked over a peat fire. While it is very popular in the British Isles, it can be difficult to find in North America, particularly if you live on the west coast. Substitute smoked sturgeon, cod or bluefish if you can't find it.

The thin tail ends of smoked haddock are oversmoked and tough. I recommend removing these bits and discarding them, but you can add them to the poaching liquid to enhance the flavor.

I like to use brown rice because I enjoy its pleasantly nutty taste and its nutritional superiority over white rice. If you prefer it, you can substitute an equal quantity of white basmati rice and reduce the simmering time to about 15 minutes.

If you are preparing this dish for someone who is sensitive to gluten, check your curry powder to make sure no wheat products have been added as filler.

Kedgeree is sometimes called *khitchuri* (see page 321).

- **Large saucepan with tight-fitting lid**

1 lb	trimmed smoked haddock	500 g
1	bay leaf	1
1 cup	heavy or whipping (35%) cream	250 mL
	Freshly ground black pepper	
2 tbsp	butter	30 mL
1	onion, finely chopped	1
2	cloves garlic	2
2	red finger chiles, thinly sliced	2
1 tbsp	curry powder	15 mL
2 tsp	minced gingerroot	10 mL
1¼ cups	brown basmati rice (see Tips, left)	300 mL
1¼ cups	chicken stock	300 mL
4	hard-cooked eggs, quartered	4
	Finely snipped fresh chives	
	Lemon wedges	

1. In a large saucepan, place fish skin side up. Add bay leaf, cream and enough water to cover. Season to taste with black pepper. Cook over medium heat until bubbles form around the edge. (Do not boil.) Cover, reduce heat to very low and simmer gently until fish flakes easily when tested with a knife, about 10 minutes. Remove from heat. Drain fish, reserving 1¼ cups (300 mL) of the cooking liquid. Discard bay leaf. Set fish aside.

2. In another large saucepan with a tight-fitting lid, melt butter over medium heat. Add onion and cook, stirring, until softened, about 3 minutes. Add garlic, finger chiles, curry powder and ginger and cook, stirring, for 1 minute. Add rice and stir to coat. Add stock and reserved cooking liquid and bring to a boil. Cover, reduce heat to very low and simmer until liquid is absorbed and rice is tender, about 40 minutes.

3. When cool enough to handle, lift off skin and flake fish.

4. Transfer rice mixture to a deep serving platter. Sprinkle flaked fish evenly over top and gently stir in. Garnish with egg quarters and sprinkle with chives to taste. Serve with lemon wedges.

Basque-Style Roasted Fish

This treatment for freshly caught fish is very popular in bistros on the Basque seaside, and it is ideal for a quick, easy weeknight meal. Any firm white fish works well—sea bream and hake are both traditional choices in that area. In the Basque region, this dish is pan-fried or grilled, but I prefer oven roasting, which allows me time to make the sauce that finishes cooking the fish.

MAKES 2 SERVINGS

GLUTEN-FREE FRIENDLY

Tips

Add the fresh chile if you are a heat seeker. A mild red chile, such as Fresno, is a good choice.

For the absolute best flavor, use high-quality sherry vinegar in this recipe.

If you prefer, you can grill the fish over high heat (for the most traditional version of this dish) or cook it under the broiler, flipping it halfway through. In either case, it will take about 5 minutes per side.

• **Preheat oven to 400°F (200°C)**

2	skin-on fish fillets (each about 6 oz/175 g)	2
	Salt and freshly ground black pepper	
5 tbsp	extra virgin olive oil, divided	75 mL
4	cloves garlic, thinly sliced	4
1 tsp	piment d'Espelette	5 mL
	Minced fresh chile (optional), see Tips, left	
2 tbsp	sherry vinegar (see Tips, left)	30 mL
1 tbsp	finely chopped fresh parsley	15 mL

1. Season fish to taste with salt and black pepper. In a large skillet, heat 1 tbsp (15 mL) of the oil over medium high-heat. Place fish, skin side up, in skillet and cook for 2 minutes. Flip and transfer skillet to preheated oven. Cook until fish flakes easily when tested with a knife, about 7 minutes. (Cooking time will depend on the thickness of the fillets.) Transfer to a warm serving platter.

2. Meanwhile, in a small saucepan, heat remaining oil, garlic, piment d'Espelette and chile (if using) over low heat until garlic is golden. Remove from heat. Stir in vinegar and parsley and pour over hot fish.

Kerala-Style Shrimp Curry

Coconut and seafood are another marriage made in heaven. This recipe, a divine union of seafood and coconut milk, reflects a style of cooking prevalent in the lovely Indian state of Kerala. Serve the curry over rice, another staple of that area.

MAKES 4 SERVINGS

GLUTEN-FREE FRIENDLY

Tips

Traditionally, this recipe would be made using only coconut milk in the sauce. I like to buy shrimp in their shells so I can make stock, which I think produces a lighter result. However, if you prefer, you can use deveined peeled shrimp, omit the shrimp stock and substitute 1 can (14 oz/400 mL) of coconut milk for the 1 cup (250 mL) called for in this version.

To make shrimp stock: In a saucepan, combine shrimp shells, 1 cup (250 mL) white wine and 1 cup (250 mL) water. Bring to a boil. Reduce heat and simmer for 15 minutes. Strain through a fine-mesh sieve into a bowl, pressing the shells with a spatula to extract as much liquid as possible. Measure 1 cup (250 mL) and use in this curry. Freeze remainder for another use.

1 lb	shrimp, peeled, deveined and shells reserved for stock (see Tips, left)	500 g
2 tbsp	freshly squeezed lemon juice	30 mL
2 tsp	ground coriander (see Tips, page 152)	10 mL
1 tsp	ground cumin	5 mL
1 tsp	coarse salt	5 mL
½ tsp	turmeric	2 mL
¼ tsp	ground dried red chile, such as cayenne pepper	1 mL
2 tbsp	coconut oil or olive oil	30 mL
1	onion, finely chopped	1
1	green bell pepper, seeded and diced	1
1	red or green finger chile, seeded and minced	1
2	cloves garlic, minced	2
1 tbsp	minced gingerroot	15 mL
1	can (14 oz/398 mL) crushed tomatoes (passata)	1
1 cup	shrimp stock (see Tips, left)	250 mL
1 cup	coconut milk	250 mL
	Salt and freshly ground black pepper	

1. In a medium bowl, combine shrimp, lemon juice, coriander, cumin, salt, turmeric and ground chile. Stir well to coat. Cover and refrigerate until ready to cook. Make shrimp stock (see Tips, left).

2. In a large skillet, heat oil over medium heat. Add onion, bell pepper and finger chile and cook, stirring, until softened, about 5 minutes. Add garlic and ginger and cook, stirring, for 1 minute. Add tomatoes, shrimp stock and coconut milk and bring to a boil. Reduce heat and simmer until slightly reduced, about 5 minutes.

3. Increase heat to medium and add shrimp and marinade. Return to a boil. Cook, stirring, until shrimp are pink and sauce is slightly thickened, about 5 minutes. Season to taste with salt and black pepper.

Paella

My paella is not traditionally Spanish. It is more like a Portuguese dish in the sense that it combines seafood and meat. But I've been making it for years and it is a family favorite—one that, I might add, I often serve to guests. Served with crusty bread, a simple green salad and some good white wine, it makes a perfect Friday night dinner with friends.

MAKES 6 SERVINGS

GLUTEN-FREE FRIENDLY

Tips

The best rice for making paella is Bomba; Valencia or Calasparra are good substitutes. In a pinch, use Arborio. Do not substitute long-grain rice, which isn't starchy enough.

Ideally, you will want 3 to 4 cherrystone clams per person, but I have made delicious iterations of this dish using 6 to 8 much smaller clams per person. You can eyeball the quantity with your fishmonger and adjust to suit your taste. The quantity of clams you use will not affect the results.

- Large skillet or paella pan

1	red bell pepper, roasted (see Tips, page 166)	1
4 cups	chicken stock	1 L
1/8 tsp	saffron, crumbled	0.5 mL
2 tbsp	olive oil	30 mL
1 lb	thinly sliced pork butt or tenderloin	500 g
8 oz	fresh (uncooked) chorizo sausage, casings removed	250 g
1	onion, finely chopped	1
4	cloves garlic, minced, divided	4
1 tsp	sweet paprika	5 mL
1½ cups	medium-grain rice (see Tips, left)	375 mL
½ cup	dry white wine	125 mL
1	can (14 oz/398 mL) diced tomatoes, with juice	1
2 lbs	fresh clams (approx.), see Tips, left	1 kg
¼ cup	butter	60 mL
24	large shrimp (approx.), peeled and deveined	24
¼ cup	finely chopped fresh parsley	60 mL

1. Seed and peel roasted red pepper and cut into thin strips.

2. In a large saucepan, combine stock and saffron. Bring to a boil. Reduce heat and simmer until ready to use.

3. In large skillet, heat oil over medium heat. Add pork, in batches if necessary, and cook, stirring, until just a hint of pink remains in center. Using a slotted spoon, transfer pork to a plate and set aside. Preheat oven to 400°F (200°C).

4. Add chorizo and onion to skillet and cook, stirring, until chorizo is no longer pink. Add half of the garlic and the paprika and cook, stirring, for 1 minute. Add rice and stir until well coated. Add wine and bring to a boil. Boil for 1 minute. Stir in tomatoes and juice, and stock mixture. Return to a boil. Reduce heat and cook, stirring, until liquid just covers the top of the rice. Stir in reserved pork.

continued on page 164

5. Arrange roasted red pepper strips over rice. Arrange clams on top. Transfer pan to preheated oven and bake until clams open, about 15 minutes. Remove from oven. Keep warm, discarding any clams that have not opened.

6. Meanwhile, in a skillet, melt butter over medium heat. Add shrimp and remaining garlic and cook, stirring, until shrimp are pink. Arrange shrimp over rice mixture. Garnish with parsley. Serve immediately.

Chile-Baked Halibut

So far as I know, this recipe has no identifiable roots. It is something I came up with years ago, as a quick and easy way to prepare halibut. The recipe is versatile and makes a great weeknight dinner. Using the recipe as a template, you can vary the seasonings to suit your needs or your taste (see Variations, below). You can also double or triple the recipe if you are serving more people; just adjust the cooking time accordingly.

Tips

If you are making this dish for people who are avoiding gluten, use gluten-free rather than regular panko.

The quantity of bread crumbs and the cooking time will vary, depending on the size and shape of your halibut steak.

You can substitute any fresh chile you have on hand for the habanero. Jalapeño, serrano, Fresno or Anaheim would all work well and provide different degrees of heat. Adjust the quantity to suit your taste.

- Preheat oven to 400°F (200°C)
- Roasting pan with rack

1 lb	skinless boneless halibut steak, patted dry	500 g
½ cup	panko bread crumbs (approx.)	125 mL

Topping

⅓ cup	mayonnaise	75 mL
2 tbsp	extra virgin olive oil	30 mL
1 tbsp	freshly squeezed lemon juice	15 mL
1	habanero pepper (see Tips, left), seeded and minced	1
½ tsp	smoked sweet paprika	2 mL

1. *Topping:* In a small bowl, stir together mayonnaise, olive oil, lemon juice, habanero pepper and paprika. Brush evenly all over fish.
2. Spread panko on a large plate and dredge fish, turning to coat all over. Place fish on rack in roasting pan and bake in preheated oven until fish flakes easily when tested with a knife, about 20 minutes (see Tips, left). Serve immediately.

Variations

Chermoula-Baked Halibut: Omit paprika. Stir ⅓ cup (75 mL) chermoula paste into topping before spreading over fish.

Berbere-Baked Halibut: Omit habanero pepper and paprika. Stir 2 tsp (10 mL) berbere spice blend into topping before spreading over fish.

Other spice mixtures or pastes, such as baharat spice blend or harissa, would also work well in the topping, as would sriracha sauce. I recommend starting with a small amount (½ tsp/2 mL) and adding in increments to suit your palate.

Portuguese-Style Seafood with Rice

Seafood and rice is a quintessential combination in Portugal, but so is seafood and pork. This recipe is a riff on one developed by chef George Mendes of Aldea, an elegant Michelin-starred restaurant in New York City, where they serve mouthwatering Portuguese-inspired food. To me, this dish seems reminiscent of *cozido*, the one-pot dinner made with rice. In any case, it is delicious. I serve it to guests, followed only by a simple salad.

MAKES 6 SERVINGS

GLUTEN-FREE FRIENDLY

Tips

To roast peppers: Brush peppers lightly with oil and place them directly on a hot grill on a preheated barbecue, or arrange them on a baking sheet and place under a preheated broiler. Grill or broil, turning 2 or 3 times, until the skin on all sides is blackened, about 20 minutes. Transfer to a heatproof bowl. Cover with a plate and let stand until cool. Using a sharp knife, lift off the skin, reserving any accumulated juices. Discard skin, stems and seeds.

Roast the peppers before you start to prepare the other ingredients. Reserve their liquid and add it to the skillet along with the clam cooking liquid in Step 5.

- Heavy saucepan with tight-fitting lid
- Dutch oven or large skillet with lid

2 tbsp	extra virgin olive oil, divided	30 mL
1	onion, finely chopped	1
½ tsp	smoked sweet paprika	2 mL
1	bay leaf	1
½ tsp	salt	2 mL
1½ cups	long-grain white rice	375 mL
1 cup	chopped peeled tomatoes, with juice	250 mL
3 cups	chicken stock or water	750 mL

Clams

1 cup	dry white wine	250 mL
4	cloves garlic, minced	4
18	littleneck clams	18

Seafood

6	sea scallops, cut in half if large, patted dry	6
1 tbsp	sweet Spanish paprika, divided	15 mL
18	large shrimp, peeled, deveined and patted dry	18
2 tbsp	grapeseed oil (approx.)	30 mL

Toppings

6 oz	dry-cured chorizo sausage, sliced very thinly	175 g
2	red bell peppers, roasted (see Tips, left), seeded, peeled and cut into strips	2
	Finely chopped fresh parsley	
	Coarse sea salt	
	Extra virgin olive oil	

Tips

If you are serving this to someone who is sensitive to gluten, check the label on your chorizo. Wheat products are often added to sausage as filler.

If you would like a bit more heat, try substituting up to ¼ tsp (1 mL) smoked hot Spanish paprika or cayenne pepper for the sweet paprika used to season the scallops and shrimp. Both are very potent, so use with caution.

Chile Savvy
The use of sweet paprika and bell peppers in this dish permits the heat in the chorizo to pop.

1. In heavy saucepan, heat oil over medium heat. Add onion, and cook, stirring, until softened, about 3 minutes. Add smoked paprika, bay leaf and salt and cook, stirring, for 1 minute. Stir in rice until well coated. Add tomatoes and juice, and stock and bring to a boil. Cover, reduce heat to very low and simmer until rice is tender and liquid is absorbed, 15 to 20 minutes. (Do not lift the lid while cooking.) Discard bay leaf.

2. *Clams:* Meanwhile, in Dutch oven, combine wine, garlic and clams. Bring to a boil. Cover, reduce heat and simmer until clams open, about 5 minutes. Remove from heat. Set aside clams and cooking liquid.

3. *Seafood:* Meanwhile, sprinkle tops of scallops with about half of the paprika. Sprinkle remainder over shrimp. In a large skillet, heat 2 tbsp (30 mL) grapeseed oil over medium-high heat. Add scallops, paprika side down, and cook, pressing down with a spatula, until browned, about 1 minute. Flip and repeat. Transfer to a plate and set aside.

4. Add more grapeseed oil to skillet, if necessary. Add shrimp and cook, stirring, until pink, about 2 minutes. Transfer to plate with scallops. Remove skillet from burner but increase heat to medium-high.

5. Using a slotted spoon, place cooked clams on plate with shrimp and scallops, reserving cooking liquid. Set aside, discarding any clams that have not opened. Return skillet to medium-high heat and add reserved cooking liquid. Bring to a boil. Cook, stirring and scraping up browned bits from bottom of skillet, until liquid is reduced, about 2 minutes. Stir into rice mixture.

6. *Toppings:* Spread rice mixture on a warm deep serving platter. Arrange chorizo and roasted pepper strips evenly over rice. Arrange clams, scallops and shrimp over top. Sprinkle to taste with parsley and salt. Drizzle lightly with extra virgin olive oil. Serve immediately.

Spaghetti Puttanesca

Depending on the source, this dish may or may not have originated with prostitutes in Italy, who found it so quick to prepare they could enjoy a meal between clients. It covers all the flavor bases: it's an addictive mix of sweet, sour, salty and pungent, with umami from the anchovies. As those ladies of the night understood, it is a perfect dinner for a busy weeknight.

MAKES 4 TO 6 SERVINGS

Tips

If you are a heat seeker, increase the hot pepper flakes to ½ tsp (2 mL).

Especially rich and delicious, San Marzanos are the Rolls-Royce of tomatoes. Authentic versions have *Denominazione di Origine Protetta* (DOP) status and are grown in volcanic soil near Naples, Italy, where they receive long hours of flavor-building sunshine. However, imitations are grown from San Marzano seeds in various locations, with differing degrees of success. Because the tomatoes play such a significant role in this recipe, I recommend you spring for the real ones. They are pricier than most but are widely available.

- Stockpot

2 tbsp	extra virgin olive oil	30 mL
4	anchovy fillets, finely chopped	4
4	cloves garlic, minced	4
¼ tsp	hot pepper flakes, preferably *peperoncino* (see Tips, left)	1 mL
3 tbsp	drained chopped capers	45 mL
½ to 1	red finger chile, minced	½ to 1
1	can (28 oz/796 mL) tomatoes, preferably San Marzano, with juice, chopped	1
¾ cup	sliced black olives	175 mL
1 tsp	finely grated lemon zest	5 mL
	Salt and freshly ground black pepper	
1 lb	spaghetti or spaghettini	500 g
¼ cup	finely chopped fresh parsley	60 mL
	Freshly grated Parmesan cheese	

1. In a large skillet, heat oil over medium heat. Add anchovies and cook, stirring, until they resemble tiny specks. Add garlic, and hot pepper flakes to taste and cook, stirring, for 1 minute. Stir in capers, finger chile to taste, and tomatoes and juice, and bring to a boil.

2. Reduce heat and simmer, uncovered, until sauce is thickened and flavors are melded, about 15 minutes. Stir in olives and lemon zest. Season to taste with salt and black pepper. Remove from heat. Set aside.

3. Meanwhile, in stockpot of boiling water, combine 1 tbsp (15 mL) salt and spaghetti. Cook according to package directions until pasta is al dente.

4. Scoop out about 1 cup (250 mL) of the pasta cooking liquid and set aside. Drain pasta. Return skillet to burner over medium heat and add about 3 tbsp (45 mL) of the reserved pasta cooking liquid to sauce. Add spaghetti and parsley and toss to coat evenly, adding more of the reserved pasta cooking liquid if necessary.

5. Transfer to a large serving bowl and garnish to taste with Parmesan. Pass additional cheese at the table.

Focus on: Chiles in Italy

The first documented use of hot peppers in Italy appears in a cookbook written by Antonio Latini in 1694. His *salsa di pomodoro alla spagnola* is a condiment composed of hot peppers, tomatoes, onion, mint and olive oil. In modern times, peppers are used quite widely in Italy, particularly in the southern parts of the country. Both sweet and hot varieties feature in rustic Italian cooking; pungent peppers are used both fresh and dried. Dried peppers appear mainly as flakes and less commonly as powder.

When hot peppers are called for in recipes, the range of heat may be unpredictable; *peperoncini*, the term used to describe them, is a catchall moniker for red Italian hot peppers. Confusingly, bell-type peppers are called *peperoni*, a term North Americans are likely to mistake for a type of spicy dried sausage. And perhaps not surprisingly, individual varieties of the same capsicum family are likely to have different names depending on the location in which they are grown or used. For instance, the same pepper is called *pepentò* in L'Aquila and *pipi russi* in Sicily.

Most of the hot peppers are what we in North America would describe as "finger chile" size, about 4 inches (10 cm) long, possibly narrow and pointed. One variety known as "little devils" has an assortment of different names depending upon the location it comes from: *diavoletti* in general, *diavulicchiu* in Basilicata, or *diavulillu* or *pipazzu* in Calabria. These peppers are, not surprisingly, tiny (about ½ inch/1 cm long) and smoking hot. They are usually dried and crushed. Sweet red peppers are usually described as *pepe rosso* or even *peperoni*. They are usually cooked in some way—fried or roasted—and tossed with olive oil. Cubanelle is a favorite variety used

for this treatment. When Cubanelle or similar types of mild, light green frying peppers are called for, bell peppers can be substituted.

Calabria and Basilicata are the regions of Italy most associated with capsicum consumption. The *peperoncino di Cayenna*, better known to North Americans as the common *C. annuum* variety cayenne, is widely used in Southern Italy. It is often added to olive oil to make chile oil for sprinkling over pizza and other dishes.

Calabria is famous for a very spicy sausage, a kind of spreadable salami known as *'nduja*. It can be used to make pasta sauce, as a spread for bruschetta or to liven up creamy polenta (a marriage made in heaven). Another well-known product of the region is *bomba calabrese*, a peppery condiment that can be used as a spread or in sauces. Since 1992, every September, the town of Diamante is liberally decorated with colorful strings of drying red peppers in preparation for the annual five-day Peperoncino Festival.

Basilicata, which lies in the instep of Italy's boot, is also known for peppers, especially *Peperoni di Senise*, a locally grown variety that was awarded Protected Geographical Indication (PGI) in 1996. This mildly spicy chile is about 4 inches (10 cm) long and pointed. It is traditionally grilled or fried and tossed in olive oil, but may also be dried. Dried Senise peppers are often fried in liberal amounts of olive oil (in which case they are known as *cruschi*) and drizzled over bread or pasta. Another of Basilicata's claims to fame is *sugna piccante*, which is lard flavored with ground "little devil" chiles and fennel seeds. It is used mainly as a spread on grilled bread.

Pad Thai

Most people associate Thai food with this delicious noodle dish, which is now enjoyed around the world. Often it is made with tofu as the main source of protein, with just a smattering of dried shrimp to add a foundation of umami. This version uses fish sauce and tamarind water to achieve a similar result.

Tip

Thai bird's-eye chiles are very hot. Finishing the dish with one fresh chile produces a mildly spicy result. If you are a heat seeker, use more to suit your taste.

Moreover ...

Although other grains, such as wheat or buckwheat, figure prominently in noodles from other parts of Asia, in Thailand, most noodles are made from rice flour. They are usually used dried (fresh rice noodles are popular in China) and come in various thicknesses. Dried rice noodles are very convenient because they do not need to be cooked. A quick soak in water is usually all it takes to make them recipe-ready.

- Fine-mesh sieve
- Large wok

¼ cup	boiling water	60 mL
2 tbsp	coconut sugar	30 mL
2 tbsp	Thai tamarind paste (about 2 oz/60 g), broken into pieces	30 mL
1	package (8 oz/250 g) thin rice noodles	1
1 tbsp	toasted sesame oil	15 mL
2 tbsp	grapeseed oil	30 mL
4	dried red Thai bird's-eye chiles	4
1 tbsp	minced garlic	15 mL
4	green onions (white and green parts), thinly sliced	4
8 oz	shrimp, peeled and deveined, cut into small pieces if necessary	250 g
2	eggs, beaten	2
2 tbsp	freshly squeezed lime juice	30 mL
1 tbsp	fish sauce	15 mL
2 cups	bean sprouts	500 mL
¼ cup	unsalted roasted peanuts, chopped	60 mL
	Thinly sliced red Thai bird's-eye chiles (see Tip, left)	
	Finely chopped fresh cilantro	
	Lime wedges	
	Roasted chile powder (optional), see Tips, page 131	

1. In a small bowl, stir boiling water with coconut sugar until sugar is dissolved. Add tamarind paste and mash well. Let stand for 30 minutes, mashing and stirring occasionally to blend. Strain through fine-mesh sieve into a bowl, pressing solids with a spatula to extract as much liquid as possible. Scrape residue off bottom of sieve into bowl. Discard solids.

2. Meanwhile, place noodles in a large bowl and cover generously with boiling water. Soak, stirring frequently, until softened but still slightly firm. Drain. Toss with sesame oil and set aside.

Tip

If you are serving this dish to someone who avoids gluten, be sure to use gluten-free fish sauce.

3. In wok, heat grapeseed oil over medium-high heat. Add dried bird's-eye chiles, garlic, green onions and shrimp and cook, stirring, for 1 minute. Add eggs and cook, without stirring, just until they begin to set, about 1 minute. Toss to combine. Add reserved tamarind water, lime juice and fish sauce and toss until everything is well coated.

4. Add noodles and bean sprouts and stir-fry until heated through, about 2 minutes. Stir in peanuts.

5. Transfer to a serving platter. Garnish to taste with thinly sliced bird's-eye chiles and cilantro. Serve with lime wedges. Pass roasted chile powder at the table.

Southeast Asian–Style Grilled Shrimp

This is a sort-of satay, but I prefer to use large shrimp and grill them individually rather than skewer them. The shrimp make a lovely main course for a warm summer night. Easy Thai-Style Peanut Sauce (page 386) is an ideal accompaniment.

Tips

To purée gingerroot or garlic quickly and easily, use a sharp-toothed rasp grater, such as those made by Microplane.

When making the peanut sauce, be sure to use gluten-free soy sauce or wheat-free tamari if you will be serving it to someone who is sensitive to gluten.

1½ lbs	jumbo shrimp (about 20 per 1 lb/500 g) in the shell	750 g
2 tbsp	coconut milk	30 mL
2 tbsp	soy sauce	30 mL
1 tbsp	coconut oil, melted	15 mL
1 tbsp	freshly squeezed lime juice	15 mL
1 tsp	puréed garlic (see Tips, left)	5 mL
1 tsp	puréed ginger	5 mL
½ tsp	ground dried red chile, such as cayenne or Kashmiri	2 mL
	Easy Thai-Style Peanut Sauce (page 386)	

1. Remove legs from shrimp and devein, leaving shells on. If you have time, brine them (see Tips, page 177). Pat dry with a paper towel.

2. Meanwhile, in a medium bowl, stir together coconut milk, soy sauce, coconut oil, lime juice, garlic, ginger and ground chile. Add prepared shrimp and toss well to coat. Let stand at room temperature for about 15 minutes.

3. Preheat barbecue to high or preheat broiler. Grill or broil shrimp, turning once, until pink and opaque throughout, about 4 minutes. Transfer to a serving platter. Serve with peanut sauce.

Malaysian-Style Shrimp Curry with Pineapple

This is my take on a traditional Nyonya dish, which I have tweaked for simplicity. In Malaysia, cooks would use dried shrimp in the spice paste and serve the shrimp with the shells and heads intact. There is a lot of liquid in this dish, so I recommend serving it in soup or pasta bowls over cooked jasmine rice.

MAKES 4 SERVINGS

GLUTEN-FREE FRIENDLY

Tips

Even after puréeing in the food processor, there will be some fibrous bits of lemongrass in the spice paste. If you prefer a smoother result, finely grate the peeled trimmed lemongrass using a rasp grater, such as those made by Microplane.

If fresh pineapple is not available, used drained canned pineapple chunks.

If you are serving this to someone who is sensitive to gluten, be sure to use gluten-free fish sauce.

- Fine-mesh sieve
- Food processor
- Wok or large skillet

1 lb	large shrimp	500 g
	Hot cooked rice	

Stock

1 cup	water	250 mL
½ cup	dry white wine	125 mL
2	slices (each ½ inch/1 cm thick) gingerroot	2

Spice Paste

1	stalk lemongrass, trimmed and cut into chunks (about 1 inch/2.5 cm)	1
¼ cup	coarsely chopped shallots	60 mL
2 tbsp	coarsely chopped roasted cashews	30 mL
2 tbsp	coconut oil	30 mL
1 tbsp	coarsely chopped gingerroot	15 mL
1	clove garlic	1
2 to 4	red Thai bird's-eye chiles	2 to 4

Sauce

1½ cups	coconut milk	375 mL
1 tbsp	coconut sugar	15 mL
1 cup	bite-size pineapple chunks (see Tips, left)	250 mL
1 tbsp	lime juice	15 mL
1 tbsp	fish sauce	15 mL
	Salt (optional)	

1. Peel and devein shrimp, reserving shells for stock. Set shrimp aside.

2. *Stock:* In a medium saucepan, combine shrimp shells, water, wine and ginger. Bring to a boil over medium-high heat. Reduce heat to low, cover and simmer for 15 minutes. Strain through fine-mesh sieve into a bowl, pressing the shells with a spatula to extract as much liquid as possible. Discard solids. Set ³⁄₄ cup (175 mL) of the shrimp stock aside, and save remainder for another use.

3. *Spice Paste:* In food processor fitted with the metal blade, combine lemongrass, shallots, cashews, coconut oil, ginger, garlic and bird's-eye chiles to taste. Purée until a smooth paste forms, stopping and scraping down the side of the bowl as necessary. If mixture is too thick, add up to 3 tbsp (45 mL) of the coconut milk for the sauce to facilitate processing.

4. *Sauce:* Heat wok over medium heat. Add spice paste and cook, stirring, until very fragrant and bubbly, about 3 minutes. Add reserved shrimp stock, coconut milk and coconut sugar and bring to a boil. Add reserved shrimp and pineapple and simmer until shrimp is pink and opaque throughout, about 5 minutes. Stir in lime juice and fish sauce. Season to taste with salt (if using). Serve immediately over hot cooked rice.

Shrimp Creole

This is a signature dish of New Orleans, but I have always found it to be a bit uneventful. To dress it up, I have added okra, which contributes texture and flavor while it thickens the sauce. I've also added a sprinkle of fresh chile for a bit of nice heat. Even so, some heat seekers may want to pass the hot sauce at the table.

MAKES 4 SERVINGS

GLUTEN-FREE FRIENDLY

Tip

Tabasco sauce, which is made on Avery Island (a short trip from New Orleans), is a good choice for the accompanying Louisiana-style hot sauce.

- **Large skillet with lid**

1 lb	deveined peeled large shrimp	500 g
2 tbsp	freshly squeezed lemon juice	30 mL
1 tsp	coarse salt	5 mL
½ tsp	freshly ground black pepper	2 mL
¼ tsp	cayenne pepper	1 mL
2 tbsp	olive oil	30 mL
1	onion, finely chopped	1
4	stalks celery, diced	4
1	green bell pepper, seeded and cut into thin strips	1
4	cloves garlic, minced	4
1 tsp	dried thyme	5 mL
2 cups	good-quality tomato sauce	500 mL
1 cup	thinly sliced (about ¼ inch/0.5 cm thick) trimmed okra	250 mL
2 tbsp	finely chopped fresh parsley	30 mL
	Salt and freshly ground black pepper	
	Thinly sliced red finger chile (optional)	
	Hot cooked rice	
	Louisiana-style hot pepper sauce (see Tip, left)	

1. In a medium bowl, combine shrimp, lemon juice, coarse salt, black pepper and cayenne pepper. Stir well to coat. Cover and refrigerate until ready to use.

2. In a large skillet, heat oil over medium heat. Add onion, celery and bell pepper and cook, stirring, until softened, about 5 minutes. Add garlic and thyme and cook, stirring, for 1 minute. Stir in tomato sauce and bring to a boil. Stir in okra. Cover, reduce heat and simmer until okra is barely tender, about 15 minutes.

3. Add shrimp mixture with liquid, parsley, and salt and black pepper to taste. Cover and cook until shrimp are pink and opaque throughout, about 5 minutes. Garnish to taste with finger chile (if using). Serve over hot cooked rice. Pass hot pepper sauce at the table.

Hunan Shrimp with Chinese Chives

Shrimp with chives is a dish that is often served in restaurants that specialize in Hunan cuisine. Hunan is one of the two provinces in China known for its love of chiles (the other is Sichuan). This version is inspired by one that appeared in Fuchsia Dunlop's *Revolutionary Chinese Cookbook*. Chinese chives, also known as garlic chives, have a strong garlic-onion flavor that is essential for this dish. Look for them in Asian markets.

MAKES 4 SERVINGS

GLUTEN-FREE FRIENDLY

Tips

To brine shrimp: Brining the shrimp before cooking makes them plump and succulent. In a medium bowl, dissolve 1 tbsp (15 mL) coarse salt in boiling water. Add cold water and enough ice cubes to bring the mixture to room temperature. Add shrimp, adding a little more cold water if necessary to ensure they are completely covered with brine. Let stand at room temperature for 15 minutes or refrigerate for up to 30 minutes. Rinse shrimp under cold running water before using in recipe.

A more authentic version of this dish would likely call for chopped salted chile peppers (see page 396) rather than hot pepper flakes. For a fiery result, use about 2 tsp (10 mL) of salted chiles, rinsed and drained.

If you don't have Chinese black rice vinegar, substitute an equal amount of balsamic vinegar or unseasoned rice vinegar.

In season, try substituting chopped fresh ramps or garlic scapes for the Chinese chives.

- Wok or large skillet

1 lb	large shrimp, peeled, deveined and preferably brined (see Tips, left)	500 g
1	egg white, beaten until frothy	1
1 tbsp	cornstarch	15 mL
1 tbsp	peanut or grapeseed oil	15 mL
Pinch	granulated sugar	Pinch
	Oil for frying	
1 tbsp	minced garlic	15 mL
1 tbsp	minced gingerroot	15 mL
1 tsp	hot pepper flakes (see Tips, left)	5 mL
1 tbsp	Chinese black rice vinegar (see Tips, left)	15 mL
1	bunch (about 3 oz/90 g) Chinese chives, coarsely chopped	1
1	red finger chile, thinly sliced	1
1 tsp	toasted sesame oil	5 mL

1. Pat shrimp dry with a paper towel. In a bowl, stir together beaten egg white, cornstarch, peanut oil and sugar. Add shrimp and toss to coat. Set aside.

2. In wok, heat oil for frying over medium-high heat. Add shrimp in a single layer (or in 2 batches) and cook until beginning to brown on the bottom, about 1 minute. Flip and cook just until coating crisps up. Using a slotted spoon, transfer to a plate. (The shrimp should be barely cooked.) Add more oil to wok, if necessary, scraping up browned bits from bottom.

3. Add garlic, ginger and hot pepper flakes to wok and cook, stirring, for 1 minute. Return shrimp to wok and drizzle vinegar over top. Add chives and cook, stirring, until shrimp are evenly coated with chives, about 30 seconds. Sprinkle finger chile over top and drizzle with sesame oil. Transfer to a serving dish and serve immediately.

Salt and Pepper Shrimp

I've seen renditions of this very simple but delicious shrimp recipe in Chinese and Vietnamese cookbooks. It is a nice option to include in a multidish meal, and it makes a great appetizer, particularly if you are looking for an ice breaker to facilitate conversation among people who haven't met. The shrimp are tastiest if you eat them whole, shells and all. Just provide lots of paper napkins to catch any drips.

GLUTEN-FREE FRIENDLY

Tips

Be sure to use gluten-free soy sauce or wheat-free tamari if you are making this dish for someone who is sensitive to gluten.

I like to brine shrimp before cooking them to ensure the most succulent results.

- Mortar and pestle, or spice grinder
- Large wok or skillet
- Candy/deep-fry thermometer

1½ lbs	large shrimp (about 20 per 1 lb/500 g) in the shell	750 g
1 cup	boiling water	250 mL
2	cloves garlic, crushed	2
2	dried red chiles, broken in half	2
2 tbsp	kosher salt	30 mL
6 cups	cold water	1.5 L
	Ice cubes	
1½ tsp	black peppercorns	7 mL
1½ tsp	Sichuan peppercorns	7 mL
3 tbsp	cornstarch	45 mL
½ tsp	granulated sugar	2 mL
2 cups	peanut or other oil for frying	500 mL
3	green onions (white and green parts), thinly sliced	3
1	red finger chile, minced	1
2 tsp	soy sauce	10 mL
	Coarse sea salt	

1. Remove legs from shrimp and devein, leaving shells on. Set aside.

2. In a large bowl, combine boiling water, garlic, chiles and salt, stirring until salt is dissolved. Add cold water and enough ice to bring the solution to room temperature. Add prepared shrimp, adding a little more cold water if necessary to ensure they are completely covered with brine. Let stand for 15 minutes.

3. Meanwhile, in a mortar using a pestle, crush black peppercorns with Sichuan peppercorns until coarse. (If you are using a spice grinder, pulse once or twice.) Set 1 tsp (5 mL) of the spice mixture aside. In a large resealable plastic bag, shake together remaining spice mixture, cornstarch and sugar until combined.

Moreover ...

I enjoy an element of freshness in this dish, so I include minced green onions and a fresh chile. However, this is a traditional street-food dish in parts of China, where it is customarily made using ground dried chiles. If you prefer, substitute about ½ tsp (2 mL) cayenne pepper or another ground dried red chile for the finger chile and add it to the spice mixture. If you are a heat seeker, you can lightly dust the dish with ground dried red chile just before serving.

4. In wok, heat oil until thermometer registers 350°F (180°C).

5. Meanwhile, remove shrimp from brine and pat dry with a paper towel. Discard brine. Add shrimp to cornstarch mixture and shake until well coated.

6. Add shrimp to hot oil, in batches, and cook, stirring, until lightly browned and opaque in center, about 2 minutes per batch. Transfer each batch to a paper towel–lined plate as it is completed. When all the shrimp have been cooked, drain oil from wok and wipe clean.

7. Return wok to medium heat. Add shrimp, green onions, finger chile and reserved spice mix and toss well to combine. Drizzle with soy sauce and toss again. Transfer to a warm serving platter and season to taste with salt. Serve immediately.

Poultry

Country Captain

In many ways, this is an American variation on Anglo-Indian cuisine. Historically, there was active commerce between ports such as Charleston, South Carolina, and the Caribbean Islands, which traded with ports in Asia. Arriving sea captains disembarked bearing an array of spices, which gradually worked their way into daily cooking. This mildly pungent dish is based on one that appears in John Martin Taylor's book *Hoppin' John's Lowcountry Cooking*. He describes it as "a fairly straightforward chicken 'curry' from northern India," which "can also be found throughout the British Isles," wherever the East India Company's "country captains" made port.

MAKES 4 SERVINGS

GLUTEN-FREE FRIENDLY

Tip

This is a wonderful way to use up leftover chicken, which is why I have kept the number of servings on the small side. If you want to make a larger portion, simply double the recipe.

- Spice grinder, or mortar and pestle

2 cups	shredded cooked chicken	500 mL
2 tbsp	dried currants	30 mL
¼ cup	toasted slivered blanched almonds	60 mL

Spice Blend

1 tsp	each coriander seeds, cumin seeds and whole allspice berries	5 mL
4	whole cloves	4
1	small piece (about ½ inch/1 cm long) cinnamon stick	1

Sauce

1 tbsp	oil	15 mL
1	onion, finely chopped	1
1	green bell pepper, seeded and cut into thin strips	1
2	cloves garlic, finely chopped	2
2 tsp	finely chopped gingerroot	10 mL
1 tsp	turmeric	5 mL
¼ tsp	cayenne pepper	1 mL
1	bay leaf	1
1	can (14 oz/398 mL) tomatoes, with juice, coarsely chopped	1
1 cup	chicken stock	250 mL

1. *Spice Blend:* In a dry deep saucepan over medium heat, toast coriander seeds, cumin seeds and allspice, stirring constantly, until fragrant, about 3 minutes. Transfer to spice grinder. Add cloves and cinnamon stick and grind to a fine powder. Set aside.

2. *Sauce:* In same saucepan, heat oil over medium heat. Add onion and bell pepper and cook, stirring, until softened, about 5 minutes. Add garlic, ginger, turmeric, cayenne, bay leaf and reserved spice blend and cook, stirring, for 1 minute. Add tomatoes and juice, and stock, and bring to a boil. Reduce heat and simmer until sauce is thickened and reduced by one-third, about 5 minutes.

3. Stir in chicken and currants and cook until chicken is heated through, about 2 minutes. Discard bay leaf.

4. Transfer to a serving dish. Garnish with almonds and serve immediately.

Hot Chicken

Fried chicken is one of the great dishes of the American South. Some say it is as deeply rooted and pervasive as kudzu, the rampantly invasive vine that nearly took over the region. My version, which my family loves, is marinated in buttermilk and seasoned with paprika and a bit of cayenne. It is mildly spicy and utterly delicious (it is, if I do say so myself, "finger-lickin' good") but certainly not likely to induce hallucinations.

And yet, that is exactly what super-chef Sean Brock seems to be searching for. He describes an "out-of-body experience" as the basic appeal of Nashville hot chicken, a version of Southern fried chicken, which has taken the country by storm. A trip to Prince's Hot Chicken Shack, a mecca for hot-chicken pilgrims, is featured in a segment of Brock's portion of the PBS series "The Mind of a Chef," and in 2014 he published an article on the subject in *Australian Gourmet Traveller* magazine. He wrote, "Hot chicken is about the cayenne powder—it travels through the bloodstream like a snake in the grass; you never see that bite coming until you step on it." (You can find his recipe online.)

Nashville hot chicken is defined by three fundamental ingredients: chicken, lard and a copious amount of cayenne pepper. Brock, who opened a Nashville branch of his highly esteemed Charleston, South Carolina, restaurant Husk in 2013, apparently got hooked on the dish more than a decade ago and whenever he's in town, he makes regular pilgrimages to Prince's. The restaurant has been around since the 1930s and this is its genesis: founder Thornton Prince, reportedly a womanizer, arrived home late one night under murky circumstances. In retaliation, his angry girlfriend made him some chicken, which she seasoned with every spice she had in the house. Surprisingly, he enjoyed the result and opened Prince's Hot Chicken Shack. The rest, as they say, is history.

Over the years, hot chicken has traveled to numerous locations, including Brooklyn, New York; Chicago; and Melbourne, Australia, where restaurants serving facsimiles of this Nashville dish have opened. The apex (or nadir, depending on your point of view) of the trend came in 2016, when KFC added hot chicken to its menu. An article in *The Tennessean* announcing the development described it as "either a sign of the apocalypse or the sincerest form of flattery." Whatever your perspective, it is probably a sign of the times.

Basque-Style Chicken

In this recipe from the Basque region of Spain, everything is usually cooked together like a fricassee; I have produced tasty results this way, but always felt that it made the chicken soggy and destroyed the texture of the beautiful (and pricey) ham. Pre-roasting the chicken separately, then adding the sauce to finish it, resolves these concerns.

MAKES 4 SERVINGS

GLUTEN-FREE FRIENDLY

Tips

When making this dish, I like to cut the breasts and large thighs in half. Pat the chicken dry before starting the recipe.

Traditionally, the piment d'Espelette in this recipe is an undernote. If you prefer a more pungent result, add a bit of minced fresh hot chile, such as finger chile, along with the bell peppers.

Use a vegetable peeler to peel the peppers.

If you can't find serrano ham, substitute prosciutto or pancetta.

Using an instant-read thermometer is the surest way to determine when your chicken is cooked. Inserted in the thickest part of the thigh, it should register 165°F (74°C).

I like to serve this with crusty roasted potatoes.

- Preheat oven to 350°F (180°C)
- Large ovenproof serving dish

3 lbs	bone-in skin-on chicken pieces, cut into serving-size pieces (see Tips, left)	750 g
¼ cup	extra virgin olive oil, divided	60 mL
1 tsp	piment d'Espelette (see Tips, left)	5 mL
1	onion, chopped	1
2	red bell peppers, peeled (see Tips, left), seeded and thinly sliced	2
1	green bell pepper, peeled, seeded and thinly sliced	1
6	cloves garlic, minced	6
½ cup	each dry white wine and chicken stock	125 mL
1	can (14 oz/398 mL) diced tomatoes	1
4 oz	thinly sliced serrano ham (about 10 slices), cut into thin strips (see Tips, left)	125 g
	Salt and freshly ground black pepper	

1. Brush chicken with about 1 tbsp (15 mL) of the oil and sprinkle evenly with piment d'Espelette.

2. In a large skillet, heat 1 tbsp (15 mL) of the remaining oil over medium heat. Add chicken, skin side down, in batches if necessary, and brown lightly on both sides, about 4 minutes per batch. Transfer to serving dish, skin side up. When all of the chicken is browned, transfer baking dish to preheated oven and roast for 20 minutes.

3. Meanwhile, add remaining oil to skillet and heat over medium-high heat. Add onion, red and green bell peppers and garlic and cook, stirring, until peppers are softened, about 5 minutes. Add wine and bring to a boil. Boil for 2 minutes, scraping up browned bits from bottom of pan. Add stock, and tomatoes and juice and bring to a boil. Stir in ham. Remove from heat and keep warm.

4. Remove chicken from oven and pour sauce over top. Return to oven and continue roasting until juices run clear when chicken is pierced with a fork (see Tips, left), about 15 minutes. Season to taste with salt and black pepper.

Chicken Paprikash

I have a very soft spot in my heart for this Hungarian classic, which I first tried as a university student at a popular restaurant close to campus. I've always loved the flavors, but found most versions to be greasy and far too heavy on the sour cream. I just love this rendition. It is quintessential comfort food served with buttered noodles or, better still, spaetzle.

MAKES 4 SERVINGS

GLUTEN-FREE FRIENDLY

Tips

If you are using prepared stock and serving this dish to people who are sensitive to gluten, be sure to check the label to ensure it is gluten-free.

The hottest type of Hungarian paprika is labeled *erős*. Sweet is identified as *különleges* (mild and delicate).

When making this dish, I like to cut the breasts and large thighs in half. Pat the chicken dry before starting the recipe.

Using an instant-read thermometer is the surest way to determine when your chicken is cooked. Inserted in the thickest part of the thigh, it should register 165°F (74°C).

- Preheat oven to 375°F (190°C)
- Large ovenproof baking dish or baking sheet
- Instant-read thermometer

1 tsp	hot Hungarian paprika (see Tips, left)	5 mL
1 tsp	coarse sea salt	5 mL
	Freshly ground black pepper	
3 lbs	bone-in skin-on chicken pieces, cut into serving-size pieces (see Tips, left)	1.5 kg
1 tbsp	olive oil	15 mL
2 tbsp	butter or oil	30 mL
2	onions, chopped	2
1	large red bell pepper, seeded and diced	1
4	cloves garlic	4
1 tsp	sweet Hungarian paprika	5 mL
1 tbsp	tomato paste	15 mL
2 cups	chicken stock	500 mL
1 tbsp	freshly squeezed lemon juice	15 mL
1 cup	sour cream	250 mL
	Salt and freshly ground black pepper	
	Finely chopped fresh dill	

1. In a small bowl, combine hot paprika, salt, and black pepper to taste. Rub all over chicken. Brush chicken with olive oil and place in baking dish. Bake in preheated oven until juices run clear when chicken is pierced, about 35 minutes.

2. Meanwhile, in a large skillet, melt butter over medium heat. Add onions and bell pepper and cook, stirring, just until onions begin to brown, about 10 minutes. Add garlic and cook, stirring, for 1 minute. Sprinkle sweet paprika evenly over top. Add tomato paste and stir well. Stir in stock and lemon juice. Bring to a boil. Reduce heat and simmer, stirring occasionally, until flavors are melded, about 5 minutes.

3. Remove from heat, stir in sour cream and season to taste with salt and black pepper. Pour over cooked chicken. Garnish to taste with dill and serve immediately.

Cuban-Style Chicken Fricasé

In some ways, this is a New World adaptation of Basque-Style Chicken (page 184). Versions were brought to Cuba by Spanish immigrants and adapted to use local ingredients, such as ají cachucha. My recipe is a bit of a riff on traditional ones but remains true to their spirit. An abundance of sweet bell peppers creates the foundation, and spicy chorizo with a hint of habanero adds the zest. I like the touch of bitterness provided by sherry vinegar, which subs for the more traditional dry sherry.

MAKES 4 SERVINGS

GLUTEN-FREE FRIENDLY

Tips

I like to use an attractive baking dish so I can bring it directly to the table to serve to guests. However, if you have a large ovenproof skillet, you can return the chicken and potatoes to the pan and bake them in it.

If you prefer, substitute an equal quantity of diced pork belly for the chorizo. Brown it before cooking the potatoes and transfer it to a plate. Return it to the skillet with the chicken.

- Preheat oven to 350°F (180°C)
- Large ovenproof baking dish (see Tips, left)

2 tbsp	oil or pure lard (approx.)	30 mL
2	potatoes, peeled and thinly sliced	2
3 lbs	bone-in skin-on chicken pieces, cut into serving-size pieces (breasts and large thighs halved) and patted dry	750 g
4 oz	fresh (uncooked) chorizo sausage (about 1), casings removed (see Tips, left)	125 g
1	onion, finely chopped	1
1	green bell or Cubanelle pepper (see Tips, opposite), seeded and cut into thin strips	1
1	red bell or Cubanelle pepper, seeded and cut into thin strips	1
4	cloves garlic	4
½ to 1	habanero pepper, seeded and minced	½ to 1
1 tsp	dried oregano	5 mL
1 tsp	ground cumin	5 mL
3 tbsp	sherry vinegar	45 mL
2 cups	jarred or canned crushed tomatoes (passata)	500 mL
1 cup	chicken stock or water	250 mL
	Salt and freshly ground black pepper	
½ cup	sliced pimento-stuffed green olives	125 mL
2 tbsp	chopped drained capers	30 mL

1. In a large skillet, heat 2 tbsp (30 mL) oil over medium-high heat. Add potatoes and cook, turning once, until crisp and beginning to turn golden. Transfer to baking dish and set aside.

2. Add more oil to skillet, if necessary. Add chicken, skin side down, in batches if necessary, and brown on both sides, about 6 minutes per batch. Transfer to baking dish, skin side up.

Tips

Feel free to substitute Shepherd or sweet Hungarian peppers for the bell peppers.

Using an instant-read thermometer is the surest way to determine when your chicken is cooked. Inserted in the thickest part of the thigh, it should register 165°F (74°C).

If you're cooking this dish for someone who can't eat gluten, read the label on your chorizo. Wheat products are often added to sausage as fillers.

3. Add chorizo, onion and green and red bell peppers to skillet and cook, stirring, until sausage is browned. Add garlic, habanero pepper to taste, oregano and cumin and cook, stirring, for 1 minute. Add sherry vinegar and bring to a boil. Stir in tomatoes and stock. Reduce heat and simmer until mixture is thickened and reduced, about 5 minutes. Season to taste with salt and black pepper.

4. Pour sauce over chicken and bake in preheated oven for 30 minutes or until juices run clear when chicken is pierced with a fork (see Tips, left). Add olives and capers and cook until warmed through. Serve immediately, being careful to ensure that each guest receives a share of the potatoes.

To Seed or Not to Seed

Whether you seed and remove the veins inside your peppers is a matter of preference. With the exception of bell peppers, I usually don't seed and devein because, in my opinion, it affects the taste and experience of the pepper. I like the texture the seeds add to a dish. The veins are the placental tissue inside the peppers, and they contain any spiciness, so removing them may be a good idea if you are heat-averse; you can also reduce the quantity of chile called for in a recipe or substitute a chile that ranks lower on the Scoville scale.

Italian Chicken Stew (*Spezzatino*)

Spezzatino is an Italian term for stew. This one, built around sweet peppers and chicken, uses red wine vinegar to add tangy flavor. I like to serve this with sautéed potatoes or plain rice.

MAKES 4 SERVINGS

GLUTEN-FREE FRIENDLY

Tips

If you're making this for someone who eats gluten-free, use an all-purpose gluten-free blend instead of the all-purpose flour.

To roast peppers: Brush peppers lightly with oil and place them directly on a hot grill on a preheated barbecue, or arrange them on a baking sheet and place under a preheated broiler. Grill or broil, turning 2 or 3 times, until the skin on all sides is blackened, about 20 minutes. Transfer to a heatproof bowl. Cover with a plate and let stand until cool. Using a sharp knife, lift off the skin, reserving any accumulated juices. Discard skin, stems and seeds.

When making this dish, I like to cut the breasts and large thighs in half. Pat the chicken dry before starting the recipe.

Using an instant-read thermometer is the surest way to determine when your chicken is cooked. Inserted in the thickest part of the thigh, it should register 165°F (74°C).

Garnish with finely chopped fresh flat-leaf (Italian) parsley for a bit of color.

- Preheat oven to 400°F (200°C)
- Ovenproof serving dish

1	each red, yellow and orange bell pepper, roasted (see Tips, left)	1
	Fresh thyme sprigs	
2	cloves garlic, thinly sliced	2
3 lbs	bone-in skin-on chicken pieces, cut into serving-size pieces (see Tips, left)	1.5 kg
2 tbsp	freshly squeezed lemon juice	30 mL
	Salt and freshly ground black pepper	
¼ cup	all-purpose flour	60 mL
2 tbsp	extra virgin olive oil	30 mL
1	onion, finely chopped	1
1	bay leaf	1
¼ tsp	hot pepper flakes	1 mL
¾ cup	dry white wine	175 mL
½ cup	chicken stock or water	125 mL
⅓ cup	red wine vinegar	75 mL

1. Seed, peel and cut roasted red, yellow and orange bell peppers into strips. Set aside.

2. Place 1 or 2 each of the thyme sprigs and garlic slices under the skin of each piece of chicken. Rub chicken with lemon juice and season to taste with salt and pepper. Dust lightly with flour on both sides; set any remaining flour aside.

3. In a skillet, heat oil over medium heat. Add chicken, skin side down, in batches, and brown lightly on both sides. Transfer to serving dish and bake in preheated oven until juices run clear when chicken is pierced, about 30 minutes.

4. Meanwhile, return skillet to medium heat. Add onion and cook, stirring, until softened, about 3 minutes. Add remaining thyme and garlic, bay leaf and hot pepper flakes and cook, stirring, for 1 minute. Add reserved flour and cook, stirring, for 1 minute. Add wine, stock and vinegar and boil, stirring, until reduced by half, about 10 minutes.

5. Add roasted peppers, reduce heat and simmer until flavors are melded. Discard bay leaf. Season to taste with salt and black pepper. Pour over chicken and serve.

Chicken Sauce Piquant

This dish is a Cajun classic. *Piquant* means spicy, but in Cajun terms it is a technique for cooking a variety of meats or seafood (such as shrimp, crabmeat or locally caught fish) in a sauce based on the "holy trinity" of onions, celery and peppers. Chef Paul Prudhomme said his mother usually used chicken or rabbit and sometimes even fresh turtle, but other cooks used more exotic offerings, such as squirrel and alligator. Don't be afraid to make extra, because this dish reheats well and the sauce actually benefits from resting.

MAKES 4 SERVINGS

GLUTEN-FREE FRIENDLY

Tips

Cajun spice blends vary dramatically in pungency. This quantity is fine for the blend I have on hand, but you may want to adjust it to suit yours. If the bottle has a name that suggests the blend will burn your socks off, reduce the quantity.

I have used a red finger chile to enhance the spice in the Cajun seasoning because these fresh peppers are readily available. If you can find fresh cayenne peppers, which are more traditional, by all means use one. A jalapeño, Fresno or hot banana pepper would work well, too.

- Large deep skillet with lid, or Dutch oven

3 lbs	bone-in skin-on chicken pieces, cut into serving-size pieces (see Tips, opposite)	1.5 kg
2 tsp	Cajun seasoning (see Tips, left)	10 mL
1 tbsp	olive oil	15 mL
2 tbsp	oil or pure lard	30 mL
2	onions, chopped	2
4	stalks celery, diced	4
1	green bell pepper, seeded and cut into thin strips	1
4	cloves garlic, minced	4
1	red finger chile, minced (see Tips, left)	1
1 tsp	dried thyme	5 mL
1	bay leaf	1
2 cups	chicken stock	500 mL
1 cup	prepared tomato sauce	250 mL
	Salt and freshly ground black pepper	
¼ cup	chopped green onions (white and green parts)	60 mL

1. Sprinkle chicken evenly with Cajun seasoning and rub in. Brush all over with olive oil.

2. In skillet, heat oil over medium heat. Add chicken, skin side down, in batches if necessary, and brown on both sides, about 6 minutes per batch. Transfer to a plate as completed.

3. Add onions, celery and bell pepper to pan and cook, stirring, until vegetables are softened and onions begin to turn golden, about 8 minutes. Add garlic, finger chile, thyme and bay leaf and cook, stirring, for 1 minute. Stir in stock and tomato sauce and bring to a boil.

4. Return chicken to pan, spooning sauce over top. Season to taste with salt and black pepper. Cover, reduce heat and simmer until juices run clear when chicken is pierced (see Tips, opposite), about 35 minutes. Discard bay leaf. Garnish with green onions.

Tagine of Chicken with Apricots

Tagine is the name for a type of earthenware vessel as well as the stew-like dishes that are cooked in it. They are popular throughout North Africa and differ among locales. This one is my own invention, but the addition of harissa gives it a Tunisian spin. I love the juxtaposition of hot and sweet flavors. It is easy enough to make for a weeknight meal, but with a tiny bit of dressing up, it is also perfect for guests (see Tips, below).

MAKES 6 SERVINGS

GLUTEN-FREE FRIENDLY

Tips

To make this tagine gluten-free, be sure to check the label on your harissa paste. Some contain wheat ingredients as fillers.

For an impressive presentation, arrange cooked couscous, millet or even New-World quinoa in a ring around the edge of a deep serving platter and fill the center with the chicken mixture. Then garnish with the cilantro and pine nuts.

Using an instant-read thermometer is the surest way to determine when your chicken is cooked. Inserted in the thickest part of the thigh, it should register 165°F (74°C).

If you prefer a more concentrated sauce, transfer the finished chicken to a platter and keep warm. Boil the cooking liquid over high heat until reduced, about 4 minutes. Return chicken to sauce before serving.

• Dutch oven

2 tbsp	olive oil	30 mL
3 lbs	bone-in skin-on chicken pieces, cut into serving-size pieces (breasts and large thighs halved)	1.5 kg
2	onions, thinly sliced on the vertical	2
4	cloves garlic, minced	4
1 tbsp	minced gingerroot	15 mL
½ tsp	sea salt	2 mL
½ tsp	cracked black peppercorns	2 mL
2	bay leaves	2
1	piece (2 inches/5 cm long) cinnamon stick	1
1 cup	chicken stock	250 mL
1 to 2 tbsp	harissa paste	15 to 30 mL
1 tbsp	liquid honey	15 mL
12	dried apricots, halved	12
¼ cup	finely chopped fresh cilantro	60 mL
¼ cup	toasted pine nuts	60 mL

1. In Dutch oven, heat oil over medium heat. Add chicken, skin side down, in batches if necessary, and lightly brown on both sides, about 3 minutes per batch. Transfer to a plate as completed and set aside.

2. Add onions to pan and cook, stirring, until softened, about 3 minutes. Add garlic, ginger, salt, peppercorns, bay leaves and cinnamon stick and cook, stirring, for 1 minute. Stir in stock, harissa to taste, and honey until blended.

3. Add apricots and chicken to sauce and bring to a boil. Cover, reduce heat and simmer until juices run clear when chicken is pierced (see Tips, left), about 30 minutes. Discard bay leaves.

4. Garnish with cilantro and pine nuts and serve immediately.

Berbere Chicken Stew

I have very fond memories of enjoying a version of this dish in Addis Ababa many years ago as part of a traditional meal. It was served over a sheet of injera, a flatbread made from fermented teff, which served as a plate, and we ate it with our fingers, sitting on the floor. It was a memorable, delightful experience.

Tips

Berbere is a spice mix that is the basis for many dishes in Ethiopia. It's a lovely combination of hot and sweet, with earthy notes that result from the inclusion of cumin. You can make your own, but prepared blends are becoming increasingly available.

Store berbere spice blend in a cool dark place in an airtight container for up to 6 months. It can also be the basis of a seasoning paste (like Thai or Indian curry pastes) when cooked with aromatics, such as onion and garlic, and other spices, such as paprika.

To toast and grind fennel seeds and allspice: Place fennel seeds and whole allspice berries in a dry skillet over medium heat and cook, stirring, until fragrant, about 3 minutes. Transfer to a spice grinder and grind (or use a mortar and pestle).

2 tbsp	freshly squeezed lemon juice	30 mL
3 lbs	bone-in skin-on chicken pieces, cut into serving-size pieces (see Tips, opposite)	1.5 kg
2 tbsp	berbere spice blend (see Tips, left), divided	30 mL
2 tbsp	oil or clarified butter (ghee)	30 mL
2	onions, finely chopped	2
1 tbsp	each minced garlic and gingerroot	15 mL
1/2 tsp	ground toasted fennel seeds (see Tips, left)	2 mL
1/2 tsp	ground toasted whole allspice berries	2 mL
3 tbsp	tomato paste	45 mL
1/2 cup	dry red wine	125 mL
1 1/2 cups	chicken stock	375 mL
6	hard-cooked eggs (optional), halved	6
	Salt and freshly ground black pepper	

1. Rub lemon juice all over chicken, then rub both sides with 1 tbsp (15 mL) of the berbere spice blend. Let stand at room temperature for 30 minutes.

2. In a skillet, heat oil over medium-high heat. Add chicken, skin side down, in batches if necessary, and brown on both sides, about 6 minutes per batch. Transfer to a plate as completed and set aside.

3. Reduce heat to medium. Add onions to pan and cook, stirring, for 3 minutes. Add garlic, ginger, fennel, allspice and remaining berbere spice blend and cook, stirring, for 1 minute. Stir in tomato paste. Add wine and cook, stirring, for 2 minutes. Add stock and bring to a boil.

4. Return chicken to pan, skin side up. Reduce heat to low. Cover and simmer until juices run clear when chicken is pierced (see Tips, opposite), about 30 minutes. Add eggs (if using) and cook until heated through, about 1 minute.

5. Using a slotted spoon, transfer chicken to a deep serving platter or dish and arrange eggs around chicken. Season sauce to taste with salt and black pepper. Pour over chicken and serve.

African Peanut Stew

This stew is a staple throughout Africa. It is lovely served over rice, but plain cooked millet is an equally delicious accompaniment. Pass hot sauce at the table.

Tips

When making this dish, I like to cut the breasts and large thighs in half. Pat the chicken dry before starting the recipe.

Using an instant-read thermometer is the surest way to determine when your chicken is cooked. Inserted in the thickest part of the thigh, it should register 165°F (74°C).

To make a vegetarian version, substitute vegetable stock for the chicken stock. Substitute 6 hard-cooked eggs for the chicken. Add them whole to the stew after the peanut butter has been stirred in and cook until heated through, if desired.

To make a vegan version, substitute 2 cups (500 mL) drained cooked black-eyed peas for the chicken and an equal quantity of vegetable stock for the chicken stock.

- Dutch oven or large deep skillet with lid

2 tbsp	oil, preferably peanut	30 mL
3 lbs	bone-in skin-on chicken pieces, cut into serving-size pieces (see Tips, left)	1.5 kg
1	large onion, finely chopped	1
1	each green and red bell pepper, seeded and cut into strips	1
1 tbsp	each minced garlic and gingerroot	15 mL
2 to 4	red bird-type chiles, such as piri-piri or Thai bird's-eye, minced	2 to 4
2 tsp	curry powder	10 mL
1 tsp	each dried thyme and salt	5 mL
1	bay leaf	1
1	sweet potato (about 1 lb/500 g), peeled and cut into 1-inch (2.5 cm) cubes	1
2 cups	chicken stock	500 mL
1	can (28 oz/796 mL) tomatoes, drained and coarsely chopped	1
1½ cups	thinly sliced trimmed okra	375 mL
1½ cups	sliced trimmed green beans	375 mL
½ cup	smooth peanut butter	125 mL
	Freshly ground black pepper	
½ cup	chopped roasted peanuts	125 mL

1. In Dutch oven, heat oil over medium-high heat. Add chicken, skin side down, in batches if necessary, and brown lightly on both sides, about 6 minutes per batch. Transfer to a plate as completed and set aside.

2. Reduce heat to medium. Add onion and green and red bell peppers to pan and cook, stirring, until softened, about 5 minutes. Add garlic, ginger, and bird chiles to taste and cook, stirring, for 1 minute. Stir in curry powder, thyme, salt and bay leaf. Add sweet potato and stir to coat.

3. Stir in stock and tomatoes. Return chicken to pan. Cover, reduce heat and simmer for 20 minutes.

4. Stir in okra and green beans. Cover and cook until juices run clear when chicken is pierced, about 10 minutes. Discard bay leaf. Stir in peanut butter and season with black pepper. Garnish with peanuts.

Senegalese Chicken in Onion Gravy (*Yassa*)

This sumptuous chicken in onion gravy is a specialty of Senegal. In my experience, it is usually made as a one-pot dish, with the chicken simmering in the onion gravy, but I came across a native Senegalese account suggesting that the chicken is often cooked separately on a grill and then topped with the gravy. That inspired this easy, delicious version.

MAKES 4 SERVINGS

GLUTEN-FREE FRIENDLY

Tips

Cooking the onions until they are meltingly soft maximizes the lushness of this dish. It's worth the time it takes.

Using an instant-read thermometer is the surest way to determine when your chicken is cooked. Inserted in the thickest part of the thigh, it should register 165°F (74°C).

> **FYI:** I use the term "gluten-free friendly" whenever I include prepared ingredients in a recipe that would otherwise be gluten-free. Manufacturers often add wheat products to prepared foods, so you need to check the label to ensure these products are actually gluten-free.

- Fine-mesh sieve
- Large deep skillet with lid
- Broiler pan

4	large onions, very thinly sliced	4
4	cloves garlic, minced	4
½ cup	freshly squeezed lime juice	125 mL
2 tbsp	soy sauce	30 mL
3½ lbs	bone-in skin-on chicken pieces, cut into serving-size pieces (breasts and large thighs halved)	1.75 kg
¼ cup	olive oil (approx.), divided	60 mL
2	carrots, chopped	2
4	stalks celery, chopped	4
1	bay leaf	1
1 tbsp	packed brown sugar	15 mL
2	red bird-type chiles, such as piri-piri or Thai bird's-eye, minced	2
1 cup	chicken stock	250 mL
	Salt and freshly ground black pepper	
1 tbsp	grainy mustard	15 mL
	Hot cooked rice, couscous or millet	

1. In a large bowl, combine onions, garlic, lime juice and soy sauce. Add chicken and toss, ensuring chicken is well coated with mixture. Cover and refrigerate overnight, turning occasionally.

2. When you are ready to cook, preheat broiler. Remove chicken from marinade and pat dry. Strain remaining marinade through fine-mesh sieve into a large bowl. Set liquid and solids aside separately.

3. In skillet, heat 3 tbsp (45 mL) of the oil over medium heat. Pat strained solids dry with a paper towel and add to pan along with carrots and celery. Stir well. Cover and reduce heat to low and cook until vegetables are softened, about 10 minutes.

4. Increase heat to medium-high. Add bay leaf and brown sugar and cook, stirring, until onions start to turn golden, about 2 minutes. Add bird chiles and stock and bring to a boil. Boil for 2 minutes. Season to taste with salt and black pepper. Cover, reduce heat and simmer until onions are meltingly tender, about 30 minutes. Discard bay leaf. Stir in mustard.

5. Meanwhile, brush chicken on all sides with remaining 1 tbsp (15 mL) olive oil. Place on broiler pan, skin side down, and broil for 15 minutes. Turn. Brush skin side with additional olive oil and broil until crisp and brown, and juices run clear when chicken is pierced (see Tips, opposite), about 15 minutes.

6. Transfer chicken to a serving platter and pour cooking juices over top. Season to taste with additional salt and black pepper. Pour onion mixture over chicken. Serve over rice, couscous or millet.

New World Arroz Con Pollo

When Spanish immigrants arrived in the Caribbean, they wanted to make their traditional dishes, so they substituted available ingredients for those they had left behind. This is one example of what we call foodways, or the evolution of culinary traditions as recipes move from one place to another. Saffron flavors and colors traditional paella; in adapting to the New World, achiote seeds assumed that role. While it is very colorful, achiote hardly compares to saffron in terms of flavor, so this dish depends on an abundance of sweet and hot peppers, olives and capers to compensate.

MAKES 4 SERVINGS

GLUTEN-FREE FRIENDLY

Tips

If you're using a skillet instead of a paella pan, it should be big enough to hold the chicken in a single layer.

Another name for annatto seeds (from the annatto tree) is achiote. Technically speaking, annatto is used to refer to products made from the seeds, such as oil or paste, which are used mostly as coloring agents.

- Preheat oven to 350°F (180°C)
- Large skillet or paella pan (see Tips, left)
- Large glass baking dish (optional)

3 lbs	bone-in skin-on chicken pieces, cut into serving-size pieces (breasts and large thighs halved)	1.5 kg
3 tbsp	olive oil	45 mL
2 tsp	annatto seeds (see Tips, left)	10 mL
1	onion, finely chopped	1
1	each red and green bell pepper, seeded and cut into strips	1
1	Scotch bonnet or habanero pepper, seeded and minced	1
4	cloves garlic, minced	4
1 tbsp	minced gingerroot	15 mL
1 tsp	dried thyme	5 mL
2	bay leaves	2
1½ cups	medium-grain Valencia-style rice, such as Bomba (see Tips, opposite)	375 mL
4 cups	chicken stock	1 L
¼ cup	pimento-stuffed green olives, thinly sliced	60 mL
¼ cup	nonpareil capers (see Tips, opposite)	60 mL
	Lime wedges (optional)	

Marinade

2 tbsp	freshly squeezed lime juice	30 mL
1 tsp	turmeric	5 mL
1 tsp	ground cumin	5 mL
1 tsp	dried oregano	5 mL
½ tsp	ground allspice	2 mL

Tips

Medium- or short-grain rice is the right choice for this dish, because it needs to absorb lots of liquid. Bomba rice is ideal, but Valencia or even Arborio will work, too.

If you prefer, you can substitute large caperberries for the tiny nonpareil capers. Slice and adjust the quantity to suit your taste.

When cooking for people who are gluten-free, always check the labels of prepared products such as chicken stock. They may contain added gluten.

1. *Marinade:* In a large bowl, stir together lime juice, turmeric, cumin, oregano and allspice. Add chicken and toss well to coat. Cover and refrigerate for at least 1 hour or for up to 4 hours.

2. In skillet, heat oil over medium-low heat. Add annatto seeds and cook, stirring, until seeds darken and oil turns deep red, about 3 minutes. Using a slotted spoon, remove seeds and discard. Remove chicken from marinade, discarding marinade. Add to pan, skin side down, in batches, and brown on both sides, about 6 minutes per batch. Transfer to a plate as completed and set aside.

3. Add onion, red and green bell peppers and Scotch bonnet pepper to skillet and cook, stirring, until peppers are softened, about 5 minutes. Add garlic and ginger and cook, stirring, for 1 minute. Add thyme and bay leaves. Add rice and cook, stirring, until well coated. Add stock and bring to a boil. Boil for 2 minutes.

4. Remove from heat. Transfer rice mixture to baking dish (if using). Arrange chicken over rice mixture in a single layer. Bake in preheated oven until juices run clear when chicken is pierced (see Tip, page 195), about 40 minutes, scattering olives and capers over top during the last 10 minutes of cooking time. Discard bay leaf. Serve with lime wedges (if using).

Chicken and Sausage Jambalaya

This dish is a Louisiana culinary icon. Like its Spanish relative, paella, jambalaya is an ever-changing mixture depending upon the cook's whim and ingredient availability. Shrimp, crayfish and chicken often star; pork, in the form of smoked sausage (especially andouille) or ham, usually plays the secondary role. According to Southern food expert James Villas, the name likely comes from the French word *jambon*, for ham, and the African word *ya*, for rice. Tomatoes are usually included, but I omitted them here to highlight the peppers.

MAKES 4 TO 6 SERVINGS

GLUTEN-FREE FRIENDLY

Tips

Cut the chicken into relatively even serving-size pieces: breasts in half, drumsticks and thighs separated. This facilitates even and relatively quick cooking.

Since Louisiana is close to east Texas, Tex-Mex influences infiltrate Cajun territory, so feel free to substitute a jalapeño pepper (or 2 if you like heat) for the red finger chile.

- Dutch oven or large deep skillet with tight-fitting lid

3 tbsp	butter or pure lard	45 mL
3 lbs	bone-in skin-on chicken pieces, cut into serving-size pieces (see Tips, left)	1.5 kg
2	onions, finely chopped	2
4	stalks celery, chopped	4
1	green bell pepper, seeded and diced	1
1	red bell pepper, seeded and diced	1
1	red finger chile (see Tips, left), minced	1
4	cloves garlic, minced	4
2 tsp	Cajun seasoning (see Tips, opposite)	10 mL
1 tsp	dried thyme (or 2 sprigs fresh thyme)	5 mL
2	bay leaves	2
	Freshly ground black pepper	
1½ cups	long-grain white rice (see Tips, opposite)	375 mL
½ cup	dry white wine (optional)	125 mL
3 cups	chicken stock	750 mL
8 oz	smoked sausage, cut into ½-inch (1 cm) cubes	250 g
	Chopped green onions (white and green parts)	
	Louisiana-style hot sauce, such as Tabasco (optional)	

1. In Dutch oven, melt butter over medium heat. Add chicken, skin side down, in batches, and brown on both sides, about 6 minutes per batch. Transfer to a plate as completed and set aside.

2. Add onions, celery and green and red bell peppers to pan and cook, stirring, until softened, about 5 minutes. Add finger chile, garlic, Cajun seasoning, thyme, bay leaves, and black pepper to taste. Cook, stirring, for 1 minute. Add rice and toss until well coated.

Tips

The heat level of different Cajun seasonings varies. If you are a heat seeker, and you know the heat level of your blend, consider increasing the quantity of it to as much as 1 tbsp (15 mL).

I recommend using heritage rice, such as Louisiana Pecan Rice, or Carolina Gold, which was grown in the American South for hundreds of years and has recently been resurrected as an artisanal product by Glenn Roberts of Anson Mills.

When cooking for people who are gluten-free, always check the labels of prepared products such as sausage and chicken stock. They may contain gluten.

3. Add wine (if using) and bring to a boil. Boil for 2 minutes. Add stock and bring to a boil. Add sausage and stir well.

4. Return chicken and accumulated juices to pan, arranging evenly over rice mixture. Cover, reduce heat to very low and cook until juices run clear when chicken is pierced (see Tip, page 195), rice is tender and liquid is absorbed, about 20 minutes. Garnish with green onions and serve immediately. Pass hot sauce at the table.

Variation

Shrimp and Ham Jambalaya: Substitute $1^1/_2$ lbs (750 g) medium shrimp, peeled, deveined and halved, for the chicken, and 8 oz (250 g) smoked ham, cut into $^1/_2$-inch (1 cm) cubes, for the sausage. Reduce the cooking time in Step 4 to 15 minutes.

Kung Pao Chicken

This dish, which is a staple in North American Chinese restaurants, is one of the most famous from Sichuan province, although I have also seen it claimed by its southern neighbor, Guizhou, as well. Apparently, the dish was created for a general, whose title was Kung Pao; legend has it that the cook was either his personal chef or a man who saved him from drowning when he was child (depending on the source). The dish traditionally uses fried dried chiles, although some suggest Sichuan peppercorns or even a combination of the two. Served with rice, it makes a spicy, inviting weekday meal.

MAKES 4 TO 6 SERVINGS

GLUTEN-FREE FRIENDLY

Tips

Use kitchen shears to quickly and easily cut the dried chiles into pieces.

Shaoxing wine is a Chinese rice wine. Although I understand there are some elegant versions, the ones that are usually available outside China are unpleasantly salty. I prefer to use dry sherry or vodka in my recipes.

Chili bean paste can be very pungent, although it adds pleasantly complex flavor in addition to its heat. Exercise discretion when using it. If you are heat-averse, omit it in this recipe.

- Wok or large skillet

1 lb	boneless skinless chicken, cubed (½ inch/1 cm)	500 g
2 tbsp	grapeseed or peanut oil (approx.)	30 mL
1	green bell pepper, seeded and cut into thin strips	1
4 to 6	dried red chiles, such as cayenne, each cut into 3 pieces (see Tips, left)	4 to 6
1 tbsp	each minced garlic and gingerroot	15 mL
½ cup	unsalted roasted peanuts, coarsely chopped	125 mL
¼ cup	thinly sliced green onions (white and green parts)	60 mL

Marinade

2 tbsp	soy sauce	30 mL
1 tbsp	cornstarch	15 mL
2 tsp	dry sherry, vodka or Shaoxing wine (see Tips, left)	10 mL
1 tsp	toasted sesame oil	5 mL
¼ tsp	granulated sugar	1 mL

Sauce

1 tbsp	soy sauce	15 mL
1 tbsp	dry sherry, vodka or Shaoxing wine	15 mL
1 tsp	unseasoned rice vinegar	5 mL
1 tsp	toasted sesame oil	5 mL
½ to 1 tsp	chili bean paste (optional), see Tips, left	2 to 5 mL

1. *Marinade:* In a small bowl, combine soy sauce, cornstarch, sherry, sesame oil and sugar. Add chicken and toss until well coated. Let stand at room temperature while you continue with the recipe.

continued on page 202

2. *Sauce:* In a separate small bowl, combine soy sauce, sherry, vinegar, sesame oil, and chili bean paste (if using) to taste. Stir well and set aside.

3. In wok, heat oil over medium-high heat. Add bell pepper, and dried chiles to taste and cook, tossing and stirring, until peppers are glossy, about 3 minutes. Add garlic and ginger and toss to combine. Using a slotted spoon, transfer to plate and set aside.

4. Add more oil to wok, if necessary. Add chicken, with marinade, in a single layer and cook, without stirring, for 1 minute. Stir-fry until chicken begins to brown. Add sauce and cook, stirring, until chicken is no longer pink in center. Add reserved bell pepper mixture and cook, stirring, until combined. Add peanuts and green onions and toss well to coat. Serve immediately.

Braised Chicken Ivory Coast–Style (*Kedjenou*)

This slow-cooked chicken stew hails from Africa's Ivory Coast, where cooks braise chicken and vegetables in a well-sealed clay pot known as a *canari*, traditionally over hot coals. According to several sources, the word *kedjenou* comes from the Baoulé language and means "to move or shake." While braising the chicken, the pot is frequently shaken vigorously to ensure that neither the chicken nor the sauce sticks to the bottom.

MAKES 6 SERVINGS

GLUTEN-FREE FRIENDLY

Tips

While it is not customary to brown the chicken, I feel it improves the flavor; plus, the crisp skin adds a pleasant textural element.

You can leave the skin on the eggplant or peel it off if you prefer.

This dish is usually served with *attiéké*, a starchy grain-like product made from cassava flour that is briefly fermented, adding pleasant tartness to the meal. Attiéké is often described as *couscous de manioc*. If you can't find it, rice, millet or semolina-based couscous also make excellent accompaniments.

When cooking for people who are gluten-free, always check the labels if using prepared products such as chicken stock. They may contain added gluten.

- Preheat oven to 325°F (160°C)
- Dutch oven

1 tbsp	oil	15 mL
12	bone-in skin-on chicken thighs	12
1	large onion, finely chopped	1
4	cloves garlic, minced	4
1 tbsp	minced gingerroot	15 mL
2	red bird-type chiles, such as piri-piri or Thai bird's-eye, minced	2
1 tsp	dried thyme	5 mL
1	bay leaf	1
1	large eggplant (about 1½ lbs/750 g), cubed (2 inches/5 cm)	1
¾ cup	jarred or canned crushed tomatoes (passata)	175 mL
¾ cup	chicken stock	175 mL
	Salt and freshly ground black pepper	

1. In Dutch oven, heat oil over medium-high heat. Add chicken, skin side down, in batches, and brown on all sides, about 4 minutes per batch. Transfer to a plate as completed and set aside.

2. Reduce heat to medium. Add onion to pan and cook, stirring, until softened. Add garlic, ginger, bird chiles, thyme and bay leaf and cook, stirring, for 1 minute. Add eggplant and toss well to coat. Stir in tomatoes and stock. Season to taste with salt and black pepper.

3. Return chicken to pan, submerging pieces in eggplant mixture. Cover and bring to a boil. Transfer to preheated oven and bake until chicken is falling off the bone, about 1½ hours. Discard bay leaf.

Jamaican Jerk Chicken

Like Portuguese grilled chicken, Jamaican jerk is iconic. Pungent yet fruity, jerk marinade is a much-loved combination of flavors—beautifully hot with lovely sweet overtones from allspice, nutmeg and cloves. This highly seasoned chicken, fresh from the grill, is one of my favorite summer dinners. This marinade is equally good with pork.

Tips

I like to freshly grind whole spices for this marinade. To make the amounts you need in the ingredient list, combine 5 tsp (25 mL) whole allspice berries, 2 tsp (10 mL) coriander seeds, 1½ tsp (7 mL) whole cloves and ½ whole nutmeg in a clean spice grinder. Grind until powdered and add to marinade as directed.

If the weather doesn't permit barbecuing, you can bake the marinated chicken. Place it in a large glass baking dish in a single layer and roast, uncovered, in a preheated 375°F (190°C) oven until juices run clear when chicken is pierced and an instant-read thermometer inserted in the thickest part of the thigh registers 165°F (74°C), about 35 minutes.

Four Scotch bonnet peppers may seem like a lot for people who aren't heat seekers, but bear in mind that you do not actually consume the marinade. I find this quantity just right, but if you are timid about heat, feel free to reduce the number to 3.

- Food processor
- Instant-read thermometer

6	green onions (white and green parts), coarsely chopped	6
4	Scotch bonnet or habanero peppers, coarsely chopped	4
4	sprigs fresh cilantro	4
4	cloves garlic, coarsely chopped	4
2 tbsp	fresh thyme leaves	30 mL
1 tbsp	minced gingerroot	15 mL
1 tbsp	ground allspice (see Tips, left)	15 mL
2 tsp	each dried oregano and sweet paprika	10 mL
1 tsp	each ground coriander, ground cloves, freshly grated nutmeg and salt	5 mL
⅓ cup	freshly squeezed lime juice (about 3 limes)	75 mL
2 tbsp	each soy sauce and olive oil	30 mL
4 lbs	bone-in skin-on chicken pieces	2 kg
	Sea salt	
	Lime wedges	

1. In food processor fitted with the metal blade, combine green onions, Scotch bonnet peppers, cilantro, garlic, thyme, ginger, allspice, oregano, paprika, coriander, cloves, nutmeg and salt. Pulse until finely chopped, about 12 times, scraping down side of bowl as necessary. Add lime juice, soy sauce and oil and process until incorporated.

2. Place 1 layer of chicken in a large nonreactive bowl or dish and cover with some of the marinade, rubbing it into the skin. Repeat layering with chicken and marinade and pour any remaining marinade over top when completed. Cover and refrigerate for at least 4 hours or up to overnight.

3. When you are ready to cook, preheat barbecue to high. Place chicken on preheated barbecue and grill, turning once, until instant-read thermometer inserted into thickest part of thigh registers 165°F (74°C). Season to taste with sea salt. Serve immediately with lime wedges.

GRILLED CHICKEN WITH CHILES

GRILLED CHICKEN WITH CHILES is a dish that resonates around the world. Italians have *pollo alla diavola*. The Portuguese call it *churrasqueira*. Moroccans love *djej mechoui*. Jamaicans do jerk chicken … and so on. I ate one of the most memorable grilled chickens of my life on an outdoor terrace overlooking the Chao Phraya River at Bangkok's Mandarin Oriental Hotel. The seasonings were complex—chile and lemongrass dominated—and, sadly, challenging to nail down. I tried to duplicate the dish when I returned home, without success.

There are two basic methods for preparing spicy grilled chicken. The first is to marinate the chicken, then grill it (see Portuguese Grilled Chicken plus variations, page 206). The second is to prepare a spice paste and work it under the skin before grilling. Following are some ideas for using the latter technique. The spice pastes make enough to season four half chicken breasts or 1 whole chicken. If you prefer, spatchcock the chicken (split it down the back and press it flat). You can also use these spice pastes to season a turkey: double or triple the recipe, depending on the size of your turkey. Twice the amount will work for a small turkey (about 10 lbs/5 kg). Cook the turkey on a rotisserie.

To work the spice pastes under the skin, use your fingers or a long blunt utensil, such as a chopstick, to loosen the skin. Spread the spice mixture under the skin as far as you can reach, working it into the meat without breaking the skin.

Preheat barbecue to high. Place chicken on preheated barbecue and grill until the outside is crisp and browned and juices run clear when pierced or until an instant-read thermometer inserted in the thickest part registers 165°F (74°C).

North African Harissa Grilled Chicken: In a small bowl, combine 2 tbsp (30 mL) harissa paste and 2 tbsp (30 mL) extra virgin olive oil. If you want to gild the lily, add 2 tbsp (30 mL) grated onion and a pinch of cinnamon. Spread under chicken skin and brush skin with olive oil. When the chicken is cooked, sprinkle with coarse sea salt, and drizzle with extra virgin olive oil and a generous squeeze of fresh lemon juice. Spicy Olive Salsa (page 374) is a particularly delicious accompaniment to this chicken.

Moroccan Djej Mechoui: In a small bowl, combine $\frac{1}{4}$ cup (60 mL) butter, softened; 2 green onions (white and green parts), finely chopped; 2 tbsp (30 mL) finely chopped cilantro (leaves and tender stems); 2 cloves garlic, minced; 2 tsp (10 mL) sweet paprika; 1 tsp (5 mL) ground cumin; and $\frac{1}{4}$ tsp (1 mL) cayenne pepper. Spread under chicken skin and brush skin with olive oil. When the chicken is cooked, sprinkle with coarse sea salt and serve with lemon wedges.

Mexican-Style Grilled Chicken: In a small heatproof bowl, soak 2 ancho or guajillo chiles in boiling water for 30 minutes. Remove stems and discard. Chop soaked chiles finely and place in a food processor fitted with the metal blade. Add 1 to 2 chipotle pepper(s) in adobo sauce; 2 tbsp (30 mL) butter, softened; 2 cloves garlic, minced; and $\frac{1}{2}$ tsp (2 mL) each dried oregano and salt. To give the chicken a distinctive red color, sprinkle with ground annatto. Brush skin with olive oil. If desired, serve with Fresh Tomato Salsa (page 358), Yucatán Habanero Salsa (page 359), Pepita Salsa (page 361) or Mexican Tomatillo Salsa (page 366).

Portuguese Grilled Chicken

Spicy grilled chicken has become a very trendy dish, probably due to the popularity of *churrasqueiras*, restaurants that specialize in chicken charcoal-grilled in the Portuguese style and usually served with incendiary piri-piri sauce on the side. I love this classic recipe, but if you feel the need for something different, consider making one of the variations that follow.

MAKES 4 TO 6 SERVINGS

GLUTEN-FREE FRIENDLY

Tips

This amount of ground chile produces a fairly mild result, so feel free to ramp up the heat if you prefer. I like to add crushed piri-piri peppers to the rub for added zest and a bit of visual appeal. They are available from specialty purveyors, such as Kalustyan's. You can also purchase jars of pickled piri-piri peppers; if you want to use them in this recipe, chop them finely and sprinkle them over the cooked chicken along with the salt.

If you can't find ground bird's-eye chiles, substitute an equal quantity of cayenne pepper.

The smoked paprika adds a pleasantly smoky flavor, but a little goes a long way. I err on the side of caution with it, but if you prefer a stronger flavor, use more.

I usually make this recipe with chicken pieces for convenience. However, for a more impressive presentation, follow these instructions, using a spatchcocked chicken (one that has been split down the backbone).

3 lbs	bone-in skin-on chicken pieces, patted dry	1.5 kg
2 tbsp	olive oil	30 mL
1/4 cup	freshly squeezed lemon juice	60 mL
	Flaky sea salt, such as Maldon	
	Extra virgin olive oil	
	Lemon wedges	
	Piri-piri sauce	

Spice Rub

1 tbsp	sweet paprika	15 mL
2 tsp	dried oregano	10 mL
1/4 tsp	ground cinnamon	1 mL
1/4 tsp	ground ginger	1 mL
1/4 tsp	ground allspice	1 mL
1/4 tsp	ground red bird-type chile, such as piri-piri or Thai bird's-eye (see Tips, left)	1 mL
1/4 tsp	sweet or hot smoked paprika (optional)	1 mL

1. *Spice Rub:* In a small bowl, combine paprika, oregano, cinnamon, ginger, allspice, ground chile and paprika (if using). Set aside.

2. Rub chicken with oil, working it into the skin. Sprinkle chicken all over with spice blend. Place in an airtight container in layers, drizzling each layer with some of the lemon juice. Cover and refrigerate overnight.

3. Thirty minutes before you are ready to cook, remove chicken from refrigerator and preheat barbecue to high. Place chicken on preheated barbecue and grill until outside is charred and juices run clear when pierced with a sharp knife (see Tips, opposite).

4. Transfer chicken to a serving platter. Season to taste with salt. Drizzle to taste with extra virgin olive oil. Serve with lemon wedges and piri-piri sauce.

Tips

If you prefer a more time-forgiving version of grilled or roasted spiced chicken, rub chicken pieces all over with olive oil. Sprinkle liberally with a spice rub. Place in an ovenproof baking dish and pour about ¼ cup (60 mL) freshly squeezed lemon juice over top. Cover with plastic wrap and let stand at room temperature for 1 hour. You can remove the chicken and grill it or transfer it to an ovenproof dish and roast it in preheated 400°F (200°C) oven until the skin is browned and crisp, about 35 minutes.

Using an instant-read thermometer is the surest way to determine when your chicken is cooked. Inserted in the thickest part of the thigh, it should register 165°F (74°C).

Variations

Baharat-Spiced Grilled Chicken: Baharat is an Arabian spice blend that is highly aromatic but not hot. Omit Spice Rub. Substitute 1 tbsp (15 mL) each Aleppo pepper and baharat spice blend. The chicken will have a pleasant fruitiness and will be more mildly spiced than the original. It is delicious with Spicy Olive Salsa (page 374).

Berbere-Spice Grilled Chicken: Omit Spice Rub. Substitute up to 2 tbsp (30 mL) berbere spice blend. This Ethiopian spice blend can be quite hot; if you are heat-averse, you may want to cut back on it a bit. Spicy Olive Salsa (page 374) is good with this chicken, too.

Cajun-Spiced Grilled Chicken: Substitute melted butter for the olive oil. Omit Spice Rub. Substitute up to 2 tbsp (30 mL) Cajun seasoning. This spice mixture can be quite hot; if you are heat-averse, you may want to use less. Serve with Tabasco sauce on the side.

Chicken alla Diavola: This is a classic Italian recipe. Omit Spice Rub. Substitute 1 tbsp (15 mL) Italian hot pepper flakes (*peperoncino*). Pass Chile Oil (page 399) at the table.

Rotisserie Chicken at Home

Any of the seasonings on this page (as well as those on page 205) are delicious for seasoning a whole chicken and cooking it on the rotisserie. In that case, I don't recommend marinating the chicken. Instead, combine the spices with 1 tbsp (15 mL) of the olive oil to make a thick paste. Use a long blunt utensil, such as a chopstick, to loosen the skin on the breast and thighs and spread the paste under the skin as far as you can reach, working it into the meat without breaking the skin. Brush the outside of the chicken thoroughly with the remaining olive oil, and truss the chicken before loading it onto the spit rods. The chicken will take about an hour to cook, but the total time will depend on the temperature of your rotisserie. The chicken is ready when an instant-read thermometer inserted into the thickest part of the thigh registers 165°F (74°C).

Chicken Shahi Korma

Kormas are curries in which the main ingredient is braised in a creamy sauce that has been enriched with nuts. The term *shahi* means "imperial," so I have included saffron.

Tips

When cooking for people who are gluten-free, always check the labels of prepared products such as chicken stock. They may contain gluten.

I like to cut the breasts and large thighs in half when making this dish.

You can substitute serrano pepper(s) for the finger chile(s). Or, if you live in an area with a well-stocked Indian market, by all means use a green jwala chile (or 2, if you are a heat seeker) in this recipe.

Using an instant-read thermometer is the surest way to determine when your chicken is cooked. Inserted in the thickest part of the thigh, it should register 165°F (74°C). If you don't have an instant-read thermometer, cook the chicken until the juices run clear when it is pierced with a sharp knife.

• Food processor

3 lbs	bone-in skinless chicken pieces, cut into serving-size pieces (see Tips, left)	1.5 kg
2 tbsp	oil	30 mL
1	onion, finely chopped	1
1 to 2	green finger chile(s), each about 3 inches (7.5 cm) long	1 to 2
1	piece (2 inches/5 cm long) cinnamon stick	1
2	green cardamom pods, bruised	2
4	whole cloves	4
1 cup	chicken stock	250 mL
¼ cup	heavy or whipping (35%) cream	60 mL
	Salt and freshly ground black pepper	

Marinade

1 cup	plain yogurt	250 mL
¾ cup	raw cashews	175 mL
3 tbsp	shredded unsweetened coconut	45 mL
2	cloves garlic, minced	2
2 tsp	minced gingerroot	10 mL
2 tsp	ground coriander	10 mL
2 tsp	ground cumin	10 mL
½ tsp	salt	2 mL
Pinch	saffron, dissolved in 2 tbsp (30 mL) hot water	Pinch

1. *Marinade:* In food processor fitted with the metal blade, combine yogurt, cashews, coconut, garlic, ginger, coriander, cumin, salt and saffron water. Place chicken in a large nonreactive bowl. Add marinade and toss well to coat. Let stand at room temperature for 30 minutes (or cover and refrigerate for up to 12 hours).

2. In a large skillet, heat oil over medium heat. Add onion and cook, stirring, until softened, about 3 minutes. Add finger chile(s) to taste, cinnamon stick, cardamom and cloves and stir well. Stir in stock and cream and bring just to a boil.

3. Add chicken with marinade, turning to coat. Reduce heat, cover and simmer (do not boil) for 30 minutes. Season with salt and black pepper.

Grilled Turkey Burgers with Chipotle Mayo

This is an easy-to-make dinner that makes the most of chiles, both in the meat and the condiment, to create a no-fuss wow factor. Served with a simple green salad, it's a great meal the whole family will enjoy.

MAKES 4 SERVINGS

Tips

You can easily substitute ground chicken for the turkey.

I like to use a combination of about 3 parts unsmoked sweet paprika to 1 part hot smoked paprika when making these burgers. Feel free to use the kind of paprika that suits your palate.

To toast cumin seeds: Place seeds in a dry skillet over medium heat and cook, stirring, until fragrant and just beginning to brown, 3 to 4 minutes. Immediately transfer to a spice grinder or a mortar and grind.

Chile Savvy

Give a spicy flourish to the burgers by adding a mix of your favorite chile powder or flakes and salt. Grated lemon or lime zest will enhance the flavors.

1 lb	ground turkey (see Tips, left)	500 g
1	small onion, minced (about ½ cup/125 mL)	1
1	egg, beaten	1
½ cup	dry bread crumbs	125 mL
1 tbsp	prepared barbecue sauce	15 mL
1 tsp	paprika (see Tips, left)	5 mL
1 tsp	ground cumin	5 mL
½ tsp	salt	2 mL
	Freshly ground black pepper	
	Hamburger buns, warmed or toasted	

Chipotle Mayo

½ cup	mayonnaise	125 mL
1	chipotle pepper in adobo sauce, finely chopped	1
1 tsp	cumin seeds, toasted and ground (see Tips, left)	5 mL

Garnishes (optional)

Sliced tomatoes

Sliced Spanish or red onion

Lettuce

Sliced avocado or guacamole

1. *Chipotle Mayo:* In a bowl, stir together mayonnaise, chipotle pepper and cumin until blended. Cover and refrigerate for 30 minutes to allow flavors to meld.

2. Preheat barbecue to high or preheat broiler. In a large bowl, combine ground turkey, onion, egg, bread crumbs, barbecue sauce, paprika, cumin, salt, and black pepper to taste. Mix until well blended. Shape into 4 patties, each about ½ inch (1 cm) thick. Place on preheated barbecue or arrange on baking sheet and place under preheated broiler. Grill or broil, turning once, until no longer pink inside, about 12 minutes.

3. Serve burgers on buns with chipotle mayo. Top with optional garnishes (if using).

Korean-Style Chicken Wings

What could be better than chicken wings bathed in spicy *koch'ujang* (a.k.a. *gochujang*), the hot red pepper paste that imbues Korean food with its unique flavor? The proliferation of restaurants specializing in Korean fried chicken has popularized this rather addictive dish. My version is grilled, which reduces the quantity of fat. Serve with beer and, perhaps, some Fresh Cucumber or Fresh Radish Kimchi (pages 81 and 82) to add some nice crunch.

MAKES 4 TO 6 SERVINGS

GLUTEN-FREE FRIENDLY

Tips

Korean red pepper powder is called *koch'ukaru* or *gochugaru*. Look for it at Korean grocery stores or specialty markets.

If you are cooking for someone who is gluten-free, make sure to purchase a gluten-free version of the pepper powder. And be sure to use gluten-free soy sauce or wheat-free tamari.

To purée gingerroot or garlic quickly and easily, use a sharp-toothed rasp grater, such as those made by Microplane.

4 lbs	chicken wings (about 16), tips removed	2 kg
1 tbsp	toasted sesame seeds	15 mL
	Flaky sea salt (optional)	

Marinade

2 tbsp	soy sauce	30 mL
1 tbsp	unseasoned rice vinegar	15 mL
1 tbsp	toasted sesame oil	15 mL
2 tsp	Korean red pepper powder (see Tips, left)	10 mL
1 tsp	granulated sugar	5 mL
1 tsp	puréed gingerroot (see Tips, left)	5 mL
1 tsp	puréed garlic	5 mL

Sauce

2 tbsp	Korean red pepper paste	30 mL
2 tbsp	unseasoned rice vinegar	30 mL
2 tbsp	liquid honey	30 mL
1 tsp	toasted sesame oil	5 mL

1. *Marinade:* In a bowl large enough to accommodate all of the chicken wings, combine soy sauce, vinegar, sesame oil, red pepper powder, sugar, ginger and garlic. Stir well to combine. Add chicken wings and toss well to coat. Cover and refrigerate for at least 4 hours or up to overnight.

2. *Sauce:* In a small bowl, stir together red pepper paste, vinegar, honey and sesame oil. Set aside.

3. When you are ready to cook, preheat barbecue to high or preheat broiler to high. Place wings on preheated barbecue or under preheated broiler. Grill or broil, turning once, until crisp and juices run clear when chicken is pierced, about 20 minutes.

4. As they are cooked, transfer wings to a large bowl. When all of the wings are cooked, add reserved sauce and toss well to coat. Sprinkle with sesame seeds and toss again.

5. Transfer to a warm serving platter. Season to taste with salt (if using). Serve immediately.

Buffalo Chicken Wings

What would a major sporting event be without a big bowl of this made-in-America classic? Legend has it they were invented at the Anchor Bar in Buffalo, New York. Many years ago, I made the required pilgrimage to try the original; let's just say I prefer my own version. Traditionally, the wings are deep-fried. I much prefer them cooked on the barbecue or under the broiler. They are tasty and just perfect for any "big game" get-together.

MAKES 4 SERVINGS

GLUTEN-FREE FRIENDLY

Tips

These wings are moderately spicy; if you prefer a five-alarm version, add more cayenne or hot pepper sauce. You can also up the heat quotient by substituting a portion (no more than 1 tsp/5 mL) of hot paprika or hot smoked paprika for some of the sweet paprika. Using smoked paprika will shift the flavor profile.

When cooking for people who are gluten-free, always check the labels of prepared products such as mayonnaise and Worcestershire sauce. They may contain gluten.

- Preheat barbecue to high or preheat broiler
- Food processor

1 tbsp	sweet paprika (see Tips, left)	15 mL
1 tsp	puréed garlic (see Tips, page 210)	5 mL
½ tsp	cayenne pepper	2 mL
½ tsp	hot pepper sauce, or to taste	2 mL
	Freshly ground black pepper	
¼ cup	unsalted butter, melted	60 mL
3 lbs	chicken wings (about 12), tips removed and patted dry	1.5 kg
	Coarse sea salt (optional)	
	Celery sticks	

Blue Cheese Sauce

½ cup	mayonnaise	125 mL
¼ cup	crumbled blue cheese (about 2 oz/60 g)	60 mL
2 tsp	freshly squeezed lemon juice	10 mL
1 tsp	minced garlic	5 mL
½ tsp	Worcestershire sauce	2 mL
	Freshly ground black pepper	

1. In a bowl large enough to accommodate all of the chicken wings, combine paprika, garlic, cayenne pepper, and hot pepper sauce and black pepper to taste. Stir well to combine. Gradually stir in melted butter until combined. Add chicken wings and toss well to coat.

2. Place wings on preheated barbecue or under broiler. Grill or broil, turning once, until crisp and juices run clear when chicken is pierced, about 20 minutes. Transfer to a serving platter. Season to taste with salt (if using).

3. *Blue Cheese Sauce:* Meanwhile, in food processor fitted with the metal blade, combine mayonnaise, blue cheese, lemon juice, garlic and Worcestershire sauce. Process until smooth. Season to taste with black pepper. Transfer to a small serving bowl.

4. Serve wings with blue cheese sauce and celery sticks.

Focus on: Chiles in North America

Chiles were most likely introduced to North America by birds, and those that took root are descendants of wild chiltepín peppers (see page 30). According to chile authority Dave DeWitt, the first domesticated chiles were probably planted in Santa Fe, New Mexico, around 1609, when the city was founded. Subsequently, a number of cultivated peppers were developed and grown in New Mexico and other parts of what eventually became the United States. For instance, in the late 1700s, both George Washington and Thomas Jefferson grew chiles on their farms at Mount Vernon and Monticello, respectively. It is likely that chiles traveled fairly quickly across the country. As DeWitt notes, "By the early 1800s, commercial seed varieties became available to the American public."

Cayenne peppers have long been a staple in the regional cooking of the American South. They are a characteristic ingredient used by the African-Americans who helped settle the Lowcountry; like the lives of the slaves and their owners, they are deeply interwoven into the culture. Louisa Stoney's *The Carolina Rice Cook Book*, which was published in 1901, was solidly based on recipes from the 1800s, many of which were sourced from African-American cooks, who made liberal use of chiles both in their cooking for the "Big House" and for themselves. But hot peppers were also used as a seasoning in northerly parts of the country. Eliza Leslie, who wrote *Directions for Cookery*, the most popular American cookbook of the 19th century (published in Philadelphia in 1837), included a recipe for lobster ketchup that contained cayenne.

Perhaps not surprisingly, chiles became particularly popular in the Southwest—so much so that in 1844, Josiah Gregg, author of the book *Commerce of the Prairies*, described the use of red pepper in New Mexico as "extravagant." Many Mexican and other Spanish-speaking people inhabited the Southwest. It had been part of both Spain and Mexico, and didn't become part of America until, along with parts of Texas and California, it was ceded to the United States after the 1846 Mexican-American War. This heritage is still reflected in the region's affection for fiery cuisine, which is characterized by moles and salsas seasoned with many varieties of chiles.

Tex-Mex cuisine is one offshoot of these historical layers. Like Southwestern cuisine (see page 141), it developed from Tejano culture. *Tejano* is the term used to describe Spanish-speaking people whose heritage was Spanish, Mexican or indigenous American, who lived in the area known as Texas when it was still part of New Spain or Mexico. Some traced their lineage to the Canary Islands and, as a result, brought Middle Eastern ingredients such as cumin and tomatoes to the table. Being Texas, beef played an important role.

When Diana Kennedy was researching her 1972 book, *The Cuisines of Mexico*, she took a look at Mexican food in America. Ingredients such as processed cheese, chili powder blends and dishes such as nachos, burritos, chile con queso and preformed taco shells filled with mixtures such as ground beef, melted cheese and chiles bore little resemblance to what she was documenting south of the border. At that point, she invented the description "Tex-Mex cuisine." By her definition, Tex-Mex was "a 'mixed plate':

continued on next page

a crisp taco filled with ground meat heavily flavored with an all-purpose chili powder; a soggy tamal covered with a sauce … (and) a few fried beans."

Fortunately, Tex-Mex evolved to better things. I recall being thrilled when, in the early 2000s, I visited Dallas and was finally able to visit the then-legendary restaurant in The Mansion on Turtle Creek. The chef, Dean Fearing, was a pioneer in marrying chile peppers with fine dining, creating such memorable dishes as lobster tacos and tortilla salads.

In 1896, the stage was set for another spin on Tejano culture—Cal-Mex Cuisine—when Emilio Ortega planted New Mexico chile seeds in Anaheim, California. The chile now known as Anaheim (a mild, long, green version of the New Mexico pod type) is most closely associated with this subset of Tex-Mex cuisine, although many other chile types, particularly the Fresno chile, are used. There is much discussion about exactly how Cal-Mex and Tex-Mex cuisines differ, but basically it seems safe to say that Cal-Mex cuisine places more emphasis on fresher, lighter ingredients, such as chicken, fish and vegetables, and makes more use of fresh cheeses, such as queso fresco, rather than heavier yellow cheeses, be they processed or Cheddar. On a recent trip to Los Angeles, I was surprised by how extensively chiles permeated restaurant meals. If they weren't visible or noted in the description of dishes, I'm pretty sure they were present in house-made chile oil, which was often added as a final flourish.

While Tex-Mex was putting down roots in the American West, Creole cooking was emerging in New Orleans. In his book *Tom Fitzmorris's New Orleans Food*, the author notes that New Orleans Creole was recognized as a unique entity in the late 1800s, when the first cookbooks were published. He suggests that this capsicum-loving cuisine is "the oldest comprehensive regional cuisine in America" and delightfully describes it as having "a French face, a Spanish soul and African hands."

Based in worldly New Orleans, Creole is the sophisticated side of Louisiana cooking. Cajun, its rural cousin, which simultaneously sprouted up in the Louisiana countryside, is quite rustic. Louisiana country cooking is defined by the so-called "holy trinity": bell peppers, onions and celery. The late celebrity chef Paul Prudhomme remembered his mother's farm kitchen in the 1940s near Opelousas, Louisiana, where fresh cayenne, banana and bell peppers were staples. Later, the family began using other hot peppers, such as jalapeño, tabasco and bird's-eye chiles. Donald Link, chef at the Cajun-inspired restaurant Cochon in New Orleans (where I ate one of my best New Orleans meals ever—and that is saying something) comments in his book *Real Cajun* that Cajun cooking is more about the flavors of chiles rather than simple heat, which is why bell peppers are so prominent. "They have a fresh green flavor and almost no heat," he writes, although to add punch he often mixes them with fiery chiles.

While working their way into the hearts, minds and stomachs of the people of Louisiana, chiles were also taking hold in other parts of America. Emilio Ortega (who, as noted, imported the first New Mexico chiles to California in 1896) opened the first commercial pepper canning operation in Ventura, California, in 1898. Today, many types of chiles are grown in various parts of the state, and all species and various types are represented—from New Mexico to wax, from ají to tabasco, and including rocoto and manzano peppers.

The Deep South is another region whose cuisine is closely associated with the use of peppers. It is characterized by diverse culinary styles, from the European/British-inspired cuisine of cosmopolitan Charleston and the plantations to Lowcountry Gullah cooking, which is the product of West African slaves who were brought to South Carolina to cultivate its rice fields. By the time the Lowcountry was settled, hot peppers were playing a significant role in its cooking, says culinary historian John Martin Taylor.

The influence of African-Americans on the food culture of the South is pervasive. Author James Villas describes their arrival, as slaves in 1619, as possibly the most "pivotal" incident in the region's gastronomic history. Not only did they "stir the pots," he says, but many of the recipes documented in early cookbooks such as *The Virginia Housewife* (published in 1824 by Mary Randolph) were their creations, although the ladies of the "Big House" were likely to take credit for them.

One of the few African-American chefs to emerge from a farming community in the South is the late Edna Lewis, who was raised in Freetown, Virginia, a self-sufficient agricultural community where cooking was a vital part of daily life. In an essay published in the now defunct *Gourmet* magazine, she attempted to define the essence of Southern food by spotlighting "a meal of early spring wild greens," which she likely seasoned simply with some form of hot pepper (see page 336).

Scott Peacock, who collaborated with Mrs. Lewis during the final years of her life, remembers growing up in Alabama, where fresh peppers grew abundantly and inevitably arrived at the dinner table. Hot peppers were often served raw, thinly sliced, as a condiment. Others, such as the Lee Brothers (food writers and purveyors of classic Southern ingredients), define hot pepper vinegar as the region's essential condiment, used to season greens, vegetables and even meat. Pimiento peppers turn up in many Southern dishes, such as salads and the iconic pimento cheese (see page 54). Pickled peppers (both hot and mild), sweet pepper relish, piccalilli seasoned with hot peppers and hot pepper jelly are all pantry staples. Pepper jelly and cream cheese on crackers is a quintessential no-fuss Southern appetizer.

Chicken Satay with Peanut Sauce

This treatment for satay is traditionally Thai. Easy to make and delicious, it's not surprising that these skewers have become a fashionable North American party food.

Tips

If you don't have fresh limes, substitute lemon zest and juice in the chicken marinade.

To make roasted chile powder: Place dried red Thai bird's-eye chiles in a dry skillet over medium heat and cook, stirring often, until fragrant and color deepens, about 3 minutes. Remove from heat and let cool. In a mortar with a pestle, or in a spice grinder, grind toasted chiles to a fine powder. Store the powder in an airtight container for up to 1 year.

- Blender or food processor
- 24 wooden skewers, soaked

¼ cup	soy sauce	60 mL
½ tsp	grated lime zest	2 mL
2 tbsp	freshly squeezed lime juice (see Tips, left)	30 mL
1 tbsp	fish sauce	15 mL
1 tbsp	oil	15 mL
1 tsp	granulated sugar	5 mL
1 tsp	Asian chile sauce, such as sriracha	5 mL
1 tsp	grated gingerroot	5 mL
1 tsp	puréed garlic (see Tips, page 210)	5 mL
2 lbs	boneless skinless chicken, cut into 1-inch (2.5 cm) cubes	1 kg
	Roasted chile powder (optional), see Tips, left	

Peanut Sauce

½ cup	smooth peanut butter	125 mL
¼ cup	warm water	60 mL
2 tbsp	chopped fresh cilantro (optional)	30 mL
1 tbsp	soy sauce	15 mL
1 tbsp	unseasoned rice vinegar	15 mL
2 tsp	toasted sesame oil	10 mL
1 tsp	granulated sugar	5 mL
1	piece (about 2 inches/5 cm long) gingerroot, cut into quarters	1
2	cloves garlic, coarsely chopped	2
1	red Thai bird's-eye chile (optional), minced	1
1 tbsp	finely chopped roasted peanuts (optional)	15 mL

1. In a bowl large enough to accommodate all of the chicken, stir together soy sauce, lime zest, lime juice, fish sauce, oil, sugar, chile sauce, ginger and garlic. Add chicken and toss well to coat. Let stand at room temperature for 30 minutes or cover and refrigerate for up to 4 hours.

Tip

Be sure to use gluten-free soy sauce or wheat-free tamari, and gluten-free fish sauce if you are making this satay for someone who is sensitive to gluten. Always check the labels of prepared sauces, such as chile sauce, to make sure no wheat products have been added.

2. *Peanut Sauce:* Meanwhile, in blender, combine peanut butter, warm water, cilantro (if using), soy sauce, vinegar, sesame oil, sugar, ginger, garlic and bird's-eye chile (if using). Blend until smooth, about 1 minute. Pour into individual serving bowls for dipping. Garnish with peanuts (if using).

3. When you're ready to cook, preheat barbecue to medium-high or preheat broiler. Remove chicken from marinade. Discard marinade. Pat chicken dry with a paper towel and thread onto prepared skewers. Place on preheated barbecue or under preheated broiler. Grill or broil, turning once, until no longer pink in center, about 3 minutes. Season to taste with roasted chile powder (if using). Serve immediately with peanut sauce.

Turkey Mole

In Mexico, no special occasion is complete without turkey cooked in mole poblano. Since the authentic version is quite a production, I'm grateful that turkey breast, which is much easier to cook than a whole bird, is now widely available. Although this mole has been greatly simplified from traditional recipes, I think it is very good.

Tips

Tomatillos are available in the Mexican food section of supermarkets. I have used canned tomatillos here for convenience, but if you want to use fresh ones, in a large saucepan, combine 4 cups (1 L) fresh tomatillos with enough water to cover. Bring to a boil, reduce heat and simmer just until tender, about 10 minutes. Drain and let cool slightly before adding to the food processor.

Ancho and other dried Mexican chiles are usually available in supermarkets and specialty food stores, in cellophane packages, near the fresh produce.

Check the label to make sure your chili powder doesn't contain gluten. Strictly speaking, it should be just a blend of spices, but some manufacturers add ingredients that contain wheat. Do the same if you are using prepared stock.

- Preheat oven to 350°F (180°C)
- Food processor
- Blender
- Instant-read thermometer
- Deep ovenproof skillet with lid, or large ovenproof serving dish

1 tbsp	extra virgin olive oil or pure lard	15 mL
1	boneless skin-on turkey breast (about 3 lbs/1.5 kg), patted dry	1
2	onions, sliced	2
3	cloves garlic, sliced	3
4	whole cloves	4
1	piece (2 inches/5 cm long) cinnamon stick	1
1 tsp	cracked black peppercorns	5 mL
½ tsp	sea salt	2 mL
1	can (28 oz/796 mL) tomatillos, drained (see Tips, left)	1
1 cup	chicken or turkey stock, divided	250 mL
½ cup	whole blanched almonds	125 mL
½ oz	unsweetened chocolate, broken in pieces	15 g
2	ancho chiles (see Tips, left)	2
	Boiling water	
½ cup	coarsely chopped fresh cilantro (leaves and tender stems)	125 mL
1 tbsp	chili powder (see Tip, opposite)	15 mL
1 to 2	jalapeño or serrano pepper(s), chopped	1 to 2

1. In skillet, heat oil over medium heat. Add turkey, skin side down, and brown on both sides, about 4 minutes. Transfer to a plate or ovenproof serving dish (if using) and set aside.

Most people associate the term *mole* with mole poblano, a sauce with a slightly murky history that usually contains chocolate. Although the origins of this classic paste are disputed, the most common story attributes its invention to enterprising nuns from the Convent of Santa Rosa in Puebla, Mexico, who hastily put together the ingredients to address a surprise visit by the archbishop. The inclusion of chocolate is a distinguishing feature of their mole, but across Mexico less-auspicious versions are widely used in everyday dishes. Prepared moles are often sold at local markets and distinguished by color— in my experience, green, yellow and black. They are fairly simple, readily available sauces, based on chiles, complementary spices and aromatics. Mexican home cooks make regular use of these preparations to jump-start a meal.

2. Add onions to pan and cook, stirring, until softened, about 3 minutes. Add garlic, cloves, cinnamon stick, peppercorns and salt and cook, stirring, for 1 minute. Transfer mixture to food processor fitted with the metal blade. Add tomatillos, $\frac{1}{2}$ cup of the stock, the almonds and chocolate and process until smooth.

3. Return turkey to skillet or add to baking dish (if using). Pour sauce over turkey. Cover and bake in preheated oven for 30 minutes.

4. Meanwhile, in a heatproof bowl, soak ancho chiles in boiling water for 30 minutes, weighing down with a cup to ensure they remain submerged. Drain, discarding soaking liquid. Remove and discard stems. Chop chiles coarsely. Transfer to blender. Add cilantro, remaining stock, chili powder, and jalapeño pepper(s) to taste and purée.

5. Remove turkey from oven. Add ancho chile mixture to dish and stir gently to combine. Cover and cook until juices run clear when turkey is pierced or instant-read thermometer inserted in thickest part registers 165°F (74°C), about 30 minutes. Discard cinnamon stick.

Beef and Veal

Hungarian Goulash

This flavorful stew, liberally seasoned with paprika, is one of Hungary's national dishes. Apparently, it originated with cattle herders—its name came from the Hungarian word *gulyás*, which means "herder." This dish can also be made with veal, pork or lamb and is often served with noodles or spaetzle. I also enjoy it with boiled potatoes or (when I have an urge to go over the top) baked new potatoes topped with sour cream and chives.

MAKES 6 SERVINGS

GLUTEN-FREE FRIENDLY

Tips

Shredded potato is a great thickener. It dissolves into the sauce and thickens the liquid while adding flavor.

If you prefer a hit of color, use half a red and half a green bell pepper instead of all red.

FYI: I use the term "gluten-free friendly" whenever I include prepared ingredients in a recipe that would otherwise be gluten-free. Manufacturers often add wheat products to prepared foods, so you need to check the label to ensure these products are actually gluten-free.

- Preheat oven to 325°F (160°C)
- Spice grinder, or mortar and pestle
- Dutch oven

1 cup	beef stock, divided	250 mL
1 tbsp	tomato paste	15 mL
2 tsp	finely grated lemon zest	10 mL
2 tbsp	pure lard, beef tallow or olive oil	30 mL
2 lbs	trimmed boneless stewing beef, cut into cubes and patted dry	1 kg
2	onions, diced	2
4	cloves garlic, minced	4
1	bay leaf	1
1	potato, peeled and shredded (see Tips, left)	1
1	red bell pepper, seeded and cut into thin strips (see Tips, left)	1
	Sour cream	

Spice Blend

2 tsp	caraway seeds	10 mL
2 tsp	coriander seeds	10 mL
2 tsp	hot Hungarian paprika (see Tips, opposite)	10 mL
1 tsp	sweet Hungarian paprika	5 mL
1 tsp	dried marjoram (see Tips, opposite)	5 mL

1. *Spice Blend:* In spice grinder, combine caraway seeds and coriander seeds. Grind until powdery. Transfer to a small bowl and stir in hot and sweet paprika and marjoram.

2. Add 2 tbsp (30 mL) of the stock, the tomato paste and lemon zest to spice blend. Mix well and set aside.

Tips

Do not cook the spice blend for too long; the paprika will become bitter.

Marjoram is traditionally used in goulash, but if you don't have it, substitute an equal quantity of dried oregano.

3. In Dutch oven, melt lard over medium-high heat. Add beef, in batches, and brown on all sides, about 4 minutes per batch. Transfer to a bowl as completed and set aside. When all beef is browned, add onions to pan and cook, stirring, until softened, about 3 minutes. Add garlic and bay leaf and cook, stirring, for 1 minute. Stir in potato. Return beef and accumulated juices to pan. Stir in reserved spice mixture and cook, stirring, for 1 minute. Add remaining stock and bring to a boil.

4. Cover and transfer to preheated oven. Bake for 1 hour. Remove from oven. Add bell pepper and return to oven. Bake until beef is very tender, about 30 minutes. Discard bay leaf.

5. Ladle into warm soup plates. Pass sour cream at the table.

To Seed or Not to Seed

Whether you seed and remove the veins inside your peppers is a matter of preference. With the exception of bell peppers, I usually don't seed and devein because, in my opinion, it affects the taste and experience of the pepper. I like the texture the seeds add to a dish. The veins are the placental tissue inside the peppers, and they contain any spiciness, so removing them may be a good idea if you are heat-averse; you can also reduce the quantity of chile called for in a recipe or substitute a chile that ranks lower on the Scoville scale.

Turkish-Style Beef with Eggplant and Zucchini (*Güveç*)

This particularly delicious recipe, a kind of Turkish ratatouille, uses the Turkish pepper paste *biber salçasi* (see page 385) to add depth to the sauce. I have served it with a pilaf studded with currants and toasted pine nuts, and it was a sumptuous combination.

MAKES 4 SERVINGS

GLUTEN-FREE FRIENDLY

Tips

A *güveç* is a type of earthenware baking dish. In Turkey, it also refers to the popular dishes that are cooked in these vessels.

To partially peel the eggplant and zucchini, use a vegetable peeler and cut lengthwise, removing strips of peel from the vegetables and leaving behind an equal amount of peel. Then cut each vegetable into quarters lengthwise, then in half crosswise.

I often like to peel bell peppers, too, when I am using them in stew-like dishes like this. Use a vegetable peeler; it's easy to do.

Use sweet or hot paprika to suit your taste.

If you don't have Turkish pepper paste, place half of a bottle of roasted red peppers in a blender along with the beef stock and purée.

When cooking for people who are gluten-free, always check the labels of prepared products such as beef stock and tomato paste. They may contain gluten.

- Preheat oven to 400°F (200°C)
- Dutch oven

2	each small eggplants and zucchini (each about 8 oz/250 g), partially peeled and cut into pieces (see Tips, left)	2
2 tbsp	olive oil (approx.)	30 mL
	Salt	
1 lb	trimmed boneless stewing beef, cut into small chunks and patted dry	500 g
1 tsp	paprika or hot pepper flakes (see Tips, left)	5 mL
1	onion, finely chopped	1
1	each red and green bell pepper (see Tips, left)	1
1 cup	beef stock	250 mL
1 tbsp	tomato paste	15 mL
1 tbsp	Turkish pepper paste (see Tips, left)	15 mL
	Freshly ground black pepper	

1. Brush eggplant and zucchini pieces liberally with olive oil and season to taste with salt. Place on a baking sheet and bake in preheated oven, turning several times, until roasted and soft, about 25 minutes. Reduce oven temperature to 350°F (180°C).

2. Meanwhile, heat remaining 2 tbsp (30 mL) oil in Dutch oven. Add beef, in batches, and brown on all sides, about 4 minutes per batch. Transfer to a plate as completed. Sprinkle paprika over beef. Set aside.

3. Add onion, and red and green bell peppers to Dutch oven. Toss well, adding additional oil if necessary. Cover, reduce heat to low and cook until vegetables are softened, about 10 minutes. Return meat and accumulated juices to pan. Add roasted eggplant and zucchini and toss well to combine.

4. In a small bowl, stir together stock, tomato paste and pepper paste until blended. Add to pan and stir well. Season to taste with salt and black pepper. Transfer to preheated oven and bake until meat is very tender, about 1 hour.

Beef Panang Curry

Along with massaman curry, Panang curry is one of the few Thai curries made with beef. This beloved dish gets its flavor from curry paste and is enriched with peanuts and coconut milk. I've cheated a bit here and used peanut butter—it is easier than roasting fresh peanuts and, in my opinion, just as good. The curry is delicious over rice.

Tips

Use prepared red curry paste or make your own (see page 392). This amount of curry paste produces a mildly pungent result. You may want to adjust the amount to suit your taste or the strength of the curry paste you are using.

When cooking for people who are gluten-free, always check the labels of prepared products such as curry paste. They may contain gluten. Be sure also to use gluten-free fish sauce.

1	can (14 oz/400 mL) coconut milk, divided	1
2 tbsp	red curry paste (see Tips, left)	30 mL
1½ lbs	trimmed boneless stewing beef, cut into cubes (about 1 inch/2.5 cm)	750 g
¼ cup	smooth natural peanut butter	60 mL
2 tbsp	fish sauce	30 mL
2 tbsp	coconut sugar	30 mL
4	dried makrut lime leaves	4
	Salt	
	Fresh basil leaves, preferably Thai	
1	red finger chile (optional), cut into paper-thin slices	1
	Roasted chile powder (optional), see Tips, page 216	

1. In a skillet over medium heat, combine 1 cup (250 mL) of the coconut milk and curry paste. Cook, stirring, until paste is dissolved and blended into liquid. Add beef and toss well to coat. Reduce heat and simmer, uncovered, until beef is very tender, about 45 minutes.

2. Stir in remaining coconut milk, peanut butter, fish sauce, coconut sugar and lime leaves. Season to taste with salt. Cook, uncovered and stirring occasionally, until flavors are melded, about 15 minutes.

3. Garnish to taste with basil, and sliced chile or roasted chile powder (if using).

Beef Rendang

Rendang is a dish from the island of Sumatra in Indonesia. It is traditionally made with beef, but other meats such as pork, chicken or even goat may be used. Its defining features are an abundance of aromatic ingredients, such as lemongrass, ginger, turmeric and coconut milk, and a fiery quantity of chiles. I've tamed the heat in this version, which has much more sauce than is customary. (I love the flavors and enjoy it over rice.) If you are a heat seeker, by all means amp it up.

Tips

To make tamarind juice: Combine 2 tbsp (30 mL) Thai tamarind paste (about 1 oz/30 g), chopped, with 3 tbsp (45 mL) boiling water. Stir well and let stand for 10 minutes. Strain through a fine-mesh sieve into a small bowl, pressing on the solids with a spatula. Scrape the paste on the underside of the sieve into the bowl, and discard solids.

If you would prefer to use tamarind concentrate instead, you will need about 2 tsp (10 mL).

Fresh turmeric root is available in Asian markets.

If you have fresh galangal root, substitute it for half of the gingerroot.

- Preheat oven to 325°F (160°C)
- Food processor
- Dutch oven

2 tbsp	coconut or other vegetable oil, divided	30 mL
2 lbs	trimmed boneless stewing beef, cut into cubes (about 1 inch/2.5 cm) and patted dry	1 kg
2 tsp	coconut sugar	10 mL
1 cup	chicken stock	250 mL
2 tbsp	tamarind juice (see Tips, left)	30 mL
1	can (14 oz/400 mL) coconut milk	1
	Salt and freshly ground black pepper	
3 tbsp	desiccated coconut	45 mL

Spice Paste

2	stalks lemongrass, trimmed and coarsely chopped	2
3	large shallots, chopped	3
4	cloves garlic, chopped	4
¼ cup	thinly sliced gingerroot (see Tips, left)	60 mL
2 tbsp	chopped turmeric root (see Tips, left)	30 mL
2	red finger chiles, chopped	2

1. *Spice Paste:* In food processor fitted with the metal blade, combine lemongrass, shallots, garlic, ginger, turmeric and finger chiles. Process until a smooth paste forms, stopping and scraping down the side of the bowl as necessary (see Tips, opposite). Set aside.

2. In Dutch oven, heat 1 tbsp (15 mL) of the oil over medium-high heat. Add beef, in batches, and brown on all sides, about 4 minutes per batch, adding more of the remaining oil as necessary between batches. Transfer to a plate as completed and set aside.

Tips

If you are having difficulty getting your aromatics to form a smooth paste in the food processor, add 1 tbsp (15 mL) or so of the coconut milk called for in the recipe and continue processing.

When cooking for people who are gluten-free, always check the labels of prepared products such as chicken stock. They may contain gluten.

3. Reduce heat to medium. Add spice paste to pan and cook, stirring, until very fragrant, about 5 minutes. Return beef and accumulated juices to pan. Sprinkle with coconut sugar and cook, stirring, until meat and spices are well combined, about 2 minutes.

4. Add stock and bring to a boil. Boil for 2 minutes. Stir in tamarind juice and coconut milk and return just to a boil. Season to taste with salt and black pepper. Cover and transfer to preheated oven. Bake until meat is very tender, about $1\frac{1}{2}$ hours.

5. Meanwhile, in a dry skillet over medium heat, toast coconut, stirring constantly, until nicely browned, about 5 minutes. Remove from heat and immediately transfer to a small bowl. Let cool.

6. Using a slotted spoon, transfer beef to a warmed serving bowl. Return Dutch oven to medium heat. Stir in toasted coconut and cook sauce, stirring, until reduced by half, about 10 minutes. Pour sauce over meat and serve.

Cuban-Style Hash (*Picadillo*)

Picadillo is Spanish for "hash." Essentially, this is a Cuban version of the good old American mélange, eaten on its own or used as a filling for empanadas. Spanish influences, specifically Andalusian, are obvious due to the addition of olives and raisins. Picadillo is often served topped with hard-cooked or fried eggs and is usually accompanied by fried plantains.

MAKES 4 TO 6 SERVINGS

GLUTEN-FREE FRIENDLY

Tips

You can substitute Cubanelle peppers for the red and green bell peppers if you like.

I have used a habanero here because these peppers are common throughout the Caribbean, and I like the slightly fruity flavor they impart to this dish. However, it may be more common to find picadillo made with jalapeño peppers, even though purists suggest that jalapeños are not used in Cuban cooking. Both chiles do a fine job of bringing heat to this dish, so use whatever is easiest or suits your taste. If you're using jalapeños, you'll need 1 to 2.

Instead of garnishing the entire dish with chopped eggs, transfer individual servings to warm soup plates or deep bowls and top each with a fried egg. Garnish liberally with parsley.

- Large skillet with lid

2 tbsp	extra virgin olive oil	30 mL
1	onion, chopped	1
1	each red and green bell pepper, seeded and thinly sliced (see Tips, left)	1
½	habanero pepper, minced (see Tips, left)	½
4	cloves garlic, minced	4
1¼ lbs	lean ground beef	625 g
1 tsp	dried Mexican oregano	5 mL
½ tsp	ground cumin (see Tips, page 233)	2 mL
1	piece (2 inches/5 cm long) cinnamon stick	1
¼ cup	dry sherry	60 mL
1	can (28 oz/796 mL) tomatoes, with juice	1
½ cup	dark raisins	125 mL
12	large pimento-stuffed green olives, sliced	12
	Salt and freshly ground black pepper	
2	hard-cooked eggs, chopped	2
	Finely chopped fresh parsley	

1. In skillet, heat oil over medium heat. Add onion, red and green bell peppers, habanero pepper and garlic and stir well. Cover, reduce heat to low and cook until vegetables are very soft, about 10 minutes.

2. Increase heat to medium-high. Add beef and cook, breaking up with a spoon, until no longer pink, about 5 minutes. Add oregano, cumin and cinnamon stick and cook, stirring, for 1 minute. Add sherry and cook, stirring, until almost all of the liquid is evaporated, about 2 minutes.

3. Add tomatoes and juice, and cook, breaking up with a spoon, until mixture comes to a boil. Reduce heat and simmer until slightly thickened, about 20 minutes. Stir in raisins, olives, and salt and black pepper to taste. Cook until olives are heated through, about 1 minute.

4. Transfer to a large deep serving platter. Sprinkle chopped eggs over top. Garnish with parsley. Serve hot.

Bobotie

I've been making this dish since the early 1990s, when I discovered a recipe in a lovely book called *Kwanzaa: An African-American Celebration of Culture and Cooking* that my husband gave me as a present. Known as South Africa's national dish, this casserole of curried meat and fruit with a custard topping is deliciously different. It makes a great dish for a buffet, as well as a main course. Bobotie is probably Indonesian-inspired and was brought to South Africa by traders from the Dutch East India Company—an interesting coincidence for our family, since my husband's heritage is Dutch.

MAKES 6 SERVINGS

GLUTEN-FREE FRIENDLY

Tip

If you have refrigerated the meat mixture in Step 1, make sure to reheat it before transferring it to the casserole dish. Otherwise your topping will set, but the casserole may not be warmed through in the given baking time.

- **Preheat oven to 350°F (180°C)**
- **8-cup (2 L) casserole dish, greased**

2 tbsp	grapeseed oil	30 mL
2 lbs	lean ground beef (see Tip, opposite)	1 kg
2	onions, finely chopped	2
1	red finger chile, minced	1
1 tbsp	minced garlic	15 mL
1 tbsp	minced gingerroot	15 mL
1 tbsp	curry powder	15 mL
2 tsp	ground cumin	10 mL
2 tsp	ground coriander	10 mL
1 tsp	salt	5 mL
	Freshly ground black pepper	
½ cup	finely chopped dried apricots	125 mL
2 tbsp	freshly squeezed lemon juice	30 mL
¼ cup	raisins (optional)	60 mL
⅓ cup	toasted slivered blanched almonds	75 mL
1 tbsp	almond flour	15 mL
1	apple, peeled and diced	1
	Chutney	

Topping

6	bay leaves	6
1 cup	whole milk or half-and-half (10%) cream	250 mL
4	eggs	4
½ tsp	salt	2 mL
¼ tsp	ground cinnamon	1 mL
¼ tsp	cayenne pepper	1 mL

1. In a large skillet, heat oil over medium-high heat. Add beef and onions and cook, stirring, until beef is no longer pink and is just starting to brown, and onions are softened, about 5 minutes. Add finger chile, garlic and ginger and cook, stirring, for 1 minute. Add curry powder, cumin, coriander, salt, and black pepper to taste. Stir well to combine. Stir in apricots, lemon juice, raisins (if using), almonds, almond flour and apple. Reduce heat to low and simmer until flavors are melded, about 5 minutes. (The dish can be made ahead to this point, covered and refrigerated overnight. See Tip, opposite.)

2. *Topping:* When you are ready to bake, transfer meat mixture to prepared casserole dish. Arrange bay leaves lengthwise down the center. In a bowl, whisk together milk, eggs, salt, cinnamon and cayenne until blended. Pour over meat mixture. Bake in preheated oven until topping is set and golden and meat mixture is bubbly, about 40 minutes. Serve immediately. Pass chutney at the table.

African-Style Beef with Plantains (Matoke)

This is a variation of an African dish known as *matoke*, which is also the name for a type of plantain grown in Africa. This recipe includes spinach, which reflects Kenyan roots.

<table>
<tr><td colspan="2">MAKES 4 TO 6 SERVINGS</td></tr>
</table>

GLUTEN-FREE FRIENDLY

Tips

In Africa, this dish would likely be made with piri-piri peppers, but any small hot chile, such as commonly available red Thai bird's-eyes, will work. Or try half of a habanero or Scotch bonnet pepper.

When cooking for people who are gluten-free, always check the label of prepared foods such as tomato paste, curry powder or beef stock to ensure they do not contain gluten. Some brands contain added wheat products.

A covered casserole dish is convenient for this recipe. If you don't have one, just cover your casserole dish with foil.

- Preheat oven to 350°F (180°C)
- 8-cup (2 L) casserole dish

3 tbsp	oil, divided	45 mL
3	yellow plantains, peeled and thinly sliced (¼ inch/0.5 cm thick)	3
1 tbsp	packed brown sugar	15 mL
¼ tsp	cayenne pepper	1 mL
3 tbsp	freshly squeezed lemon juice	45 mL
4 cups	tightly packed spinach leaves, coarsely chopped	1 L
1 lb	lean ground beef	500 g
1	large onion, finely chopped	1
1	green bell pepper, seeded and cut into strips	1
4	cloves garlic, minced	4
1 tbsp	minced gingerroot	15 mL
1 to 2	bird-type chile(s), minced (see Tips, left)	1 to 2
2 tbsp	tomato paste	30 mL
1 tbsp	curry powder	15 mL
½ tsp	salt	2 mL
¾ cup	beef stock	175 mL

1. In a large skillet, heat 2 tbsp (30 mL) of the oil over medium heat. Add plantains, in batches, and brown on both sides, about 3 minutes per batch. Transfer to a large bowl as completed. When all are browned, return to pan. Sprinkle with brown sugar and cayenne. Add lemon juice and toss well. Return to bowl and stir in spinach. Set aside.

2. Add remaining oil to pan. Add beef, onion and bell pepper and cook, stirring, until beef is no longer pink, about 5 minutes. Add garlic, ginger, and bird chile(s) to taste and cook, stirring, for 1 minute. Stir in tomato paste, curry powder and salt. Add stock and bring to a boil. Reduce heat and simmer for 5 minutes. Spread plantain mixture in casserole dish. Top with beef. Cover and bake until plantains are tender, about 45 minutes.

Peppery Meatloaf with Couscous

This is not a traditional recipe by any stretch of the imagination, but I love the range of mouthwatering tastes it delivers. The combination of old-fashioned meatloaf with Mediterranean flavors, such as red peppers, paprika, cumin and coriander, is sensational. I like to serve it with baked potatoes in their skins and a tossed salad.

MAKES 8 SERVINGS

GLUTEN-FREE FRIENDLY

Tips

Use sweet or hot Italian sausage depending on your spiciness preference.

For the best flavor, toast whole cumin and coriander seeds and grind them yourself. To toast seeds, spread them in a dry skillet over medium heat and cook, stirring, until fragrant, about 3 minutes. Transfer to a mortar or a spice grinder and grind.

You can substitute spelt or barley couscous for the whole wheat version.

If you are making this meatloaf for someone who is gluten-intolerant, substitute quinoa or millet for the couscous. For the best flavor, toast millet lightly in the dry saucepan before beginning Step 1.

- Preheat oven to 350°F (180°C)
- 9- by 5-inch (23 by 12.5 cm) loaf pan
- Instant-read thermometer

¾ cup	water	175 mL
½ cup	beef stock or water	125 mL
¾ cup	whole wheat couscous	175 mL
1 lb	lean ground beef	500 g
8 oz	Italian sausage (see Tips, left), casings removed, crumbled	250 g
1	onion, diced	1
1	red bell pepper, seeded and diced	1
½ cup	finely chopped fresh parsley	125 mL
2	eggs, beaten	2
1 cup	prepared tomato sauce, divided	250 mL
1 tbsp	sweet paprika	15 mL
1 tbsp	ground cumin (see Tips, left)	15 mL
1 tsp	ground coriander	5 mL
½ tsp	salt	2 mL
¼ tsp	cayenne pepper	1 mL

1. In a medium saucepan, bring water and stock to a boil. Gradually stir in couscous. Cover, remove from heat and let stand until couscous is tender and water is absorbed, about 15 minutes. Fluff with a fork before using.

2. In a large bowl, combine ground beef, sausage, onion, bell pepper, parsley, eggs, all but 2 tbsp (30 mL) of the tomato sauce, paprika, cumin, coriander, salt, cayenne pepper and prepared couscous. Using your hands, mix until well blended. Transfer to loaf pan and spread remaining tomato sauce over top. Bake in preheated oven until instant-read thermometer inserted in center registers 165°F (74°C), about 1 hour.

3. Cut meatloaf into slices and serve immediately.

Guatemalan-Style Beef in Chile-Spiked Tomato Sauce

This is my version of a classic Guatemalan dish called *hilachas*, in which a combination of tomatoes and tomatillos are often used as braising liquids. I have simplified the traditional technique, which often calls for simmering the beef prior to cooking and shredding it. I prefer to build a bit of a *fond* by browning it first (the browned bits on the bottom of the pan deepen the flavor of the sauce). This beef is particularly delicious served with polenta, but tortillas are also a nice accompaniment.

MAKES 6 SERVINGS

GLUTEN-FREE FRIENDLY

Tips

Tomatillos are available in the Mexican food section of supermarkets. I have used canned tomatillos here for convenience, but if you want to use fresh ones, in a medium saucepan, combine 8 fresh tomatillos with enough water to cover. Bring to a boil, reduce heat and simmer just until tender, about 10 minutes. Drain and let cool slightly before adding to the recipe.

To roast peppers: Brush peppers lightly with oil and place them directly on a hot grill on a preheated barbecue, or arrange them on a baking sheet and place under a preheated broiler. Grill or broil, turning 2 or 3 times, until the skin on all sides is blackened, about 20 minutes. Transfer to a heatproof bowl. Cover with a plate and let stand until cool. Using a sharp knife, lift off the skin, reserving any accumulated juices. Discard skin, stems and seeds.

- Preheat oven to 325°F (160°C)
- Dutch oven

2	dried ají panca, or pasilla or guajillo chiles	2
	Boiling water	
2 tbsp	grapeseed oil or pure lard (approx.)	30 mL
2 lbs	trimmed boneless stewing beef, cut into cubes and patted dry	1 kg
1	large white onion, finely chopped	1
6	cloves garlic, minced	6
1	serrano or jalapeño pepper, minced	1
1 tbsp	ground cumin	15 mL
1 tsp	dried oregano	5 mL
1	bay leaf	1
1	can (14 oz/398 mL) crushed tomatoes (passata)	1
1	can (11 oz/312 g) tomatillos, drained (see Tips, left)	1
½ cup	beef stock	125 mL
	Salt and freshly ground black pepper	
1	each red and green bell pepper, roasted (see Tips, left)	1
	Warm tortillas (optional)	

1. In a small heatproof bowl, soak ají panca in boiling water for 30 minutes, weighing down with a cup to ensure they remain submerged. Drain, discarding soaking liquid. Remove and discard stems. Chop peppers finely. Set aside.

2. In Dutch oven, heat 2 tbsp (30 mL) oil over medium-high heat. Add beef, in batches, and brown on all sides, about 4 minutes per batch. Transfer to a bowl as completed and set aside.

Tip

Substitute different peppers for the bell peppers to suit your taste. Cubanelle, sweet Hungarian, Shepherd or, if you are a heat seeker, poblano peppers, are all possibilities.

3. Reduce heat to medium, adding more oil if necessary. Add onion and cook, stirring, until softened, about 3 minutes. Add garlic, serrano pepper, cumin, oregano, bay leaf and soaked dried peppers and cook, stirring, for 1 minute. Stir in tomatoes, tomatillos and stock and bring to a boil. Return beef and accumulated juices to pan and return to a boil. Season to taste with salt and black pepper. Transfer to preheated oven and cook until meat is very tender, about 1¹/₂ hours. Discard bay leaf.

4. Meanwhile, seed, peel and cut roasted red peppers into strips. Stir into beef mixture. Serve with tortillas (if using).

Chili con Carne

By the time chili con carne was emerging as an American obsession, the concept was well ensconced in Hispanic culture. No recipes have survived, but anthropological evidence indicates that indigenous peoples in South and Central America were likely cooking meat with chile peppers and other seasonings long before Columbus set sail for the New World. Certainly, the Spanish were no strangers to marinating meats in pungent spices, which they had been doing since medieval times. But how this dish, chili, actually came into being is the stuff of legend. There are many fragments of information, but no one knows exactly how and when it was born.

We do know that in 1731, a group of immigrants from the Canary Islands settled in what is now San Antonio, Texas, and that the women in that community prepared a Spanish stew that resembled chili. By the early 1800s, the gruel fed to prisoners in Texas jails consisted of beef boiled with chile peppers and other spices. In 1845, an article in *The American Whig Review* described a "frontier meal of beef … seasoned to scalding heat with red pepper … and thin Mexican cakes, called Tortillas." Another article published in *Scribner's Magazine* in 1894 described a homestead dinner of jerked beef "broken up and fried in grease with scalding hot chilchipines (a fiery pepper growing wild in Texas and Mexico)." Chili's mystique likely owes a lot to the chuck-wagon culture of cattle drives, which began in the mid-1850s, and the he-man image of brawny cowboys who cooked their freshly killed or even dried beef along with foraged produce, such as the chiltepín peppers (see page 30) that grew wild on the Texas borderlands.

Before chili could become a cultural icon, it needed to become a successful commodity. By the second half of the 19th century, San Antonio's *Plaza de Armas* (Military Plaza) had lost its martial presence and become, according to one historian, "the liveliest spot in Texas." Cooking on portable stoves (or perhaps warming up dishes they had made at home), a group of women sold chili con carne, along with other Mexican specialties. They soon became known as "the chili queens." Writers, including Stephen Crane, author of the civil war novel *The Red Badge of Courage*, contributed to their legendary status. He described their offerings as "pounded firebrick from Hades." By 1893, San Antonio chili supposedly went national with a stand at the Chicago World's Fair, although that story may be apocryphal. In any case, the dish was destined to become popular because Catholic priests preached about the dangers of chile peppers, which they identified as aphrodisiacs.

continued on next page

The chili stalls continued to operate in Military Plaza until September 12, 1937, when the San Antonio Health Department established new sanitary regulations and closed them down. But by that time, chili was deeply rooted in the American landscape. Chili joints started to spring up in Texas around the turn of the 20th century and soon spread across the country. A pot of chili made with copious amounts of beans is a cheap and nourishing meal, so it's not surprising that during the Great Depression countless people ate at their local chili parlors, which by that time were located in virtually every town.

Failing that, they could open a can. In 1895, a businessman named Lyman T. Davis began selling chili prepared by his Mexican cook, from the back of a wagon in downtown Corsicana, Texas. In 1921, he started canning his product, naming it after his pet wolf, Kaiser Bill. Wolf Brand Chili is still manufactured; after many changes of ownership, the company is currently owned by ConAgra Foods.

No doubt the chili queens would be astounded to see how their humble creation has evolved. Lyman T. Davis was not the only person to make a business out of the dish. One of its most famous iterations was developed in 1922 by Tom Kiradjieff, a Greek restaurateur in Cincinnati, who (it appears) valued the more-is-better approach to recipe development. After finding the market for Greek food was not substantial enough to support his establishment, he changed directions and created a ground-beef chili that could be tailored to customers' tastes with add-ons, such as onions, kidney beans, shredded cheese, oyster crackers and even hot dogs. Patrons wanting the entire package ordered the "five-way" version. In my opinion, his secret weapon was the use of cinnamon in the tomato sauce base—a classic Mediterranean flavor combination that, at the time, probably seemed exotic in Cincinnati.

Cookbook authors have also boarded the chili wagon. There have been many single-subject books on the subject (full disclosure: I own one myself), beginning with the volume entitled *With or Without Beans* that Joe E. Cooper published in 1952. That same year, chili cook-offs were launched at the State Fair of Texas. When Lyndon Johnson was president, in the late 1960s, his wife, Lady Bird, had cards printed with his favorite chili recipe, which she reported were "almost as popular as the government pamphlet on the care and feeding of children." In 1977, the state legislature proclaimed chili the official "state food of Texas."

One of chili's most legendary incarnations was developed at Chasen's, a restaurant in Hollywood that counted among its fans political figures and celebrities ranging from former U.S. President John F. Kennedy to Frank Sinatra. Elizabeth Taylor ensured its immortality when she had Chasen's chili flown to her in Rome while she was filming *Cleopatra*. It's a fairly classic beef and bean chili, so it's difficult to see what made it so special—except, perhaps, the addition of fatty pork shoulder, which, along with the beef, is sautéed in half a cup of butter!

Cincinnati Chili

Cincinnati chili (see opposite) resembles the kind of ground-beef-based chili, made with red kidney beans, which I enjoyed with toast while growing up. Despite the popularity of this dish, I was not in love with any of the recipes I found. I put my own spin on it, which may offend true aficionados.

(see opposite)

MAKES 4 TO 6 SERVINGS

Tips

The chili in this recipe acts like a kind of sauce, served over hot spaghetti and/or beans. The oyster crackers add a pleasant crunchy texture and are probably an essential component of the experience.

Tom Kiradjieff, the creator of Cincinnati chili, appears to have used cayenne pepper in his original recipe, but I prefer the fresh flavor of jalapeño in the sauce.

1 tbsp	olive oil	15 mL
1 lb	ground beef	500 g
1	onion, chopped	1
2	stalks celery, thinly sliced	2
1	green bell pepper, finely chopped	1
1	jalapeño pepper, minced (or ½ tsp/ 2 mL cayenne pepper), see Tips, left	1
4	cloves garlic, minced	4
1	bay leaf	1
1 tbsp	chili powder blend	15 mL
2 tsp	ground cumin	10 mL
½ tsp	ground cinnamon	2 mL
1 tsp	salt	5 mL
½ tsp	freshly ground black pepper	2 mL
1	can (28 oz/796 mL) tomatoes, with juice, coarsely chopped	1
1 tbsp	Worcestershire sauce	15 mL
12 oz	spaghetti, cooked, drained and tossed with 1 tbsp (15 mL) butter or extra virgin olive oil	375 g
2 cups	drained cooked red kidney beans (optional)	500 mL
	Oyster crackers	
	Shredded Cheddar cheese	
	Finely chopped green onion (white and green parts)	

1. In a large skillet, heat oil over medium heat. Add beef, onion, celery and bell pepper and cook, stirring, until beef is no longer pink and vegetables are softened, about 7 minutes. Add jalapeño pepper, garlic, bay leaf, chili powder, cumin, cinnamon, salt and black pepper and cook, stirring, for 1 minute. Add tomatoes and juice, and bring to a boil.

2. Reduce heat and simmer until flavors are melded, about 20 minutes. Stir in Worcestershire sauce. Discard bay leaf.

3. Place spaghetti and beans (if using) in a large serving bowl. Add chili and toss well to combine. Pass oyster crackers, cheese and green onion for garnishing at the table.

Original San Antonio Chili

If you are looking for the ground beef chili your mother made for Friday night dinner, this isn't it. If instead you want to taste what amounts to a fabulous, highly spiced beef stew, then I highly recommend this chili. Leftovers reheat well.

GLUTEN-FREE FRIENDLY

Tips

To reconstitute dried chiles, remove the stems and place in a heatproof bowl. Add 2 cups (500 mL) boiling beef stock and soak for 30 minutes, weighing the chiles down with a cup to ensure they remain submerged.

If you want to make a version of this dish that is similar to the one made by former U.S. President Lyndon Johnson, substitute venison for the beef. You can also cube a beef chuck roast and use it in place of the stewing beef.

Moreover ...

The very first San Antonio chili contained neither tomatoes nor beans, making it reminiscent of some South American adobos. This probably isn't surprising, because the "chili queens" (see page 235) certainly had Hispanic roots. This is my slightly amended version of the recipe that is held in the research library of the Institute of Texan Cultures.

- Blender
- Dutch oven

2	each ancho and guajillo chiles, reconstituted (see Tips, left)	2
½ cup	fresh cilantro leaves and tender stems	125 mL
2 tbsp	pure lard or oil	30 mL
1 lb	each trimmed boneless stewing beef and stewing pork, cut into ½-inch (1 cm) cubes and patted dry (see Tips, left)	500 g
2	onions, thinly sliced on the vertical	2
6	cloves garlic, minced	6
1 tbsp	each ground cumin and dried Mexican oregano	15 mL
	Salt and freshly ground black pepper	
1	serrano or jalapeño pepper, thinly sliced (optional)	1
6	green onions (white and green parts), very thinly sliced (optional)	6
	Crumbled Mexican cheese, such as soft cotija	

1. Transfer reconstituted chiles with liquid to blender. Add cilantro and purée until smooth. Set aside.

2. Meanwhile, in Dutch oven, melt lard over medium-high heat. Add beef and pork, in batches, and brown on all sides, about 2 minutes per batch. Transfer to a plate as completed and set aside. Reduce heat to medium.

3. Preheat oven to 325°F (160°C). Add sliced onions to pan and cook, stirring, until softened, about 4 minutes. Add garlic, cumin and oregano and cook, stirring, for 1 minute. Return beef and pork to pan. Add reserved ancho and guajillo chile mixture and stir well. Season to taste with salt and black pepper. Bring to a boil. Cover and transfer to preheated oven. Bake until meat is very tender, about 2 hours.

4. Ladle into warm soup plates. Garnish with serrano pepper (if using) and green onions (if using). Sprinkle with cheese.

Meatballs Paprikash

This is a traditional dish in Hungary and Czechoslovakia. I love the flavors in this sauce— paprika, sweet peppers and tomatoes, with just a hint of caraway seed. Served over hot buttered noodles sprinkled with poppy seeds (if you're so inclined), this dish is positively ambrosial.

- Preheat oven to 325°F (160°C)
- Food processor
- Dutch oven

¾ cup	cold water	175 mL
½ cup	fine bulgur	125 mL
1	onion, quartered	1
2	cloves garlic, chopped	2
½ cup	fresh parsley leaves	125 mL
1 tsp	salt	5 mL
	Freshly ground black pepper	
1 lb	lean ground beef	500 g
1 lb	ground pork	500 g
1	egg, beaten	1
2 tbsp	olive oil, divided	30 mL
2	onions, finely chopped	2
2	red bell peppers, seeded and diced	2
4	cloves garlic, minced	4
1 tsp	caraway seeds, ground	5 mL
½ tsp	salt	2 mL
½ tsp	cracked black peppercorns	2 mL
1 tbsp	sweet or hot Hungarian paprika	15 mL
1	can (28 oz/796 mL) tomatoes, with juice, coarsely chopped	1
1 cup	beef stock	250 mL
½ cup	finely chopped fresh dill	125 mL
	Sour cream (optional)	

1. In a medium bowl, combine cold water and bulgur. Stir well and set aside until liquid is absorbed, about 10 minutes.

2. Meanwhile, in food processor fitted with the metal blade, combine quartered onion, garlic, parsley, salt, and black pepper to taste. Process until onion is very finely chopped. Add beef, pork, egg and soaked bulgur and pulse until combined. Shape mixture into 18 equal balls.

Chile Savvy

The caraway seed and dill in this dish add bitterness, which is appealingly complex. Don't be too heavy-handed with the hot paprika or you will cancel it out.

3. In Dutch oven, heat 1 tbsp (15 mL) of the oil over medium-high heat. Add meatballs, in batches, and cook, turning, until browned on all sides, about 5 minutes per batch. Transfer to a plate as completed and set aside.

4. Reduce heat to medium. Add remaining oil to pan. Add finely chopped onions and bell peppers and cook, stirring, until softened, about 5 minutes. Add garlic, ground caraway, salt and peppercorns and cook, stirring, for 1 minute. Stir in paprika. Add tomatoes and juice, and stock and bring to a boil.

5. Return meatballs and accumulated juices to pan and return to a boil. Cover and transfer to preheated oven. Bake for 1 hour.

6. Just before serving, garnish with dill. Drizzle sour cream (if using) over top to taste.

Catalan Meatballs

These meatballs are a staple in Spain, where they are probably most popular as tapas—but larger versions also make an excellent main course. Perhaps not surprisingly, a version of this dish shows up in France's southern Pays Catalans region, where many Catalan people reside. There the dish is known as *boles de picolat*.

Tips

To serve this dish as tapas, divide the mixture into 36 meatballs. Reduce the browning time to 4 minutes and the cooking time to 10 minutes. Double the amount of flour for dredging.

If you are making these meatballs for someone who is avoiding gluten, substitute ¼ cup (60 mL) almond flour mixed with ¼ cup (60 mL) sorghum or brown rice flour for the all-purpose flour.

- **Large skillet with lid**

1 tbsp	olive oil or pure lard	15 mL
2 oz	slab bacon, diced	60 g

Meatballs

1 lb	lean ground beef	500 g
8 oz	ground pork	250 g
¼ cup	all-purpose flour (approx.)	60 mL
4	cloves garlic, minced	4
1	egg, beaten	1
2 tsp	sweet paprika	10 mL
½ tsp	sea salt	2 mL
¼ tsp	freshly grated nutmeg	1 mL
	Freshly ground black pepper	

Sauce

1	onion, finely chopped	1
1	bay leaf	1
1	red finger chile, thinly sliced	1
½ tsp	salt	2 mL
½ tsp	cracked black peppercorns	2 mL
1	piece (2 inches/5 cm long) cinnamon stick	1
2 tbsp	all-purpose flour	30 mL
2 tbsp	tomato paste	30 mL
2 cups	beef stock	500 mL
½ cup	sliced pimento-stuffed green olives	125 mL
¼ cup	finely chopped fresh parsley	60 mL

1. *Meatballs:* In a large bowl, combine beef, pork, ¼ cup (60 mL) flour, garlic, egg, paprika, salt, nutmeg, and black pepper to taste. Mix well. Shape into 18 equal balls. Spread additional flour on a plate and dredge meatballs until lightly coated. Discard any excess flour.

2. In a large skillet, heat oil over medium heat. Add bacon and cook, stirring, until lightly browned, about 5 minutes. Using a slotted spoon, transfer to a plate and set aside.

3. Add meatballs to pan, in batches, and cook, turning, until lightly browned on all sides, about 6 minutes per batch. Transfer to a plate as completed and set aside.

4. *Sauce:* Add onion to pan and cook, stirring, until softened, about 3 minutes. Add bay leaf, finger chile, salt, peppercorns and cinnamon stick and cook, stirring, for 1 minute. Stir in flour and tomato paste. Add stock and bring to a boil. Cook, stirring, until sauce is slightly reduced and thickened, about 5 minutes.

5. Return meatballs and bacon to pan. Cover and cook until meatballs are no longer pink inside, about 15 minutes. Add olives and stir well. Cover and cook until olives are heated through and flavors are melded, about 5 minutes. Discard bay leaf. Garnish with parsley.

Mexican Meatballs

These simple meatballs are revved up with the addition of zesty chipotle chiles. I find that two chiles provide a nice punch. If you're a heat seeker, use three; if you are heat-averse, stick with one.

MAKES 8 MAIN-COURSE SERVINGS

GLUTEN-FREE FRIENDLY

Tips

If you are making this dish for people who are gluten-free, be sure to check the labels of prepared products such as chicken or beef stock, tomato paste and chipotle chiles in adobo sauce. Some brands contain gluten.

To serve this dish as tapas, divide the mixture into 48 meatballs. Reduce the browning time to 4 minutes and the cooking time to 10 minutes. Double the amount of flour for dredging.

- **Blender**

1 lb	lean ground beef	500 g
1 lb	ground pork	500 g
1	onion, finely chopped	1
½ cup	almond flour, divided	125 mL
2 tsp	dried oregano	10 mL
1 tsp	ground cumin	5 mL
½ tsp	sea salt	2 mL
	Freshly ground black pepper	
1	egg, beaten	1
1 tbsp	oil or pure lard	15 mL
	Finely chopped fresh cilantro	

Sauce

2	ancho chiles, stems removed	2
1 cup	boiling chicken or beef stock	250 mL
¼ cup	fresh cilantro leaves and tender stems	60 mL
1 tbsp	oil or pure lard	15 mL
¼ cup	minced onion	60 mL
4	stalks celery, diced	4
4	cloves garlic, minced	4
2 tsp	dried Mexican oregano	10 mL
1 tsp	ground cumin	5 mL
½ tsp	sea salt	2 mL
½ tsp	freshly ground black pepper	2 mL
¼ cup	tomato paste	60 mL
1	can (14 oz/398 mL) tomatoes, with juice, coarsely chopped	1
1 to 2	chipotle chile(s) in abobo sauce, minced	1 to 2

1. In a large bowl, combine beef, pork, onion, ¼ cup (60 mL) of the almond flour, oregano, cumin, salt, and black pepper to taste. Mix well. Add egg and, using your hands, mix until well combined. Shape mixture into 24 equal balls. Spread remaining flour evenly over a plate and dredge meatballs in it until lightly coated. Discard any excess flour.

Moreover ...

Mexican food expert Diana Kennedy says that every region in Mexico has its unique way of making *albóndigas*, or meatballs. Often, they turn up in soup. They are also frequently served as part of a stew-like dish, simmered in tomato sauce. Chipotle peppers are a common seasoning. Although I prefer to use more than one type of chile, which I feel adds complexity to the sauce, in one version I've seen, the sauce is based on dried chipotle peppers with heavily charred roasted tomatoes.

2. In a large skillet, heat oil over medium-high heat. Add meatballs to pan, in batches, and cook, turning, until lightly browned on all sides, about 6 minutes per batch. Transfer to a plate as completed and set aside.

3. *Sauce:* Meanwhile, in a heatproof bowl, soak ancho chiles in boiling stock for 30 minutes, weighing down with a cup to ensure they remain submerged. Transfer to blender. Add cilantro and purée until smooth. Set aside.

4. Reduce heat to medium. Add oil to pan. Add onion and celery and cook, stirring and scraping up browned bits from bottom of pan, until softened, about 5 minutes. Add garlic, oregano, cumin, salt and black pepper and cook, stirring, for 1 minute. Stir in tomato paste. Add tomatoes and juice, chipotle chile(s) to taste, and reserved ancho chile purée and cook, stirring, until mixture comes to a boil.

5. Return meatballs to pan. Cover and simmer until meatballs are no longer pink inside, about 20 minutes. Garnish with chopped cilantro.

Turkish-Style Stuffed Peppers (Etli Biber Dolmasi)

It is hard to believe that these peppers taste so sensational. This is an example of how Turkish cooks artfully combine simple ingredients to create outstanding results.

Tips

Choose a casserole dish that will hold the peppers snugly. If you don't have a covered one, simply cover the top with foil.

To prepare the peppers, using a sharp knife, cut off the tops and discard. Remove the seeds and membranes. A grapefruit spoon makes easy work of this job.

When cooking for people who are gluten-free, always check the label of prepared foods such as tomato paste and beef stock to ensure they do not contain added wheat products.

When pouring the sauce over the stuffed peppers, let the excess run down the sides and into the casserole dish.

If desired, top the peppers with a dollop of plain Greek-style yogurt before serving.

Chile Savvy

The addition of Aleppo pepper, sumac and a bit of dill distinguishes these peppers. The bittersweet mix of flavors is superb.

- Preheat oven to 350°F (180°C)
- Covered casserole dish (see Tips, left)

6	small green bell peppers, tops, seeds and membranes removed (see Tips, left)	6
1 cup	cooked brown or white rice	250 mL
1 tbsp	olive oil	15 mL
2	onions, finely chopped	2
1 lb	ground beef or lamb	500 g
4	cloves garlic, minced	4
2 tsp	dried oregano	10 mL
1 tsp	Aleppo pepper	5 mL
½ tsp	ground allspice	2 mL
2 tbsp	toasted pine nuts	30 mL
2 tbsp	tomato paste	30 mL
½ cup	finely chopped fresh dill	125 mL
	Salt and cracked black peppercorns	

Sauce

1	can (14 oz/398 mL) puréed tomatoes	1
1 cup	beef stock	250 mL
1 tsp	ground sumac	5 mL
	Extra virgin olive oil	

1. In a large skillet, heat oil over medium heat. Add onions and beef and cook, stirring, until beef is no longer pink, about 7 minutes. Add garlic, oregano, Aleppo pepper and allspice, and cook, stirring, for 1 minute. Stir in pine nuts and tomato paste and cook, stirring, for 1 minute. Stir in dill and cooked rice. Season to taste with salt and cracked pepper.

2. Using a spoon, fill peppers with meat mixture, dividing equally. Arrange peppers upright in baking dish.

3. *Sauce:* In a large measuring cup, combine tomatoes, stock and sumac. Pour over peppers, dividing equally. Drizzle olive oil over top.

4. Cover and bake in preheated oven until peppers are tender and sauce is bubbly, about 1 hour. Spoon into bowls.

Country Fried Steak

Depending on the source you consult, this is a typical dish from the American South or West. It is thought to have originated with German or Austrian immigrants to Texas, who were basing their fried steaks on schnitzel. Traditionally, the gravy was made with copious amounts of milk, but I find that using stock, with a finish of cream, produces a more flavorful result.

Tips

For convenience, I have made smaller portions in this recipe—accompanied by a heaping mound of mashed potatoes, they make a satisfying weekday dinner. If you have more people to feed, you can easily double or triple the recipe.

You can adjust the spiciness to suit your palate by playing with the paprika, as well as by changing the quantity of jalapeño. If you like heat, use hot paprika or a combination of hot and sweet. You can include or omit the cayenne. And if your jalapeño peppers are tame (which can happen; taste a tiny bit before using), add a second one.

If you're making this dish for people who are gluten-intolerant, substitute an all-purpose gluten-free blend for the all-purpose flour. And always check the label of prepared foods such as chicken or beef stock to ensure they do not contain added wheat products.

¼ cup	all-purpose flour	60 mL
2 tsp	paprika (see Tips, left)	10 mL
¼ tsp	cayenne pepper (optional)	1 mL
	Salt and freshly ground black pepper	
1 lb	beef flat iron steak, pounded until thin	500 g
2 tbsp	oil or pure lard	30 mL
1	onion, finely chopped	1
2	cloves garlic, minced	2
1 to 2	jalapeño pepper(s), minced	1 to 2
1½ cups	chicken or beef stock	375 mL
¼ cup	heavy or whipping (35%) cream	60 mL
	Finely chopped fresh parsley	

1. On a large plate or sheet of waxed paper, combine flour, paprika and cayenne (if using). Season to taste with salt and black pepper. Dredge steak in flour mixture, turning to coat all over. Set any remaining flour mixture aside.

2. In a large skillet, heat oil over medium-high heat. Add steak and cook, turning once, until desired degree of doneness is achieved. Transfer to a deep serving platter and keep warm.

3. Reduce heat to medium. Add onion to pan, and cook, stirring, until softened, about 3 minutes. Add garlic, and jalapeño pepper(s) to taste and cook, stirring, for 1 minute. Add reserved flour mixture and cook, stirring, for 1 minute. Stir in stock. Bring to a boil. Cook, stirring, until slightly thickened, about 4 minutes. Stir in cream. Season to taste with additional salt and black pepper.

4. Pour gravy over steak and garnish to taste with parsley. To serve, cut steak into thin slices.

Chinese Beef with Orange

Here is a fresh-flavored version of a Chinese restaurant classic, which I believe is Sichuan in origin. It is an easy weekday meal, perfect with a bowl of steaming rice.

Tips

I have a wok that is large enough to accommodate the beef in a single layer. If you don't, cook the beef in 2 batches, using half each of the oil and aromatics for each batch. Return the entire amount to the wok when adding the sauce.

I use grapeseed oil to cook the beef because it is unrefined and has a high smoke point. If you prefer, use another high-heat-tolerant oil, such as peanut.

If you like, you can substitute the same amount of finely chopped reconstituted dried orange peel for the fresh zest. (Look for it in Asian markets; it will provide a more intense orange flavor.) Soak the dried peel in warm water until softened, about 20 minutes. Reserve the soaking liquid and add it to the sauce. Cut the peel into thin strips and add to the recipe.

Be sure to use gluten-free soy sauce or wheat-free tamari if you are making this dish for someone who is sensitive to gluten.

- Wok or large skillet (see Tips, left)

1½ lbs	thinly sliced beef for stir-fry (flank, skirt or sirloin)	750 g
2 tbsp	grapeseed oil (see Tips, left)	30 mL
1 tsp	sesame oil	5 mL
2 tbsp	finely chopped green onions (white and green parts)	30 mL
	Orange slices	

Marinade

¼ cup	soy sauce	60 mL
2 tbsp	dry sherry, vodka or Shaoxing wine	30 mL
2 tbsp	cornstarch	30 mL

Aromatics

2 tbsp	grated orange zest (about 2 oranges)	30 mL
1 tbsp	each minced garlic and gingerroot	15 mL
1 to 2	red Thai bird's-eye chile(s), minced	1 to 2

Sauce

½ cup	orange juice	125 mL
1 tbsp	granulated sugar	15 mL

1. *Marinade:* In a bowl large enough to accommodate all of the beef, stir together soy sauce, sherry and cornstarch. Transfer ¼ cup (60 mL) of mixture to a separate small bowl and set aside. Add beef to remainder and toss well to coat. Let stand for 15 minutes at room temperature.

2. *Aromatics:* Meanwhile, in a small bowl, combine orange zest, garlic, ginger, and bird's-eye chile(s) to taste. Set aside.

3. *Sauce:* Stir orange juice and sugar into reserved marinade.

4. In wok, heat grapeseed oil over medium-high heat. Add beef in a single layer and cook, without stirring, for about 30 seconds. Sprinkle aromatics over top. Toss well. Cook, stirring, until just a hint of pink remains inside beef, about 1½ minutes. Add sauce and cook until beef is no longer pink inside and sauce is thickened, about 1 minute.

5. Transfer to a serving platter. Drizzle with sesame oil and sprinkle green onions evenly over top. Garnish with orange slices.

Sichuan-Style Beef with Celery

This easy-to-make stir-fry is a lovely weeknight meal, but it also works well as part of a multidish Chinese meal. Serve with plenty of hot rice.

Tips

If you can find Chinese celery, which is more aromatic than regular celery, use it. It is rather stringy, so be sure to peel it before adding it to the dish.

Shaoxing wine is a Chinese rice wine. Although I understand there are some elegant versions, the ones that are usually available outside China are unpleasantly salty. I prefer to use dry sherry or vodka in my recipes.

- Wok or large skillet (see Tips, page 249)

1 lb	thinly sliced beef for stir-fry (flank, skirt or sirloin)	500 g
2 tbsp	grapeseed oil (see Tips, page 249)	30 mL
3 cups	thinly sliced celery (see Tips, left)	750 mL
½ cup	finely diced red bell pepper	125 mL
	Chinese Salted Chiles (page 396), optional	

Marinade

2 tbsp	soy sauce	30 mL
1 tbsp	dry sherry, vodka or Shaoxing wine (see Tips, left)	15 mL
2 tsp	cornstarch	10 mL
1 tsp	granulated sugar	5 mL
	Freshly ground black pepper	

Aromatics

1 tbsp	minced garlic	15 mL
1 tbsp	minced gingerroot	15 mL
2 tsp	Sichuan chili bean paste (see Tips, left)	10 mL

Sauce

¼ cup	chicken stock	60 mL
2 tbsp	soy sauce	30 mL
1 tbsp	vodka, dry sherry or Shaoxing wine	15 mL
2 tsp	cornstarch	10 mL
2 tsp	Chinese black rice vinegar	10 mL
1 tsp	granulated sugar	5 mL

1. *Marinade:* In a bowl large enough to accommodate all of the beef, stir together soy sauce, sherry, cornstarch, sugar, and black pepper to taste. Add beef and toss well to coat. Let stand at room temperature for 30 minutes.

2. *Aromatics:* Meanwhile, in a small bowl, combine garlic, ginger and chili bean paste. Set aside.

3. *Sauce:* In another small bowl, stir together stock, soy sauce, vodka, cornstarch, vinegar and sugar. Set aside.

Tip

Be sure to use gluten-free soy sauce or wheat-free tamari if you are making this dish for someone who is sensitive to gluten. Also, check the label of all prepared foods, such as chicken stock or chili bean paste, to make sure they are gluten-free. Some brands contain added wheat products.

Chile Savvy

Chile bean paste, made from fermented soybeans and fiery chiles, is a Sichuan staple. It adds deep umami flavor, but use it sparingly— too much makes dishes unpleasantly hot.

4. In wok, heat oil over medium-high heat. Add celery and bell pepper and cook, stirring, until vegetables just begin to soften and become glossy, about 3 minutes. Using a slotted spoon, transfer to a plate and set aside.

5. Add aromatics to pan and cook, stirring, until fragrant, about 30 seconds. Add beef with marinade, spreading evenly in a single layer and cook, without stirring, for 30 seconds. Toss well to combine. Cook, stirring, until just a hint of pink remains inside beef, about 1 minute.

6. Return reserved celery mixture to wok. Add sauce and cook, stirring, until beef is no longer pink inside, about 2 minutes. Transfer to a serving platter and serve immediately. Pass salted chiles at the table (if using).

Variation

Sichuan-Style Pork with Celery: Substitute thinly sliced pork tenderloin or butt for the beef.

Focus on: Chiles in China

Like Japan, China is not known for its chile intake, although chiles feature prominently in the cuisines of several regions, particularly the provinces of Hunan and Sichuan. They are also used in Taiwan.

Having traveled in China, without visiting either Hunan or Sichuan, I found that chiles are more widely used than I expected them to be. They turn up in many dishes, both as a garnish and an ingredient. And, of course, they are hidden in many prepared sauces, such as hoisin sauce, hot bean pastes and shacha sauce, which are widely used.

No one knows for certain how chiles arrived in China; it's possible they came via the Silk Road, the ancient trade route connecting Asia and Europe, or perhaps through southwest Asia. We do know that they arrived in the country in the 16th century and were not immediately embraced. The citizens initially described the fiery plants as "barbarian peppers." At first, they were used purely as ornamentals; in 1591, one writer described them as having round red fruits that were "incredibly beautiful."

According to Sichuan food expert Fuchsia Dunlop, chiles were not widely cultivated in that province until the early 19th century, but once available they were quickly adopted for culinary use. Sichuan food works strenuously to create a balanced flavor profile. However, liberal use of pungent red chiles plus Sichuan pepper ensures that the results are appealingly zesty. (Sichuan pepper is not a capsicum but rather a member of the Rutaceae family; it is the dried berries of trees in the *Zanthoxylum* genus, also known as "prickly ash.")

I traveled in China in 2014. While I didn't visit either Hunan or Sichuan province, which are noted for pungent dishes—such as kung pao chicken, General Tso's chicken, ma-po tofu, *shui zhu yu* (fish in chile oil) and Chongqing hot pot—I easily found restaurants that specialized in these cuisines everywhere I visited. At the time of my visit, Sichuan cuisine was having a moment, and even our Chinese guide, who seemed to have an aversion to his country's food, recommended a popular new Sichuan restaurant near our hotel in Shanghai. Restaurants devoted to Sichuan cooking are well represented throughout the country. Traveling in the countryside, it was not uncommon to see ristras (see page 31) strung up and drying in the sun.

The other great chile-eating region, aside from Sichuan, is Hunan, the native province of Chairman Mao, who enjoyed chiles so much he reportedly sprinkled them over watermelon and commented "No chiles, no revolution." I am oversimplifying to say they are used much as they are in Sichuan because the preparation methods differ. I have a sense that more fresh chiles, including sweet peppers, are used. When I visited a farmers' market in Yangshuo, which is located in Guangxi, a province bordering Hunan, vendors were selling several varieties of fresh red, green and yellow chiles. A red chile, about 5 inches (12.5 cm) long and sharply pointed, possibly a close relative of the cayenne pepper, seemed to dominate. Dried chiles were coarsely ground and made into chile oil. With a view toward experiencing authentic local food, my daughter and I took an afternoon cooking class in the countryside. Not only did we use an abundance of capsicum in the dishes we created, but also we were told that chiles—fresh, dried or pickled—figure prominently in that region's cuisine.

Chopped salted chiles (see page 396) seem to be a unique product associated with Hunan. This homemade condiment is added to stir-fries and tossed with noodles, among other uses. As in Sichuan, pickled chiles, chile oils and chile pastes are widely used. According to Bruce Cost, author of *Asian Ingredients*, chili bean sauce is used more than soy sauce in Sichuan and Hunan cooking. And even hoisin sauce, which is not associated with pungency, contains some dried red chile.

Parts of China have significant Muslim populations whose citizens enjoy spicy food. Aside from the Terra-Cotta Army, my favorite memories of the city of Xi'an revolve around its Muslim quarter, where a wide variety of chile-spiked dishes are hawked on the colorful streets—everything from grilled meats to handmade noodles. It is fun to watch the vendors hand-stretching noodles, to order, which are then cooked and served with various sauces and inevitably accompanied by a bottle of pungent chile oil (a fixture on every table, to ensure a fiery finish). These culinary vendors also serve a variety of kebabs, basted with chile sauce and sprinkled, I believe, with chile-infused salt.

According to Deh-Ta Hsiung, a Chinese food scholar, the spiciest pepper, loved in both Sichuan and Hunan, is a very hot fingertip chile known as "To the Sky" because it faces the sky as it grows. But many other types of chiles are grown and used in China. An article in the English-language newspaper *Beijing Today* noted that by 2002, more than 2,000 varieties of chiles were grown in China. In 2013, according to FAOSTAT, the statistics division of the Food and Agriculture Organization of the United Nations (FAO), China was the second-largest pepper-producing area in the world after India. That year, it produced more than 15 million tons of peppers.

Beef Fajitas

Fajitas are, basically, beef tacos, traditionally made from strips of grilled skirt steak. They are a Tex-Mex cowboy-style classic, but in recent years their popularity as fast food has tarnished their luster. The skirt is a part of a steer that is too small to market commercially, so it was traditionally given to herders working both sides of the border between Texas and Mexico. They cooked it over campfires and wrapped the juicy meat in tortillas and topped it with a spicy sauce, such as pico de gallo (see page 358). Fajitas are fun, and kids love rolling them up and adding their own fixings.

MAKES 4 TO 6 SERVINGS

GLUTEN-FREE FRIENDLY

Tips

If you can't find New Mexico or ancho chile powder, use regular chili powder in this recipe. Or grind a dried chile in a spice grinder.

To toast cumin seeds: Place seeds in a dry skillet over medium heat and cook, stirring, until fragrant and just beginning to brown, 3 to 4 minutes. Immediately transfer to a spice grinder or a mortar and grind.

Annatto seeds, also known as achiote, have a mild peppery flavor and can easily be ground in a mortar or a spice grinder. If you can't find them, substitute sweet paprika.

Any leftover meat reheats nicely. In fact, it seems to benefit from an overnight rest in its seasoned juices.

Optional condiments: Finish your fajita with any (or all) of the following: Fresh Tomato Salsa (page 358), Texas-Style Hot Sauce (page 360), Mexican Tomatillo Salsa (page 366) or sour cream.

1	batch Roasted Red Pepper Strips (*Rajas*), page 368	1
1 lb	boneless beef skirt, hangar or top sirloin steak, cut into long strips about 1 inch (2.5 cm) wide	500 g
1 tbsp	New Mexico or ancho chile powder (see Tips, left)	15 mL
2 tsp	cumin seeds, toasted and ground (see Tips, left)	10 mL
1 tsp	ground annatto seeds (see Tips, left)	5 mL
½ tsp	freshly ground black pepper	2 mL
¼ tsp	hot smoked paprika	1 mL
2 tbsp	olive oil, divided	30 mL
8	large green onions (white with a bit of green parts)	8
	Sea salt	
	Freshly squeezed lime juice	
	Extra virgin olive oil	
8	small (6-inch/15 cm) corn tortillas	8

1. Pat beef dry with a paper towel. In a small bowl, stir together chile powder, cumin, ground annatto, black pepper and paprika. Rub all over beef. Brush with 1 tbsp (15 mL) of the oil. Let stand at room temperature for 30 minutes.

2. When you are ready to cook, preheat barbecue to high or grill pan to medium-high. Drizzle 1 tsp (5 mL) of the remaining oil over the green onions and toss to coat. Grill green onions until lightly browned. Transfer to a plate.

3. Add beef to grill or pan and cook to desired doneness. Transfer to a cutting board and let cool slightly. Cut into thin strips, each about 2 inches (5 cm) long and ¼ inch (0.5 cm) wide. Season with salt and drizzle with lime juice to taste. Drizzle remaining oil over green onions.

4. To serve, pass warm tortillas, beef, red pepper strips, green onions and optional condiments (see Tips, left) at the table.

Ropa Vieja

This Cuban dish, which translates literally as "old clothes," is beef that is cooked twice; once until it is tender enough to shred and then in a flavorful sauce. It is served with rice or often used as a filling for tortillas. I like to serve it with an island-inspired rice, such as Caribbean Peas and Rice (page 350) or Cuban-Style Black Beans and Yellow Rice (page 355), with warm tortillas on the side. A robust red Spanish Rioja makes a nice wine accompaniment.

MAKES 6 TO 8 SERVINGS

GLUTEN-FREE FRIENDLY

Tips

You can also use flat iron steaks in this recipe; they are smaller, however, so you will probably need 4 to reach the 2 lbs (1 kg) you need.

Drained jarred pimentos are traditionally used in this recipe, but if you prefer, you can substitute a diced seeded roasted red bell pepper. The flavor will be slightly less intense.

When cooking for people who are gluten-free, always check the labels of prepared foods such as beef stock to ensure they do not contain added wheat products.

- Large skillet with lid
- Fine-mesh sieve

1	onion, thinly sliced	1
4	cloves garlic, thinly sliced	4
2	bay leaves	2
1 tsp	dried oregano	5 mL
4	whole allspice berries	4
½ tsp	salt	2 mL
½ tsp	black peppercorns	2 mL
2 cups	beef stock	500 mL
1	large (about 2 lbs/1 kg) beef flank steak (see Tips, left)	1
1 tbsp	oil or pure lard	15 mL
1	large onion	1
4	cloves garlic	4
1	Cubanelle or green bell pepper, seeded and diced	1
½ to 1	habanero pepper, minced	½ to 1
2 tsp	ground cumin	10 mL
1 tsp	ground oregano	5 mL
2 tbsp	dry sherry	30 mL
1 tbsp	tomato paste	15 mL
1	can (14 oz/398 mL) diced tomatoes, with juice	1
	Salt and freshly ground black pepper	
½ cup	finely chopped drained jarred pimentos (see Tips, left)	125 mL

1. Place onion, garlic, bay leaves, oregano, allspice, salt and black peppercorns in skillet. Pour in stock and top with steak. (Steak should fit in a single layer and be covered with stock; if your steak is too large, cut it to fit. If necessary, add water to cover.) Bring to a boil. Reduce heat, cover and simmer until meat is tender, about 1½ hours.

2. Transfer meat to a cutting board and set aside. Strain cooking liquid through a fine-mesh sieve into a bowl, pressing solids with a spatula to extract as much liquid as possible. Set aside. When meat is cool enough to handle, using 2 forks or your hands, shred.

3. In a medium skillet, heat oil over medium heat. Add onion, garlic, Cubanelle pepper, and habanero pepper to taste and cook, stirring, until softened, about 5 minutes. Add cumin and oregano and cook, stirring, for 1 minute. Add sherry and cook, stirring, until liquid is evaporated, about 1 minute. Stir in tomato paste, tomatoes and juice, and $1\frac{1}{2}$ cups (375 mL) of the reserved cooking liquid. Bring to a boil.

4. Reduce heat and simmer, uncovered, until liquid is reduced and mixture is thickened, about 20 minutes. Add reserved shredded beef and stir well to coat. Cover and simmer until meat is heated through, about 10 minutes. Season to taste with salt and black pepper. Transfer to a serving dish. Garnish with pimentos.

Jamaican Beef Patties

These patties are sold as street food in Jamaica, as well as in many North American cities. They are great for parties, but they are so delicious that I like to serve them for regular dinners, as well. A tossed green salad or (for a more authentic touch) coleslaw is all you need to complete the meal.

MAKES TWELVE 6-INCH (15 CM) PATTIES

Tips

If you don't have a round cutter, you can use a small plate or a bowl to cut out rounds, or cut them freehand with a knife.

If you prefer to make patties to serve as party food or an appetizer, use a smaller cutter and adjust the quantity of filling accordingly. You may need to reduce the baking time slightly.

These patties freeze well. If you want to freeze them, complete the recipe up to the end of Step 4. Wrap them tightly in foil and enclose in a resealable freezer bag and freeze for up to 2 weeks. Bake from frozen, increasing baking time to about 35 minutes.

If your patties start to get too brown before they're finished baking, cover them loosely with a piece of tented foil.

- Preheat oven to 400°F (200°C)
- Food processor
- 6-inch (15 cm) round cutter (see Tips, left)
- 2 baking sheets, lined with parchment paper

1 tbsp	oil	15 mL
12 oz	lean ground beef	375 g
1	small onion, finely chopped	1
4	cloves garlic, minced	4
1 tbsp	minced gingerroot	15 mL
1	Scotch bonnet or habanero pepper, seeded and minced	1
2 tsp	curry powder	10 mL
½ tsp	ground allspice	2 mL
1 tbsp	tomato paste	15 mL
1 cup	green peas, thawed if frozen	250 mL
	Salt and freshly ground black pepper	
2	green onions (white and green parts), chopped	2
	Hot sauce	

Pastry

3 cups	all-purpose flour	750 mL
1 tsp	curry powder	5 mL
1 tsp	baking powder	5 mL
½ tsp	salt	2 mL
1 cup	cold butter, cubed	250 mL
¼ cup	ice water (approx.)	60 mL
1	egg	1
1 tbsp	water	15 mL

1. In a large skillet, heat oil over medium heat. Add beef and onion and cook, stirring, beef is no longer pink, about 5 minutes. Add garlic, ginger, Scotch bonnet pepper, curry powder and allspice and cook, stirring, for 1 minute. Stir in tomato paste and peas. Reduce heat and simmer until peas are tender, about 3 minutes. Season to taste with salt and pepper. Remove from heat. Let cool.

Years ago, I had the good fortune to visit Jamaica with a native citizen whose extended family had properties around the island. We sampled Blue Mountain coffee grown on a relative's farm, fresh fish purchased directly from a boy who had recently reeled it in and fish cakes prepared by a family cook and finished with homemade hot sauce. I enjoyed everything I ate but my most memorable experiences revolve around discovering home-cooked saltfish and ackee for breakfast, jerk chicken and pork cooked over barbecues made from oil drums, and versions of these patties, prepared in ramshackle kitchens that appeared to sprout up all over the island.

2. *Pastry:* Meanwhile, in food processor fitted with the metal blade, combine flour, curry powder, baking powder and salt. Process until blended. Add butter and process until mixture resembles rolled oats, about 10 seconds. Pour ice water into a glass measuring cup and, with motor running, slowly pour through the feed tube in a steady stream just until the dough begins to come together. (You may not use all of the ice water.) Turn dough out onto a clean work surface and knead into a ball. Refrigerate for about 20 minutes to firm up.

3. When you are ready to bake, preheat oven to 400°F (200°C). On lightly floured work surface, roll out dough to generous $1/16$-inch (2 mm) thickness. Using cutter, cut into rounds (see Tips, opposite) and place on prepared baking sheets, spacing about 2 inches (5 cm) apart. Reroll and cut scraps as necessary.

4. In small bowl, beat egg with water to make egg wash. Brush edges of rounds with some of the egg wash. Place about $1/4$ cup (60 mL) of the beef mixture in center of each round and sprinkle with about $1/2$ tsp (2 mL) of the chopped green onions. Fold dough in half and pinch edges together to seal. Using the tines of a fork, crimp edges. Brush tops with remaining egg wash. Using a fork, pierce a few holes in the center of each patty.

5. Bake in preheated oven until golden brown, about 25 minutes. Let cool slightly before serving. Pass hot sauce at the table.

Italian-Style Veal with Peppers

This Italian-inspired stew is easy to make and very flavorful. I like to serve it over creamy polenta, with sautéed broccoli rabe on the side.

Tips

This quantity of hot pepper flakes produces a mild bit of heat. If you prefer, increase the quantity.

If you're making this dish for someone who is gluten intolerant, substitute an all-purpose gluten-free blend for the all-purpose flour. And be sure to check the labels of prepared foods such as tomato paste and stock to ensure they do not contain added wheat products.

- Preheat oven to 325°F (160°C)
- Dutch oven

1 tbsp	olive oil (approx.)	15 mL
3 oz	pancetta, diced (¼ inch/0.5 cm)	90 g
2 lbs	trimmed boneless stewing veal, cut into cubes (1 inch /2.5 cm) and patted dry	1 kg
1	onion, finely chopped	1
2	red bell peppers, seeded and diced	2
4	cloves garlic, chopped	4
1½ tbsp	finely chopped fresh rosemary	22 mL
1 tsp	salt (approx.)	5 mL
½ tsp	freshly ground black pepper (approx.)	2 mL
¼ tsp	hot pepper flakes, such as *peperoncino*	1 mL
2 tbsp	tomato paste	30 mL
2 tbsp	all-purpose flour	30 mL
½ cup	dry white wine	125 mL
1 cup	veal or chicken stock	250 mL
	Finely chopped fresh parsley	

1. In Dutch oven, heat oil over medium heat. Add pancetta and cook, stirring, until crisp, about 3 minutes. Using a slotted spoon, transfer to a bowl.

2. Add veal to pan, in batches, and cook, stirring and adding more oil as necessary, just until beginning to brown, about 2 minutes per batch. Using a slotted spoon, transfer to plate.

3. Add onion, bell peppers and garlic to pan and cook, stirring, until softened, about 5 minutes. Add rosemary, 1 tsp (5 mL) salt, ½ tsp (2 mL) black pepper and hot pepper flakes and cook, stirring, for 1 minute. Stir in tomato paste. Sprinkle flour over top and cook, stirring, for 1 minute. Stir in wine and bring to a boil. Boil for 2 minutes. Add stock and return to a boil. Reduce heat and simmer, stirring, until thickened, about 5 minutes. Return veal and pancetta with accumulated juices to pan. Return to a simmer. Season to taste with additional salt and black pepper.

4. Cover and transfer to preheated oven. Cook until veal is very tender, about 1½ hours. Garnish to taste with parsley and serve immediately.

Basque Veal Stew (Axoa)

This dish is a specialty of the village of Espelette in the Basque region of France. Seasoned with piment d'Espelette, it is a very mild-tasting dish, so if you are looking for pungency, this is probably not for you. Fried potatoes are a traditional accompaniment.

Tips

Axoa is usually made in the style of a blanquette of veal, which means the veal is not browned. However, in the interest of bumping up the flavor and adding heft to the sauce, I have dredged the meat in flour and lightly browned it.

Use milder hot peppers, such as Anaheim, poblano, padrón or shishito, in this stew. You could even use hot banana peppers. If you have access to authentic Basque peppers, try *pimiento de Gernika*.

For an even prettier presentation, use a combination of different colored bell peppers rather than all red. Green, orange and yellow are all lovely.

If you're making this dish for someone who is gluten intolerant, substitute an all-purpose gluten-free blend for the all-purpose flour. And be sure to check the labels of prepared foods such as chicken stock to ensure they do not contain added wheat products.

• Dutch oven

2 lbs	trimmed boneless stewing veal, cut into 1-inch (2.5 cm) cubes	1 kg
¼ cup	all-purpose flour	60 mL
¼ cup	olive oil (approx.)	60 mL
2	onions, thinly sliced on the vertical	2
2	red bell peppers, seeded and thinly sliced (see Tips, left)	2
2	medium-hot green peppers (see Tips, left)	2
4	cloves garlic, minced	4
1 tsp	piment d'Espelette (approx.)	5 mL
1 cup	dry white wine	250 mL
1 cup	chicken stock	250 mL
½ tsp	finely grated lemon zest	2 mL
4	sprigs fresh thyme	4
	Salt and freshly ground black pepper	

1. In a plastic bag, combine veal and flour. Shake until meat is well dredged in flour.

2. In Dutch oven, heat ¼ cup (60 mL) oil over medium-high heat. Add dredged veal, in batches, and sauté quickly on all sides, transferring to a plate as completed, about 2 minutes per batch. (Do not let the meat brown; you just want the flour to become crusty and turn, at most, light golden.) Discard any excess flour. Reduce heat to medium.

3. Add up to 1 tbsp (15 mL) more oil to pan, if necessary. Add onions, bell peppers and green hot peppers and toss well to coat. Cover, reduce heat to low and cook until vegetables are tender, about 10 minutes.

4. Preheat oven to 350°F (180°C). Uncover pan and stir well. Increase heat to medium-high. Stir in garlic and piment d'Espelette. Stir in wine and bring to a boil. Boil for 2 minutes. Stir in stock. Return veal and accumulated juices to pan. Stir in lemon zest and thyme. Season to taste with salt and black pepper. Return to a boil.

5. Cover and transfer to preheated oven. Cook until meat is very tender, about 1 hour. Pass additional piment d'Espelette at the table.

Pork and Lamb

Portuguese Roast Pork

Sweet red peppers are practically a staple food in Portugal. Often, they are roasted and transformed into *massa de pimentão*, a paste that is frequently used as a marinade for meats, especially pork. This dish, which features pork marinated in a savory homemade version of that paste and roasted, is popular in different forms throughout Portugal. It is usually made with loin, but I prefer the results I get with a good-quality pork butt. It's particularly delicious accompanied by fried potatoes.

MAKES 4 TO 6 SERVINGS

GLUTEN-FREE FRIENDLY

Tips

Piri-piri pepper flakes are available from specialty markets or online. If you can't find them, substitute Italian *peperoncino* flakes, which are less spicy.

Use smoked hot or sweet paprika to suit your taste.

The pork butt I buy from my butcher is from a heritage breed and is perfectly done when cooked to this temperature. Usually pork butt or shoulder is cooked slightly longer. If you prefer, remove it from the oven when the temperature reaches 160°F (71°C).

- Dutch oven
- Instant-read thermometer

2 cups	dry white wine, divided	500 mL
½ cup	Portuguese Pepper Paste (page 384)	125 mL
6	cloves garlic, puréed (see Tips, page 270)	6
2	bay leaves, crumbled	2
1 tsp	salt	5 mL
½ to 1 tsp	piri-piri pepper flakes (see Tips, left)	2 to 5 mL
½ tsp	smoked paprika (see Tips, left)	2 mL
1	trimmed boneless pork butt (3 lbs/1.5 kg)	1
2 tbsp	olive oil	30 mL

1. In a small bowl, stir together ½ cup (125 mL) of the wine, the pepper paste, garlic, bay leaves, salt, piri-piri pepper flakes to taste and paprika.

2. Using the tip of a sharp knife, prick pork all over. Using your fingers, rub pepper mixture all over pork. Transfer to a bowl. Cover and refrigerate overnight or for up to 48 hours.

3. When you are ready to cook, preheat oven to 325°F (160°C). Remove pork from refrigerator and let stand at room temperature for 30 minutes. Using a slotted spoon, remove pork from marinade, scraping marinade back into bowl. Transfer to a plate. Stir remaining wine into marinade and set aside.

4. In Dutch oven, heat oil over medium-high heat. Add pork and brown on all sides. Pour reserved marinade mixture over top and bring to a boil. Cover and transfer to preheated oven. Bake until instant-read thermometer inserted into thickest part registers 150°F (66°C), about 1½ hours (see Tips, left). Remove from oven and let rest for 10 minutes. Thinly slice pork and serve immediately.

Pork Adobo Cusco-Style (*Chancho en Adobo al Estilo de Cusco*)

This is an adaptation of a recipe that appears in Maricel Presilla's wonderful cookbook *Gran Cocina Latina*. She notes that the dried ají panca provide the bright red color and that the authentic recipe employs *chicha de jora*, a fermented corn beverage, to add acidity. I have used vinegar instead, and the result is still superb. I serve this pork with polenta; quinoa is another good choice as a side dish.

MAKES 6 SERVINGS

GLUTEN-FREE FRIENDLY

Tips

If you can't find ají panca and/or ají mirasol, substitute widely available guajillo peppers for some or all of the amount of dried peppers called for.

Latin American recipes sometimes suggest using achiote-infused lard or oil for frying meat. It is very easy to make and imparts a rosy color to dishes, with a hint of achiote flavor. To make ½ cup (125 mL), in a large saucepan, melt ½ cup (125 mL) pure lard or heat grapeseed oil over medium heat. Add 2 tbsp (30 mL) crushed achiote seeds and cook, stirring, until bubbling. Remove from heat. Using a fine-mesh sieve, strain into a bowl. Discard seeds. Cover and refrigerate any leftovers for up to 1 month.

When I make this dish, I cut the pork into 6 crosswise slices, each about 1 inch (2.5 cm) wide. They resemble large, flatter filets of beef. If you prefer, cut the pork into large chunks.

- Blender
- Dutch oven

3	dried ají panca (see Tips, left)	3
3	dried ají mirasol	3
4 cups	boiling water	1 L
2 cups	chicken stock	500 mL
½ cup	fresh cilantro leaves and tender stems	125 mL
2 tbsp	cider vinegar	30 mL
6	cloves garlic, minced	6
1 tbsp	ground cumin	15 mL
1 tbsp	dried oregano	15 mL
1 tsp	salt	5 mL
2 tbsp	pure lard or grapeseed oil (approx.)	30 mL
3 lbs	trimmed boneless pork butt, sliced or cut into chunks (see Tips, left)	1.5 kg
1	onion, thinly sliced	1

1. In a bowl, soak dried chiles in boiling water for 30 minutes, weighing down with a cup to ensure they remain submerged. Drain, reserving 2 cups (500 mL) of the liquid.

2. Transfer soaked peppers to blender. Add stock, cilantro, vinegar, garlic, cumin, oregano, salt and reserved soaking liquid. Purée until smooth. Set aside.

3. Preheat oven to 325°F (160°C). In Dutch oven, heat 2 tbsp (30 mL) lard over medium-high heat. Add pork, in batches, and sauté, adding more lard if necessary, until lightly browned on all sides, about 4 minutes per batch. Transfer to a plate as completed and set aside.

4. Reduce heat to medium, Add onion to pan and cook, stirring, until softened, about 3 minutes. Add reserved chile mixture and stir well. Return pork and accumulated juices to pan. Bring to a boil. Cover and transfer to preheated oven. Bake until pork is very tender, about 2 hours.

Pork in Tablecloth-Stainer Sauce (Mancha Manteles)

I've been making variations on this traditional Mexican recipe for years. Other regions have laid claim to it, but this relatively mild mole seems to be Oaxacan in origin. (It is one of the "seven moles of Oaxaca," according to Mexican food expert Diana Kennedy.) The dish is often made with poultry or pork and is distinguished from other established moles by the addition of fruit, such as pineapple and banana. Traditionally, it was made with dried local chiles, but, according to Kennedy, most modern cooks use readily available ancho and guajillo peppers.

MAKES 8 SERVINGS

GLUTEN-FREE FRIENDLY

Tip

The herb usually identified as Mexican oregano is a different plant from the Mediterranean version (*Origanum vulgare*). Although there is one variety of so-called Mexican oregano that belongs to that family, most likely the version you purchase will be *Lippia graveolens* or *L. berlandieri*, which are part of the verbena family. In any case, Mexican oregano, which is sun-dried, provides a similar but more robust flavor than its European counterpart. It tends to have particularly strong citrus notes.

- Preheat oven to 325°F (160°C)
- Blender
- Fine-mesh sieve
- Dutch oven

2	each ancho and guajillo chiles	2
	Boiling water	
1 cup	chicken stock	250 mL
1 tbsp	cider vinegar	15 mL
1 tbsp	olive oil or pure lard	15 mL
1	trimmed boneless pork shoulder or butt (about 3½ lbs/1.75 kg), patted dry	1
2	onions, thinly sliced on the vertical	2
4	cloves garlic, minced	4
1 tbsp	dried Mexican oregano (see Tip, left)	15 mL
1	piece (about 3 inches/7.5 cm long) cinnamon stick	1
2	apples, peeled, cored and thinly sliced	2
1	can (28 oz/796 mL) tomatoes, with juice, coarsely chopped	1
	Salt and freshly ground black pepper	
1 cup	pineapple chunks (see Tips, opposite)	250 mL
2	bananas, sliced	2

1. In a dry skillet, in batches if necessary, toast chiles over medium heat, turning frequently, until they are lightly charred and fragrant, about 4 minutes. Transfer to a bowl and cover with boiling water. Let stand for 30 minutes, weighing down with a cup to ensure they remain submerged. Drain and discard soaking liquid. Remove and discard stems. Chop chiles coarsely.

Tips

You can use fresh pineapple or drained canned pineapple chunks in this recipe.

If you are serving this dish to someone who is gluten-free, be sure to check the label if you are using prepared chicken stock. Some manufacturers add wheat-based products.

2. Transfer chopped chiles to blender. Add stock and vinegar and purée until smooth. Strain through sieve into a bowl, pressing solids through with a spatula. Set aside.

3. While chiles are soaking, in Dutch oven, heat oil over medium heat. Add pork and brown on all sides, about 8 minutes. Transfer to a plate and set aside.

4. Add onions to pan and cook, stirring often, until golden and starting to brown, about 10 minutes. Add garlic, oregano and cinnamon stick and cook, stirring, for 1 minute. Stir in apples. Add tomatoes and juice, and reserved chile mixture and bring to a boil. Reduce heat and simmer for 5 minutes. Return pork to pan. Cover and transfer to preheated oven. Bake until pork is very tender, about 2 hours.

5. Stir in pineapple and bananas and bake until warmed through, about 15 minutes.

To Seed or Not to Seed

Whether you seed and remove the veins inside your peppers is a matter of preference. With the exception of bell peppers, I usually don't seed and devein because, in my opinion, it affects the taste and experience of the pepper. I like the texture the seeds add to a dish. The veins are the placental tissue inside the peppers, and they contain any spiciness, so removing them may be a good idea if you are heat-averse; you can also reduce the quantity of chile called for in a recipe or substitute a chile that ranks lower on the Scoville scale.

Haitian-Style Pork (*Griot*)

This famous Haitian dish features pork that is marinated in a mixture of chiles and bitter orange juice and braised, then removed from the cooking juices and crisped in a skillet. It is served with Haiti's answer to sauerkraut, spicy *Pikliz* (page 409).

Tip

Although the pork is pleasant on its own, pikliz really makes the dish. I do not recommend serving it without this accompaniment.

> **FYI:** I use the term "gluten-free friendly" whenever I include prepared ingredients in a recipe that would otherwise be gluten-free. Manufacturers often add wheat products to prepared foods, so you need to check the label to ensure these products are actually gluten-free.

- Blender
- Dutch oven

3 lbs	trimmed boneless pork butt	1.5 kg
2 tbsp	grapeseed oil (see Tips, page 274), divided	30 mL
1	onion, thinly sliced	1
1	green bell pepper, seeded and diced	1
1	red bell pepper, seeded and diced	1
1 tsp	packed dark brown sugar	5 mL
½ cup	chicken stock	125 mL
	Salt and freshly ground black pepper	
	Finely snipped fresh chives	
	Haitian-Style Pickled Cabbage (*Pikliz*), page 409	

Marinade

½ cup	freshly squeezed orange juice	125 mL
2 tbsp	freshly squeezed lemon juice	30 mL
2 tbsp	freshly squeezed lime juice	30 mL
1	onion, coarsely chopped	1
4	cloves garlic	4
1	Scotch bonnet or habanero pepper	1
1 tsp	dried thyme	5 mL
1 tsp	salt	5 mL
	Freshly ground black pepper	

1. *Marinade:* In blender, combine orange juice, lemon juice, lime juice, onion, garlic, Scotch bonnet pepper, thyme, salt, and black pepper to taste. Purée until smooth. Set aside.

2. On a cutting board, cut pork in half crosswise. Cut each half lengthwise into halves and each half lengthwise into quarters. (You will end up with 16 long, narrow pieces.) Place pork in a large bowl or baking dish and cover with reserved marinade. Toss well to ensure all pieces of pork are covered with marinade. Cover and refrigerate for 24 hours, stirring occasionally to distribute liquid.

3. Preheat oven to 325°F (160°C). Meanwhile, in Dutch oven, heat 1 tbsp (15 mL) of the oil over medium heat. Add onion, and green and red bell peppers and cook, stirring, until softened, about 5 minutes. Stir in brown sugar and stock. Add pork with marinade and bring to a boil. Season to taste with salt and black pepper. Transfer pan to preheated oven. Bake until very tender, about $1\frac{1}{2}$ hours.

4. Transfer pan to stovetop. In a large skillet that can accommodate the pork in a single layer, heat remaining oil over medium-high heat. Using a slotted spoon, transfer pork to skillet and brown on all sides, about 6 minutes total. Meanwhile, bring cooking liquid to a boil. Boil until reduced by half, about 6 minutes.

5. Transfer fried pork to a warm serving platter. Pour reduced cooking liquid over top. Garnish to taste with chives. Serve with pikliz.

Portuguese Pork with Clams (Porco à Alentejana)

This is Portugal's national dish—if you haven't tried it, prepare for a treat. The combination of succulent pork, briny clams and spicy chorizo is to die for. I love to serve this with a version of hash brown potatoes.

Tips

If you are making this dish for people who are gluten-intolerant, be sure to check the label on your chorizo. Many prepared sausages contain added gluten.

To purée garlic quickly and easily, use a sharp-toothed rasp grater, such as those made by Microplane.

Vary the paprika to suit your taste. You can use less sweet and more hot smoked—just maintain the total amount. The pungency of your chorizo will also influence the quantity of hot paprika you use.

- Large Dutch oven

2 lbs	trimmed boneless pork butt, cut into 1-inch (2.5 cm) cubes and patted dry	1 kg
1 cup	dry white wine	250 mL
2	bay leaves	2
2 tbsp	extra virgin olive oil or pure lard	30 mL
1	onion, diced	1
4 oz	dry-cured chorizo, thinly sliced (¼ inch/0.5 cm)	125 g
1	can (14 oz/398 mL) diced tomatoes, with juice	1
	Salt and freshly ground black pepper	
24	large clams, scrubbed	24
¼ cup	finely chopped fresh parsley	60 mL

Seasoning Paste

4	cloves garlic, puréed (see Tips, left)	4
2 tbsp	sweet paprika	30 mL
2 tbsp	olive oil	30 mL
½ tsp	smoked hot paprika (see Tips, left)	2 mL

1. *Seasoning Paste:* In a small bowl, stir together garlic, sweet paprika, oil and smoked paprika.

2. Using the tip of a sharp knife, prick pork all over. Using your fingers, rub seasoning paste all over pork. Transfer to a large bowl. Add wine and bay leaves and turn to coat. Cover and refrigerate overnight.

3. When you are ready to cook, preheat oven to 325°F (160°C). Remove pork from refrigerator and let stand at room temperature for 30 minutes. Using a slotted spoon, remove pork from marinade, reserving marinade. Pat pork dry with a paper towel and set aside on a plate.

continued on page 272

4. In Dutch oven, heat oil over medium-high heat. Add pork, in batches, and brown on all sides, about 4 minutes per batch. Transfer to a plate as completed and set aside.

5. Reduce heat to medium. Add onion to pan and cook, stirring, until softened, about 3 minutes. Add chorizo and toss well. Add reserved marinade, and tomatoes and juice, and bring to a boil. Boil for 2 minutes. Return pork to pan and season to taste with salt and black pepper. Cover and transfer to preheated oven. Bake until pork is very tender, about 1 hour.

6. Add clams to pan, arranging evenly over pork. Cover and bake until clams have opened, about 7 minutes. (The cooking time will depend on the size of the clams.)

7. Remove from oven. Discard bay leaves and any clams that have not opened. Garnish with parsley and serve immediately.

Currywurst

Although chiles likely won't spring to mind when you think about German food, sausages might. So it may not be completely surprising to learn that in that country a dish called *currywurst* is extremely popular. It is fast food, as ubiquitous as the North American hamburger with fries, and has been described as "an icon of German popular culture." In Frankfurt, which I visit every year, my first stop after arriving on an overnight flight is always a take-out place, where I enjoy a yummy rendition at a picnic table on the pedestrian mall.

The origins of currywurst are a variation on the theme of Anglo-Indian cuisine (see page 94). This dish was invented in Berlin at the end of the Second World War by a woman named Herta Heuwer. The story goes that some British soldiers, missing the Indian cuisine they had become accustomed to back home, brought curry powder and Worcestershire sauce to their foreign posting. American soldiers brought ketchup. The servicemen passed all of these ingredients along to Frau Heuwer, who used them as the basis for an original sauce, which she served over cooked sausages and sold from a street stand. It was a brilliant marketing strategy, because the city was in ruins and the abundance of construction workers brought in for rebuilding were desperate for tasty fast food.

The components of currywurst vary, but not too much. Basically, it is boiled pork sausage, usually bratwurst, which is subsequently fried and topped with a spicy curry-flavored ketchup-type sauce. It is usually served on a bun, often with fries or fried onions. (I like sauerkraut on the side.) It is a fascinating example of a very simple idea taking hold. By 1951, Frau Heuwer had patented her sauce; today, there are more than 200 currywurst outlets in Berlin alone, with countless others scattered across Germany. In the spirit of the original creation, most are down-to-earth mom-and-pop outlets, but there are some upscale spots that offer premium libations, such as champagne, with their currywurst.

An article in *The New York Times* described the popularity of the dish as "a political statement," a symbol of Germany's desire to see itself as an egalitarian country. Briefly, with the influx of Turkish guest workers to the country, it appeared that currywurst's iconic status might be challenged by the *doner kebab* (another term for a Greek gyro), but that threat never materialized. Every year at the Volkswagen plant in Wolfsburg alone, 3.5 million currywursts are served to employees.

In 2009, the Deutsches Currywurst Museum Berlin opened. Approximately 350,000 people visit every year because, as the museum's director stated in an article published upon its opening, "No other German dish inspires such excitement."

Pork Colombo

Pork Colombo is a Christmas specialty on Caribbean islands such as Martinique and Guadeloupe. In broad terms, it is pork in a curry-type sauce; the difference is that the seasoning is Sri Lankan, supposedly brought to the islands by Tamil laborers. I have created my own spice blend instead of using Sri Lankan curry powder, which contains cinnamon and allspice, and tends to be higher on the sweet scale than I'd like for this dish. I've based it on a blend that appears in Ian Hemphill's book *The Spice and Herb Bible*, although I have introduced some recipe-specific tweaks.

MAKES 6 SERVINGS

GLUTEN-FREE FRIENDLY

Tips

I like to use expeller-pressed grapeseed oil for sautéing because it is unrefined and has a high smoke point. If you don't have or want to use grapeseed oil, substitute another oil that has a high smoke point, such as refined canola oil.

Sweet potato makes a good and convenient substitute for the butternut squash.

If you are serving this dish to someone who is gluten-free, be sure to check the label if you are using prepared chicken stock. Some manufacturers add wheat-based products.

- Dutch oven

2 lbs	trimmed boneless pork shoulder or butt, cut into 1-inch (2.5 cm) cubes	1 kg
6	cloves garlic, minced	6
1 tbsp	white wine vinegar	15 mL
2 tbsp	grapeseed oil (approx.), see Tips, left	30 mL
1	large onion, finely chopped	1
1 tbsp	raw cane sugar, such as Demerara	15 mL
1	green bell pepper, seeded and diced	1
½ to 1	Scotch bonnet or habanero pepper, minced	½ to 1
1	bay leaf	1
4 cups	cubed (about 1 inch/2.5 cm) peeled seeded butternut squash (see Tips, left)	1 L
1½ cups	chicken stock	375 mL
	Salt and freshly ground black pepper	
2 tbsp	finely chopped fresh parsley	30 mL
2 tbsp	freshly squeezed lime juice	30 mL
2 tsp	chopped fresh thyme	10 mL

Spice Blend

1 tsp	ground coriander	5 mL
1 tsp	ground cumin	5 mL
1 tsp	ground allspice	5 mL
1 tsp	ground cinnamon	5 mL
1 tsp	turmeric	5 mL
¼ tsp	cayenne pepper	1 mL

1. *Spice Blend:* In a small bowl, stir together coriander, cumin, allspice, cinnamon, turmeric and cayenne. Set aside.

2. In a bowl, combine pork, garlic and vinegar. Toss well to combine and let stand at room temperature for 1 hour.

Moreover ...

The spice blend I have prepared for this recipe is a variation of "Colombo powder," which is a fixture on the islands of Martinique and Guadeloupe. There, it's used to season a variety of one-pot dishes that feature fish, seafood, chicken or pork, as well as starches such as plantains, yams and rice. Food scholar Jessica B. Harris calls it a "legacy" of the islands' history of borrowing from the native peoples, the original French settlers, the African slaves and the indentured Tamils, all of whom left their stamp on the region's foodways. In addition to the spices I have used here, Colombo powder may also contain fenugreek, and dried mango or tamarind, and is more likely to get its heat from black pepper and brown mustard than from chile. The name Colombo (for the city in Sri Lanka) is used to describe the spice blend and any dish that uses it. According to food historian Alan Davidson, in Guadeloupe it is even used to describe an event: "Please come to my Colombo on such and such a day at such and such a time."

3. Preheat oven to 325°F (160°C). In Dutch oven, heat 2 tbsp (30 mL) oil over medium-high heat. Add pork, in batches (reserving any remaining marinade), and brown lightly on all sides, about 4 minutes per batch. Transfer to a plate as completed and set aside.

4. Reduce heat to medium. Add more oil to pan, if necessary. Add onion and cook, stirring, until softened, about 2 minutes. Stir in sugar. Add bell pepper, Scotch bonnet pepper to taste, and reserved marinade and cook, stirring, until bell pepper is softened, about 3 minutes. Add bay leaf and reserved spice blend and cook, stirring, for 1 minute. Return pork and accumulated juices to pan. Add squash and stir well to coat. Stir in stock and bring to a boil. Season to taste with salt and black pepper. Cover and transfer to preheated oven. Bake until pork is very tender, about $1\frac{1}{2}$ hours.

5. Remove from oven. Discard bay leaf. Stir in parsley, lime juice and thyme. Season to taste with additional salt and black pepper if desired.

Variation

If you want to stretch this dish or turn it into a one-pot meal (with rice), add 1 to 2 cups (250 to 500 mL) drained cooked black beans along with the stock.

Pork Vindaloo

This recipe is a quintessential example of Goan cuisine, which marries Portuguese and Indian influences. I was under the impression that vindaloo was, by definition, fiery. However, according to my friend Raghavan Iyer, the word *vindaloo* comes from the Portuguese *vinha d'alho*, the term for a marinade of wine and garlic, which means the resulting curry can be pleasantly mild. This version is moderately hot, but the heat can be adjusted.

Tips

For this recipe, cut the pork into large cubes, about 2 inches (5 cm).

Four dried red chiles in the marinade produce a pleasantly spiced dish—about a four on a scale of one to 10. If you are a heat seeker, adjust upward accordingly.

If you are serving this dish to someone who is gluten-free, be sure to check the label if you are using prepared chicken stock. Some manufacturers add wheat-based products.

When using cilantro as a garnish, use only the leaves and tender stems. For marinades, the stems (and sometimes the roots) may be used.

- Blender
- Dutch oven

2 lbs	trimmed boneless pork butt, cubed	1 kg
4	bay leaves	4
2 tbsp	clarified butter (ghee), approx.	30 mL
1 cup	chicken stock	250 mL
	Finely chopped fresh cilantro	

Marinade

1	onion, quartered	1
4	dried red chiles (see Tips, left)	4
6	cloves garlic	6
½ cup	cider vinegar	125 mL
2 tbsp	chopped gingerroot	30 mL
1 tbsp	each ground cumin and coriander	15 mL
1 tsp	salt	5 mL

1. *Marinade:* In blender, combine onion, dried chiles, garlic, vinegar, ginger, cumin, coriander and salt. Purée until smooth, adding a bit of water to thin if necessary.

2. Using a fork, prick pork all over. In a large resealable plastic bag, combine pork, marinade and bay leaves. Seal bag and gently massage marinade into pork. Let stand at room temperature for at least 30 minutes or refrigerate overnight.

3. Preheat oven to 325°F (160°C). Using a spatula, scrape off as much marinade from the meat as possible and reserve.

4. In Dutch oven, heat clarified butter over medium-high heat. Add pork, in batches, and brown on all sides, adding more clarified butter if necessary, about 4 minutes per batch. Transfer to a plate as completed and set aside.

5. When all has been browned, add stock and reserved marinade to pan and bring to a boil. Boil until slightly reduced, about 2 minutes. Return pork and juices to pan and return to a boil. Cover and transfer to preheated oven. Bake until pork is very tender, about 1½ hours.

6. Discard bay leaves. Garnish pork to taste with cilantro.

Chairman Mao's Braised Pork

This Hunan dish was supposedly Mao Zedong's favorite dish. I can understand why—it is very easy to make and very delicious. It makes a superb main course, served with plenty of hot rice and a green vegetable. It's also lovely in smaller portions as part of a multiplate Chinese meal. I have based this version on the one that appeared in Fuchsia Dunlop's *Revolutionary Chinese Cookbook*.

MAKES 4 TO 8 SERVINGS

GLUTEN-FREE FRIENDLY

Tips

Shaoxing wine is a Chinese rice wine. Although I understand there are some elegant versions, the ones that are usually available outside China are unpleasantly salty. I prefer to use dry sherry or vodka in my recipes.

Be sure to use gluten-free soy sauce or wheat-free tamari if you are making this dish for someone who is sensitive to gluten.

- Preheat oven to 325°F (160°C)
- Dutch oven

1	piece (2 lbs/1 kg) fresh pork belly	1
2 tbsp	peanut or grapeseed oil	30 mL
2 tbsp	granulated sugar	30 mL
2 tbsp	dry sherry, vodka or Shaoxing wine (see Tips, left)	30 mL
1 cup	chicken stock	250 mL
4	cloves garlic, sliced	4
1	piece (1 inch/2.5 cm long) gingerroot, cut into 4 slices	1
1	piece (2 inches/5 cm long) cinnamon stick	1
1	whole star anise	1
2	dried red chiles, broken into pieces	2
8	black peppercorns	8
3 tbsp	soy sauce	45 mL
3 tbsp	Chinese black rice vinegar	45 mL
6	green onions (white and green parts), thinly sliced	6

1. Cut pork belly into 8 thick pieces, each about $1^1/_2$ by $3^1/_2$ inches (4 by 8.5 cm). Set aside.

2. In Dutch oven, heat oil over medium heat. Add sugar and stir to combine. Cook, tipping the pot to ensure even browning, until mixture is a deep copper color. Standing well back, add sherry. Once mixture stops sputtering, add pork belly, turning to coat well.

3. Add stock, garlic, ginger, cinnamon stick, star anise, dried chiles and peppercorns. Bring to a boil. Cover and transfer to preheated oven. Bake until pork belly is very tender and cooked through, about 1 hour.

4. Transfer pan to stove top. Using tongs, transfer pork belly to a warm deep serving platter and keep warm. Bring liquid in pan to a boil. Boil for 2 minutes. Remove from heat. Stir in soy sauce, vinegar and green onions. Pour over pork belly and serve immediately.

Focus on: Chiles in India

Chiles are so much a part of Indian cooking that it is startling to be reminded that they are not indigenous to the subcontinent. Capsicums arrived in India around 1498, when Portuguese traders landed in what is today Goa. Over the next century or two, their use spread to other parts of the country. Interestingly, the northeastern parts of India were particularly welcoming to capsicums, and many wild varieties that flourished initially took root in these areas.

In India, like Mexico, the culinary use of chiles is something of an art: there are many regional types of capsicums and some have very specific uses. Both green and ripe chiles give Indian food its piquancy. They are used fresh in chutneys and dishes such as salads. Dried red chiles are one of the most significant and widely used spices. They are often powdered for use on their own or as a component of blends, such as *podis* (often called "dry chutneys"), *sambars* and various types of *masala*.

Whether visible or buried in a sauce, chiles are part of practically every meal as well as *chaat*, the ubiquitous street food that my friend Suneeta Vaswani calls "love at first bite." Chiles appear in chutneys, and in dishes featuring pulses, eggs, vegetables, meat and fish—not to mention salads, drinks and unique mouthwatering treats, such as *dosa*, a type of savory crêpe. When the British arrived in India, they expanded chiles' footprint, morphing into an entirely new entity with the advent of Anglo-Indian cuisine (see page 94).

Today, India is the world's largest producer and exporter of spices. Within that framework, chiles rule, having replaced black pepper as that country's largest spice export some time ago.

Between 2014 and 2015, 347,000 tons of chiles were exported. This represents an 11% increase in quantity (almost 30% in value) over the previous year. Much of that production was shipped to the United States, a full-circle journey back to the New World, where the plants originated.

It is an understatement to say that Indian people consume a large quantity of chiles—well over 1 million tons of them are produced annually and most are consumed domestically. *C. annuum* and *C. frutescens* are the two main cultivated species. The common *C. annuum* varieties often resemble cayenne peppers, and one of the most common is the Kashmiri chile. However, genuine Kashmiri chiles (those actually grown in Kashmir) are in very short supply, so the name has become a generic term for medium-long dried red chile peppers and the powder made from them. If you are purchasing a product labeled "Kashmiri chile powder," there is a good chance it was ground from dried byadagi chiles. This long, pointed, bright red varietal visually resembles the chile de árbol, and its powdered form is often sold as Kashmiri chile powder.

Byadagi chiles may trace their origins back to the same varieties of peppers from which Hungarian paprika is made. Recently, they were awarded Geographical Indication (GI) status in India to ensure the high quality associated with regional production. However, due to environmental challenges, their production is in decline.

Another widely used Indian chile from the paprika family is reshampatti. This flat, broad pepper, which is a deep shade of maroon, is popular in northern India. It is usually sold ground.

Various tiny but powerful bird-type peppers are the most common varieties of the *C. frutescens* species in India. They may be cultivated or wild. One type, kanthari, is grown in the southern state of Kerala. Predictably, there are green and red versions, but the ivory white one is worth noting because of its unusual color.

India's most notorious chile is the bhut jolokia (also known as the naga jolokia or naga mircha). A hybrid of the *C. frutescens* and *C. chinense* species, the so-called "ghost pepper" enjoyed a brief reign as the world's hottest pepper. In her highly entertaining *New Yorker* article on the search for the world's hottest chile, Lauren Collins suggests that the bhut jolokia had been "whispered about for years among chiliheads" and was the object of an intense search that resembled a quest for a "vegetable Loch Ness monster." However, Anandita Dutta Tamuly, who achieved a Guinness World Record for eating an extraordinary quantity of bhut jolokia chiles (see page 21) has been eating these firebombs since 1988, when she was five years old and her mother fed her chile paste to cure an infection; apparently it worked. The pepper originated in Nagaland, a region of northeastern India near Assam, where Tamuly grew up, so presumably it was proliferating in that area while chileheads were in hot pursuit. Under the name naga mircha, it was recently awarded GI status to protect its purity.

Every region in India has its favorite chiles. Guntur chiles are group of cultivars belonging to the *C. annuum* species, the most popular of which is Guntur Sannam, a flat red variety known for its pungency. It is used fresh as well as dried. It, too, was recently awarded GI status, along with products such as Darjeeling tea and specific types of Arabica coffee.

One of the largest chile markets in the world is located in Guntur, in the southern state of Andhra Pradesh. It has about 15 acres (6 hectares) devoted entirely to chile commerce. In 2008, a devastating fire destroyed much of the market and that year's harvest. Bringing the blaze under control was extremely difficult because, not surprisingly, the firefighters were overcome by the pungent fumes of burning chiles.

The Pusa Jwala, or jwala chile (*jwala* meaning "volcano" in Hindi), is one of the most common chiles in India. It is often found in Indian markets elsewhere, likely because market gardeners are growing it locally. It is bright green, long (about 4 inches/10 cm) and narrow, with a slightly bumpy exterior and a curvy tail. Often called hot finger chile, it is used fresh, usually when green, but occasionally when ripened to red.

Hunan-Style Pork with Peppers

Hunan is one of two provinces in China that are noted for their fiery cuisine (the other is Sichuan). While the ingredients in this stir-fry—pork, peppers and fermented black beans—are traditionally used in Hunan cooking, I have taken many liberties with the approach. The black beans and the pickled chiles add depth to the flavor of this otherwise straightforward stir-fry, which makes a great weeknight meal over rice. It is also an excellent addition to a multidish Chinese dinner.

MAKES 4 SERVINGS

GLUTEN-FREE FRIENDLY

Tips

Be sure to use gluten-free soy sauce or wheat-free tamari if you are making this dish for someone who is sensitive to gluten. Also check the labels of any prepared ingredients, such as stock, because they can contain added wheat ingredients.

I like to use expeller-pressed grapeseed oil because it is unrefined, but if you prefer, substitute another oil that has a high smoke point, such as refined canola oil.

• Wok or large skillet

12 oz	trimmed boneless pork (butt or tenderloin), thinly sliced	375 g
2 tbsp	grapeseed oil (see Tips, left)	30 mL
2	green bell peppers, thinly sliced	2
½ tsp	Chinese Salted Chiles (page 396), approx.	2 mL
2	green onions (white and green parts), thinly sliced	2

Marinade

2 tbsp	soy sauce	30 mL
1 tbsp	dry sherry, vodka or Shaoxing wine (see Tips, page 277)	15 mL
1 tsp	granulated sugar	5 mL
1 tsp	cornstarch	5 mL
	Freshly ground black pepper	

Aromatics

2 tbsp	drained fermented black beans, rinsed and chopped	30 mL
1 tbsp	minced gingerroot	15 mL
1 tbsp	minced garlic	15 mL

Sauce

2 tbsp	chicken stock or water	30 mL
1 tbsp	soy sauce	15 mL
1 tbsp	Chinese black rice vinegar	15 mL
1 tsp	granulated sugar	5 mL

1. *Marinade:* In a bowl large enough to accommodate all of the pork, stir together soy sauce, sherry, sugar, cornstarch, and black pepper to taste. Add pork and toss well to coat. Cover and let stand at room temperature for 30 minutes.

2. *Aromatics:* Meanwhile, in a small bowl, combine fermented black beans, ginger and garlic. Set aside.

continued on page 282

Tip

If you don't have Chinese Salted Chiles (page 396), use a pickled chile, such as piri-piri or malagueta. Adjust the quantity you add to this recipe to suit the heat level of your chile.

3. *Sauce:* In another small bowl, stir together stock, soy sauce, vinegar and sugar. Set aside.

4. In wok, heat oil over medium-high heat. Add bell peppers and stir-fry until glossy and softened, about 2 minutes. Transfer to a plate and set aside.

5. Add pork and marinade to wok, spreading evenly in a single layer and cook, without stirring, until edges of pork begin to firm up, about 1 minute. Add aromatics and stir-fry until pork is almost cooked but still pink in center, about 1 minute. Return peppers to wok. Stir in sauce and $1/2$ tsp (2 mL) salted chiles. Stir-fry just until ingredients are well combined and pork is cooked to desired degree of doneness.

6. Transfer to a warm serving platter. Garnish with green onions. Pass additional salted chiles at the table.

Pasta all'Amatriciana

This famous Italian chile-spiced pasta dish is probably from the town of Amatrice, hence its name, but the Romans lay claim to it, too. This version, which my husband makes all the time, appeared with a slight modification in chef John Coletta's book, *250 True Italian Pasta Dishes*.

MAKES 4 TO 6 SERVINGS

Tips

Guanciale is bacon made from pork cheek. It is cured but not smoked, and is essential to make this dish authentic. If you can't find it, substitute pancetta.

According to chef John Coletta, the California-grown red finger chile (also called the Dutch or Holland chile) makes an acceptable substitute for the medium-hot Italian red finger chile traditionally used in this recipe.

Especially rich and delicious, San Marzanos are the Rolls-Royce of tomatoes. Authentic versions have *Denominazione di Origine Protetta* (DOP) status and are grown in volcanic soil near Naples, Italy, where they receive long hours of flavor-building sunshine. However, imitations are grown from San Marzano seeds in various locations, with differing degrees of success. Because the tomatoes play such a significant role in this recipe, I recommend you spring for the real ones. They are pricier than most but are widely available.

If you can't find bucatini, substitute thick spaghetti.

- Stockpot

3 tbsp	extra virgin olive oil	45 mL
½ cup	finely diced guanciale (see Tips, left)	125 mL
¾ cup	dry white wine, preferably Italian	175 mL
½ tsp	minced Italian red finger chile (see Tips, left)	2 mL
1	can (28 oz/796 mL) San Marzano tomatoes (see Tips, left)	1
	Salt and freshly ground black pepper	
1 tbsp	salt	15 mL
1 lb	dried bucatini (see Tips, left)	500 g
¾ cup	grated pecorino Romano cheese, divided	175 mL

1. In large skillet, heat oil over medium heat. Add guanciale and cook, stirring, until lightly browned, about 5 minutes. Add wine and finger chile and cook, stirring often, until wine is reduced by half. Stir in tomatoes, and salt and black pepper to taste. Reduce heat and simmer gently until sauce is thickened, about 30 minutes.

2. Meanwhile, bring stockpot filled with water to a boil. Add 1 tbsp (15 mL) salt and bucatini to boiling water. Cook according to package directions, uncovered, over medium-high heat until pasta is almost al dente. Scoop out about 1 cup (250 mL) of the pasta cooking liquid and set aside. Drain pasta and set aside.

3. When sauce has finished cooking, stir in 2 tbsp (30 mL) of the reserved cooking liquid. Add bucatini and cook, tossing with tongs to coat evenly and adding more of the reserved cooking liquid if necessary, until pasta is al dente, about 3 minutes. Add half of the cheese and toss well to coat. Season to taste with additional salt and black pepper.

4. Transfer to a warm large serving bowl and sprinkle with remaining cheese. Serve immediately.

Malaysian-Style Sweet-and-Sour Pork

There is a large population of people of Chinese descent in Malaysia and Singapore. Some are associated with their own style of cooking (Nyonya), but, for the most part, this group prepares fairly traditional Chinese food, adding their own local spin. This delicious riff on sweet-and-sour spareribs, which was inspired by a recipe from Southeast Asian culinary expert Rosemary Brissenden, is one of those dishes.

MAKES 4 SERVINGS

GLUTEN-FREE FRIENDLY

Tip

Be sure to use gluten-free soy sauce or wheat-free tamari if you are making this dish for someone who is sensitive to gluten.

- Wok or large skillet
- Candy/deep-fry thermometer

1 lb	pork tenderloin	500 g
1 tbsp	soy sauce	15 mL
1 tbsp	dry sherry, vodka or Shaoxing wine (see Tips, page 277)	15 mL
	Oil for frying	
	Salt and freshly ground black pepper	
	Thinly sliced red finger chile	
½ cup	pineapple chunks (optional), see Tips, opposite	125 mL

Sweet-and-Sour Sauce

1 cup	water	250 mL
⅓ cup	granulated sugar	75 mL
¼ cup	unseasoned rice vinegar	60 mL
2 tbsp	soy sauce	30 mL
1½ tbsp	cornstarch	22 mL
	Salt and freshly ground black pepper	

Coating

¼ cup	brown or white rice flour	60 mL
2 tbsp	cornstarch	30 mL

1. Cut pork into ½-inch (1 cm) thick slices. In a medium bowl, stir soy sauce with sherry. Add pork and toss well to coat. Set aside.

2. *Sweet-and-Sour Sauce:* In a saucepan large enough to accommodate all of the pork, combine water, sugar, vinegar, soy sauce, cornstarch, and salt and black pepper to taste. Bring to a boil over medium heat, stirring constantly. Reduce heat and simmer until thickened, about 1 minute. Remove from heat and keep warm.

Tips

Use fresh pineapple or drained canned chunks; the choice is up to you.

This recipe makes quite a bit of sauce, but I like to have extra to enjoy with an abundance of rice.

3. Meanwhile, pour enough oil into wok to come about 2 inches (10 cm) up side of pan. (Ideally, it should cover the pork slices when they are added in a single layer.) Heat until thermometer registers 350°F (180°C), or a grain of rice dropped into the hot oil floats to the top and begins to sizzle.

4. *Coating:* In a large resealable plastic bag, toss rice flour with cornstarch until combined. Drain pork, discarding any excess marinade. Add to flour mixture and toss well to coat.

5. Using tongs, fry pork, in batches and turning if necessary, until browned and crisp, about 3 minutes per batch. Transfer to a paper towel–lined plate as completed. Season to taste with salt and black pepper.

6. Drain off and discard all but 1 tbsp (15 mL) oil from wok. Return wok to medium heat. Add finger chile to taste and cook, stirring, for 30 seconds. Add sauce and cook, stirring, until slightly thickened. Stir in pork and accumulated juices, and pineapple (if using). Transfer to a warm serving platter and serve immediately.

Brazilian-Style Cassoulet (Feijoada)

Reputed to be the national dish of Brazil, *feijoada* apparently has its roots in plantation cooking; it was originally made by slaves, traditionally from leftover bits of meat, such as pigs' feet, tails and ears, and beef tongues, which were often smoked or dried. Today, it is a special-occasion dish, probably because making it is a fair bit of work. This much-simplified version makes enough for a crowd (or ample leftovers) and reheats splendidly. The spiciness comes from the chorizo, not the hot sauce, which you may or may not choose to include. It is quite rich, so serve it over plenty of hot cooked rice.

MAKES ABOUT 12 SERVINGS

GLUTEN-FREE FRIENDLY

Tips

If you are cooking for someone who is sensitive to gluten, check labels on packaged ingredients, such as stock, sausages and jerky. They can contain gluten.

To soak the dried beans for this recipe, place them in a large bowl and add about 12 cups (3 L) of water. Let stand at room temperature for 6 hours or overnight. Drain and rinse thoroughly before using.

- Large Dutch oven (see Tips, page 294)
- Blender

3 cups	dried black beans, soaked, rinsed and drained (see Tips, left)	750 mL
1½ lbs	smoked ham hock (approx.)	750 g
8 oz	slab bacon, diced	250 g
8 oz	smoked pork chop or pork ribs	250 g
4 oz	beef jerky	125 g
4 cups	chicken stock	1 L
4 oz	dry-cured chorizo sausage, thinly sliced	125 g
1 tbsp	olive oil	15 mL
1 lb	fresh (uncooked) chorizo sausage, casings removed	500 g
2	onions, finely chopped	2
6	cloves garlic	6
2	bay leaves	2

Pepper and Lime Hot Sauce (optional)

⅓ cup	freshly squeezed lime juice	75 mL
2 tsp	white vinegar	10 mL
½ tsp	salt	2 mL
4	green onions (white parts only), minced	4
10	pickled malagueta peppers, drained and minced	10
1	clove garlic, minced	1
2 tbsp	extra virgin olive oil	30 mL

Moreover ...

I have become a huge fan of pickled malagueta peppers since discovering them several years ago while shopping at that delightful New York food emporium Kalustyan's. I am rarely without a jar in the fridge so I can be sure to have these pungent Brazilian fireballs on hand for adding to dishes such as deviled eggs and homemade hot sauce. I now have a local source, but if you can't locate them, pickled piri-piri peppers make a fine substitute. That member of the *C. frutescens* family is a very close relative and probably a direct descendent of the malagueta, which arrived in Africa from Brazil via Portuguese traders.

1. In Dutch oven, combine beans, ham hock, bacon, pork chop and jerky. Add stock plus enough water to cover meat mixture and bring just to a boil. Reduce heat and simmer, skimming off scum from surface as necessary, until meats are tender, about $1\frac{1}{2}$ hours.

2. Remove ham hock and pork chop from pan and let cool. Once cool, remove meat from bones and cut into thin slices. Scoop out about 2 cups (500 mL) of the cooked beans and a bit of liquid, transfer to blender and purée until smooth. Return to pan along with sliced meat. If mixture is a bit watery, simmer for a few minutes to reduce to desired consistency. Add dry-cured chorizo and continue to simmer.

3. Meanwhile, in a skillet, heat oil over medium heat. Add fresh chorizo and onions and cook, stirring, until onions are softened and chorizo is no longer pink, about 5 minutes. Add garlic and bay leaves and cook, stirring for 1 minute. Add to Dutch oven, cover and return to a simmer. Simmer until flavors are blended, about 30 minutes. Discard bay leaves.

4. *Pepper and Lime Hot Sauce (if using):* Meanwhile, in a small bowl, combine lime juice, vinegar and salt, stirring until salt is dissolved. Stir in green onions, malagueta peppers and garlic. Whisk in olive oil until combined. Serve with feijoada.

Indonesian-Style Fried Rice (Nasi Goreng)

Nasi goreng is Indonesia's national dish. At its simplest, it is cold leftover rice, seasoned with sweet soy sauce (kecap manis) and whatever leftovers and spices the cook has on hand. Often it is topped with a fried egg and served for breakfast. Of course, it can be much more elaborate, depending on the circumstances under which it will be served. My version leans toward simplicity, making it a quick and easy weekday meal.

MAKES 4 SERVINGS

Tips

It is more authentic to use jasmine rice in this dish, but I prefer brown rice.

If you don't have kecap manis, mix together 1½ tbsp (22 mL) each soy sauce and pure maple syrup to use in place of it.

Make sure you save any leftovers, because they reheat well for lunch the next day.

Look for ready-to-cook shrimp chips at Asian markets. They are a tasty snack or accompaniment to fried rice, and they just need a quick fry to make them crispy and delicious.

To make Fried Shrimp Chips: Pour enough oil into a wok or large saucepan to come about 1 inch (2.5 cm) up the side of the pan. Heat until hot but not smoking, or until candy/deep-fry thermometer registers about 350°F (180°C). (Do not overheat. If the oil is too hot, the chips will curl up and cook unevenly.) Add shrimp chips, 2 at a time, and fry, turning constantly with tongs, until they are puffed all over, about 20 seconds. Transfer to a paper towel–lined plate and let drain.

- Wok or large skillet

2 cups	cold cooked rice (see Tips, left)	500 mL
2 tbsp	oil	30 mL
8 oz	deveined peeled shrimp, chopped	250 g
1	onion, finely chopped	1
8 oz	ground pork	250 g
4	cloves garlic, minced	4
1 to 2	red Thai bird's-eye chile(s), minced	1 to 2
3 tbsp	kecap manis (see Tips, left)	45 mL
1 tbsp	fish sauce	15 mL
4	fried eggs	4
	Fried Shrimp Chips (see Tips, left), optional	
	Sriracha sauce (optional)	

1. In wok, heat oil over medium-high heat. Add shrimp and cook, stirring, until pink and opaque throughout, about 1 minute. Using a slotted spoon, transfer to a plate.

2. Add onion and pork to wok and cook, stirring, until pork is no longer pink and onion is softened, about 5 minutes. Reduce heat to medium. Add garlic, and bird's-eye chile(s) to taste and cook, stirring, for 1 minute. Add rice, kecap manis and fish sauce and cook, stirring and breaking up any clumps with a wooden spoon, until rice is heated through. Return shrimp to pan and toss well to combine.

3. Spoon rice mixture onto 4 warm serving plates and top each with 1 of the fried eggs. Serve with shrimp chips (if using). Pass sriracha sauce (if using) at the table.

Spanish-Style Baked Eggs with Chorizo

The Spanish have many wonderful ways with eggs, not the least of which is their famous tortilla. They make various combinations of scrambled eggs with chorizo, tomatoes and peppers and serve them on bread like crostini, often as tapas. In this recipe, I have played with that idea to produce this dish. It is delicious with just a simple salad.

MAKES 4 SERVINGS

GLUTEN-FREE FRIENDLY

Tips

If you're cooking this dish for someone who can't eat gluten, read the label on your chorizo. Wheat products are often added to sausage as fillers.

If you don't have mini-cocottes on hand, use wide-mouth 8-oz (250 mL) canning jars, greased.

Vary the type of paprika to suit your taste—either sweet or smoked is delicious. Use hot with caution if your chorizo is spicy.

Use a vegetable peeler to peel the pepper.

Crushed tomatoes are often identified as passata.

If you prefer a result that resembles scrambled eggs, beat the eggs with sea salt and freshly ground black pepper before adding them to the cocottes. Omit the final seasoning with salt and pepper.

The eggs are even more tasty topped with your favorite hot sauce. Pass it at the table.

- Preheat oven to 350°F (180°C)
- Four 8-oz (250 mL) mini-cocottes, greased (see Tips, left)

2 tbsp	extra virgin olive oil	30 mL
2	cooled drained cooked potatoes, thinly sliced	2
½ tsp	paprika (approx.), see Tips, left	2 mL
1	onion, thinly sliced	1
½	red bell pepper, peeled (see Tips, left), seeded and diced	½
½	red finger chile (optional), seeded and minced	½
2	cloves garlic, minced	2
1 cup	jarred or canned crushed tomatoes	250 mL
1 cup	sweet green peas, thawed if frozen	250 mL
8 oz	dry-cured chorizo sausage, thinly sliced	250 g
8	eggs	8
	Finely chopped fresh parsley	
	Flaky sea salt and freshly ground black pepper	

1. In a skillet, heat oil over medium heat. Add potatoes and cook, turning once, until nicely browned on both sides, about 4 minutes. Sprinkle ½ tsp (2 mL) paprika over top and transfer to prepared cocottes, creating as solid a layer as possible on the bottom.

2. Return skillet to medium heat, adding more oil if necessary. Add onion, bell pepper and finger chile (if using) and cook, stirring, until softened, about 5 minutes. Add garlic and cook, stirring, for 1 minute. Add tomatoes and peas and bring to a boil. Stir in chorizo. Divide equally among cocottes.

3. Break 2 eggs into each. Sprinkle with additional paprika. Bake in preheated oven until eggs are just set, about 12 minutes. Garnish with parsley. Season with salt and freshly ground pepper.

Middle Eastern–Style Omelet (*Eggah*)

This is my interpretation of an egg dish served across the Middle East. It most closely resembles a Spanish tortilla or an Italian frittata. This particular iteration is a bit of a mash-up: the spicy sausages are a Tunisian touch, according to Middle Eastern cuisine expert Claudia Roden. If you make the Variations (below), the potatoes takes the dish into Persian territory.

MAKES 4 SERVINGS

GLUTEN-FREE FRIENDLY

Tips

Eggah does not resemble a French-style omelet, because the filling is abundant and the eggs are firmly cooked. Eggah is never served *baveuse*, the French term for "runny."

Butter, not olive oil, is often the preferred fat for cooking eggah in the Middle East.

Vary the quantity of harissa to suit your taste, bearing in mind that the sausage is also spicy.

You can easily double this recipe. Use a 12-inch (30 cm) skillet and adjust the cooking time accordingly.

To ensure this omelet is gluten-free, be sure to check the label on your harissa paste and your sausage. Some products contain wheat ingredients as fillers.

I like to serve this as a weekday dinner with a salad, but you could cut it into small wedges to serve as an appetizer. Like a Spanish tortilla, this omelet can be eaten hot or cold, which makes it great for picnics.

- 10-inch (25 cm) ovenproof skillet with lid, greased

2 tbsp	olive oil or butter (see Tips, left)	30 mL
8 oz	merguez sausage, casings removed	250 g
1	onion, finely chopped	1
2	cloves garlic, minced	2
1 tbsp	tomato paste	15 mL
1 tsp	harissa paste (approx.), see Tips, left	5 mL
6	eggs	6
¼ cup	finely chopped fresh parsley	60 mL
	Salt and freshly ground black pepper	

1. In prepared skillet, heat oil over medium heat. Add sausage and onion and cook, stirring, until sausage is lightly browned and cooked through, about 5 minutes. Stir in garlic, tomato paste and harissa. Reduce heat to low.

2. In a medium bowl, lightly beat eggs with parsley. Season to taste with salt and black pepper. Add to pan and stir well, ensuring contents are evenly distributed over bottom of pan. Cover and cook until eggs are almost set, about 10 minutes.

3. Meanwhile, preheat broiler. When eggs are almost set, place pan under preheated broiler and broil until the top is firm and lightly browned, about 2 minutes.

4. Slip omelet onto a serving plate. Cut into wedges.

Variations

Persian-Style Eggah: Cook, peel and cut 1 potato into ½-inch (1 cm) cubes. In a skillet, heat 2 tbsp (30 mL) oil over medium-high heat and cook potato until browned, about 6 minutes. Season to taste with salt, freshly ground black pepper, and sweet paprika or Aleppo pepper. Add to sausage mixture just before adding the eggs.

Vegetarian Eggah: Substitute 2 cooked potatoes for the sausage; cube and brown as for Persian-Style Eggah (above). Adjust the quantity of harissa paste accordingly.

American-Style Rubbed Ribs with Mop

Here is an easy method for producing ribs with layer after layer of flavor: season them with a rub and bake them at a low temperature. They are then ready to be finished on the barbecue. Adding the meat's cooking juices to your "mop" sauce and grilling the ribs over high heat make for a finger-licking summertime meal.

Moreover ...

Probably because I grew up in the north, I had no idea where the terms "mop" or "mop sauce" originated. So I experienced a Eureka! moment watching the "Lowcountry BBQ" episode of the PBS series "The Mind of a Chef" in which chef Sean Brock explains them. When you are cooking a very large piece of meat, the most expedient way to slather sauce on it is to put the stuff in a bucket and use a brand-new floor mop to spread it. Of course! Why hadn't I guessed that?

- Preheat oven to 325°F (160°C)
- Spice grinder, or mortar and pestle

2	racks baby back ribs, membrane removed	2
1 cup	Chile-Spiked Barbecue Sauce (page 383)	250 mL

Spice Rub

1 tsp	fennel seeds	5 mL
1 tsp	cumin seeds	5 mL
1 tsp	coriander seeds	5 mL
1 tsp	black peppercorns	5 mL
1 tsp	dried oregano	5 mL
1 tbsp	sweet paprika	15 mL
1 tsp	garlic powder or onion powder	5 mL
½ tsp	cayenne pepper	2 mL
½ tsp	salt	2 mL

1. *Spice Rub:* In a dry skillet over medium heat, toast fennel, cumin and coriander seeds, stirring constantly, until fragrant, about 3 minutes. Transfer to spice grinder. Add peppercorns and oregano and grind to a powder. Pour into a small bowl. Stir in paprika, garlic powder, cayenne and salt until well combined. Rub evenly all over ribs.

2. Place 1 rack of ribs on a large sheet of foil. Fold foil over to make a tight packet and place on a baking sheet. Repeat with second rack of ribs. Bake in preheated oven for 1 hour.

3. Preheat barbecue to high or preheat broiler. Remove ribs from foil and return to baking sheet, reserving cooking juices.

4. In a small bowl, stir reserved cooking juices with barbecue sauce until blended. Brush sauce evenly all over ribs and place on preheated grill or under preheated broiler. Grill or broil, basting occasionally with any remaining sauce, until nicely glazed.

5. Cut into individual rib portions and serve immediately.

Spicy Sausage

Sausages, both fresh and cured, were one of the world's first convenience foods. Usually made from a ground meat mix stuffed into casings, they are a quick way of adding complex flavors to any dish. It's not surprising then that many varieties are liberally seasoned with varying amounts of pungent chiles.

The most familiar examples of the genre probably come from Italian *salumi*—cured meats such as pancetta, coppa, capicolo and various types of salami and soppressata, not to mention the famous Calabrian spread *'nduja*. In Spain and Portugal, there is chorizo, an often mouth-burning pork sausage that can be dry-cured or fresh. In the Basque region of France, the milder chorizo is flavored with piment d'Espelette. Mexico does its own version, usually seasoned with ancho and pasilla chiles. It is traditionally sold fresh, not cured, but it may be pungent. There is also a Mexican green chorizo, which is liberally seasoned with fresh herbs such as parsley and cilantro. Nowadays, vegan versions of fresh chorizo are turning up. Some are spicy, but I am not certain they are authentically Mexican. When I made green chorizo with Diana Kennedy, the queen of Mexican cuisine, many years ago, the mixture contained pork in addition to herbs.

Merguez is a spicy fresh sausage that is popular in North Africa. It is usually made from lamb and seasoned with chile peppers and/or harissa paste, as well as other traditional spices, such as cumin and sumac. In China, the province of Sichuan is known for highly spiced sausages seasoned with pungent ground chiles and (sometimes) spicy chili bean paste. Hungary is also renowned for spicy sausages such as *kolbász*, which are liberally spiked with paprika of varying heat levels.

Cape Verde Sausage Stew (Cachupa)

Cape Verde is a collection of islands off the west coast of Africa, and *cachupa* is their national dish. There are many different versions, but most are based on some kind of pork or perhaps freshly caught fish, although vegetables may be substituted. Since Cape Verde was a Portuguese colony, this rendition contains chorizo. Because sausage is relatively pricy, the result is probably deserving of the description *cachupa rica*, which means it was prepared when the family was feeling prosperous.

MAKES 8 TO 10 SERVINGS

GLUTEN-FREE FRIENDLY

Tips

You will need a Dutch oven with a capacity of at least 5 quarts (5 L) to accommodate the volume of this dish.

This stew is traditionally made with pork belly, which means it is rather fatty. If you prefer a leaner result, use trimmed boneless pork butt.

If you are cooking for someone who is gluten-free, check labels on packaged ingredients, such as sausage and stock. They may contain added gluten.

To make 1 cup (250 mL) of cooked red kidney beans: soak and cook ½ cup (125 mL) dried red kidney beans, or use half of a can (14 to 19 oz/398 to 540 mL) of red kidney beans. Drain and rinse the beans before using.

- Preheat oven to 325°F (160°C)
- Large Dutch oven (see Tips, left)

1 tbsp	oil	15 mL
1	onion, finely chopped	1
4	cloves garlic, minced	4
2	bay leaves	2
1	can (14 oz/ 398 mL) tomatoes, with juice	1
2 cups	chicken stock	500 mL
1	piece (1 lb/500 g) fresh pork belly (see Tips, left), cut into 6 pieces	1
1	small green cabbage (about 1 lb/500 g), cored and quartered	1
1	sweet potato, peeled and cut into chunks (about 1 inch/2.5 cm)	1
1	can (15 oz/425 g) hominy, drained	1
1 cup	drained cooked red kidney beans (see Tips, left)	250 mL
8 oz	dry-cured chorizo sausage, thinly sliced	250 g

1. In Dutch oven, heat oil over medium heat. Add onion and cook, stirring, until softened, about 3 minutes. Add garlic and bay leaves and cook, stirring, for 1 minute. Add tomatoes and juice, and stock and bring to a boil. Add pork belly and return to a boil. Reduce heat and simmer for 30 minutes.

2. Stir in cabbage, sweet potato, hominy, kidney beans and chorizo and return to a boil. Cover and transfer to preheated oven. Bake until pork is very tender and vegetables are tender, about 30 minutes.

3. Remove from oven. Let pan stand, covered, at room temperature for about 30 minutes before serving. Discard bay leaves.

Kentucky Burgoo

Traditionally made with game, particularly squirrel, burgoo is Kentucky's state dish. While they omit squirrel from their recipe, Southern food experts the Lee Brothers include lamb shank to produce what they describe as "deep holler," a distinctly gamy flavor. I've always made my burgoo with beef and chicken, but taking a page from their playbook, I've used lamb shanks in this version. The flavors are excellent.

MAKES 6 TO 8 SERVINGS

GLUTEN-FREE FRIENDLY

Tips

This recipe was tested using 3 small lamb shanks, each halved. If your lamb shanks are large, you may want to have your butcher cut them into smaller pieces, perhaps thirds.

If you have some robust stalks of fresh thyme, substitute 2, including the stems, for the dried version.

If you prefer, substitute an extra 1 cup (250 mL) of chicken stock plus 1 tbsp (15 mL) lemon juice for the white wine.

- Preheat oven to 325°F (160°C)
- Dutch oven

4 oz	slab bacon, diced	125 g
2 lbs	lamb shanks, sliced (see Tips, left)	1 kg
6 to 8	bone-in chicken thighs	6 to 8
3	onions, finely chopped	3
2	carrots, diced	2
2	stalks celery, diced	2
6	cloves garlic, minced	6
1 tsp	salt	5 mL
1 tsp	cracked black peppercorns	5 mL
1 tsp	dried thyme (see Tips, left)	5 mL
2	bay leaves	2
2	dried red hot peppers, split lengthwise	2
1 cup	dry white wine (see Tips, left)	250 mL
1	potato, peeled and shredded	1
1	can (28 oz/796 mL) tomatoes, with juice	1
2 cups	chicken stock	500 mL
1 cup	thinly sliced trimmed okra (see Tips, opposite)	250 mL
1 cup	corn kernels	250 mL
1	red bell pepper, seeded and diced	1
1	green bell pepper, seeded and diced	1
1 to 2	jalapeño pepper(s), seeded and minced (see Tips, opposite)	1 to 2
	Salt and freshly ground black pepper	
	Worcestershire sauce	
	Finely chopped fresh parsley	

Tips

Okra, a tropical vegetable, has great flavor but becomes unpleasantly sticky when overcooked. Choose young okra pods that are 2 to 4 inches (5 to 10 cm) long and don't feel sticky to the touch. (If they are sticky, they are too ripe.) Gently scrub the pods and cut off the top and tail before slicing.

A burgoo should be spicy, but my version is less heavy on the chile peppers than some. If you like heat, use the second jalapeño. You could also stir in a little cayenne pepper—or a hotter fresh chile, seeded and diced—with the garlic in Step 2.

When cooking for people who are eating gluten-free, always check the labels if using prepared products such as chicken stock and Worcestershire sauce. They may contain added gluten.

1. In Dutch oven over medium-high heat, sauté bacon until crisp. Using a slotted spoon, transfer to a plate and set aside. Add lamb to pan, in batches, and cook, stirring, until lightly browned on all sides, about 4 minutes per batch. Transfer to a plate as completed and set aside. Add chicken to pan, in batches, and brown on all sides, about 4 minutes per batch. Transfer to a plate as completed and set aside.

2. Reduce heat to medium. Add onions, carrots and celery to pan and cook, stirring, until softened, about 7 minutes. Add garlic, salt, peppercorns, thyme, bay leaves and dried hot peppers and cook, stirring, for 1 minute. Add wine and bring to a boil. Boil, stirring and scraping up browned bits from bottom of pan, for 2 minutes.

3. Stir in potato, and tomatoes and juice, and bring to a boil. Return bacon, lamb and chicken to pan. Pour in stock and enough water to cover meat mixture. Return to a boil.

4. Cover and transfer to preheated oven. Bake until lamb is very tender, about $1^1/_2$ hours.

5. Remove from oven. Add okra, corn, red and green bell peppers, and jalapeño pepper(s) to taste and stir well. Cover, return to oven and bake until corn is tender, about 20 minutes. Discard bay leaves. Season to taste with salt, black pepper and Worcestershire sauce. Garnish to taste with parsley.

Cape Malay Lamb Curry

South Africa's Cape Malay community is a unique blend of various ethnicities: Indonesian, South Asian and African, to name just three. Not surprisingly, the resulting culture, which might be described as "fusion," is distinctive, particularly in areas such as music and cuisine. In cooking, the key flavors are based on blends of spices, such as turmeric, cardamom, ginger, garlic, coriander, cumin, cinnamon and, of course, chiles. Serve this delicious curry with your favorite kind of hot cooked rice.

MAKES 4 TO 6 SERVINGS

GLUTEN-FREE FRIENDLY

Tip

This recipe produces a mildly pungent curry. If you prefer one that's a bit spicier, increase the quantity of chiles.

- Preheat oven to 325°F (160°C)
- Dutch oven
- Spice grinder, or mortar and pestle

2 tbsp	oil, divided	30 mL
2 lbs	trimmed boneless stewing lamb, cut into cubes (about 1 inch/2.5 cm)	1 kg
2	onions, finely chopped	2
4	cloves garlic, minced	4
1 tbsp	minced gingerroot	15 mL
1 tsp	turmeric	5 mL
1 tsp	salt	5 mL
1	piece (about 2 inches/5 cm long) cinnamon stick	1
8	whole cloves	8
4	black cardamom pods, crushed	4
2	dried red hot peppers, crumbled	2
1 tbsp	tomato paste	15 mL
2	large potatoes, peeled and cut into small chunks	2
1	can (14 oz/398 mL) diced tomatoes, with juice	1
2 cups	chicken stock (approx.)	500 mL
	Salt and freshly ground black pepper	
	Finely chopped fresh cilantro	
	Minced green finger chile (optional)	

Spice Blend

1 tbsp	cumin seeds	15 mL
1 tbsp	coriander seeds	15 mL
1 tsp	fennel seeds	5 mL

Tip

When cooking for people who are gluten-free, always check the labels if using prepared products such as chicken stock. They may contain added gluten.

1. *Spice Blend:* In Dutch oven, toast cumin, coriander and fennel seeds, stirring, until fragrant, about 3 minutes. Transfer to spice grinder and grind to a powder. Set aside.

2. In same Dutch oven, heat 1 tbsp (15 mL) of the oil over medium-high heat. Add lamb, in batches and adding more of the remaining oil as necessary, and sauté until browned on all sides, about 4 minutes per batch. Transfer to a plate as completed and set aside.

3. Reduce heat to medium. Add onions and cook, stirring, until softened, about 3 minutes. Add garlic, ginger, turmeric, salt, cinnamon stick, cloves, cardamom, dried hot peppers and spice blend and cook, stirring, for 1 minute. Stir in tomato paste.

4. Return lamb and accumulated juices to pan and stir well to coat. Stir in potatoes, tomatoes and juice, and stock. Bring to a boil. Cover and transfer to preheated oven. Bake until lamb and potatoes are very tender, about $1\frac{1}{2}$ hours.

5. Season to taste with salt and black pepper. Garnish to taste with cilantro, and fresh chile (if using).

Kashmiri-Style Lamb Curry (Rogan Josh)

Because this curry originated in Kashmir, I recommend using Kashmiri chile powder if you can find it. It is milder than cayenne, the flavor is lovely and it colors the dish a beautiful shade of red. Serve this as the centerpiece of an Indian meal, with rice, naan and raita.

MAKES 6 SERVINGS

GLUTEN-FREE FRIENDLY

Tips

If you don't have almond flour, substitute an equal quantity of all-purpose flour.

Dried Kashmiri chiles, whole and ground, are widely available in Indian markets.

If you can't find Kashmiri chile powder, for every 1 tsp (5 mL) called for, substitute 1½ tsp (7 mL) sweet paprika and ½ tsp (2 mL) cayenne pepper.

- Dutch oven
- Spice grinder, or mortar and pestle

1½ lbs	boneless leg of lamb, cut into cubes	750 g
2 tbsp	clarified butter (ghee) or oil	30 mL
1	onion, finely chopped	1
1	bay leaf	1
1 tsp	turmeric	10 mL
1	piece (2 inches/5 cm long) cinnamon stick	1
2 tbsp	almond flour (see Tips, left)	30 mL
2 tsp	Kashmiri chile powder (see Tips, left)	10 mL
2 cups	chicken stock	500 mL
2 tbsp	tomato paste	30 mL
1½ cups	diced (½ inch/1 cm) seeded peeled butternut squash (about 12 oz/375 g)	375 mL
½ cup	frozen sweet green peas	125 mL
	Finely chopped fresh cilantro	

Marinade

1 cup	plain full-fat Greek-style yogurt	250 mL
2 tbsp	freshly squeezed lime juice	30 mL
1 tbsp	minced gingerroot	15 mL
1 tbsp	minced garlic	15 mL
1 tsp	salt	5 mL

Spice Blend

2 tsp	cumin seeds	10 mL
2 tsp	coriander seeds	10 mL
2 tsp	fennel seeds	10 mL

1. *Marinade:* In a bowl large enough to accommodate all of the lamb, stir together yogurt, lime juice, ginger, garlic and salt. Add lamb and toss well to coat. Let stand at room temperature for at least 30 minutes or cover and refrigerate overnight.

Chile Savvy

Kashmiri chiles are a type of *C. annuum* chile that originated in Kashmir, India. However, like cayenne, this term has become a catchall for any dried red chile of medium length and heat.

2. *Spice Blend:* Meanwhile, in Dutch oven, toast cumin, coriander and fennel seeds until fragrant, about 3 minutes. Transfer to spice grinder and grind to a powder. Set aside.

3. In same Dutch oven, heat clarified butter over medium heat. Add onion and cook, stirring, until softened, about 3 minutes. Add spice blend, bay leaf, turmeric and cinnamon stick and cook, stirring, until fragrant, about 30 seconds. Add lamb and marinade and cook, stirring often, until yogurt thickens and begins to dry, about 15 minutes. Stir in almond flour and chile powder until lamb is well coated.

4. Stir in stock and tomato paste and bring to a boil. Reduce heat, cover and simmer for 30 minutes. Stir in squash. Cover and cook until squash is almost tender, about 15 minutes. Stir in peas and cook until tender, about 5 minutes. Discard bay leaf. Garnish to taste with cilantro and serve immediately.

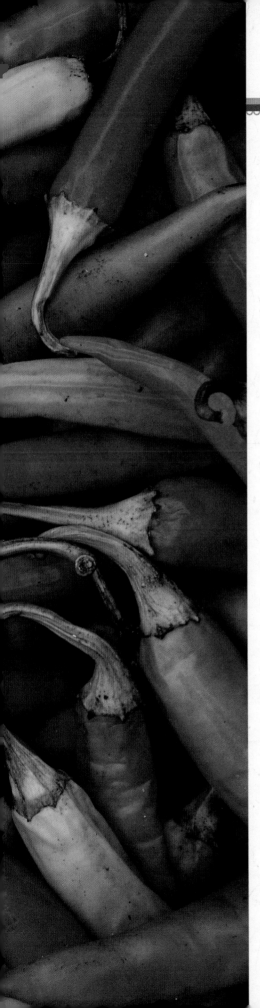

Meatless Mains

Caribbean Pepper Pot

This Caribbean-inspired soupy vegetable stew is very different from Philadelphia pepper pot, which was originally made with tripe and black peppercorns. The island version contains a hodgepodge of local ingredients. The coconut milk produces a nicely spicy, lusciously creamy sauce. This recipe makes a large quantity, so it's ideal for a buffet; leftovers also keep well.

MAKES 10 TO 12 SERVINGS

VEGAN FRIENDLY

GLUTEN-FREE FRIENDLY

Tips

If you are cooking for someone who is gluten-free, check labels on packaged ingredients, such as stock. They can contain gluten.

This dish is typically made with a variety of *Capsicum chinense*, such as Scotch bonnet or habanero peppers. However, in *The Carolina Rice Cook Book*, which was published in 1901, Louisa Stoney calls for chopped pickled or fresh long red peppers to make her pepper pot, a version that is similar to the ones made in the Caribbean, so feel free to consider red finger chiles as an option.

To make 3 cups (750 mL) of cooked red kidney beans: Soak and cook 1½ cups (375 mL) dried red kidney beans, or use 1½ cans (each 14 to 19 oz/398 to 540 mL) of red kidney beans. Drain and rinse before using.

Callaloo, also known as pigweed or amaranth leaves, is becoming increasingly available from greengrocers. Look for it in farmers' markets, as well.

• Dutch oven

1 tbsp	oil	15 mL
2	onions, thinly sliced on the vertical	2
4	cloves garlic, minced	4
2 tbsp	minced gingerroot	30 mL
2	Scotch bonnet peppers, minced	2
1 tbsp	each sweet paprika, ground cumin and dried oregano	15 mL
1 tsp	each ground allspice, dried thyme and salt	5 mL
2	bay leaves	2
1 tbsp	packed brown sugar	15 mL
½ cup	brown long-grain rice	125 mL
1	can (28 oz/796 mL) diced tomatoes, with juice	1
4 cups	cubed (1 inch/2.5 cm) seeded peeled butternut squash (about 1)	1 L
3 cups	drained cooked red kidney beans	750 mL
2 cups	vegetable stock or water	500 mL
4 cups	chopped trimmed callaloo or kale	1 L
1	can (14 oz/400 mL) coconut milk	1
	Salt and freshly ground black pepper	
	Finely chopped fresh cilantro (optional)	

1. In Dutch oven, heat oil over medium heat. Add onions and cook, stirring, until softened, about 3 minutes. Add garlic, ginger and Scotch bonnet peppers and cook, stirring, for 1 minute. Add paprika, cumin, oregano, allspice, thyme, salt and bay leaves and cook, stirring, for 1 minute. Stir in brown sugar. Add rice and cook, stirring, until well coated.

2. Add tomatoes and juice, squash, beans and stock and bring to a boil. Reduce heat and simmer until squash is tender, about 30 minutes.

3. Stir in callaloo and coconut milk. Cover and cook until callaloo and rice are tender, about 15 minutes. Discard bay leaves. Season to taste with additional salt and black pepper. Garnish to taste with cilantro (if using).

Spanish-Style Poor Man's Potatoes (*Patatas a lo Pobre*)

This classic Spanish dish consists of potatoes seasoned with caramelized onions and an abundance of peppers and olive oil. It is rustic and delicious. As the name implies, it is meant to be served as a main course, without expensive meat. I enjoy it as a main dish with a green salad on the side, but it also makes a tasty accompaniment to simple grilled meat.

MAKES 4 MAIN-COURSE SERVINGS

VEGAN FRIENDLY

GLUTEN-FREE FRIENDLY

Tips

If you don't have an ovenproof skillet, use a 13- by 9-inch (33 by 23 cm) glass baking dish. After browning the potatoes in a regular skillet, transfer them to the baking dish and set aside. Complete the recipe, transferring the pepper mixture to the baking dish.

You can easily turn this into a meat-based dish by adding 4 oz (125 g) dry-cured chorizo, thinly sliced. Use chorizo that is spiced to suit your taste (mild or hot) and stir it in just before garnishing with the parsley.

- Preheat oven to 375°F (190°C)
- Large ovenproof skillet (see Tips, left)

½ cup	extra virgin olive oil, divided	125 mL
2 lbs	waxy potatoes, cut into ½-inch (1 cm) slices	1 kg
½ tsp	hot smoked paprika	2 mL
2	onions, thinly sliced on the vertical	2
4	cloves garlic, minced	4
2	bay leaves	2
1	green bell pepper, seeded and thinly sliced	1
1	red bell pepper, seeded and thinly sliced	1
	Salt and freshly ground black pepper	
	Finely chopped parsley leaves	

1. In skillet, heat 2 tbsp (30 mL) of the oil over medium heat. Add potatoes and cook, turning, until lightly browned on both sides, about 5 minutes. Sprinkle with paprika. Transfer to a plate and set aside.

2. Add onions to pan and cook, stirring and adding more of the remaining oil as necessary, for 2 minutes. Reduce heat and cook, stirring occasionally, until onions are golden, about 5 minutes. Add garlic and bay leaves and cook, stirring, for 1 minute. Add green and red bell peppers and cook, stirring, until tender, about 5 minutes. Return potatoes to pan and stir well to combine. Season to taste with salt and black pepper.

3. Pour remaining oil over potato mixture and transfer to preheated oven. Bake until potatoes are tender, about 20 minutes. Discard bay leaves. Garnish with parsley.

Variation

Substitute small new potatoes for the waxy potatoes called for in the recipe. Depending on their size, cut them in half or into thirds before browning in Step 1.

Malaysian-Style Eggplant Curry (Brinjal Curry)

This Malaysian specialty is usually made with a large round eggplant known as *dayak*, which is slightly sour. By all means, use that variety if you have access to it. I find that regular Italian eggplant works just fine in this recipe, though.

MAKES 4 SERVINGS

VEGAN FRIENDLY

GLUTEN-FREE FRIENDLY

Tips

After trimming and peeling off the tough outer layers of the lemongrass, grate the inner core with a sharp-toothed grater, such as those made by Microplane.

I have used miso rather than traditional fish sauce so that this recipe is vegan friendly. I like brown rice miso because it is gluten-free; if you are not sensitive to gluten, any miso will work well in this recipe. If you aren't a vegetarian, you could substitute an equal quantity of fish sauce.

1 tbsp	coarse sea salt	15 mL
1	large eggplant, peeled and cubed	1
¼ cup	coconut oil (approx.), divided	60 mL
1	onion, chopped	1
2	cloves garlic, minced	2
1	stalk lemongrass, trimmed and grated (see Tips, left)	1
3	dried red chiles, broken into thirds	3
1 tbsp	miso paste (see Tips, left)	15 mL
1 cup	coconut milk	250 mL
	Salt and freshly ground black pepper	
	Thinly sliced red or green finger chile, or minced red Thai bird's-eye chile	

1. Bring a large saucepan of water to a boil. Add salt and return to a boil. Add eggplant and return to a boil. Boil for 2 minutes. Drain and let cool enough to handle. Using your hands, squeeze out the excess moisture. Transfer eggplant to a clean tea towel and pat dry.

2. In a skillet, heat 2 tbsp (30 mL) of the oil over medium heat. Add half of the eggplant and cook, stirring, until browned on all sides, about 4 minutes. Transfer to a plate as completed and set aside. Repeat with remaining eggplant and oil.

3. Add onion to pan and cook, stirring and adding more oil if necessary, until softened, about 3 minutes. Add garlic, lemongrass and dried chiles and cook, stirring, for 1 minute. Stir in miso. Return eggplant to pan and toss well to coat. Stir in coconut milk and bring to a boil.

4. Reduce heat and simmer until eggplant is meltingly tender, about 20 minutes. Season to taste with salt (if necessary) and black pepper. Garnish to taste with finger chile.

Caramelized Tempeh with Chiles

Tempeh is a fermented soybean cake. It was invented in Indonesia, where it has been a staple for centuries. Not surprisingly, this classic chile-spiced treatment is also Indonesian and delivers a delicious balance of hot and sweet tastes. Serve a simple vegetable side with the tempeh and rice.

MAKES 4 SERVINGS

VEGAN FRIENDLY

GLUTEN-FREE FRIENDLY

Tips

If you're cooking for people who are avoiding gluten, check your tempeh to make sure it is free of grains, such as wheat. Also use gluten-free soy sauce or wheat-free tamari.

To make tamarind water: In a small saucepan, combine 1 cup (250 mL) water and 2 tbsp (30 mL) chopped tamarind pulp. Bring to a boil. Reduce heat and simmer for 5 minutes. Strain through a fine-mesh sieve into a bowl, using the back of a spoon to press the solids and remove as much liquid as possible. Discard solids. Measure ¾ cup (175 mL) of the liquid and use in recipe, discarding any excess.

¾ cup	tamarind water (see Tips, left)	175 mL
1 cup	peanut oil	250 mL
1 lb	tempeh, thinly sliced (about ½ inch/1 cm)	500 g
2	shallots, thinly sliced	2
4	cloves garlic, thinly sliced	4
1 tbsp	minced gingerroot	15 mL
1 to 2	red finger chile(s), thinly sliced	1 to 2
¼ cup	coconut sugar	60 mL
2 tbsp	soy sauce	30 mL
	Hot cooked rice	

1. Make tamarind water and set aside. In a skillet, heat oil over medium-high heat. Add tempeh, in batches if necessary, and cook, turning, just until golden on both sides, about 4 minutes per batch. Transfer to a paper towel–lined plate as completed and let drain. Set aside.

2. Drain all but 2 tbsp (30 mL) of the oil from pan. Reduce heat to low. Add shallots, garlic and ginger and cook, stirring, until softened, about 4 minutes. Add finger chile(s) to taste, and coconut sugar and cook, stirring, until sugar is dissolved.

3. Stir in reserved tamarind water and soy sauce. Bring to a boil. Reduce heat and simmer until mixture is thickened to the consistency of liquid honey, about 3 minutes. Return tempeh to pan and turn to coat with sauce. Cook until heated through, about 2 minutes. Serve with rice.

Indonesian Mixed Vegetables (Gado Gado)

Gado gado means "mixture" in Indonesian, and there are many different versions of this dish throughout that country. Some are salads of raw ingredients, while others are main-course meals with blanched vegetables and fried tofu or tempeh. It may be garnished with crispy fried shallots or accompanied by fried shrimp chips, and is usually finished with cooked eggs and peanut sauce. I have tailored this version to make it suitable for vegans, but you can adjust the recipe to suit your needs.

MAKES 4 SERVINGS

VEGAN FRIENDLY

GLUTEN-FREE FRIENDLY

Tip

If you are avoiding gluten, be sure to use gluten-free kecap manis, and gluten-free soy sauce or wheat-free tamari.

- Food processor

2 tbsp	peanut oil	30 mL
1	block (1 lb/500 g) firm tofu, cut into strips (about 1 inch/2.5 cm wide by ½ inch/1 cm thick)	1
2	hard-cooked eggs (optional), quartered	2
	Toasted sesame oil	

Vegetables

½	small head green cabbage, cored and thinly sliced	½
2 cups	bean sprouts	500 mL
2 cups	sliced (about 2 inches/5 cm long) trimmed green beans (about 8 oz/250 g)	500 mL
1	red bell pepper, seeded and diced	1
2	carrots, shredded	2
12	sprigs watercress	12

Peanut Sauce

½ cup	roasted peanuts	125 mL
1	red Thai bird's-eye chile, chopped	1
1	clove garlic, chopped	1
1 tbsp	coconut sugar	15 mL
⅓ cup	water	75 mL
½ cup	coconut milk	125 mL
2 tbsp	kecap manis (see Tips, opposite)	30 mL
2 tsp	unseasoned rice vinegar	10 mL

1. In a large skillet, heat oil over medium-high heat. Add tofu, in batches if necessary, and fry, turning once, until golden on both sides, about 5 minutes. Transfer to a paper towel–lined plate and let drain. Set aside.

Tips

If you don't have kecap manis, substitute 1 tbsp + 1 tsp (20 mL) soy sauce mixed with 2 tsp (10 mL) maple syrup. It will have a similar sweet-salty taste.

If you're cooking for someone with a peanut allergy (who doesn't mind a little fish sauce), substitute Coconut Sambal (page 376) for the peanut sauce.

2. *Vegetables:* Bring a large saucepan of salted water to a boil. Add cabbage and return to a boil. Boil for 3 minutes. Using a slotted spoon, scoop out cabbage and scatter evenly on a deep serving platter.

3. Add bean sprouts to boiling water and return to a boil. Cook for 10 seconds. Using a slotted spoon, scoop out bean sprouts and arrange evenly over cabbage.

4. Add green beans to boiling water and return to a boil. Cook until tender-crisp, about 4 minutes. Drain and arrange evenly over bean sprouts.

5. Sprinkle bell pepper and shredded carrots evenly over green beans. Surround with watercress. Garnish with tofu, and egg quarters (if using). Drizzle with sesame oil.

6. *Peanut Sauce:* In food processor fitted with the metal blade, process peanuts until finely ground. Add bird's-eye chile, garlic and coconut sugar and pulse to combine. Add water and pulse to form a paste. Transfer to a small saucepan. Stir in coconut milk and cook, stirring, until thickened, about 5 minutes. Remove from heat. Stir in kecap manis and vinegar. Pour evenly over vegetable mixture.

Variations

Indonesian peanut sauce is traditionally made with fish sauce or dried shrimp paste (blachan). I have used kecap manis, a sweet soy sauce, to make the recipe suitable for vegetarians. If you are not cooking for vegetarians, you can substitute 2 tbsp (30 mL) fish sauce for the kecap manis.

If you are serving this dish to pescetarians, feel free to add some fried shrimp chips (see Tips, page 288), along with the eggs and tofu.

Spinach and Tomato Dal

Dal can be pungent or very tame, and it plays a significant role in Indian cuisine. This mildly spiced version makes a delicious main course over hot cooked rice; it can also be served as a side dish.

Tips

Dal is the word for both split pulses (such as split peas or red lentils) and the dishes made from them.

If you are cooking for someone who is gluten-free, check labels on packaged ingredients, such as stock. They can contain gluten.

To rinse split peas before cooking them: Place split peas in the saucepan in which they will be cooked and cover with water. Using your hands, rub the peas together until the water becomes very cloudy. Drain. Repeat 3 more times or until the water is clear. Proceed with Step 1.

You will need about 8 cups (2 L) chopped fresh spinach leaves. For convenience, you can substitute 1 package (10 oz/300 g) frozen spinach, thawed, for the fresh.

The yogurt adds a pleasantly creamy finish—if you are avoiding dairy, you can omit it or substitute a vegan version.

- Mortar and pestle, or spice grinder

1 cup	yellow split peas, rinsed and drained (see Tips, left)	250 mL
1 tbsp	each cumin seeds and coriander seeds	15 mL
2 tbsp	clarified butter (ghee) or oil	30 mL
1	onion, finely chopped	1
1 tbsp	each minced garlic and gingerroot	15 mL
1 tsp	salt	5 mL
½ to 1 tsp	red chile powder, such as Kashmiri	2 to 5 mL
½ tsp	turmeric	2 mL
	Freshly ground black pepper	
1	can (28 oz/796 mL) tomatoes, with juice, coarsely chopped	1
1 cup	vegetable stock or water	250 mL
1 tbsp	freshly squeezed lemon juice	15 mL
8 oz	trimmed fresh spinach leaves, chopped	250 g
	Plain dairy or vegan yogurt (optional)	

1. In a large saucepan, combine rinsed split peas with 4 cups (1 L) fresh water. Bring to a boil. Skim off any foam. Reduce heat to low, partially cover and simmer until peas are very tender, about 30 minutes. Drain.

2. In another large saucepan, toast cumin and coriander seeds over medium heat, stirring, until fragrant, about 3 minutes. Transfer to mortar and grind to a powder.

3. In same pan, heat clarified butter over medium heat. Add onion and cook, stirring, until softened, about 3 minutes. Add garlic and ginger and cook, stirring, for 1 minute. Stir in salt, chile powder to taste, turmeric and reserved cumin mixture. Season to taste with black pepper. Stir in tomatoes and juice, and bring to a boil. Stir in drained cooked split peas, stock and lemon juice. Reduce heat and simmer until flavors are melded, about 5 minutes.

4. Add spinach, in batches, stirring to submerge each before adding the next. Cover and cook until spinach is wilted, about 5 minutes.

5. Ladle into warm serving bowls. Drizzle to taste with yogurt (if using).

Moroccan Chickpea Soup (*Harira*)

This traditional Moroccan soup, often made with lamb, is usually served during Ramadan, at the end of a day of fasting. In my opinion, this vegetarian version is equally robust. Served with warm pitas, it makes a great light dinner. A salad of shredded carrots topped with a sprinkle of currants adds color to the meal and complements its Middle Eastern flavors.

MAKES 6 SERVINGS

VEGAN FRIENDLY

GLUTEN-FREE FRIENDLY

Tips

If you are cooking for someone who is gluten-free, check labels on packaged ingredients, such as stock. They can contain gluten.

To make 2 cups (500 mL) of cooked chickpeas: Soak and cook 1 cup (250 mL) dried chickpeas, or use 1 can (14 to 19 oz/398 to 540 mL) chickpeas. Drain and rinse before using.

Use the type of lentil you prefer or have on hand. Red, green or brown all work well in this soup. For red lentils, reduce the cooking time in Step 2 to about 20 minutes.

There is a modest amount of harissa in this soup, which produces a mildly seasoned result. Since harissa provides a concentrated hit of capsaicin and prepared versions vary in terms of their pungency, I recommend starting with a small amount. You can always add more at the table to suit your taste.

- Large stockpot or Dutch oven

1 tbsp	oil	15 mL
2	onions, coarsely chopped	2
4	stalks celery, diced	4
2	carrots, diced	2
4	cloves garlic, minced	4
1 tbsp	minced gingerroot	15 mL
1 tsp	each turmeric, ground cumin and ground coriander	5 mL
Pinch	saffron	Pinch
1	piece (about 2 inches/5 cm long) cinnamon stick	1
1	can (28 oz/796 mL) diced tomatoes, with juice	1
4 cups	vegetable stock	1 L
2 cups	drained cooked chickpeas (see Tips, left)	500 mL
½ cup	lentils (see Tips, left), rinsed	125 mL
3 cups	chopped trimmed spinach leaves	750 mL
¼ tsp	harissa paste (approx.), see Tips, left	1 mL
2 tbsp	freshly squeezed lemon juice	30 mL
	Salt and freshly ground black pepper	
½ cup	finely chopped fresh parsley	125 mL

1. In stockpot, heat oil over medium heat. Add onions, celery and carrots and cook, stirring, until softened, about 5 minutes. Add garlic, ginger, turmeric, cumin, coriander, saffron and cinnamon stick and cook, stirring, for 1 minute. Add tomatoes and juice, and stock and bring to a boil.

2. Add chickpeas and lentils and return to a boil. Cover, reduce heat and simmer until lentils are tender, about 30 minutes. Stir in spinach and harissa. Cover and cook until spinach is wilted, about 5 minutes. Add lemon juice and season to taste with salt and black pepper. Return to a boil. Stir in parsley.

3. Ladle into warm serving bowls. Pass additional harissa paste at the table.

Jollof Rice

This dish is a staple of West African countries, such as Nigeria. As is the case with jambalaya, which it is thought to have inspired, every cook has his or her own spin. Many versions include tomatoes and are spiked with tomato paste, onions and hot red chiles. Meat, usually in the form of chicken, is often added or served alongside. If you are not serving this dish to vegetarians, pick up a rotisserie chicken on your way home, slice it up and serve it alongside the rice for an easy dinner. The meal may be delicious enough to merit a bottle of wine.

MAKES 6 SERVINGS

VEGAN FRIENDLY

GLUTEN-FREE FRIENDLY

Tips

If you have leftover Roasted Pepper Strips (*Rajas*) (page 368), substitute 1½ cups (375 mL) of them, chopped, for the green bell pepper. Mixed roasted peppers produce a particularly luscious result—I've used a combination of red and green bell and poblano.

In Africa, a fiery fatalii chile would likely be added to this dish, because West Africans like their joloff rice very spicy. The Scotch bonnet or habanero is a good alternative. If you are heat-averse, feel free to reduce the quantity of chile to taste.

In Africa, palm oil is used to soften the vegetables. It adds an interesting orangish hue to the dish. If you can find a sustainable version (see Tips, page 114), use it here.

If you prefer, substitute an equal quantity of long-grain brown rice for the white. After boiling for 1 minute (Step 2) reduce heat to low and simmer for 20 minutes before completing the recipe.

- Large heavy saucepan or Dutch oven

2 tbsp	oil	30 mL
1	onion, finely chopped	1
1	green bell pepper, seeded and diced (see Tips, left)	1
1	Scotch bonnet or habanero pepper (see Tips, left), minced	1
4	cloves garlic, minced	4
1 tsp	dried thyme	5 mL
1 tsp	curry powder	5 mL
1	bay leaf	1
2 cups	long-grain white rice (see Tips, left)	500 mL
4 cups	vegetable stock	1 L
2 cups	canned or jarred crushed tomatoes (passata)	500 mL
2 cups	frozen sweet green peas	500 mL
2 tbsp	tomato paste	30 mL

1. In saucepan, heat oil over medium heat. Add onion and bell pepper and cook, stirring, until softened, about 5 minutes. Add Scotch bonnet pepper, garlic, thyme, curry powder and bay leaf and cook, stirring, for 1 minute. Add rice and toss well to coat.

2. Stir in stock and bring to a boil. Boil for 1 minute. Stir in tomatoes, peas and tomato paste. Cover, reduce heat to low and simmer until rice is very tender, about 20 minutes. Discard bay leaf. Serve immediately.

Focus on: Chiles in Africa

One of the few things you can say for sure about chiles in Africa is that they are used extensively. The continent is too broad and diverse to generalize otherwise, and many—if not most—people grow their own in household gardens, making it challenging to document the varieties that are actually used. However, there is little doubt that the African love of smoldering hot peppers has influenced cuisine in the Americas and, ultimately, around the world.

Chiles reached the continent thanks to Portuguese traders. When they arrived in the New World, usually as slaves, Africans brought their love of fiery foods with them, influencing the cuisines of places such as Brazil, the American South and Cuba. For instance, jollof rice (page 313), which originated in West Africa, is thought to be the progenitor of dishes such as Moors and Christians (page 320), jambalaya (page 198) and feijoada (page 286), among many others.

Today, numerous varieties of chiles are grown throughout Africa, from Angola to Zimbabwe and in every country in between. The most widely used chiles in Africa are likely a type of cultivated bird pepper belonging to the C. frutescens species, often called piri-piri. These tiny peppers have a volcanic effect. The term piri-piri refers not only to the pepper but also to the eponymous sauce and many of the dishes cooked in it. Piri-piri sauce is widely used in parts of previously Portuguese Africa and in Portugal, as well. Piri-piri is also the national dish of Mozambique—made with shrimp, chicken or fish and often cooked in coconut milk, it invariably includes a healthy measure of piri-piri sauce. Since 1987, thanks to Nando's, a fast-food restaurant chain with a "Mozambican/Portuguese theme," piri-piri sauce is actively represented in at least 30 countries throughout the world.

The dishes in which chiles are used range widely, depending on the locale. In North Africa, for instance, peppers are used in much the same way and in many of the same dishes that characterize Middle Eastern cuisine (see page 122). In Kenya, Indian influences are strong. The first time I ever consumed curry to cool off was on a sweltering day in Mombasa, possibly not far from where they grow the pepper of the same name. I don't know if my lunch contained Mombasa chiles, which are supposedly sweat-inducing, but to my surprise the curry did make me feel more comfortable. One popular dish in Kenya is a particularly pungent stew called kima. It is made from chopped beef seasoned with red chile powder, among other spices, and is strongly reminiscent of Indian keema.

Ethiopia (and, to some extent, its neighbor Eritrea) is probably an entity unto itself. Its cuisine makes liberal use of a signature spice blend called berbere. (Berbere can also be made into a paste that works like Thai curry pastes, but with a different flavor profile.) Berbere turns up in dishes featuring a wide array of ingredients, from eggs and lentils to ground meat. It is even used to season kita firfir, a spiced flatbread often eaten for breakfast.

Nigerian food is legendary for its spiciness. It is a subject that crops up in the work of one of my favorite authors, Chimamanda Ngozi Adichie. She often mentions chile cravings in her novels, and when her characters are not in Nigeria they are likely to express longings for a fiery bowl of joloff rice. In Nigeria, as well as in Senegal, a dish of the West African Hausa people known as suya or *dibi Hausa* is very popular. It is skewers of grilled meat, such as lamb, that are sprinkled with a dry mixture of peanuts and spices, including ground chile. I assume the blend is the same as or similar to the one I know as *tsire*, which I have used use as a coating for fish or chicken.

I have a recipe for *thiebou jenn*, the national dish of Senegal. I found it intriguing because it calls for a liberal amount of Scotch bonnet pepper—in my experience, that is a Jamaican ingredient. Many other recipes for regional dishes from this part of the world also call for Scotch bonnet peppers, which I initially found peculiar. Then I realized that during the slave trade, many West Africans were transported to Caribbean islands, such as Jamaica, to work on plantations. They took their love of spicy foods with them and, when slavery ended, some of their descendants returned to Africa with seeds of their favorite chiles, which they planted.

This scenario provides a plausible explanation for the unusual presence of the fatalii chile, one of the few members of the *C. chinense* family found in Africa. It has been described as an African version of the Scotch bonnet pepper.

Chile experts Dave DeWitt and Paul Bosland believe the fatalii was developed in Central Africa from peppers brought to Africa by former slaves who had returned from the Americas. They comment on its exceptionally fruity flavor and particularly intense heat, thanks to the alkaloid dihydrocapsaicin it contains.

Not surprisingly, hot sauces are widely used throughout West Africa. Moyo sauce, a fresh tomato salsa with a smoking amount of hot chile pepper, is a popular street-food condiment. In Senegal, kani sauce (which may be cooked or served raw) is used on just about everything, especially popular street-food snacks, such as *accara* (fritters made from black-eyed peas). Also known as *confiture de piment*, kani sauce is a salsa of tomatoes, onion, garlic and other spices, and some variety of an incendiary *C. chinense* chile. Another popular street food is deep-fried plantains sprinkled with chile and other spices, known as *kelewele* in Ghana and *aloco* in Ivory Coast.

In South Africa, Cape Malay is famous for its distinctive peppery cuisine. It features many signature curry-type dishes, such as Bobotie (page 230) and Cape Malay Lamb Curry (page 298).

Vegetable Couscous

Couscous is eaten across North Africa. It is often cooked with smen, a type of clarified butter made from naturally curdled cream, which adds a deep umami note to dishes. If you are not cooking for vegans and can find this special ingredient, by all means use it. If you can't find it, melted clarified butter, or ghee, will add a more subtle but still lovely flavor. If you do not consume dairy, extra virgin olive oil works just fine in its place.

Tip

Since harissa is a prepared product, its heat level can vary. Start with the amount called for in the ingredient list. Taste the dish after adding the vegetables and stock and increase the quantity, if desired.

1 tbsp	oil	15 mL
1	onion, finely chopped	1
1	red bell pepper, seeded and diced	1
2	cloves garlic, minced	2
2 tsp	minced gingerroot	10 mL
1 tsp	ground cumin	5 mL
1 tsp	sweet paprika	5 mL
1 tsp	salt	5 mL
½ tsp	harissa paste (see Tip, left)	2 mL
1	can (14 oz/398 mL) diced tomatoes, with juice	1
2	carrots, quartered lengthwise and cut into 2-inch (5 cm) pieces	2
1	small zucchini (about 6 oz/175 g) peeled, quartered lengthwise and cut into 2-inch (5 cm) pieces	1
1	sweet potato (about 8 oz/250 g), peeled, quartered lengthwise and cut into 2-inch (5 cm) pieces	1
1	white turnip (about 6 oz/175 g), peeled and cut into small chunks	1
2 cups	vegetable stock or water, divided	500 mL
1 cup	whole wheat, spelt or barley couscous	250 mL
2 tbsp	melted smen, clarified butter (ghee) or olive oil	30 mL
	Finely chopped fresh parsley	

1. In a skillet, heat oil over medium heat. Add onion and cook, stirring, until softened, about 3 minutes. Add bell pepper, garlic and ginger and cook, stirring, for 1 minute. Stir in cumin, paprika, salt and harissa. Add tomatoes and juice, and stir well to combine.

2. Add carrots, zucchini, sweet potato and turnip and stir to coat. Add $\frac{1}{2}$ cup (125 mL) of the stock and bring to a boil. Cover, reduce heat and simmer until vegetables are tender, about 20 minutes.

3. Meanwhile, in a saucepan, bring remaining stock to a boil. Add couscous in a steady stream, stirring constantly. Remove from heat. Cover and let stand until tender and liquid is absorbed, about 15 minutes. Fluff with a fork, using your fingers to break up any lumps.

4. Arrange couscous in a ring around the edge of a deep serving platter, leaving the center hollow. Arrange vegetable mixture in center and drizzle melted smen evenly over vegetables and couscous. Garnish to taste with parsley.

To Seed or Not to Seed

Whether you seed and remove the veins inside your peppers is a matter of preference. With the exception of bell peppers, I usually don't seed and devein because, in my opinion, it affects the taste and experience of the pepper. I like the texture the seeds add to a dish. The veins are the placental tissue inside the peppers, and they contain any spiciness, so removing them may be a good idea if you are heat-averse; you can also reduce the quantity of chile called for in a recipe or substitute a chile that ranks lower on the Scoville scale.

North African Lentils and Rice (Mujaddara)

The ingredients in this North African mélange of lentils, rice and fried onions vary depending on the country of origin. It is an excellent main dish for vegetarians and makes a delicious addition to a buffet. I like to use brown or green lentils, but I have seen it made with red lentils—even black ones in some cases.

Tips

If you are cooking for someone who is sensitive to gluten, check labels on packaged ingredients, such as stock. They can contain gluten.

You'll need to cook ¾ cup (175 mL) raw rice to produce the amount of cooked called for in the ingredient list. I use brown rice because it is more nutritious, but white rice is traditional.

If your onions start to stick to the pan when they are crisping up, add water, 1 tbsp (15 mL) at a time.

Spicy yogurt makes a delicious, creamy topping.

To make spicy yogurt: In a small bowl, stir together 1 cup (250 mL) plain Greek-style yogurt, 2 tsp (10 mL) Aleppo pepper, and 1 tsp (5 mL) each ground cumin and coriander. Drizzle some over finished dish and serve remainder alongside.

- Large saucepan with tight-fitting lid
- Food processor

3 cups	vegetable stock or water	750 mL
1 cup	dried brown lentils	250 mL
½ cup	extra virgin olive oil, divided	125 mL
4	cloves garlic, chopped	4
1 tbsp	ground cumin	15 mL
½ to 1	red finger chile, coarsely chopped	½ to 1
1½ cups	hot cooked rice (see Tips, left)	375 mL
	Salt and freshly ground black pepper	
2 tbsp	finely chopped fresh parsley or mint	30 mL

Caramelized Onions

1 tbsp	butter	15 mL
1 tbsp	olive oil	15 mL
4	onions, thinly sliced (about 2 lbs/1 kg)	4

1. In saucepan, combine stock, lentils, 2 tbsp (30 mL) of the oil and garlic. Bring to a boil. Skim off foam. Cover, reduce heat and simmer until lentils are tender, about 30 minutes.

2. Transfer to food processor fitted with the metal blade. Add cumin, and finger chile to taste and purée until creamy.

3. Transfer to a serving bowl and add cooked rice. Stir in remaining oil. Season to taste with salt and black pepper.

4. *Caramelized Onions:* Meanwhile, in a large skillet, heat butter and oil over low heat. Add onions and toss until well coated. Cook, stirring occasionally, until onions are very soft, about 20 minutes. Increase heat to medium-high and cook, stirring, until caramelized, about 10 minutes. Increase heat to high and continue to cook, stirring and watching closely to make sure they don't burn, until onions begin to crisp (see Tips, left).

5. Ladle lentil mixture into bowls. Top with onions and garnish with parsley. Serve at room temperature.

Vegetarian Indonesian-Style Fried Rice (*Nasi Goreng*)

In Indonesia, where it qualifies as the national dish, *nasi goreng* is first and foremost a way of using up leftover rice—which is just another way of saying anything goes. I have enjoyed it for breakfast, topped with a fried egg and prepared by an Indonesian chef as a matter of national pride. The dish was mouthwatering.

MAKES 4 SERVINGS

VEGAN FRIENDLY

GLUTEN-FREE FRIENDLY

Tips

Brown or white rice will work in this recipe; use whichever suits your preference.

If you are cooking for people who are gluten-intolerant, be sure to use gluten-free soy sauce or wheat-free tamari.

Sriracha and sambal oelek are good choices for hot sauce.

If you're not cooking for vegetarians, you might like to serve this dish with fried shrimp chips (see Tips, page 288) on the side, and/or Coconut Sambal (page 376), which contains fish sauce, instead of the hot sauce. You can also add leftover cooked meat, such as steak or roast chicken, if you like.

- Fine-mesh sieve

3 cups	cold cooked rice, preferably jasmine	750 mL
2 cups	cooked sliced green beans	500 mL
¼ cup	boiling water	60 mL
1 tbsp	Thai tamarind paste, chopped	15 mL
2 tbsp	soy sauce	30 mL
2 tsp	coconut sugar	10 mL
2 tbsp	coconut oil or peanut oil	30 mL
3 tbsp	chopped shallots	45 mL
1	carrot, shredded	1
1	small red bell pepper, seeded and minced	1
1 to 2	red Thai bird's-eye chile(s), minced	1 to 2
1 tbsp	each minced garlic and gingerroot	15 mL
1 tbsp	tomato paste	15 mL
	Salt	
	Fried eggs (optional)	
	Hot sauce (see Tips, left)	

1. In a small bowl, combine boiling water and tamarind paste. Let stand for 30 minutes. Strain through fine-mesh sieve into a small bowl, pressing on the solids with a spatula. Scrape the paste on the underside of the sieve into the bowl, and discard solids. Set tamarind juice aside.

2. In a small bowl, stir soy sauce with coconut sugar. Set aside.

3. In a large skillet, heat oil over medium heat. Add shallots, carrot, bell pepper, and birds-eye chile(s) to taste and cook, stirring, until softened, about 3 minutes. Add garlic and ginger and cook, stirring, for 1 minute. Stir in tomato paste.

4. Stir in cooked rice, breaking up any clumps. Toss until well coated. (Do not brown.) Stir in tamarind juice, soy sauce mixture and green beans. Season with salt.

5. Spoon rice mixture onto warm serving plates; top each with a fried egg (if using). Pass hot sauce at the table.

Moors and Christians

This is a dish that likely originated with West African slaves brought to the Americas. Its origins are disputed, but today it is usually identified as Cuban (and sometimes Caribbean). For a Cuban touch, spoon the rice mixture onto plates, top with a fried egg and accompany with fried plantains. This dish is also delicious cold.

MAKES 4 MAIN-COURSE SERVINGS

VEGAN FRIENDLY

GLUTEN-FREE FRIENDLY

Tips

If you are cooking for someone who is gluten-free, check labels on packaged ingredients, such as stock. They can contain gluten.

The addition of a mildly spicy chile, such as Cubanelle, is not common in this recipe, but I think it adds a pleasant bite.

The cooking time for the rice will vary, depending upon the type you use. Allow about 15 minutes for white rice and 40 minutes for brown.

To serve as a main course, top each serving with a fried egg and fried plantains on the side. To serve as a rice salad, cover and refrigerate until chilled, about 4 hours.

• Heavy saucepan with tight-fitting lid

1	red bell pepper, roasted	1
1	green bell pepper, roasted	1
1	Cubanelle or poblano pepper (optional), roasted (see Tips, left and page 361)	1
2 tbsp	extra virgin olive, divided	30 mL
1	onion, chopped	1
4	cloves garlic, minced	4
1 tsp	each dried oregano and ground cumin	5 mL
1 cup	white or brown long-grain rice	250 mL
1 tbsp	tomato paste	15 mL
2 cups	vegetable stock or water	500 mL
1 cup	warm drained cooked black beans	250 mL
2 tbsp	freshly squeezed lime juice	30 mL
	Salt and freshly ground black pepper	
2 tbsp	finely chopped fresh cilantro	30 mL
2	green onions (white and green parts), finely chopped	2
	Hot sauce	

1. Peel, seed and dice roasted red and green bell peppers, and roasted Cubanelle pepper (if using). Set aside.

2. In saucepan, heat 1 tbsp (15 mL) of the oil over medium heat. Add onion and cook, stirring, until softened, about 3 minutes. Add garlic, oregano and cumin and cook, stirring, for 1 minute. Add rice and toss well to coat. Stir in tomato paste. Stir in stock and bring to a boil. Reduce heat and simmer until liquid is absorbed and rice is tender (see Tips, left).

3. In a medium bowl, combine beans, remaining oil, lime juice and reserved roasted peppers. Stir well to combine. Stir into rice mixture. Season to taste with salt and black pepper.

4. Garnish with cilantro and green onions. Serve with hot sauce on the side.

Khitchuri with Peppers

A vegetarian version of kedgeree (see page 159), *khitchuri* is a kind of South Asian casserole that's often made from leftovers. Traditionally, it contains spiced rice and lentils—I like to use red lentils because they dissolve in the liquid, adding creaminess to the sauce. This recipe makes a particularly delicious main course topped with a mélange of peppers and tomatoes. Expect requests for seconds. A green salad and warm naan will complete the meal.

MAKES 6 SERVINGS

VEGAN FRIENDLY

GLUTEN-FREE FRIENDLY

Tips

Use brown basmati or another long-grain brown rice. Rinse and thoroughly drain before using.

I like to use red lentils because they dissolve in the liquid, adding creaminess to the sauce.

For the best flavor, toast and grind whole cumin seeds rather than buying ground cumin. Simply toast the seeds in a dry skillet over medium heat until fragrant, about 3 minutes. Immediately transfer to a spice grinder or mortar and pestle, and grind to a powder.

You can substitute 2 cups (500 mL) halved cherry tomatoes for the chopped tomatoes.

The rice mixture will be liquidy even when the rice is fully cooked, so serve everything in soup plates.

2 tbsp	clarified butter (ghee) or olive oil, divided	30 mL
1	onion, finely chopped	1
2	cloves garlic, minced	2
2 tsp	curry powder	10 mL
1	bay leaf	1
1	piece (2 inches/5 cm long) cinnamon stick	1
1 cup	brown rice, rinsed and drained	250 mL
1 cup	red lentils	250 mL
4 cups	vegetable stock	1 L
2	green bell peppers, seeded and diced	2
1	red or green finger chile	1
½ tsp	ground cumin (see Tips, left)	2 mL
½ tsp	each salt and freshly ground black pepper	2 mL
4	small tomatoes (see Tips, left), peeled and chopped	4
⅓ cup	ketchup	75 mL
3	hard-cooked eggs (optional), sliced	3

1. In a saucepan, heat 1 tbsp (15 mL) of the clarified butter over medium heat. Add onion and cook, stirring, until softened, about 3 minutes. Add garlic, curry powder, bay leaf and cinnamon stick and cook, stirring, for 1 minute. Add rice and lentils and stir well to coat. Stir in stock and bring to a boil. Reduce heat, cover and simmer until rice is tender, about 50 minutes. Discard bay leaf.

2. Meanwhile, in a skillet, heat remaining clarified butter over medium heat. Add bell peppers, finger chile, cumin, salt and black pepper and cook, stirring, until peppers are softened, about 5 minutes. Add tomatoes and cook, stirring, for 1 minute. Stir in ketchup. Reduce heat and simmer, stirring occasionally, until flavors are melded, about 10 minutes. Season to taste with salt and black pepper.

3. Spread rice evenly on a warm, deep serving platter. Arrange peppers over top. Garnish with eggs (if using).

Mushroom Biryani

It takes a bit of time to make a good biryani, so this delicious vegetarian version is probably a dish to save for a special occasion. Usually, meat is layered with the seasoned rice, but nice meaty mushrooms make an excellent substitute. Biryani makes a great addition to a potluck or buffet lineup. And don't worry about leftovers—they reheat beautifully.

MAKES 6 TO 8 SERVINGS

VEGETARIAN FRIENDLY

GLUTEN-FREE FRIENDLY

Tips

For the best flavor, use whole coriander and cumin seeds and toast them until fragrant in a dry skillet. Then transfer to a mortar or a spice grinder and grind to a powder for use in this recipe.

You can leave the whole spices in the rice while it bakes or remove them beforehand, if you prefer.

- Preheat oven to 325°F (160°C)
- 10-cup (2.5 L) ovenproof casserole dish, preferably with lid

2 cups	white basmati rice	500 mL
½ tsp	salt	2 mL
8	whole cloves	8
4	black cardamom pods, crushed	4
1	piece (about 2 inches/5 cm long) cinnamon stick	1
2 tbsp	butter or clarified butter (ghee), melted	30 mL
	Freshly ground black pepper	
¼ cup	finely chopped fresh cilantro	60 mL

Mushrooms

¼ cup	clarified butter (ghee), divided (approx.)	60 mL
¼ cup	slivered blanched almonds	60 mL
2 lbs	cremini mushrooms, thinly sliced	1 kg
1	green bell pepper, seeded and diced	1
2	shallots, finely chopped	2
4	stalks celery, diced	4
4	cloves garlic, minced	4
1 tbsp	minced gingerroot	15 mL
1 tsp	salt	5 mL
1 tsp	turmeric	5 mL
1 tsp	ground coriander (see Tips, left)	5 mL
1 tsp	ground cumin	5 mL
½ tsp	Kashmiri chile powder or cayenne pepper	2 mL
1 cup	plain full-fat yogurt	250 mL

1. Rinse rice thoroughly under cold running water. Drain and transfer to a large bowl. Add water to cover generously and let stand for 30 minutes. Drain and rinse.

Moreover ...

Although the results depend on the cook, in general terms biryani is one of the less pungent dishes in India's culinary cupboard. Its origins are murky and legends are plentiful, but it is probably Persian in origin because it stems from the tradition of *dum pukht* cooking. I was introduced to this method, which originated in the 16th century and reflects India's Mughal heritage, when I traveled in India several years ago. Basically, it's an Indian form of braising: food is cooked in a clay pot that has been sealed with a flour-and-water paste. The results represent the best of slow cooking; they are highly seasoned and aromatic. The chicken dish we ate one night was billed as "resplendent"—like much of Indian culture, this description was a bit over the top but not entirely inaccurate. While I wouldn't presume to use that word for my recipe for mushroom biryani, it is very good and an excellent choice if you are cooking for people who are heat-averse.

2. In a large saucepan, bring 6 cups (1.5 L) water to a rolling boil. Add salt, cloves, cardamom, cinnamon stick and drained rice. Return to a boil and cook for 5 minutes. Drain and return to bowl in which the rice was soaked. And melted butter and toss well to coat. Set aside.

3. *Mushrooms:* In a large skillet, heat 1 tbsp (15 mL) of the clarified butter over medium heat. Add almonds and cook, stirring, until golden. Using a slotted spoon, transfer almonds to a plate and set aside.

4. Add remaining clarified butter to skillet and increase heat to medium-high. Add mushrooms and cook, stirring, until they release their liquid, about 7 minutes. Transfer mushrooms and liquid to a small bowl and set aside.

5. Reduce heat to medium. Add additional clarified butter to skillet, if necessary. Add bell pepper, shallots and celery and cook, stirring, until softened, about 5 minutes. Add garlic, ginger, salt, turmeric, coriander, cumin and chile powder and cook, stirring, for 1 minute. Return mushrooms and liquid to skillet and stir in yogurt. Remove from heat.

6. Spread half of the rice mixture in casserole dish. Top with mushroom mixture. Cover with remaining rice mixture. Season liberally to taste with black pepper. Cover tightly with lid (or foil if your casserole dish does not have a lid) and transfer to preheated oven. Bake until rice is tender, about 35 minutes. Garnish with reserved toasted almonds and cilantro.

Singapore Noodles

Rice noodles, peppers, bean sprouts and a curry-flavored sauce are the base for this street-food favorite. You can add a number of other ingredients to suit your taste.

Tips

If you are making this recipe for vegans, be sure to use sugar that has not been filtered through bone char.

This is a vegetarian version of a dish commonly made with shrimp. If you like, add 6 oz (175 g) of cooked small shrimp along with the sauce and noodles in Step 4. Or cook deveined peeled shrimp in the oil in Step 4 before adding the peppers. Cook, stirring, until they turn pink, then transfer them to a plate with a slotted spoon and set aside. Continue with the recipe, returning the shrimp to the wok along with the noodles.

You can also add sliced cooked chicken, beef or char siu (Chinese barbecued pork), or just about any other ingredient that strikes your fancy.

- Large wok or skillet

4 oz	snow peas	125 g
1	pkg (8 oz/250 g) thin rice noodles	1
	Boiling water	
1 tbsp	toasted sesame oil (approx.)	15 mL
2 tbsp	peanut or coconut oil	30 mL
1	red bell pepper, seeded and thinly sliced	1
1	red or green finger chile, thinly sliced	1
¼ cup	green onions (white and green parts separated), thinly sliced	60 mL
1 tbsp	each minced garlic and gingerroot	15 mL
1 tbsp	curry powder	15 mL
2	carrots, shredded	2
½ cup	bean sprouts	125 mL

Sauce

½ cup	soy sauce	125 mL
2 tbsp	unseasoned rice vinegar	30 mL
2 tsp	granulated sugar	10 mL

1. Peel strings off edges of snow peas and discard. Trim off stems. In saucepan of boiling water, blanch snow peas for 2 minutes. Transfer to bowl of ice water and let cool. Slice diagonally into thirds and set aside.

2. *Sauce:* In a small bowl, stir together soy sauce, vinegar and sugar. Set aside.

3. Place noodles in a large bowl and cover generously with boiling water. Soak, stirring frequently, until softened, about 5 minutes. Drain and return to bowl. Toss with 1 tbsp (15 mL) sesame oil and set aside.

4. In wok, heat peanut oil over medium heat. Add bell pepper and finger chile and cook, stirring, until softened, about 3 minutes. Add white part of green onions, garlic and ginger and cook, stirring, for 1 minute. Add curry powder and reserved sauce and stir well. Stir in noodles.

5. Add reserved snow peas, carrots and bean sprouts and cook, tossing, until heated through, about 2 minutes. Garnish with green parts of green onions.

Middle Eastern Eggs with Peppers and Tomatoes (*Shakshouka*)

This dish is a kind of Middle Eastern *pipérade* (see page 31). It is very is popular in North African countries, such as Tunisia, Morocco and Algeria; in Turkey, the dish is known as *menemen*. It is conventionally thought to include onions, peppers, tomatoes and garlic. Eggplant and zucchini often make an appearance, and sometimes spicy merguez sausage is added. In his book *North African Cookery*, Arto der Haroutunian included recipes using carrots and cauliflower; he even had a fish version.

MAKES 2 TO 3 SERVINGS

VEGETARIAN FRIENDLY

GLUTEN-FREE FRIENDLY

Tips

To make this dish gluten-free, be sure to check the label on your harissa paste. Some contain wheat ingredients as fillers.

For convenience, or if tomatoes are not in season, substitute 1 can (14 oz/398 mL) diced tomatoes, with juice, for the fresh tomatoes.

- 10-inch (25 cm) skillet

1 tbsp	olive oil	15 mL
1	onion, finely chopped	1
2	green bell peppers, thinly sliced	2
2	cloves garlic	2
1 tsp	ground cumin	5 mL
3	tomatoes, peeled and diced (see Tips, left)	3
1 tsp	harissa paste, or to taste (optional)	5 mL
	Salt and freshly ground black pepper	
4 to 6	eggs	4 to 6

1. In a skillet, heat oil over medium heat. Add onion and bell peppers and cook, stirring, until softened, about 5 minutes. Add garlic and cumin and cook, stirring, for 1 minute.

2. Stir in tomatoes, and harissa to taste (if using). Season to taste with salt and black pepper. Simmer until slightly thickened, about 5 minutes.

3. Using the back of a spoon, make 4 to 6 (depending on the number of eggs you are cooking) depressions in the pepper mixture, leaving as much space as possible between each. Break 1 egg into each depression. Cover and cook until whites are opaque and yolks are still runny, about 6 minutes. Season to taste with salt and black pepper.

Variations

If you prefer, lightly whisk the eggs before adding them to the pepper mixture. Adjust the cooking time, if necessary; cook until eggs are scrambled and opaque.

If you are not cooking for vegetarians, you might like to add 8 oz (250 g) merguez sausage, cut into 1-inch (2.5 cm) thick slices, along with the bell peppers. Reduce the amount of harissa or omit it.

Tortilla with Potato and Peppers

This spin on tortilla, a traditional Spanish tapas dish resembling an omelet, enhances the traditional potato-and-egg combination with green and red bell peppers, a finger chile and a liberal amount of sharp cheese. Traditionally, it is served cold or at room temperature, but it's nice warm, too.

- Large ovenproof nonstick skillet with lid

1	potato (8 oz/250 g), scrubbed	1
2 tbsp	extra virgin olive oil	30 mL
1	red onion, thinly sliced on the vertical	1
1	red bell pepper, seeded and diced	1
1	green bell pepper, seeded and diced	1
1	red finger chile, seeded and minced	1
2	cloves garlic, minced	2
	Salt and freshly ground black pepper	
6	eggs	6
1 cup	shredded Manchego or other sharp (aged) cheese, such as Cheddar	250 mL

1. Place potato in a microwave-safe dish and add cold water to a depth of about $1/2$ inch (1 cm). Cover and microwave on High for 3 minutes. Let cool, covered, for at least 5 minutes before running under cold water. Let cool. Cut into $1/2$-inch (1 cm) cubes and set aside.

2. In skillet, heat oil over medium heat. Add potato, onion, red and green bell peppers, finger chile and garlic and cook, stirring, until peppers are softened and potato and onion are just beginning to brown, about 8 minutes. Season to taste with salt and black pepper.

3. Preheat broiler. In a medium bowl, beat eggs. Pour over onion mixture in skillet and sprinkle cheese evenly over top. Reduce heat to low, partially cover and cook until eggs are set, about 6 minutes. Uncover and transfer to preheated oven. Broil until top is nicely browned.

4. Slide tortilla onto a large plate and cut into wedges. Serve warm or at room temperature.

Variation

Tortilla with Potato, Peppers and Chorizo: Reduce Manchego cheese to $1/2$ cup (125 mL). Add 6 oz (175 g) dry-cured chorizo, diced, along with the eggs.

Focus on: Chiles in Spain

Spain is the fifth-largest producer of peppers in the world today, and a surprising number of the varieties grown there have been awarded *Denominación de Origen Protegida* (DOP) status. Peppers in many forms are widely used throughout the country: they are eaten fresh, preserved, or dried and ground into powders, such as the famous Spanish paprika.

Sweet peppers often appear as part of *sofrito*, a base sauce that contains a number of aromatic ingredients, such as onion, garlic, tomatoes, paprika and peppers. They are also regularly featured in classic Spanish dishes, such as Tortilla with Potato and Peppers (page 327), and various dressed pepper salads and tapas. While pungent peppers are less likely to turn up in recipes, their voice is still heard, particularly in the Basque region. Padrón peppers (see page 77)—those plump green bullets with the unpredictable temperament—seem to have become ubiquitous around the world, so it's easy to forget that they originated in Galicia, where they are known as *pimiento de Herbón* in Spanish or *pemento de Herbón* in Galician. Spicy dry-cured chorizo sausage is also used widely and, of course, the Spanish paprika that characterizes it is among the best in the world.

In recent years, small scarlet piquillo peppers have also been flexing their muscles and traveling well beyond their original station in life. Their name means "little beak," for their triangular shape. These melt-in-your-mouth capsicums from the town of Lodosa in the Navarre region are almost sugary, with just the faintest hint of heat. They are lightly smoked over beech wood, then peeled and packed in cans or jars. Piquillo peppers are now exported in such significant quantities that they have been called the "red gold" of Lodosa. They are usually served stuffed (see page 78), often with a filling of salt cod. Another traditional presentation is to simmer them briefly in their juices with sautéed garlic. Their smaller relative, the cristal pepper, also from Navarre, is even more highly valued.

The *pimiento Riojano*—also known as *pimiento Najerano*, after the city of Nájera, where it was originally cultivated—has been awarded *Indicación Geográfica Protegida* (IGP) status, another mark bestowed on products grown in a specific region that adhere to special quality and production-method controls. The pimiento Riojano has been grown in La Rioja since the mid-19th century. This mild, longish (about 6 inches/15 cm), slightly wide, deep-red pepper is cone-shaped. It is hand-harvested and roasted in wood-fired ovens, which imbue it with a smoky flavor. It is enjoyed fresh or canned in its own juices. Every fall, Nájera holds a celebratory festival in its honor.

The ñora is a fat, round pepper that is always used dried and is frequently sold already ground. When whole, the dried pepper resembles the Mexican cascabel chile. The ñora pepper is cultivated along the eastern coast of Spain, near Valencia, Catalonia and Murcia. There, the ground pepper takes the place of sweet paprika in regional dishes. It has a distinctive sweet flavor and an intense red color, and traditionally seasons romesco sauce (see page 388), a Catalonian specialty.

In her book *The Food of Spain*, Claudia Roden says that dried choricero peppers from the Basque country are similar in flavor to the ñora pepper. She describes these peppers as dried, smoky and just a tad spicy. Rehydrated choricero peppers and their liquid are often puréed and added to soups and stews in Basque cooking, and a thick red paste made from them is bottled and sold. It is often used to season chorizo.

Pimiento de Gernika, another famous pepper from the Basque region with IGP status, resembles the padrón pepper. It is a bit larger, on the fat side and, like the padrón, often served stir-fried and sprinkled with coarse sea salt. I have read that this pepper was originally much more pungent, but that its heat has diminished over the years due to changing growing conditions. Pimiento de Gernika is traditionally picked when ripe, strung into ristras (see page 31) and left to dry.

Mildly pungent, with a hint of sweetness, the guindilla is another traditional Basque chile. When green, it is often preserved and used to make *pintxos*, a variety of tapas. To make the Gilda, a classic pintxo supposedly named after the character played by Rita Hayworth in the 1940s noir film of the same name, the peppers are speared on wooden skewers with olives, anchovies and chunks of red bell pepper. If allowed to ripen, guindilla chiles intensify in spiciness and may be fried in olive oil and garlic. When dried, they are ground into *pimentón picante*.

Another popular pepper in Basque country is *piment d'Anglet*, also known as *doux des Landes*. It is a large sweet pepper that is often fried in olive oil and served sprinkled with salt. It may also be stuffed, and frequently turns up in *piperada*, a Basque specialty (see page 330). Throughout Spain, there are many more varieties of anonymous chiles, which Basque chef Gerald Hirigoyen describes as *piments du pays*. They are regularly used in everyday dishes, such as omelets and salads.

Spanish-Style Eggs with Pepper Sauce (*Piperada*)

I've been making versions of this Basque dish for decades, ever since I discovered Julia Child's omelet-based rendition. This luscious combination of peppers and tomatoes is always so good, especially when those ingredients are in season. Combined with ham, eggs and/or bread, it makes a fabulous dish for lunch or brunch. If you want to bump it up a notch, there are some delicious variations, opposite.

MAKES 4 SERVINGS

VEGETARIAN FRIENDLY

GLUTEN-FREE FRIENDLY

Tips

I much prefer the flavor of roasted bell peppers in this dish, but if you're pressed for time, slice raw bell peppers and add them to the pan along with the onions.

I like having a hot chile pepper in the mix, but many people like a tamer version of this dish; if you are heat-averse, feel free to omit it. If you do like a bit of heat but don't have a fresh chile on hand, add ½ tsp (2 mL) hot paprika, ground ñora pepper or hot pepper flakes along with the garlic.

To make 2 cups (500 mL) of diced tomatoes, you'll need about 3 medium tomatoes. Use any kind you like; Roma or plum tomatoes work particularly well.

If you're not cooking for vegetarians, add thinly sliced cured or smoked ham, cut into strips, to taste after the garlic is cooked. Cook the ham, stirring, for 1 minute, before adding the tomatoes.

- **Nonstick skillet**

1 tbsp	butter	15 mL
8	large eggs, beaten, divided	8
2 tbsp	finely chopped fresh parsley	30 mL

Pepper Sauce

2	red or green bell peppers (or 1 of each color), roasted (see Tips, page 361 and left)	2
2 tbsp	olive oil	30 mL
1	onion, finely chopped	1
2	cloves garlic, minced	2
1	red finger chile, thinly sliced (see Tips, left)	1
2 cups	diced peeled cored tomatoes (see Tips, left)	500 mL
	Salt and freshly ground black pepper	

1. *Pepper Sauce:* Peel, seed and slice roasted red peppers. Set aside. In a large skillet, heat oil over medium-high heat. Add onion and sauté until beginning to turn golden, about 5 minutes. Reduce heat to medium. Add garlic and finger chile and cook, stirring, for 1 minute. Add tomatoes and cook, stirring occasionally, until slightly thickened, about 10 minutes. Stir in reserved roasted peppers and season to taste with salt and black pepper.

2. Meanwhile, in nonstick skillet, melt half of the butter over medium heat. Add half of the eggs and cook, without stirring, until bottom solidifies. Using a spatula, lift the edge of the omelet away from the pan, allowing the uncooked eggs to flow underneath. Cook until omelet reaches desired degree of doneness, about 3 minutes. Slip onto a large warm serving plate. Repeat with remaining butter and eggs.

3. Divide pepper mixture evenly between omelets, pouring onto one half of each. Fold uncovered half over pepper mixture and garnish with parsley. Cut each omelet in half.

Tip

To serve this dish as tapas, cut finished omelets into pieces. Halve a baguette horizontally, then cut crosswise into generous pieces (about 3 inches/7.5 cm long). Brush cut sides with extra virgin olive oil and broil until golden. Transfer to individual serving plates. Spoon pepper mixture over bread and top with omelet pieces. Garnish with parsley.

Variations

Piperada en Cocottes: Complete Step 1. Preheat oven to 400°F (200°C). Butter 4 large ramekins. Cut toasted baguette into pieces small enough to fit in bottoms of prepared ramekins. Spoon pepper mixture over bread. Break 1 egg into each ramekin. Bake in preheated oven until eggs are just set, 10 to 12 minutes. Garnish with parsley.

Piperada with Scrambled Eggs: Complete Step 1. Whisk 2 tbsp (30 mL) heavy or whipping (35%) cream into beaten eggs. In a small skillet, melt 1 tbsp (15 mL) butter over low heat. Add egg mixture and cook, stirring constantly, until eggs are scrambled. Remove from heat and season to taste with salt and black pepper. Spoon eggs over 4 slices of hot buttered toast and top with pepper mixture. Garnish with parsley.

Ethiopian Lentils with Eggs

This is a version of *mesir wat*, a traditional Ethiopian lentil dish that is seasoned with berbere spice blend and served over injera flatbread. The eggs make it a complete meal.

MAKES 6 SERVINGS

VEGETARIAN FRIENDLY

GLUTEN-FREE FRIENDLY

Tips

If you are cooking for people who are gluten-intolerant, be sure to use gluten-free soy sauce or wheat-free tamari.

Berbere spice blend is fairly widely available. Look for it in markets that have a good spice section, in specialty shops such as Kalustyan's, or online.

- Large saucepan or Dutch oven

1 tbsp	olive oil	15 mL
1	onion, finely chopped	1
1 tbsp	each minced garlic and gingerroot	15 mL
1 tbsp	berbere spice blend (see Tips, left)	15 mL
1 cup	dried red lentils, rinsed	250 mL
1	can (14 oz/398 mL) diced tomatoes, with juice	1
4 cups	vegetable stock or water	1 L
6	hard-cooked eggs	6
	Finely chopped fresh parsley or cilantro	

1. In saucepan, heat oil over medium heat. Add onion and cook, stirring, until softened, about 3 minutes. Add garlic, ginger and berbere spice blend and cook, stirring, for 1 minute. Stir in lentils. Add tomatoes and juice, and stock and bring to a boil. Reduce heat, cover and simmer until lentils are tender, about 25 minutes.

2. Peel eggs and prick each in several places. Add to lentils. Cover and simmer for 10 minutes. Garnish with parsley.

Sides

Down-Home Okra and Tomatoes

Okra and tomatoes, often spiced with some kind of chile, is common throughout the American South. Okra is one of the crops that traveled with African slaves, as part of their victuals onboard the ships that carried them to North America. This recipe was inspired by one that Southern food expert John Martin Taylor originated. He defines its provenance as Lowcountry Creole. He recommends serving this mixture over hot grits, but it also makes a great companion to grilled meats, such as pork chops.

- Large saucepan or Dutch oven

4 oz	slab bacon, diced	125 g
1	onion, thinly sliced	1
2	cloves garlic, minced	2
1	red or green finger chile, thinly sliced	1
1 tbsp	tomato paste	15 mL
1	can (28 oz/796 mL) tomatoes, with juice, coarsely chopped	1
½ cup	chicken stock or water	125 mL
3 cups	thinly sliced trimmed okra (about 1 lb/500 g)	750 mL

1. In saucepan, sauté bacon over medium-high heat until crisp. Using a slotted spoon, transfer to a paper towel–lined plate and let drain. Reduce heat to medium.

2. Add onion to pan and cook, stirring, until softened, about 2 minutes. Add garlic and finger chile and cook, stirring, for 1 minute. Stir in tomato paste.

3. Add tomatoes and juice, and stock and stir well to combine. Bring to a boil. Boil for 2 minutes. Add okra and return to a boil. Reduce heat and simmer until okra is tender, about 10 minutes. Stir in reserved bacon and serve immediately.

African-Style Collard Greens (*Sukuma Wiki*)

Sukuma wiki is, apparently, Swahili for "stretch the week"—an indication of how this recipe is used to make limited ingredients go further. It is particularly popular in Kenya, where it is often made with kale instead of collards. It makes a delicious accompaniment to simple grilled or roasted meat.

MAKES 4 SERVINGS

VEGAN FRIENDLY

GLUTEN-FREE FRIENDLY

Tips

The coconut milk adds a pleasant creaminess to the sauce, but is not essential to the success of this dish.

If you prefer, and are not cooking for vegetarians, you can substitute chicken or beef stock for the cooking liquid from the collard greens.

1 lb	trimmed collard greens (about 2 bunches), cut into strips	500 g
1 tbsp	oil	15 mL
1	onion, finely chopped	1
1 to 2	red Thai bird's-eye chile(s) or other bird-type chile(s), minced	1 to 2
1	can (14 oz/398 mL) diced tomatoes, with juice	1
1 tsp	salt	5 mL
2 tbsp	freshly squeezed lemon juice	30 mL
1 tbsp	tapioca flour	15 mL
¼ cup	coconut milk (optional)	60 mL
	Freshly ground black pepper	

1. In a large saucepan, combine prepared collard greens and enough water to cover. Bring to a boil. Reduce heat and simmer until greens are just tender, about 10 minutes. Drain, reserving ½ cup (125 mL) of the cooking liquid. Set greens and cooking liquid aside.

2. In same saucepan, heat oil over medium heat. Add onion and cook, stirring, until softened, about 3 minutes. Add chile(s) to taste and cook, stirring, for 1 minute. Add tomatoes and juice, reserved cooking liquid and salt. Bring to a boil. Stir in reserved cooked greens. Cover and simmer until greens are tender enough to suit your taste, about 10 minutes.

3. In a small bowl, stir lemon juice with tapioca flour until smooth. Stir into greens mixture and cook, stirring, until liquid is thickened, about 1 minute. Stir in coconut milk (if using). Season to taste with additional salt and black pepper.

Wilted Spinach with Pickled Peppers

This is a riff on a recipe immortalized many years ago by the late Edna Lewis, chef extraordinaire and chronicler of the foodways of the American South. This dish is dead-easy to whip up and a perfect solution if you are tired of the same-old sides with your meals. All you need is a few simple ingredients, including a jar of pickled peppers, which I always keep on hand in the fridge.

MAKES 4 SERVINGS

VEGAN FRIENDLY

GLUTEN-FREE FRIENDLY

Tips

To reduce spattering, dry your washed spinach in a salad spinner before sautéing it.

I like to use sliced pickled banana peppers in this recipe, but any kind of sliced or minced pickled pepper will work. Vary the quantity to suit your heat tolerance.

2	bunches spinach (about 18 oz/560 g total)	2
2 tbsp	extra virgin olive oil	30 mL
2	cloves garlic, thinly sliced	2
1 tbsp	drained chopped oil-packed sun-dried tomatoes	15 mL
2 tbsp	drained sliced pickled banana peppers	30 mL
	Salt and freshly ground black pepper	

1. Trim tough stems off spinach and discard (see Tips, left). In a large skillet, heat oil over medium heat. Add garlic and toss to coat. (Do not brown.) Add spinach and increase heat to medium-high. Cook, tossing, until spinach is wilted, about 5 minutes.
2. Stir in sun-dried tomatoes and pickled peppers. Transfer to a warm serving platter. Season to taste with salt and black pepper. Serve immediately.

To Seed or Not to Seed

Whether you seed and remove the veins inside your peppers is a matter of preference. With the exception of bell peppers, I usually don't seed and devein because, in my opinion, it affects the taste and experience of the pepper. I like the texture the seeds add to a dish. The veins are the placental tissue inside the peppers, and they contain any spiciness, so removing them may be a good idea if you are heat-averse; you can also reduce the quantity of chile called for in a recipe or substitute a chile that ranks lower on the Scoville scale.

Kashmiri-Style Spinach with Mushrooms

A recipe created by my friend Suneeta Vaswani for her *Complete Book of Indian Cooking* is the inspiration for this dish. I'm sure she would be appalled to learn that I use prepared curry powder, but it is an easy way to enhance the flavor of the mushrooms. This dish makes a great accompaniment to just about anything, in my opinion.

MAKES 4 SERVINGS

VEGAN FRIENDLY

GLUTEN-FREE FRIENDLY

Tips

Suneeta uses mustard oil for frying, which adds extra flavor to the dish. I find vegetable oil and clarified butter (ghee) work well, too.

If you are avoiding gluten, check your curry powder to make sure it does not contain any wheat products.

2 tbsp	oil (see Tips, left)	30 mL
1 tsp	brown mustard seeds	5 mL
8 oz	mushrooms, trimmed and sliced	250 g
2	cloves garlic, minced	2
½ tsp	curry powder	2 mL
1	red finger chile, minced	1
1 tbsp	freshly squeezed lemon juice	15 mL
	Salt	
1 lb	trimmed spinach leaves	500 g
	Freshly ground black pepper	

1. In a skillet, heat oil over medium-high heat. Add mustard seeds, immediately cover and cook, shaking the pan, until the seeds stop popping.

2. Reduce heat to medium and add mushrooms. Cook, stirring, until mushrooms release their liquid, about 5 minutes.

3. Add garlic, curry powder and finger chile and stir well to combine. Sprinkle lemon juice evenly over top and season to taste with salt. Add spinach and cook, stirring, until wilted, about 4 minutes. Remove from heat and season to taste with additional salt and black pepper.

Rum-Roasted Onions

If you are looking for a slightly different side dish, try this. I believe the origins of this recipe are Caribbean or Creole. When I was developing it, I had in my mind an old Creole recipe for Spanish onions baked in beef stock and spiked with bourbon. I let my imagination run a bit wild with that, and this is the tasty result.

MAKES 4 SERVINGS

VEGETARIAN FRIENDLY

GLUTEN-FREE FRIENDLY

Tips

Cajun seasoning, like all spice blends, varies in potency from brand to brand. Use the quantity that suits yours best. If you are avoiding gluten, check the label to make sure it does not contain any wheat products.

Save any leftovers of this dish—they make a scrumptious topping for pizza.

¼ cup	butter	60 mL
3	white onions, thinly sliced	3
2 tbsp	raw cane sugar, such as Demerara	30 mL
2 tsp	fresh thyme leaves	10 mL
½ to 1 tsp	Cajun seasoning (see Tips, left)	2 to 5 mL
½ cup	dark rum	125 mL
½ cup	water	125 mL
2 tbsp	freshly squeezed lemon juice	30 mL
	Hot sauce	

1. In a skillet, melt butter over medium heat. Add onions and cook, stirring, until softened, about 5 minutes. Stir in sugar, thyme, and Cajun seasoning to taste and cook, stirring, for 1 minute. Add rum, water and lemon juice and stir well to combine.

2. Reduce heat and simmer, stirring occasionally, until onions are golden and almost all of the liquid is absorbed, about 45 minutes.

3. Spoon into warm serving bowl. Pass hot sauce at the table.

Indian-Style Lima Beans

If you are looking for a side dish that holds well and is perfect for a buffet, these highly seasoned lima beans are just the thing. They're also good at adding a dash of interesting spice to an otherwise bland meal.

MAKES 4 TO 6 SERVINGS

VEGAN FRIENDLY

GLUTEN-FREE FRIENDLY

Tips

If you have time, soak and cook dried lima beans. After cooking, scoop out about 1 cup (250 mL) of the cooking liquid and set it aside to add to the recipe. If you're rushed, substitute frozen lima beans, saving the same amount of the cooking water, or canned lima beans, using the liquid from the can.

Raw cashews are usually used in Indian cooking, but I have made this dish using roasted salted cashews with equally delicious results.

One finger chile produces a nicely spicy dish. If you are a heat seeker, increase the quantity to suit your taste.

This recipe can easily be doubled if you are preparing it for a buffet.

• Food processor

2 cups	drained cooked lima beans (see Tips, left)	500 mL
	Lima bean cooking liquid (see Tips, left)	
½ cup	cashews (see Tips, left)	125 mL
¼ cup	desiccated coconut	60 mL
1 tbsp	minced gingerroot	15 mL
1 tbsp	minced garlic	15 mL
1	red or green finger chile (see Tips, left), minced	1
2 tsp	ground cumin	10 mL
1 tsp	salt	5 mL
1 tbsp	oil or clarified butter (ghee)	15 mL
1	onion, finely chopped	1
1	can (14 oz/398 mL) diced tomatoes, with juice	1
2 tbsp	finely chopped fresh cilantro	30 mL

1. In food processor fitted with the metal blade, combine cashews, coconut, ginger, garlic, finger chile, cumin and salt. Process until a chunky paste forms. Set aside.

2. In a skillet, heat oil over medium heat. Add onion and cook, stirring, until softened, about 3 minutes. Add reserved cashew paste and cook, stirring, for 2 minutes. Stir in tomatoes and juice, and lima beans. Add enough of the lima bean cooking liquid to cover. (You should need ½ to ¾ cup/125 to 175 mL.) Bring to a boil.

3. Reduce heat, cover and simmer until flavors are melded and sauce is thickened, about 20 minutes. Transfer to a warm serving bowl. Garnish with cilantro.

Indonesian Green Beans

This is an extremely popular side dish in Indonesia, where it is often served as an accompaniment to rendang (see page 226) or as a main dish over rice. It makes a creative, tasty side with grilled meat or fish.

(see page 226)

MAKES 4 SERVINGS

VEGAN FRIENDLY

GLUTEN-FREE FRIENDLY

Tip

This dish is often made with long beans. However, it has also become a fixture in Dutch-Indonesian cuisine, which uses French green beans. Both are delicious.

- Wok or large skillet

1 tbsp	coconut oil	15 mL
¼ cup	finely chopped shallots	60 mL
1 tbsp	minced gingerroot	15 mL
1	clove garlic, minced	1
1 to 2	red Thai bird's-eye chile(s), minced	1 to 2
1 lb	green beans (see Tip, left), trimmed and cut diagonally into 2-inch (10 cm) pieces	500 g
3	Roma or plum tomatoes, peeled, cored and diced	3
1 cup	coconut milk	250 mL
1 tsp	coconut sugar	5 mL
	Salt	
	Chopped roasted peanuts (optional)	

1. In wok, heat oil over medium heat. Add shallots, ginger, garlic, and chile(s) to taste and cook, stirring, until fragrant and shallots are just beginning to brown, about 5 minutes.

2. Add green beans and toss until coated with the spice paste and beginning to turn glossy, about 2 minutes. Stir in tomatoes, coconut milk and coconut sugar and bring to a boil. Reduce heat, cover and simmer until green beans are tender, about 10 minutes. Season to taste with salt. Garnish to taste with peanuts (if using).

Variation

If you prefer, substitute ¼ to 1 tsp (1 to 5 mL) sriracha sauce or sambal oelek for the bird's-eye chile(s).

Vegetable Ragù (*Ciambotta*)

This Italian stew, a close relative of ratatouille, is distinguished by the addition of potatoes and, the farther south you travel in Italy, chiles. *Ciambotta* is similar to the Lebanese dish *maghmoor*, which uses chickpeas rather than potatoes.

MAKES 6 SERVINGS

VEGAN FRIENDLY

GLUTEN-FREE FRIENDLY

Tips

To sweat eggplant: Place cubed eggplant in a colander and sprinkle liberally with salt. Let stand until the moisture comes to the surface, 30 minutes to 1 hour. Rinse thoroughly under cold running water. If time is short, skip the sweating and blanch the pieces for 1 to 2 minutes in heavily salted water and rinse under cold running water. In both cases, after rinsing, use your hands to squeeze out the excess moisture.

To sweat zucchini: Place sliced zucchini in a colander and sprinkle liberally with salt. Let stand until the moisture comes to the surface, about 20 minutes. Rinse thoroughly under cold running water.

Drain sweated vegetables and pat dry with a paper towel before using.

I like to use small new potatoes, cut in half. If yours are larger, slice them thinly.

This stew is an excellent accompaniment to grilled meats or robust fish, such as swordfish. I especially like to make it when new potatoes are in season.

- Preheat oven to 325°F (160°C)
- Dutch oven

2	small Italian eggplants (about 1¼ lbs/ 625 g total), cubed and sweated	2
2	zucchini, quartered lengthwise, cut into 1-inch (2.5 cm) slices and sweated	2
¼ cup	extra virgin olive oil (approx.)	60 mL
1 lb	small new potatoes, scrubbed and cut in half (see Tips, left)	500 g
2	red bell peppers, seeded and cut into thin strips	2
1	onion, thinly sliced	1
6	cloves garlic, minced	6
1 tsp	hot pepper flakes, preferably *peperoncino*	5 mL
½ tsp	dried oregano	2 mL
1	can (28 oz/796 mL) tomatoes, with juice, coarsely chopped	1
	Salt and freshly ground black pepper	
	Finely chopped fresh parsley or basil	

1. In Dutch oven, heat 2 tbsp (30 mL) oil over medium heat. Add eggplant, in batches, and cook, stirring and adding more oil as necessary, until lightly browned on all sides, about 4 minutes per batch. Transfer to a plate as completed.

2. Add zucchini, in batches, and cook, stirring and adding more oil as necessary, just until lightly browned, about 4 minutes per batch. Transfer to a plate as completed. Add potatoes, cut side down, in batches, and brown lightly on one side, about 2 minutes per batch. Transfer to a plate.

3. Add remaining oil to pan. Add bell peppers and onion and cook, stirring, until softened, about 5 minutes. Add garlic, hot pepper flakes and oregano and cook, stirring, for 1 minute. Stir in tomatoes and juice, and bring to a boil. Add reserved eggplant, zucchini and potatoes. Season to taste with salt and black pepper. Return to a boil.

4. Cover and transfer pan to preheated oven. Bake until potatoes are tender, about 1 hour. Let cool to room temperature. Garnish to taste with parsley.

Gujarati-Style Creamed Corn

This traditional recipe from the Indian state of Gujarat has many variations. I prefer to thicken it with yogurt—rather than evaporated milk, coconut milk, heavy cream, dried coconut or chickpea flour—which produces a dish resembling a corn curry. It is lovely with grilled meat and many other main dishes.

MAKES 6 SERVINGS

VEGETARIAN FRIENDLY

GLUTEN-FREE FRIENDLY

Tips

For convenience, you can substitute an equal quantity of ground cumin, coriander and fennel and skip Step 1.

Obviously, this recipe is tastiest when made with fresh corn kernels cut from the cobs. But frozen corn kernels work very well and allow this dish to be a year-round treat.

I have seen this recipe made with pieces of fresh corn on the cob (though I have not tried it myself). Substitute 4 cobs of corn for the kernels. Cut them into about 3-inch (7.5 cm) long chunks and blanch in boiling salted water for 4 minutes. (If you are not using them immediately, leave them in the hot water until you're ready to use them to prevent the kernels from puckering.) Complete steps 1 and 2 of the recipe. Stir in yogurt, add corn and complete Step 4.

- Spice grinder, or mortar and pestle

2 tsp	cumin seeds (see Tips, left)	10 mL
2 tsp	coriander seeds	10 mL
1 tsp	fennel seeds	10 mL
1 tbsp	oil or butter	15 mL
1	large onion, chopped	1
2 tbsp	minced garlic	30 mL
1 tbsp	minced gingerroot	15 mL
1	red or green finger chile, minced	1
1 tsp	coconut sugar	5 mL
4 cups	corn kernels, thawed if frozen, or 4 corn cobs (see Tips, left)	1 L
1 cup	water	250 mL
1 cup	plain full-fat Greek-style yogurt	250 mL
	Salt and freshly ground black pepper	
¼ cup	finely chopped fresh cilantro (leaves and tender stems)	60 mL

1. In a dry large saucepan over medium-low heat, toast cumin, coriander and fennel seeds until fragrant, about 3 minutes. Transfer to spice grinder and grind to a fine powder. Set aside.

2. In same saucepan, heat oil over medium heat. Add onion and cook, stirring, until softened. Add garlic, ginger and finger chile and cook, stirring, for 1 minute. Add reserved ground spices and coconut sugar and cook, stirring, for 1 minute.

3. Add corn and water. Bring to a boil. Cover, reduce heat and simmer until corn is tender, about 4 minutes.

4. Add yogurt and cook, stirring, until heated through and flavors are blended, about 2 minutes. Season to taste with salt and black pepper. Garnish with cilantro.

Creamed Summer Corn with Chile

I have been stirring up this version of creamed corn for years. I suspect I got the idea from a canned product: those corn "niblets" seasoned with diced peppers that my mother used when I was a child. It has always been a family favorite, but I knew it was a true hit when a friend, who is an award-winning cookbook author, requested it on a return visit to my home. This side is very easy and delicious to make when corn is in season.

MAKES 6 SERVINGS

VEGETARIAN FRIENDLY

GLUTEN-FREE FRIENDLY

Tip

If you are cooking for someone who is gluten-free, check labels on packaged ingredients, such as stock. They can contain gluten.

- Saucepan with tight-fitting lid

2 tbsp	butter	30 mL
¼ cup	finely chopped shallots	60 mL
1	serrano or jalapeño pepper, seeded and diced	1
4 cups	fresh corn kernels	1 L
¼ cup	chicken stock or water	60 mL
2 tbsp	heavy or whipping (35%) cream	30 mL
	Salt and freshly ground black pepper	

1. In saucepan, melt butter over medium heat. Add shallots and cook, stirring, until softened, about 3 minutes. Stir in serrano pepper, corn and stock. Reduce heat to low, cover and cook until corn is tender, about 10 minutes.

2. Stir in cream. Season to taste with salt and black pepper.

Paraguayan Corn Pudding (Sopa Paraguaya)

The name of this traditional recipe is rather odd: *sopa* means "soup" in Spanish, but is also used to describe a type of corn bread in Paraguay, where it is a special-occasion dish. This bread is denser and moister than North American corn bread—more like a corn pudding, which is why I've called it that. I love it as a side with barbecued meats.

MAKES 12 SERVINGS

VEGETARIAN FRIENDLY

GLUTEN-FREE FRIENDLY

Tips

If you don't have a stand mixer, use a large mixing bowl and a hand mixer to combine the ingredients and to beat the egg whites.

You can use any medium-hot chile, such as jalapeño or ají amarillo, in place of the serrano peppers.

Moreover ...

Legend has it that this recipe was named because a chef mistakenly added too much cornmeal to thicken his soup. Fortunately, he enjoyed the bread-like result, but kept the moniker *sopa paraguaya* (Paraguayan soup) because he had soup on his mind.

- Preheat oven to 375°F (190°C), with rack in center
- Stand mixer (see Tips, left)
- 9-inch (23 cm) square glass baking dish, greased and dusted lightly with cornmeal

1	onion, chopped	1
1	red or green bell pepper, seeded and diced	1
1	serrano pepper, minced	1
¾ cup	water	175 mL
1 tsp	salt	5 mL
3 tbsp	butter, softened	45 mL
1 tbsp	granulated sugar	15 mL
4	eggs, separated	4
6 oz	cotija cheese or queso fresco, crumbled	175 g
1 cup	corn kernels, thawed if frozen	250 mL
¼ tsp	cayenne pepper	1 mL
1½ cups	stone-ground cornmeal	375 mL
1 cup	buttermilk	250 mL

1. In a saucepan, combine onion, bell pepper, serrano pepper, water and salt. Bring to a boil. Cover, reduce heat and simmer until onion is very soft, about 10 minutes. Remove from heat. Let cool.

2. In bowl of stand mixer, beat butter with sugar on medium speed until creamy. Add egg yolks, 1 at time, beating each until incorporated before adding the next. Beat in cheese, corn, cayenne and reserved onion mixture (including liquid). Alternately beat in cornmeal and buttermilk, making 3 additions of each, until incorporated.

3. In a clean mixer bowl, on high speed, beat egg whites until soft peaks form. Fold into cornmeal mixture.

4. Pour batter into prepared baking dish. Bake in preheated oven until a toothpick inserted in the center comes out clean, about 45 minutes.

Focus on: Chiles in South America and the Caribbean

Latin America is the birthplace of chile peppers. It is thought that the wild species that grew in parts of Bolivia and what is now Peru were the ancestors of the thousands of varieties of capsicums we recognize today. Thanks to birds, who dispersed their seeds (see page 23), and later to traders, peppers gradually moved north. Along with beans, corn and squash, capsicums were one of the first crops to be cultivated in this part of the world.

Today, the cuisines of Latin America, including the Caribbean, are a melting pot of native and European influences. There is great diversity among the countries, but they share certain culinary commonalities—chiefly, their preponderant use of chiles. For instance, I was amused to learn that when Peruvian artist Marcos Zapata painted his version of *The Last Supper* in 1753, the devout men were feasting on *chicha*, a drink made from maize; roasted guinea pig (or wild chinchilla, depending upon your source) and an assortment of fruits and vegetables that included chiles.

Thanks to Spanish and Portuguese settlers, many classic dishes in South America are built on *sofrito*, a foundation of sautéed onions, garlic and peppers, both sweet and hot. Although its execution varies from place to place, ceviche (raw fish lightly cured in citrus juice) and its Japanese-inspired Peruvian cousin, *tiradito*, invariably includes a fresh pungent chile of local origin. *Pepiáns* (stews thickened with ground pumpkin seeds) and moles, which are generally cooked sauces (guacamole being the notable exception), often rely on not just one but a combination of different chiles to achieve their mouthwatering results.

Chiles in various forms also play a significant role in the culture of grilled and roasted meat that dominates parts of South America. This style of cooking is called *churrasco* in Portuguese and *churrasco* or *asado* in Spanish. Chiles are a component of the freshly made chimichurris (see pages 371 and 372), prepared hot sauces and dried spice blends that accompany the main course. Feijoada, Brazil's national dish (see page 286), is a mouthwatering combination of meats, beans and spices; to gild the lily, it is usually finished with a chile-lime hot sauce.

Many of the chiles routinely used in South America, while not unique to that continent, have not traveled extensively to other parts of the world. For instance, you may find it difficult to acquire fresh ají amarillo, a workhorse in the South American kitchen and the most widely used member of the *C. baccatum* species. This small yellow-orange pepper, which is medium hot, has a delightful fruity flavor. However, if you have access to a good Latin American market, you may be able to find frozen and dried versions, as well as prepared ají amarillo paste. (These are also available online.) The relatively mild ají mirasol, whose name means "looking at the sun" in Spanish, is another member of the *C. baccatum* species. Dried versions are quite widely available.

Another species of chile commonly used in South America that is not widely available elsewhere is *C. pubescens*. These sturdy peppers, also known as rocoto or locoto depending on where they originate, resemble small squarish pears. They are quite hot, ranging from 50,000 to 100,000 SHU. They come in red, yellow and orange varieties. Milder versions are often stuffed and baked.

The malagueta pepper, a tiny firebomb that is a staple of Brazil's Bahian cuisine, is a member of the *C. frutescens* species; piri-piri, Thai bird's-eye and tabasco are better-known examples of this species. You can find pickled malagueta peppers online and in Latin American markets.

A love of fiery chiles extends to parts of the Caribbean, including Jamaica, Trinidad, Haiti and Barbados, where the most pungent varieties of the *C. chinense* species occupy a starring role. These peppers are usually relatives of the habanero and feature in local specialties, such as Jamaican jerk chicken (page 204), Haitian *pikliz* (see page 409), Barbados's famous mustard-based Bajan pepper sauce and Trinidadian mother-in-law relish (a spicy condiment made from carrots and bitter melon, along with other vegetables and possibly fruits). The chiles used in these signature recipes include Scotch bonnet, Congo, goat and bonney peppers.

On some of the Spanish-speaking islands, notably Puerto Rico and Cuba, milder peppers are more widely used, often in recipes that employ sofrito as the base. Although meekly pungent peppers, such as ají cachucha, are occasionally mentioned, sweet mild peppers, such as bell and Cubanelle, are kitchen mainstays. If dried capsicum is used at all, it is usually in the form of paprika. Bottled pimentos often show up in recipes, as do pimento-stuffed olives.

Puerto Rican cuisine is noted for being flavorful but not spicy. However, the island is known for *pique*, a hot pepper sauce made from the ají caballero, a tiny firebomb. Also known as "gentleman peppers," caballeros are macerated whole in vinegar, preferably made from pineapple. The resulting spicy liquid is judiciously sprinkled over food.

Cuba has a reputation for relatively tame food, but—possibly due to an influx of Haitians in the early part of the 20th century—I've found references to the use of ají caballero and a number of rather exotic *picante* peppers, such as *ají guaguao* (a small and fiery chile). The use of jalapeño peppers in Cuban cuisine is controversial; purists say never, but they do turn up in supposedly reliable recipes.

The culinary heritage of these islands is based on political upheaval and a variety of diverse elements. Native traditions laid the foundation, but immigration and colonial domination, not to mention personal experience, have stirred the pot, so to speak. Substantial numbers of Cubans and Puerto Ricans have spent most of their lives in the United States, and traditional recipes may bear the stamp of this experience. I recall the story of an Italian-American friend, who searched in vain for a lasagna recipe that would produce a result as "authentic" as her nonna's; when the notes for her nonna's recipe turned up, she discovered that the secret ingredient was Kraft cheese.

Calabrese-Style Fried Potatoes with Peppers (*Patate Fritte con Peperoni*)

If you are looking for the perfect partner to serve with plain-Jane grilled or roasted meat or fish, this Italian version of fried potatoes with peppers is deliciously different. You can use any combination of sweet or even mildly hot peppers (throw in a hot banana pepper for more spice), but I recommend varying the colors for a pretty presentation.

MAKES 4 TO 6 SERVINGS

VEGAN FRIENDLY

GLUTEN-FREE FRIENDLY

Tips

I like to use a combination of red, green, orange and yellow bell peppers. You can also use any combination of bell, Shepherd and/or Cubanelle peppers; if you like heat, make 1 a hot banana pepper.

If you don't have a finger chile, you can substitute hot pepper flakes; I would use 1 tsp (5 mL), but you can add more if you are a heat seeker.

To ensure the potatoes cook properly, they need to be sliced very thinly. I use a mandoline for this job. You can peel the potatoes or leave the skins on to suit your taste.

The peppers will cook better in the oil if you peel them, but this isn't strictly necessary. It is quite easy: a vegetable peeler does a good job.

4 to 5	bell, Shepherd or Cubanelle peppers (see Tips, left)	4 to 5
1	red or green finger chile (see Tips, left)	1
½ cup	extra virgin olive oil	125 mL
4	cloves garlic, thinly sliced	4
	Salt and freshly ground black pepper	
2 lbs	floury potatoes (about 4 medium), very thinly sliced (see Tips, left)	1 kg
	Hot pepper flakes, preferably *peperoncino* (optional)	
	Finely chopped fresh parsley (optional)	

1. Peel (see Tips, left), seed and cut bell peppers into thin strips. Thinly slice finger chile. In a skillet, heat oil over medium heat. Add bell peppers, finger chile and garlic and cook, stirring, until peppers are softened, about 5 minutes. Using a slotted spoon, transfer to a plate. Season to taste with salt and black pepper and set aside.

2. Add potatoes to pan, in batches. Spread first batch evenly across the bottom and cook for 1 minute. Move to 1 side of the pan and repeat with remaining batches of potatoes. Continue to cook potatoes, turning often, until evenly browned on all sides, about 10 minutes.

3. Return peppers to pan. Stir well to combine. Season to taste with hot pepper flakes (if using).

4. Using a slotted spoon, transfer potato mixture to a warm serving platter. Season to taste with additional salt and black pepper. Garnish to taste with parsley (if using). Serve immediately.

Caribbean Peas and Rice

This is a deliciously rich and spicy rice, inspired by traditional recipes from the Caribbean. It is excellent as part of a buffet, and the chiles and coconut help it liven up even the plainest main course.

MAKES 6 TO 8 SERVINGS

VEGAN FRIENDLY

GLUTEN-FREE FRIENDLY

Tip

To make 2 cups (500 mL) of cooked black-eyed peas: Soak and cook 1 cup (250 mL) dried black-eyed peas, or use 1 can (14 to 19 oz/398 to 540 mL) of black-eyed peas. Drain and rinse before using.

2 cups	drained cooked black-eyed peas (see Tip, left)	500 mL
1½ cups	coconut milk	375 mL
1 cup	water	250 mL
1 tsp	salt	5 mL
1	piece (2 inches/5 cm long) cinnamon stick	1
4	green onions (white and green parts), thinly sliced	4
½ to 1	Scotch bonnet or habanero pepper, minced	½ to 1
1 cup	long-grain brown rice	250 mL

1. In a saucepan, bring coconut milk, water, salt and cinnamon stick to a rapid boil. Stir in green onions, Scotch bonnet pepper to taste, and rice and return to a boil. Reduce heat, cover and simmer until rice is tender and most of the liquid is absorbed, about 35 minutes.

2. Stir in black-eyed peas. Cover and return to simmer. Cook until black-eyed peas are heated through and liquid is absorbed, about 7 minutes. Discard cinnamon stick. Serve immediately.

Dirty Rice

This Cajun rice dish is based on the so-called "holy trinity" of peppers, onions and celery, and "dirtied" with chopped chicken livers (and sometimes giblets). It almost always includes a jolt of pungent pepper. I like to use Cajun seasoning in the rice mixture, then add pickled peppers and/or hot sauce to the finished dish. Dirty rice is tasty with grilled meats, but is also substantial enough to serve as a main course with a salad.

Tips

If you are preparing this dish for someone who is sensitive to gluten, check the label on your Cajun seasoning to ensure it contains no added wheat products.

Prepared Cajun seasoning blends vary dramatically in pungency. The amount called for here is a safe quantity using the blend I have. You may want to spice up your result if yours is milder or reduce the quantity if your blend is particularly fiery. I recommend tasting the vegetable mixture before adding the rice and adjusting the seasoning, if desired.

2 cups	hot cooked rice	500 mL
2 tbsp	oil, divided	30 mL
4 oz	chicken livers, trimmed	125 g
1	onion, finely chopped	1
4	stalks celery, thinly sliced	4
1	green bell pepper, seeded and diced	1
3	cloves garlic, minced	3
1 tsp	dried thyme	5 mL
1 tsp	Cajun seasoning (see Tips, left)	5 mL
	Thinly sliced green onions (white and green parts)	
	Chopped pickled hot peppers (optional)	
	Hot sauce (optional)	

1. In a large skillet, heat 1 tbsp (15 mL) of the oil over medium-high heat. Add chicken livers and cook, tossing, until nicely browned but still a little pink inside, about 5 minutes. Using a slotted spoon, transfer to a plate and let cool. Chop finely and set aside.

2. Reduce heat to medium and add remaining oil to pan. Add onion, celery and bell pepper and cook, stirring, until softened, about 5 minutes. Add garlic, thyme and Cajun seasoning and cook, stirring, for 1 minute. Return chicken livers to pan and stir well. Add rice and toss well to combine.

3. Transfer to a warm serving dish. Garnish to taste with green onion, and pickled hot peppers (if using). Pass hot sauce (if using) at the table.

Roasted Red Pepper Risotto

I am particularly fond of this recipe because it uses nutritious brown rice to produce a creamy, luscious risotto. The addition of sweet roasted red peppers is a colorful and tasty finishing touch. This dish makes a terrific centerpiece for a simple dinner for last-minute guests. Pick up a rotisserie chicken or two (or a vegetable stir-fry) to go with it, along with a precooked vegetable, such as asparagus in vinaigrette. Whip this risotto up, then open a bottle of wine and everyone will think you're amazing.

MAKES 6 SERVINGS

VEGETARIAN FRIENDLY

GLUTEN-FREE FRIENDLY

Tips

If you are preparing this dish for someone who is sensitive to gluten, and you are using prepared grated Parmesan to save time, check the label to ensure it contains no added wheat products. You should also check the labels of any other prepared products, such as stocks or deli meats, because manufacturers often add products derived from wheat.

To shorten the cooking time, soak the rice in 1 cup (250 mL) of water for at least 3 hours or overnight. Drain before using in the recipe. If you want to retain more nutrients, substitute the soaking liquid for an equal amount of the stock called for in the recipe and bring it to a simmer along with the stock.

● **Heavy saucepan with tight-fitting lid**

3 cups	vegetable or chicken stock (approx.)	750 mL
1 tbsp	olive oil	15 mL
1	onion, finely chopped	1
2 tbsp	diced pancetta (optional)	30 mL
$\frac{1}{2}$ tsp	sweet or hot paprika	2 mL
$\frac{1}{4}$ tsp	freshly ground black pepper	1 mL
1 cup	short-grain (sweet) brown rice	250 mL
$\frac{1}{2}$ cup	dry white wine, or chicken or vegetable stock	125 mL
$\frac{3}{4}$ cup	diced roasted red peppers (about 2)	175 mL
2 tbsp	freshly grated Parmesan cheese (see Tips, left)	30 mL

1. In a small saucepan, bring stock to a boil. Reduce heat to as low as possible and maintain at a simmer.

2. In heavy saucepan, heat oil over medium heat. Add onion and pancetta (if using) and cook, stirring, until onion is softened, about 3 minutes. Stir in paprika and black pepper. Add rice and stir until well coated. Add wine and cook, stirring, until wine is evaporated, about 2 minutes.

3. Using a ladle, add stock about $\frac{1}{2}$ cup (125 mL) at a time, stirring until liquid is absorbed. Continue adding stock in increments and stirring until rice is almost tender. (You may not need the entire amount of stock; this should take about 30 minutes.)

4. Stir in roasted red peppers. Cover, remove from heat and let stand for 10 minutes to allow rice to steam. Stir in cheese. Serve immediately.

Chile-Spiked Cheese Grits

Grits are one of my favorite foods from the American South. The chiles and cheese in this version are a Tex-Mex–style flourish, and it sure works for me. I like to serve these grits as an accompaniment to grilled meats, shrimp or fish, or even a platter of roasted vegetables.

Tips

Grits are very sticky. A saucepan with a nonstick finish helps with cleanup. If you prefer, after completing Step 1, transfer the mixture to a greased ovenproof casserole dish and cover with foil.

Be sure to use whole-grain grits. Not only are the refined version devoid of nutrients, but they also become a gluey mush when cooked using this method.

- Preheat oven to 350°F (180°C)
- Ovenproof saucepan with lid (see Tips, left)

1¾ cups	water	425 mL
1½ cups	whole milk	375 mL
1 to 2	jalapeño or serrano pepper(s)	1 to 2
1 tsp	salt	5 mL
¾ cup	coarse stone-ground grits (see Tips, left)	175 mL
1½ cups	shredded Monterey Jack or mild Cheddar cheese	375 mL

1. In saucepan over medium heat, bring water, milk, jalapeño pepper(s) to taste and salt just to a boil. Gradually add grits, stirring until smooth and mixture is well blended.

2. Cover and transfer to preheated oven. Bake until grits are thickened and tender, about 40 minutes. Stir in cheese. Serve immediately.

Spicy Roasted Potatoes

I have an easy way to liven up a humdrum dinner. In a saucepan of boiling water, cook scrubbed potatoes in their skins just until fork-tender. Let cool, then peel and cut each lengthwise into 4 wedges. Pour extra virgin olive oil onto a large plate (about 1 tbsp/15 mL per potato) and roll potatoes in the oil until evenly coated. Sprinkle evenly with hot paprika or your favorite chile-based spice blend (such as Cajun or berbere). Arrange on a baking sheet and roast in a preheated 350°F (180°C) oven, turning 2 or 3 times, until potatoes are nicely browned, about 35 minutes. Season with plenty of flaky sea salt.

Home-Style Hash Browns

This is my own recipe for hash brown potatoes, and it is a family favorite. I have two simple secrets that turn this simple potato dish into something extra special: plenty of sweet, juicy caramelized onions and a generous sprinkling of sweet and hot paprika. Make sure the potatoes get nice and crisp when you fry them.

Tips

You can peel the potatoes or leave the skin on—the choice is yours. This dish works best if the potatoes have been cooked ahead and refrigerated until cool. If they are freshly cooked, dry them out a bit after draining them: return them to the warm dry saucepan, cover with a clean kitchen towel and set aside.

I use grapeseed oil because it is unrefined and has a high smoke point. If you prefer, use another high heat–tolerant oil, such as refined canola oil.

I like to use Hungarian paprika in this recipe because it comes in a number of different heat levels. However, the dish would still be delicious made with a mix of regular sweet paprika and $1/4$ to $1/2$ tsp (1 to 2 mL) cayenne pepper.

- Large skillet with lid

2 lbs	potatoes, cooked, cooled and cut into 1-inch (2.5 cm) cubes (see Tips, left)	1 kg
2 tbsp	butter or olive oil	30 mL
4	onions, thinly sliced on the vertical	4
	Salt and freshly ground black pepper	
$1/4$ cup	grapeseed oil (see Tips, left)	60 mL
2 tsp	sweet Hungarian paprika (see Tips, left)	10 mL
$1/2$ tsp	hot Hungarian paprika	2 mL
	Finely chopped fresh parsley (optional)	

1. In skillet over medium heat, melt butter. Add onions and toss until well coated. Reduce heat to very low, cover and cook, stirring occasionally, until onions begin to turn golden, about 20 minutes. Increase heat to medium and cook, stirring, until onions are evenly caramelized, about 10 minutes. Season to taste with salt and black pepper. Transfer to a bowl and set aside.

2. Add oil to pan and increase heat to medium-high. Add potatoes in a single layer. Sprinkle evenly with sweet and hot paprika and toss well to coat with oil. Cook, turning, until nicely browned and crisp on all sides, about 6 minutes.

3. Reduce heat to medium. Return caramelized onions to pan. Toss well to combine. Season to taste with additional salt and black pepper. Transfer to a warm serving dish. Garnish to taste with parsley (if using) and serve immediately.

Variation

If you prefer, you can add some fresh peppers to your hash browns. Omit the hot paprika and add 1 jalapeño, or $1/2$ to 1 green or red bell pepper, seeded and minced, to the onions during the final 5 minutes of caramelization.

Cuban-Style Black Beans and Yellow Rice

Beans and rice is a staple dish across the Caribbean. This version is a classic treatment in Cuba, where it is often prepared using leftover beans. It is a delicious side with roasted or grilled meat or fish. Leftovers reheat well and make a nutritious lunch.

MAKES 6 TO 8 SERVINGS

VEGAN FRIENDLY

GLUTEN-FREE FRIENDLY

Tips

If you are making this recipe for vegans, be sure to use sugar that has not been filtered through bone char.

If you are preparing this dish for someone who is sensitive to gluten, check the label on your curry powder to ensure it contains no added wheat products.

To make 2 cups (500 mL) of cooked black beans: Soak and cook 1 cup (250 mL) dried black beans, or use 1 can (14 to 19 oz/398 to 540 mL) of black beans. Drain and rinse before adding to recipe.

If you are using white rice, simmer it for about 15 minutes. Brown rice will take about 40 minutes.

2 cups	drained cooked black beans (see Tips, left)	500 mL
	Finely chopped fresh parsley	

Yellow Rice

2 cups	water	500 mL
1 cup	long-grain brown or white rice	250 mL
2 tsp	curry powder	10 mL
1 tsp	granulated sugar	5 mL
½ tsp	salt	2 mL

Sofrito

2 tbsp	olive oil	30 mL
1	onion, finely chopped	1
2	green bell or Cubanelle peppers, seeded and diced	2
4	cloves garlic, minced	4
2 tsp	dried oregano	10 mL
2 tsp	ground cumin	10 mL
1 tsp	salt	5 mL
1	bay leaf	1
1 tbsp	sherry vinegar	15 mL

1. *Yellow Rice:* In a saucepan, bring water to a boil. Stir in rice, curry powder, sugar and salt. Return to a boil. Cover, reduce heat to very low and simmer until rice is tender (see Tips, left).

2. *Sofrito:* Meanwhile, in a large skillet, heat oil over medium heat. Add onion, bell pepper and garlic and cook, stirring, until vegetables are softened, about 5 minutes. Add oregano, cumin, salt and bay leaf and cook, stirring, for 1 minute. Stir in vinegar and black beans and heat until beans are warmed through. Remove from heat. Discard bay leaf.

3. Add warm cooked rice to skillet and toss well to combine. Transfer to a warm serving dish. Garnish to taste with parsley.

Fresh Salsas, Sambals and Chutneys

Fresh Tomato Salsa (Salsa Mexicana Cruda)

This basic Mexican-style fresh salsa is often called pico de gallo in the United States. Make it when tomatoes are in season and at their most luscious—otherwise the results are likely to be disappointing. It is the perfect finish for many dishes and is even delicious with store-bought tortilla chips.

MAKES ABOUT 2¼ CUPS (560 ML)

VEGAN FRIENDLY

GLUTEN-FREE FRIENDLY

Tips

Use fewer or more chiles to suit your taste. This quantity produces a pleasantly spicy salsa.

Using puréed rather than minced garlic ensures it will evenly distribute throughout the salsa, producing just a welcome hint of flavor. To purée garlic quickly and easily, use a sharp-toothed rasp grater, such as those made by Microplane, or put the garlic through a garlic press.

This is fresh salsa, which means its appeal is very similar to that of fresh fruit—use it as quickly as possible once the flavors have melded. Left to stand, the tomatoes become soggy and the onion and garlic start to dominate.

I don't recommend using a food processor to chop the ingredients for this salsa; it would destroy the texture of the tomatoes.

2 cups	diced (¼ inch/0.5 cm) ripe field tomatoes	500 mL
¼ cup	very finely chopped red or green onion	60 mL
¼ cup	very finely chopped fresh cilantro	60 mL
2	serrano or jalapeño peppers, minced (see Tips, left)	2
1	clove garlic, puréed (see Tips, left and page 360)	1
1 tbsp	freshly squeezed lime juice	15 mL
½ to 1 tsp	fine sea salt (see below)	2 to 5 mL

1. In a medium bowl, combine tomatoes, onion, cilantro, serrano peppers to taste, garlic, lime juice and sea salt to taste. Toss to combine. Let stand at room temperature until flavors are melded, about 15 minutes. Serve within 3 hours of making (see Tips, left).

TASTY TIDBIT

I always use pure sea salt rather than refined table salt in fresh sauces like this. It has a clean, crisp taste and enhanced mineral content, unlike table salt, which has a bitter, acrid taste and contains unpleasant additives that prevent caking.

Yucatán Habanero Salsa

About 10 years ago I went on a culinary trip around Yucatán. Bitter orange juice and habanero chiles were constant companions. Here, they marry up in a very simple but elegant salsa, which, among other uses, makes a perfect finish for a grilled steak. I have made a small quantity in this recipe—just enough for a dinner for two. Feel free to multiply the amounts to suit your needs.

MAKES ABOUT ⅓ CUP (75 ML)

VEGAN FRIENDLY

GLUTEN-FREE FRIENDLY

Tip

If you have access to fresh Seville (bitter) oranges, by all means substitute 2 tbsp (30 mL) of the juice for the lime and orange juice called for here.

1	small tomato, diced	1
2	green onions (white and green parts), diced	2
½	habanero pepper, seeded and minced	½
1 tbsp	freshly squeezed orange juice	15 mL
2 tsp	freshly squeezed lime juice	10 mL
	Salt	

1. In a small bowl, combine tomato, onions, habanero pepper, orange juice and lime juice. Season with salt. Toss to combine. Transfer to a serving bowl and serve immediately.

Fresh Salsas for the Table

Throughout Latin America, fresh sauces liberally seasoned with pungent peppers are a fixture on many tables. The ingredients are usually chopped by hand, though some versions call for ingredients to be crushed in a vessel, such as a mortar, or *molcajete*. Using a blender or food processor would ruin the desired slightly chunky texture.

The chiles used for seasoning in these sauces reflect the local bounty. In Mexico, fresh tomato or tomatillo salsa is likely to be made with serrano peppers, but I often make them with jalapeños. Habanero peppers are abundant in the Yucatán Peninsula and often turn up in fresh salsas there. If you are using a habanero or one of its close relatives, such as the Scotch bonnet, I'd suggest substituting only half of one pepper in recipes that call for either serranos or jalapeños

In South America, the use of fresh salsas as table sauces varies from region to region. Many are onion- rather than tomato-based. In Bolivia, people make a version known as *llajwa* that is similar to pico de gallo; it is based on tomatoes and onions, but the chiles are likely to be rocotos.

Texas-Style Hot Sauce

This is a Texas version of pico de gallo. It is an all-purpose table sauce, made for spooning over grilled meats or casseroles that need a little livening up, or for dipping things, such as roasted vegetables. It keeps in the refrigerator for up to 1 month.

Tip

As garlic ages, the germ in the center of the clove increases in size and becomes bitter. While this bitterness is not particularly noticeable in cooked dishes, it imparts an unpleasant flavor when garlic is used raw. I always remove it before chopping.

- Food processor

3	Roma or plum tomatoes	3
¼	sweet onion, such as Texas 1015 or Vidalia, halved	¼
2	jalapeño peppers, quartered	2
2	cloves garlic, chopped (see Tip, left)	2
2 tbsp	red wine vinegar	30 mL
2 tbsp	extra virgin olive oil	30 mL
	Salt and freshly ground black pepper	

1. Peel, core and halve tomatoes. Set aside.

2. In food processor fitted with the metal blade, combine onion, jalapeño peppers, garlic, vinegar and oil. Pulse until vegetables are finely chopped and well combined. Add tomatoes and pulse to chop, just until combined but still chunky. (Don't overprocess; you don't want a purée.) Season to taste with salt and black pepper.

3. Transfer to a serving bowl and serve immediately, or transfer to an airtight container and refrigerate for up to 1 month.

Variation

If you prefer, substitute New Mexico–type chiles, such as Hatch or Sandia, or even fresh cayenne peppers for the jalapeños. Adjust the quantity to taste.

To Seed or Not to Seed

Whether you seed and remove the veins inside your peppers is a matter of preference. With the exception of bell peppers, I usually don't seed and devein because, in my opinion, it affects the taste and experience of the pepper. I like the texture the seeds add to a dish. The veins are the placental tissue inside the peppers, and they contain any spiciness, so removing them may be a good idea if you are heat-averse; you can also reduce the quantity of chile called for in a recipe or substitute a chile that ranks lower on the Scoville scale.

Pepita Salsa

This is my version of a salsa made from pan-roasted pumpkin seeds that is popular in Yucatán. According to Mexican food authority Diana Kennedy, the ruling Mayans regularly enjoyed stews made with pumpkin seeds and tomatoes before the time of the Spanish conquest. Here, that combination is used as a finishing touch for grilled meats or as a dip to serve with tortilla chips.

MAKES ABOUT 1 CUP (250 ML)

VEGAN FRIENDLY

GLUTEN-FREE FRIENDLY

Tip

To roast peppers: Brush peppers lightly with oil and place them directly on a hot grill on a preheated barbecue, or arrange them on a baking sheet and place under a preheated broiler. Grill or broil, turning 2 or 3 times, until the skin on all sides is blackened, about 20 minutes. Transfer to a heatproof bowl. Cover with a plate and let stand until cool. Using a sharp knife, lift off the skin, reserving any accumulated juices. Discard skin, stems and seeds.

- **Food processor**

1	poblano pepper, roasted (see Tip, left)	1
⅓ cup	raw pumpkin seeds (pepitas)	75 mL
1 cup	fresh parsley leaves	250 mL
1	small tomato, cored, seeded and chopped	1
1	green onion (white and green parts), coarsely chopped	1
½	clove garlic (see Tip, opposite)	½
1 tsp	cider vinegar	5 mL

1. Peel and coarsely chop poblano pepper. Set aside.
2. In a dry small skillet over medium heat, toast pumpkin seeds, stirring, just until fragrant and starting to pop, about 3 minutes. Immediately remove from heat. Transfer to food processor fitted with the metal blade.
3. Add reserved poblano pepper, parsley, tomato, onion, garlic and vinegar. Pulse until vegetables are chopped and well combined. (Don't overprocess; you don't want a purée.) Serve immediately.

Avocado Corn Salsa

This salsa resembles guacamole, which is actually a salsa (technically, it's not a dip, but it appears in the appetizer chapter of this book because that is how it is traditionally used in North America). This preparation might appear as a kind of salad, served over lettuce or perhaps stuffed into roasted poblano peppers, or as a finishing touch with a meat dish, such as carnitas, which is one of my favorite uses for guacamole. Refreshing and delicious, it is also perfect on its own with crisp tostadas or tortilla chips.

**MAKES ABOUT
4 CUPS (1 L)**

VEGAN FRIENDLY

GLUTEN-FREE FRIENDLY

Tips

If you have cold-pressed avocado oil, feel free to substitute it for the olive oil.

For best results, don't dice your avocados until you have completed the rest of the chopping. Add the cubes to the remaining ingredients and toss immediately to prevent oxidation (browning).

1½ cups	cooled cooked corn kernels	375 mL
1 tsp	extra virgin olive oil (see Tips, left)	5 mL
2	avocados, pitted, peeled and diced (see Tips, left)	2
½	red bell pepper, diced	½
½ cup	finely diced red onion	125 mL
½ to 1	habanero pepper, seeded and diced	½ to 1
¼ cup	freshly squeezed lime juice (about 1 lime)	60 mL
¼ cup	freshly squeezed orange juice (about ½ orange)	60 mL
2 tbsp	minced fresh oregano	30 mL
	Salt and freshly ground black pepper	

1. In a medium bowl, combine corn and oil. Toss well to combine. Add avocados, bell pepper, onion, habanero pepper to taste, lime juice, orange juice and oregano. Toss well to combine. Season to taste with salt and black pepper. Refrigerate until flavors are melded, about 30 minutes. Serve immediately.

Tortilla Chips and Salsa

In his book *The Hot Sauce Cookbook*, Tex-Mex expert Robb Walsh writes that the idea of serving chips with salsa originated in Texas in the 1970s. The forerunner, a popular bar snack at the time, was hot sauce sprinkled on buttered saltines or corn chips. In 1966, tortilla chips were introduced to the mass market by Frito-Lay. While bottled salsas were available, their role was limited to use in cooked dishes. A classic appetizer of the 1950s—chips and dip—served as the inspiration that moved them on to greater things. Gradually, tortilla chips stepped in for potato chips and variations on the theme of tomato-based salsa replaced cream cheese–based dips. Et voilà, a new trend was born.

Creole Sauce (*Salsa Criolla Cruda*)

This raw "Creole" sauce pops up throughout Latin America, the Caribbean and as far north as the southern United States. Since Creole is strongly associated with New Orleans, it may be a misnomer, or perhaps the sauce originated there and traveled to other locations, where it became popular. I have taken my cue from the American South and emphasized sweet onion in the mix. There, they serve this sauce with fried fish, but it is also tasty with boiled seafood, such as shrimp. You can also pour it over fresh fish before steaming.

MAKES ABOUT 1½ CUPS (375 ML)

VEGAN FRIENDLY

GLUTEN-FREE FRIENDLY

Tips

To make paper-thin slices, you'll need to use a mandoline.

I have called for a finger chile here because they are widely available, but you can use pretty much whatever fresh chile is available: cayenne, ají amarillo, Dutch (Holland) or even Anaheim (for a milder version). I often make this recipe with half of a habanero pepper, but a whole jalapeño or serrano pepper would probably work well, too.

To purée garlic, use a sharp-toothed rasp grater, such as those made by Microplane.

1	sweet onion, such as Vidalia, cut in paper-thin slices (see Tips, left)	1
1	large tomato, cored, peeled and finely chopped	1
¼ cup	finely chopped fresh parsley	60 mL
1	red finger chile, minced (see Tips, left)	1
1	clove garlic, puréed (see Tips, left and page 360)	1
2 tbsp	red wine vinegar	30 mL
½ tsp	dried oregano	2 mL
¼ cup	extra virgin olive oil	60 mL
	Salt and freshly ground black pepper	

1. In a medium bowl, combine onion, tomato, parsley, finger chile, garlic, vinegar and oregano. Toss well to combine. Add oil and toss again. Season to taste with salt and black pepper. Let stand at room temperature until flavors are melded, about 20 minutes. Serve immediately.

Thai-Style Grilled Chile Salsa (Nam Prik Num)

This recipe hails from northern Thailand. It is a kind of all-purpose sauce: you can use it as a dip for rice crackers or raw vegetables, or as a topping for plain rice or noodles, or stir-fried vegetables. Depending on the chile you use, it can be a bit fiery—that's to be expected, as it is Thai, after all.

MAKES ABOUT 2 CUPS (500 ML)

GLUTEN-FREE FRIENDLY

Tips

You want a relatively large and not-too-hot chile for this salsa—that is the best substitute for the *prik num* chile that would likely be used in this recipe in Thailand. Heat levels will vary depending on your choice, but reliable options include Anaheim or Hungarian wax peppers, as well as the hot banana peppers called for in the ingredient list. For a milder version, substitute half Cubanelle peppers for the hotter variety.

A grill basket is helpful for roasting the garlic and shallots on the barbecue, because it will keep small pieces from falling through the grate. The garlic will likely be done before the shallots, in which case just remove it and set it aside.

Be sure to use gluten-free fish sauce if you are making this salsa for someone who is sensitive to gluten.

- Preheat barbecue to high or preheat broiler
- Grill basket or baking sheet
- Food processor

5	hot banana peppers (see Tips, left)	5
2	shallots, peeled and quartered	2
8	cloves garlic, peeled and halved (see Tip, page 360)	8
8 oz	cherry tomatoes (about 1½ cups/375 mL)	250 g
2 tbsp	finely chopped fresh cilantro	30 mL
2 tbsp	freshly squeezed lime juice	30 mL
1 tbsp	fish sauce	15 mL
	Salt	

1. Place banana peppers, shallots and garlic in a grill basket on preheated barbecue or arrange on a baking sheet and place under preheated broiler. Grill or broil, turning occasionally to ensure even cooking, until shallots and garlic are blackened and pepper skin is blistered, about 8 minutes for garlic and shallots, and 10 minutes for peppers.

2. Transfer peppers to a bowl, cover with a plate and let cool enough to handle. Remove stems and lift off skins. Transfer peppers along with accumulated juices to food processor fitted with the metal blade.

3. Add shallots and garlic and pulse until chopped and well combined, 5 or 6 times. Add tomatoes, cilantro, lime juice and fish sauce and pulse until chopped and well combined, about 5 times. Season to taste with salt. Transfer to a serving bowl and let stand at room temperature until the flavors are melded, about 30 minutes. Serve immediately.

From top: Thai-Style Grilled Chile Salsa *(Nam Prik Num)*, opposite, and Mexican Tomatillo Salsa *(Salsa Verde)*, page 366

Mexican Tomatillo Salsa (Salsa Verde)

This Mexican-style salsa is made with cooked tomatillos instead of tomatoes. Although you can use drained canned tomatillos, the taste is much brighter when you make it with fresh ones. Increasingly, this bitter fruit is being grown throughout North America, so look for it at farmers' markets. Serve the salsa (pictured on page 365) with homemade or store-bought tortilla chips.

**MAKES ABOUT
1 CUP (250 ML)**

VEGAN FRIENDLY

GLUTEN-FREE FRIENDLY

Tips

If you're buying fresh tomatillos, this is the quantity in a pint (500 mL) basket.

If you prefer, substitute jalapeño peppers for the serranos.

As garlic ages, the germ in the center of the clove increases in size and becomes bitter. While this bitterness is not particularly noticeable in cooked dishes, it imparts an unpleasant flavor when garlic is used raw. I always remove it before chopping.

• Food processor

2 cups	fresh tomatillos (about 9), husked (see Tips, left)	500 mL
2 to 4	serrano peppers, coarsely chopped (see Tips, left)	2 to 4
½ cup	packed fresh cilantro leaves	125 mL
2 tbsp	coarsely chopped red or green onion	30 mL
1	clove garlic, coarsely chopped (see Tips, left)	1
½ tsp	salt	2 mL

1. In a small saucepan over medium heat, combine tomatillos with enough water to cover. Bring to a boil. Reduce heat and simmer just until tender, about 10 minutes. Drain, let cool slightly and transfer to food processor fitted with the metal blade. Pulse until chopped, 2 or 3 times.

2. Add serrano peppers to taste, cilantro, onion, garlic and salt. Pulse until jalapeños are finely chopped and mixture is well combined, about 10 times.

3. Transfer to a serving bowl and let stand at room temperature until flavors are melded, about 15 minutes. Serve within 3 hours of making.

Puerto Rican Sweet Pepper Salsa
(Salsa de Ají Dulce)

I have modeled this salsa on one that is popular in Puerto Rico, where it is usually made with Cubanelle peppers. Any sweet, mild chile will work well (see Tip, left).

**MAKES ABOUT
1 CUP (250 ML)**

VEGAN FRIENDLY

GLUTEN-FREE FRIENDLY

Tip

Mild green bell or red Shepherd peppers can be substituted for the Cubanelles. To make a spicier version of this salsa, omit the habanero and use Anaheim peppers in place of the Cubanelles.

2	mild green chiles, such as Cubanelle (see Tip, left), seeded and diced	2
¼	habanero pepper (or ½ jalapeño or serrano pepper), seeded and minced	¼
2 tbsp	minced red onion	30 mL
2 tbsp	finely chopped fresh cilantro (leaves and tender stems)	30 mL
1 tbsp	freshly squeezed lime juice	15 mL
1	clove garlic, puréed (see Tips, opposite and page 363)	1
¼ tsp	dried oregano	1 mL
¼ tsp	ground cumin	1 mL
	Salt	

1. In a medium bowl, combine green chiles, habanero pepper, onion, cilantro, lime juice, garlic, oregano and cumin. Toss well to combine. Season to taste with salt. Transfer to a serving bowl and serve immediately.

Roasted Pepper Strips (*Rajas*)

This is simply a recipe for roasted peppers, but I have included it as a stand-alone because, in culinary terms, *rajas* have a specific significance. The word means "slices" in Spanish and is used to describe strips of roasted peppers, usually poblano or bell, which are added to other dishes, such as tacos, as an ingredient or a garnish. I also like to serve them as something approaching a condiment. They are an easy-to-make flourish for grilled meats and a tasty addition to hamburgers.

MAKES ABOUT 1 CUP (250 ML)

VEGAN FRIENDLY

GLUTEN-FREE FRIENDLY

Tips

Use the technique in Step 1 to roast peppers for use in recipes. Substitute any type of pepper to suit the dish you're making.

You can easily multiply this recipe to make as many of the peppers as you need.

- Preheat barbecue to high or preheat broiler

4	poblano peppers (see Tips, left)	4
	Oil for brushing	
	Extra virgin olive oil	

1. Brush peppers lightly with oil. Place directly on preheated barbecue, or arrange on a baking sheet and place under preheated broiler. Grill or broil, turning 2 or 3 times, until the skin on all sides is blackened, about 20 minutes. Transfer to a heatproof bowl. Cover with a plate and let stand until cool.

2. Using a sharp knife, lift off pepper skin, reserving any accumulated juices. Cut peppers in half lengthwise and scrape out seeds (and veins if desired). Cut peppers in half crosswise. Cut into strips about $\frac{1}{4}$ inch (0.5 cm) wide and place in a bowl. Add reserved juices and extra virgin olive oil to taste. Toss well to combine. Use immediately or cover and refrigerate for up to 2 days.

Variations

Hamburger-Topper Rajas: When using rajas as a condiment, I like to combine sweet and hot peppers. For a hamburger topping, 1 each red and green bell pepper with 2 hot banana peppers is a perfect blend. If you are looking for something a bit spicier, add 1 jalapeño to the 4 poblanos called for in the ingredient list. The combinations are endless.

Rajas Salsa: Roast a mix of bell, poblano and jalapeño peppers and cut into rajas as directed. Place in a serving bowl and add 1 clove garlic, puréed; 1 tomato, cored, peeled and diced; 1 tbsp (15 mL) freshly squeezed lime juice; and salt to taste. Toss well to combine. Garnish to taste with finely chopped fresh cilantro.

West Indian Green Sauce (Salsa Verde)

Fresh green salsas, which reflect the herb-based salsas of South America, are also popular throughout the Caribbean. This recipe reminds me of an Italian fresh green sauce I often make in the summer that is based on arugula. This salsa verde is a wonderful finishing touch with simple grilled meats, such as chicken or pork.

MAKES ABOUT ¾ CUP (175 ML)

GLUTEN-FREE FRIENDLY

Tip

Chopping the ingredients coarsely before adding them to the food processor ensures they will combine easily without puréeing. You want this salsa to have lots of texture.

Chile Savvy

Barbados is famous for its mustard-based Bajan pepper sauces, which are made with incendiary bonney peppers, a habanero relative.

- Food processor

1 cup	loosely packed fresh cilantro leaves and tender stems	250 mL
1 cup	loosely packed fresh parsley leaves	250 mL
¼ cup	loosely packed fresh thyme leaves and tender stems	60 mL
4	green onions (white and a bit of the green parts), coarsely chopped	4
1	clove garlic, chopped (see Tips, page 366)	1
1 tbsp	drained capers	15 mL
3	anchovy fillets, coarsely chopped	3
½ to 1	Scotch bonnet or habanero pepper, coarsely chopped	½ to 1
½ tsp	finely grated lime zest	2 mL
1 tbsp	freshly squeezed lime juice	15 mL
1 tbsp	extra virgin olive oil	15 mL
	Salt	

1. In food processor fitted with the metal blade, combine cilantro, parsley, thyme, onions, garlic, capers, anchovies, Scotch bonnet pepper to taste and lime zest. Pulse, stopping and scraping down the side of the bowl as necessary, just until combined.

2. Add lime juice and olive oil and pulse just until combined. (Do not overprocess.) Season to taste with salt and pulse just until combined. Transfer to a serving bowl and let stand at room temperature until flavors are melded, about 30 minutes. Serve immediately.

Sauce Chien

The origins of its rather odd name (which means "dog sauce") are not clear, but this spicy condiment is a fixture on islands of the French West Indies, such as Martinique and Guadeloupe. A jumped-up version of the classic French vinaigrette, it is delicious over simple grilled foods. Good choices include white fish such as snapper (assuming you can find some that is sustainably caught), seafood such as lobster and shrimp, chicken breasts and even grilled vegetables.

MAKES ABOUT ¾ CUP (175 ML)

VEGAN FRIENDLY

GLUTEN-FREE FRIENDLY

Tip

I always use pure sea salt rather than refined table salt in fresh sauces like this. It has a clean, crisp taste and enhanced mineral content, unlike table salt, which has a bitter, acrid taste and contains unpleasant additives that prevent caking.

- Food processor

6	green onions (white and a bit of the green parts)	6
¼ cup	packed fresh parsley leaves	60 mL
½ to 1	Scotch bonnet or habanero pepper	½ to 1
2	cloves garlic	2
1 tsp	finely chopped gingerroot	5 mL
½ tsp	fresh thyme leaves	2 mL
¼ cup	freshly squeezed lime juice	60 mL
2 tbsp	extra virgin olive oil	30 mL
¼ cup	boiling water	60 mL
½ tsp	fine sea salt (see Tip, left)	2 mL
	Freshly ground black pepper	

1. In food processor fitted with the metal blade, combine onions, parsley, Scotch bonnet pepper to taste, garlic, ginger and thyme. Pulse, stopping and scraping down the side of the bowl as necessary, until finely chopped. Add lime juice and oil and process until smooth and blended.

2. With motor running, pour boiling water through the feed tube in a slow, steady steam until the mixture is emulsified. Add salt, and black pepper to taste, and pulse until blended.

3. Transfer to a serving bowl and let stand at room temperature until flavors are melded, about 15 minutes. If you're not serving immediately, cover and refrigerate for up to 3 days.

Variations

Substitute freshly squeezed lemon juice for the lime juice and serve the sauce over grilled sliced beef, such as a côte de boeuf.

Substitute red wine vinegar for the lime juice and serve the sauce with grilled lamb chops.

Green Chimichurri Sauce

This sauce (pictured on page 373) is ubiquitous in South America, where it is a significant player in the art of *churrasco*: meat, most often beef, that is grilled over charcoal or a wood fire. Parsley is the traditional base, but cooks vary the herbs and spices. I flavor my green chimichurri heavily with robust, earthy oregano, which is what the gauchos use, according to famous Argentinean churrasco chef Francis Mallman. Chile is not typically added in Argentina, he says, but this seems to be a very purist approach in practice. Pass the sauce at the table or use it as a marinade (see Tips, below).

MAKES ABOUT 2 CUPS (500 ML)

VEGAN FRIENDLY

GLUTEN-FREE FRIENDLY

Tips

Fresh ají amarillo or manzano chiles are rarely available in my part of the world, but if you can find them, by all means use them, to taste, in this sauce.

If you are using chimichurri as a marinade, scoop out about half of the batch and add ½ cup (125 mL) water. Mix well. Spread over meat, cover and refrigerate until you are ready to cook.

In North America, a version of chimichurri containing cilantro and mint is popular as an accompaniment for grilled lamb.

Moreover ...

It is amusing to note that chile peppers do not grow well in the country of Chile. The climate is too chilly (pardon the pun) for them.

- Food processor

4 cups	fresh parsley leaves (about 1 bunch)	1 L
½ cup	fresh oregano leaves	125 mL
½	red onion, sliced	½
4	cloves garlic, coarsely chopped	4
1	ají amarillo, manzano chile, habanero pepper or long red chile (see Tips, left)	1
½ cup	extra virgin olive oil	125 mL
¼ cup	red wine vinegar	60 mL
	Salt	

1. In food processor fitted with the metal blade, combine parsley, oregano, onion, garlic and ají amarillo. Pulse, stopping and scraping down the side of the bowl as necessary, until chopped and well combined, about 10 times. Scrape down the side of the bowl.

2. With motor running, pour oil and vinegar through the feed tube in a slow steady stream until the mixture is well blended. Season to taste with salt and pulse until blended.

3. Transfer to a serving bowl. Serve immediately or cover and refrigerate for up to 1 week.

Variations

Substitute 1 cup (250 mL) fresh cilantro leaves and tender stems for the oregano.

Substitute 4 green onions (white and green parts) for the red onion.

Red Chimichurri Sauce

Whenever I'm serving a mixed grill to guests, I like to provide a couple of different finishing sauces. This version of chimichurri, which likely has a direct link to immigrants from the Basque part of Spain who settled in Argentina, substitutes cilantro for parsley and adds red bell pepper and smoked paprika to the blend. Although chimichurri is usually served with beef, it is a great all-purpose sauce and makes an excellent accent to grilled chicken and fish.

MAKES ABOUT ¾ CUP (175 ML)

VEGAN FRIENDLY

GLUTEN-FREE FRIENDLY

Tips

Although I like the flavor of smoked paprika, I find that it can easily overwhelm a dish—I've chosen to be cautious in this recipe. If you prefer a smokier sauce, go ahead and increase the quantity.

I grind a dried chile de árbol, which I usually have on hand, in a spice grinder, which yields about ½ tsp (2 mL) of powder. If you have access to a fresh Latin American pepper, such as ají amarillo, or dried Argentinean ground red pepper, such as *ají molido*, substitute it, to taste. Even a fresh red finger chile, added along with the bell pepper, would work well in this sauce.

- Food processor

2 cups	fresh cilantro leaves	500 mL
½	red bell pepper, seeded and chopped	½
4	green onions (white and a bit of the green parts), coarsely chopped	4
3	cloves garlic, coarsely chopped	3
2 tbsp	red wine vinegar	30 mL
1 tbsp	extra virgin olive oil	15 mL
½ tsp	dried Mexican oregano (see Tip, page 266)	2 mL
½ tsp	smoked sweet paprika (see Tips, left)	2 mL
1	dried chile de árbol, ground (see Tips, left)	1
	Salt and freshly ground black pepper	

1. In food processor fitted with the metal blade, combine cilantro, bell pepper, onions and garlic. Pulse until chopped and well combined, about 10 times. Scrape down the side of the bowl.

2. Add vinegar, oil, oregano, paprika and chile de árbol and pulse until blended. Season to taste with salt and black pepper and pulse until blended.

3. Transfer to a serving bowl. Serve immediately or cover and refrigerate for up to 1 week.

Variation

If you happen to have merkén on hand (see box, page 374), substitute 2 tsp (10 mL) of it for the oregano, paprika and chile de árbol called for in this recipe.

From top: Red Chimichurri Sauce, opposite, and Green Chimichurri Sauce, page 371

Merkén

Merkén is a Chilean spice blend based on a local pepper called *cacho de cabra* ("goat's horn"), which is smoked and ground. It often appears in prepared hot sauces, as well. The smoked pepper is traditionally an artisanal product, prepared by the indigenous Mapuche people, who string the peppers into brightly colored ristras (see page 31) and smoke them over wood fires in their huts.

The dried smoked peppers are ground with lightly smoked cumin, oregano, coriander and salt (and perhaps other secret spices). You can buy merkén in local markets in Chile. Use it to season *sofrito*, in dry rubs for meats or as a finishing spice. To create a deliciously different beverage, add it to hot chocolate. The Chilean chef Jorge Pacheco uses it to flavor pasta dough and adds it to batter for fried fish.

Spicy Olive Salsa

This delightful salsa, which has an intriguing nutty flavor, is the perfect finish for any grilled meat flavored with Middle Eastern spices.

**MAKES ABOUT
1 CUP (250 ML)**

VEGAN FRIENDLY

GLUTEN-FREE FRIENDLY

Tip

If you don't have Aleppo pepper, substitute 1 tsp (5 mL) sweet paprika and ⅛ tsp (0.5 mL) hot paprika or cayenne pepper.

● Food processor

½ cup	coarsely chopped green olives	125 mL
½ cup	packed fresh parsley leaves	125 mL
2	green onions (white and green parts), coarsely chopped	2
½	red finger chile, coarsely chopped	½
⅓ cup	walnut halves, toasted	75 mL
2 tbsp	chopped unsalted pistachios	30 mL
1 tsp	Aleppo pepper (see Tip, left)	5 mL
2 tbsp	extra virgin olive oil	30 mL
2 tbsp	freshly squeezed lemon juice	30 mL
	Salt and freshly ground black pepper	

1. In food processor fitted with the metal blade, combine olives, parsley, onions, finger chile, walnuts, pistachios and Aleppo pepper. Pulse, stopping and scraping down the side of the bowl as necessary, until chopped and well combined, about 12 times.

2. Add oil and lemon juice and pulse until blended, about 6 times. Season to taste with salt and black pepper.

3. Transfer to a serving bowl and let stand at room temperature until flavors are melded, about 30 minutes. Serve immediately or cover and refrigerate for up to 5 days.

Yemeni-Style Fresh Chile Sauce (Zhoug)

This fresh green salsa comes from Yemen but is popular throughout the Middle East. It is often served as an accompaniment to falafels, but it is also delicious served alongside grilled meats, fish and poultry. Zhoug usually contains fiery chiles exclusively, but I prefer to mitigate the heat with the addition of half of a bell pepper.

MAKES ABOUT ¾ CUP (175 ML)

VEGAN FRIENDLY

GLUTEN-FREE FRIENDLY

Tips

Peppers are easy to peel. Use a sharp vegetable peeler to remove the skin.

If you are a heat seeker, substitute an additional jalapeño for the bell pepper.

Zhoug is typically made with fiery green chiles. I have used jalapeño peppers here because they are readily available, but feel free to substitute any hot green chile, in the amount that suits your heat tolerance.

FYI: I use the term "gluten-free friendly" whenever I include prepared ingredients in a recipe that would otherwise be gluten-free. Manufacturers often add wheat products to prepared foods, so you need to check the label to ensure these products are actually gluten-free.

- Food processor

½ cup	fresh cilantro leaves and tender stems	125 mL
½ cup	fresh parsley leaves	125 mL
½	green bell pepper, peeled (see Tips, left), seeded and cut into chunks	½
2	jalapeño peppers, peeled, seeded and cut into chunks (see Tips, left)	2
2	cloves garlic, coarsely chopped	2
1 tsp	ground cumin (see Tip, page 379)	5 mL
3 tbsp	extra virgin olive oil	45 mL
	Salt and freshly ground black pepper	

1. In food processor fitted with the metal blade, combine cilantro, parsley, bell pepper, jalapeño peppers, garlic and cumin. Pulse until chopped and well combined, about 15 times. Scrape down the side of the bowl. Add oil and pulse until blended, about 5 times. Season to taste with salt and black pepper.

2. Transfer to a serving bowl. Serve immediately or cover and refrigerate for up to 1 week.

Coconut Sambal (*Sambal Kelapa*)

This fresh coconut salsa is very popular in Sri Lanka. It is an excellent accompaniment to curries with Sri Lankan seasoning (such as Pork Colombo, page 274); a wide variety of rice dishes; and hoppers, the local version of pancakes that is often served for breakfast or lunch. In Sri Lanka, sambal kelapa accompanies almost everything, like ketchup does in North America. Although it is not traditional to toast the coconut, I enjoy the intensified flavor.

MAKES ABOUT ½ CUP (125 ML)

GLUTEN-FREE FRIENDLY

Tips

Be sure to use gluten-free fish sauce if you are making this sambal for someone who is sensitive to gluten.

You can purchase frozen shredded young coconut in Asian markets. Thaw and pat it dry before using it.

Be sure to stir the coconut constantly as it toasts; otherwise, some bits will become overly browned. Once it is nicely toasted, immediately remove it from the pan because the residual heat will continue to cook it.

To purée garlic easily, use a sharp-toothed rasp grater, such as those made by Microplane.

• Food processor with mini work bowl

1 cup	shredded young coconut, thawed if frozen (see Tips, left)	250 mL
2	green onions (white and green parts), chopped	2
1 to 2	red Thai bird's-eye chile(s), chopped	1 to 2
1	clove garlic, puréed (see Tips, left)	1
¼ cup	freshly squeezed lime juice	60 mL
1 tbsp	fish sauce	15 mL
2 tsp	coconut sugar	10 mL
	Salt	

1. In a skillet over medium heat, toast coconut, stirring constantly, until fragrant and caramel-colored, about 10 minutes. Transfer to food processor fitted with the metal blade and let cool slightly.

2. Add green onions, bird's-eye chile(s) to taste, garlic, lime juice, fish sauce and coconut sugar to food processor. Pulse until chopped and well combined, about 6 times. Season to taste with salt and pulse until combined.

3. Transfer to a serving bowl and let stand until flavors are melded, about 20 minutes. Serve immediately.

Peanut Sambal (*Sambal Bubuk Dari Kacang*)

This uncooked sambal is particularly easy to make. Serve it with satay or *gado gado* (page 308), or as an accompaniment to rice or other dishes.

Moreover ...

In his excellent book *Cradle of Flavor*, James Oseland writes that Southeast Asian sambals can contain a multitude of ingredients in addition to chiles. He also points out that, although they vary regionally, they are most often used for seasoning rice.

- Fine-mesh sieve
- Food processor

¼ cup	boiling water	60 mL
1 tbsp	Thai tamarind paste, chopped	15 mL
¼ cup	peanut oil	60 mL
1 cup	raw peanuts	250 mL
1 to 2	anchovy fillets, minced	1 to 2
1	red Thai bird's-eye chile, chopped	1
1	clove garlic, puréed (see Tips, opposite)	1
2 tbsp	unseasoned rice vinegar	30 mL
1 tsp	coconut sugar	5 mL
	Salt	
	Water or coconut milk	

1. In a small bowl, combine boiling water and tamarind paste. Mash paste into water and let stand until flavors are infused, about 20 minutes. Strain through sieve into a small bowl, pressing on the solids with a spatula. Scrape the paste on the underside of the sieve into the bowl, and discard solids. Set aside.

2. In a small skillet, heat oil over medium heat. Add peanuts and cook, stirring, until golden, about 3 minutes. Using a slotted spoon, transfer to a paper towel–lined plate. Let cool.

3. Transfer peanuts to food processor fitted with the metal blade. Add anchovies to taste, bird's-eye chile, garlic, vinegar, coconut sugar and reserved tamarind water. Pulse until ingredients are chopped and well combined. (Don't purée the peanuts; they should retain some texture.) Season to taste with salt, if necessary, and pulse once or twice to blend. If mixture seems dry, thin with water to desired consistency.

4. Transfer to a serving bowl. Serve immediately.

Cilantro Mint Chutney

This recipe is adapted from one that appeared in *Easy Indian Cooking* by my friend Suneeta Vaswani. It makes a very fresh-tasting salsa-style sauce that is delicious on tortilla chips. It also makes a wonderful dipping sauce for cold boiled shrimp or roti.

MAKES 1 CUP (250 ML)

VEGAN FRIENDLY

GLUTEN-FREE FRIENDLY

Tip

If you are making this chutney for vegans, be sure to use sugar that has not been filtered through bone char.

- Food processor

4 cups	loosely packed fresh cilantro leaves	1 L
1	red or green finger chile, coarsely chopped	1
½ cup	fresh mint leaves	125 mL
¼ cup	freshly squeezed lime juice	60 mL
2 tbsp	minced gingerroot	30 mL
2 tsp	granulated sugar	10 mL
1 tsp	each minced garlic and ground cumin	5 mL
½ tsp	salt	2 mL

1. In food processor fitted with the metal blade, combine cilantro, finger chile, mint, lime juice, ginger, sugar, garlic, cumin and salt. Purée until smooth, stopping and scraping down the side of the bowl as necessary.
2. Transfer to a serving bowl. Serve immediately.

Yogurt Mint Chutney

Thanks again to my friend Suneeta Vaswani for allowing me to use this recipe, which appeared in her book *Easy Indian Cooking*. It is so simple to make and utterly delicious. This is an all-purpose chutney, but it is particularly good as a dipping sauce for samosas.

MAKES ABOUT 1 CUP (250 ML)

VEGETARIAN FRIENDLY

GLUTEN-FREE FRIENDLY

- Blender

1 cup	plain yogurt, divided	250 mL
½ to 1	red or green finger chile	½ to 1
8	fresh mint leaves	8
2 tbsp	fresh cilantro leaves	30 mL
¼ tsp	salt, or to taste	1 mL

1. In blender, combine ¼ cup (60 mL) of the yogurt, finger chile to taste, mint, cilantro and salt. Blend to make a smooth paste.
2. Transfer to a serving bowl. Stir in remaining yogurt. Cover and refrigerate until chilled before serving, about 2 hours. If not using immediately, refrigerate for up to 1 week.

Date and Tamarind Chutney

This Indian-inspired treat, loosely based on a traditional recipe called *imli chutney*, is luscious. Indian cooks often used ground dried red pepper, such as Kashmiri, to season this condiment, but I prefer the brightness a fresh pepper adds. It's amazing served with slightly sweet crackers, such as fruit-and-nut crisps or British-style oat biscuits. If you want to keep the experience geographically contained, serve it on an Indian bread, such as naan.

MAKES ABOUT 1½ CUPS (375 ML)

VEGAN FRIENDLY

GLUTEN-FREE FRIENDLY

Tip

To toast and grind cumin: Toasting and grinding cumin yourself ensures the best flavor. In a dry skillet over medium heat, toast cumin seeds, stirring, until fragrant, about 3 minutes. Immediately transfer to a mortar or a spice grinder and grind to a powder.

• Food processor

1 cup	hot water	250 mL
1 tsp	raw cane sugar, such as Demerara	5 mL
2 oz	Thai tamarind purée, broken into pieces (about 2 tbsp/30 mL)	60 g
8 oz	pitted soft dates, such as Medjool (about 1 cup/250 mL)	250 g
1	red finger chile, seeded and coarsely chopped	1
½ tsp	ground cumin (see Tip, left)	2 mL

1. In a small bowl, combine hot water and sugar, stirring until sugar is dissolved. Add tamarind purée and let stand for 30 minutes.

2. In food processor fitted with the metal blade, combine dates, finger chile, cumin and tamarind mixture. Purée until smooth and creamy, about 1 minute. If mixture is too thick, add a little bit more water and pulse until smooth.

3. Transfer to a serving bowl. Serve immediately or cover and refrigerate for up to 1 week.

Sauces, Marinades, Dressings and Condiments

Arabian-Style Tomato Sauce (Dakkous)

This Arabian version of all-purpose tomato sauce with a kick is one of my favorite indulgences during the dark days of winter, when fresh, ripe tomatoes are scarce. In the Middle East, is traditionally served with main courses, such as lamb and rice, or as a dipping sauce for grilled vegetables. I also like to serve it with Fried Fish in Spicy Chickpea Batter (page 152).

**MAKES ABOUT
1 CUP (250 ML)**

VEGAN FRIENDLY

GLUTEN-FREE FRIENDLY

FYI: I use the term "gluten-free friendly" whenever I include prepared ingredients in a recipe that would otherwise be gluten-free. Manufacturers often add wheat products to prepared foods, so you need to check the label to ensure these products are actually gluten-free.

2 tbsp	extra virgin olive oil	30 mL
3	red finger chiles, minced	3
4	cloves garlic, chopped	4
1½ cups	canned or jarred crushed tomatoes (passata)	375 mL
1 tbsp	tomato paste	15 mL
1	piece (2 inches/5 cm long) cinnamon stick	1
	Salt and freshly ground black pepper	

1. In a small skillet, heat oil over medium heat. Add chiles and garlic and cook, stirring, for 1 minute. Stir in crushed tomatoes, tomato paste and cinnamon stick and cook, stirring occasionally, until sauce is thickened, about 30 minutes.

2. Remove from heat. Season to taste with salt and black pepper. Serve warm.

To Seed or Not to Seed

Whether you seed and remove the veins inside your peppers is a matter of preference. With the exception of bell peppers, I usually don't seed and devein because, in my opinion, it affects the taste and experience of the pepper. I like the texture the seeds add to a dish. The veins are the placental tissue inside the peppers, and they contain any spiciness, so removing them may be a good idea if you are heat-averse; you can also reduce the quantity of chile called for in a recipe or substitute a chile that ranks lower on the Scoville scale.

Chile-Spiked Barbecue Sauce

Sure, you can purchase flavorful barbecue sauce, but if you want to know exactly what is in it, you need to make your own. I really like the flavors in this sauce, which are nicely balanced—there are sweet, sour and spicy notes, with a bit of umami in the form of Worcestershire sauce thrown in. Use it wherever barbecue sauce is called for. It is particularly good with American-Style Rubbed Ribs with Mop (page 292).

MAKES ABOUT 2 CUPS (500 ML)

VEGAN FRIENDLY

GLUTEN-FREE FRIENDLY

Tip

If you're making this recipe for a vegan or vegetarian, be sure to use vegan Worcestershire sauce. You should also check to make sure it is gluten-free if you are serving the sauce to people who are sensitive to gluten.

- Blender or food processor

2 tbsp	oil	30 mL
1	onion, finely chopped	1
4	cloves garlic, minced	4
1	jalapeño pepper, minced	1
1 tbsp	dried oregano	15 mL
1 tsp	chipotle chile powder	5 mL
1 cup	canned or jarred crushed tomatoes (passata)	250 mL
1	can (5½ oz/156 mL) tomato paste	1
⅓ cup	raw cane sugar, such as Demerara	75 mL
¼ cup	red wine vinegar	60 mL
2 tbsp	Worcestershire sauce	30 mL
2 tbsp	Dijon mustard	30 mL
	Salt and freshly ground black pepper	

1. In a medium saucepan, heat oil over medium heat. Add onion and cook, stirring, until softened, about 3 minutes. Add garlic, jalapeño pepper, oregano and chipotle chile powder and cook, stirring, for 1 minute. Add crushed tomatoes, tomato paste, sugar, vinegar, Worcestershire sauce and mustard and bring to a boil. Reduce heat and simmer, stirring occasionally, until thickened, about 30 minutes. Season to taste with salt and black pepper.

2. Remove from heat. Let cool slightly. Transfer sauce to blender and purée until smooth. Transfer to an airtight container. Store in the refrigerator for up to 2 months or freeze for up to 1 year.

Portuguese Pepper Paste (Massa de Pimentão)

Portuguese cuisine uses red pepper pastes that are much like the Turkish ones. Often made from salt-cured peppers, they are included in marinades (see Portuguese Roast Pork, page 264), sauces, soups and stews to add a burst of flavor. Home cooks keep them on hand; they are likely to have both a sweet and a pungent version at the ready. This is a simplified adaptation that allows for the addition of heat, if you like.

MAKES ABOUT ½ CUP (125 ML)

VEGAN FRIENDLY

GLUTEN-FREE FRIENDLY

Tips

I have called for Thai bird's-eye peppers because they are readily available. However, piri-piri peppers, a close relative, would be the traditional choice. I have never seen fresh piri-piris in North America, but they are available in dried or preserved form at specialty markets. Preserved piri-piri peppers could be substituted for the fresh chiles in this recipe, or try adding the dried flakes for extra oomph.

To roast peppers: Brush peppers lightly with oil and place them directly on a hot grill on a preheated barbecue, or arrange them on a baking sheet and place under a preheated broiler. Grill or broil, turning 2 or 3 times, until the skin on all sides is blackened, about 20 minutes. Transfer to a heatproof bowl. Cover with a plate and let stand until cool. Using a sharp knife, lift off the skin, reserving any accumulated juices. Discard skin, stems and seeds.

- Blender
- 4-oz (125 mL) preserving jar with lid, sterilized (see Tip, page 396)

2	red bell peppers, roasted (see Tips, left), seeded and peeled	2
2	red Thai bird's-eye chiles (optional)	2
1	clove garlic	1
2 tbsp	extra virgin olive oil	30 mL
	Salt	

1. In blender, combine roasted red peppers, bird's-eye chiles (if using), garlic, oil, and salt to taste. Purée until smooth.
2. Spoon into prepared jar. Wipe rim and screw on lid. Store in the refrigerator for up to 2 weeks.

Turkish-Style Red Pepper Paste (*Biber Salçasi*)

In Turkey, healthy dollops of this paste are added to recipes for the same reason that we add tomato paste in North America: to give depth, richness and a certain *je ne sais quoi*. The mixture is ubiquitous in Turkish markets, where it is sold (along with the equally popular tomato paste) *au naturel*; both resemble large blocks of tomato aspic. Cooks have their own recipes, which can be made with sweet or hot peppers, and sometimes herbs. This is my basic version.

MAKES ABOUT 1½ CUPS (375 ML)

VEGAN FRIENDLY

GLUTEN-FREE FRIENDLY

Tips

If you are making this recipe for vegans, be sure to use sugar that has not been filtered through bone char.

Although it is more work, the easiest and most thorough way to peel peppers is by roasting them, then sweating and lifting off the skin (see Tips, opposite). However, you can do a decent job on raw peppers using a vegetable or tomato peeler—the curvy areas on the tops and bottoms of bell peppers are the only challenge. Some people use a method similar to peeling a tomato: using a sharp knife, make a number of small slits in the skin of the pepper (do not pierce the flesh.) Submerge pepper in boiling water until the skin loosens, about 10 minutes. Immerse in a bowl of ice water, then lift off the skins.

Any sweet red pepper, such as pimiento or Shepherd, works well in this paste. Use whatever is in season.

- Food processor
- Three 4-oz (125 mL) preserving jars with lids, sterilized (see Tip, page 396)

1½ lbs	red bell peppers, peeled (see Tips, left), seeded and veins removed	750 g
1 tbsp	white wine vinegar, cider vinegar or quince vinegar	15 mL
1 tsp	granulated sugar	5 mL
1 tsp	salt	5 mL
	Olive oil	

1. In food processor fitted with the metal blade, purée prepared bell peppers until smooth.
2. Transfer to a medium saucepan. Add vinegar, sugar and salt. Cook over low heat, stirring often, until mixture is reduced to a thick paste, about 45 minutes.
3. Spoon into prepared jars. Add enough oil to completely cover the surface of the paste. Wipe rims and screw on lids. Store in the refrigerator for up to 2 months, adding fresh olive oil every time you use some of the paste.

Variation

This paste is excellent in a variety of dishes, including casseroles and stews. Try mixing it with a little cream or sour cream and swirling it into soups, or adding it as a finishing touch to other dishes (see Chile-Spiked Crema, page 400, for inspiration).

Easy Thai-Style Peanut Sauce

This sauce is very easy to make and has a multitude of uses. It is a great accompaniment to shrimp, chicken or pork satay. Or toss it with hot cooked noodles and garnish liberally with green onions for an instant main course. It's also a fabulous dip for fresh vegetables, such as broccoli, carrot sticks or cucumber slices.

MAKES ABOUT 1½ CUPS (375 ML)

VEGAN FRIENDLY

GLUTEN-FREE FRIENDLY

Tips

Use salted or unsalted peanuts to suit your taste.

Be sure to use gluten-free soy sauce or wheat-free tamari if you are making this dish for someone who is sensitive to gluten.

- Food processor

2	green onions (white and green parts), thickly sliced	2
1 tbsp	minced gingerroot	15 mL
1 tbsp	minced garlic	15 mL
1 to 2	red Thai bird's-eye chile(s), sliced	1 to 2
2 tbsp	soy sauce	30 mL
2 tbsp	unseasoned rice vinegar	30 mL
½ cup	crunchy peanut butter	125 mL
½ cup	coconut milk	125 mL
1 tsp	coconut sugar	5 mL
1 tbsp	finely chopped roasted peanuts (optional), see Tips, left	15 mL
	Roasted chile powder (optional), see Tips, page 131	

1. In food processor fitted with the metal blade, combine onions, ginger, garlic, bird's-eye chile(s) to taste, soy sauce and vinegar. Pulse until onions and peppers(s) are very finely chopped, stopping and scraping down the side of the bowl as necessary.

2. Add peanut butter, coconut milk and coconut sugar and process until blended. Use immediately if tossing with noodles or adding to other dishes. If serving as a dip or accompaniment to grilled meats, transfer to a serving bowl and garnish with roasted peanuts (if using) and season to taste with roasted chile powder (if using).

Variation

For a more intense and complex flavor, in a small saucepan, bring ½ cup (125 mL) coconut milk to a boil over medium heat. Stir in 2 tsp (10 mL) Thai-Style Red Curry Paste (page 392). Cook, stirring, until paste is dissolved. Substitute this mixture for the coconut milk in Step 2. Adjust the quantity of bird's-eye chiles to suit your taste. (I recommend 1 if you're adding this infused coconut milk.)

GRILLED CALÇOTS

UNLESS YOU LIVE in Spain's Catalonia region, it is unlikely you will be able to source calçots, a type of green onion grown there. Formally recognized as Calçot de Valls, these onions have earned Protected Geographical Indication status, or *Indicación Geográfica Protegida* (IGP) in Spanish.

However, you can serve a delicious alternative by grilling green onions and then wrapping them in newspaper to steam (an integral part of the Catalonian ritual that celebrates the annual calçot harvest). Heat a grill pan or barbecue to high. Toss about 2 bunches of green onions, trimmed, with 2 tbsp (30 mL) extra virgin olive oil. Grill, turning as necessary, until onions are nicely charred and soft. Wrap in newspaper and set aside to steam for 10 minutes. Sprinkle liberally with flaky sea salt and serve with Romesco Sauce (page 388) for dipping. Don't forget to pass the napkins.

Romesco Sauce

This classic Catalan sauce is often thickened with fried bread; here, I have used almonds, which are also traditional and make the recipe gluten-free. Romesco sauce is a wonderful finish for grilled fish and seafood (especially shrimp), poultry and meat (especially pork) and even vegetables. It is actually a slight variation on a sauce served in the province of Tarragona in Catalonia, where it stars in an annual celebration along with a local onion known as the *calçot*, which is grilled (see page 387).

(see page 387).

MAKES ABOUT 3 CUPS (750 ML)

VEGAN FRIENDLY

GLUTEN-FREE FRIENDLY

Tips

To toast almonds: In a dry skillet over medium heat, toast almonds, stirring constantly, until golden brown, about 5 minutes. Immediately transfer to a small bowl to prevent burning.

Ñora is the traditional pepper used to season romesco sauce, but paprika or another mild dried chile makes a very acceptable substitute.

Chile Savvy

For a deliciously different dish, serve Romesco Sauce with grilled shishito or padrón peppers (see page 77) as dippers.

- Preheat oven to 425°F (220°C)
- Food processor

6	cloves garlic (unpeeled)	6
6	Roma or plum tomatoes (about 1 lb/500 g)	6
1	red bell pepper	1
	Olive oil for brushing	
½ cup	whole blanched almonds, lightly toasted (see Tips, left)	125 mL
2 tsp	ground ñora pepper or sweet paprika (see Tips, left)	10 mL
1	red finger chile, chopped (optional)	1
½ cup	extra virgin olive oil	125 mL
2 tbsp	red wine vinegar	30 mL
	Salt and freshly ground black pepper	

1. Place garlic, tomatoes and bell pepper on a baking sheet and brush with oil. Roast in preheated oven until garlic and tomatoes are browned and wrinkled, and pepper is blackened, about 25 minutes. (The garlic and tomatoes will be done before the pepper; remove them as completed.)

2. Transfer garlic and tomatoes to a plate and let cool. Place pepper in a bowl and cover with a plate. Set aside to sweat. When vegetables are cool, squeeze garlic out of skins; lift skins off tomatoes, if desired; and peel and seed pepper. Transfer to food processor fitted with the metal blade.

3. Add almonds, ñora pepper and finger chile (if using). Process until vegetables are puréed and almonds are finely chopped. Add oil and vinegar and process until blended. Season to taste with salt and black pepper.

4. Transfer to a sauceboat. Cover and refrigerate until flavors are developed, at least 4 hours or up to 2 days.

Harissa

Harissa is a hot pepper paste that is used extensively in North African cuisine. It is available in specialty shops across North America, but it is very easy to make your own. Prepared harissa sometimes contains gluten; this homemade one does not.

MAKES ABOUT ½ CUP (125 ML)

VEGAN FRIENDLY

GLUTEN-FREE FRIENDLY

Tips

If you have a mini-bowl attachment for your food processor, this is the perfect time to use it.

You need sun-dried tomatoes that have been rehydrated for this recipe. The easiest option is sun-dried tomatoes packed in extra virgin olive oil, which just need to be drained. You can also use dry-packed sun-dried tomatoes; soak them in 1 cup (250 mL) of boiling water for 15 minutes, then drain before using.

- Food processor or blender (see Tips, left)
- Spice grinder, or mortar and pestle
- 4-oz (125 mL) preserving jar with lid, sterilized (see Tip, page 396)

12	dried red chiles, such as cayenne or Kashmiri, stems removed	12
	Boiling water	
2 tsp	caraway seeds	10 mL
2 tsp	coriander seeds	10 mL
1 tsp	cumin seeds	5 mL
2	prepared sun-dried tomatoes (see Tips, left)	2
2	cloves garlic	2
2 tbsp	freshly squeezed lemon juice	30 mL
½ tsp	sea salt	2 mL
¼ cup	extra virgin olive oil	60 mL

1. Place dried chiles in a medium heatproof bowl and cover generously with boiling water. Let stand until softened, about 30 minutes, weighing down with a cup to ensure they stay submerged. Drain. Transfer chiles to food processor fitted with the metal blade.

2. Meanwhile, in a small skillet over medium heat, toast caraway, coriander and cumin seeds, stirring, until fragrant, about 3 minutes. Transfer to spice grinder and grind to a powder. Add to chiles in food processor.

3. Add sun-dried tomatoes, garlic, lemon juice and salt and pulse until chopped. Add olive oil and process, stopping and scraping down the side of the bowl 3 or 4 times, until the mixture forms an almost-smooth paste. (Some seeds and bits of chile pepper will remain.)

4. Spoon into prepared jar. Wipe rim and screw on lid. Store in the refrigerator for up to 1 month, adding fresh olive oil every time you use some of the paste.

Dersa

This Algerian sauce resembles Harissa (opposite). It's traditionally made by crushing dried hot peppers, paprika, garlic, salt, cumin and perhaps cinnamon in a mortar and blending the mixture with olive oil. It is often combined with water and used to cook vegetables or meat. Here, I have added tomatoes and used prepared harissa to create an all-purpose sauce that can be used like a spicy tomato sauce as the base for other dishes.

Tips

To make this sauce gluten-free, be sure to check the label on your harissa paste. Some contain wheat ingredients as fillers. You can also make your own (opposite).

If you'd like a spicier result, increase the harissa paste to 1 tsp (5 mL).

To toast and grind cumin: Toasting and grinding cumin yourself ensures the best flavor. In a dry skillet over medium heat, toast cumin seeds, stirring, until fragrant, about 3 minutes. Immediately transfer to a mortar or a spice grinder and grind to a powder.

Use this sauce as a base for a variety of cooked vegetables (see Variations, right, for some ideas) and garnish the dish with parsley, cilantro or mint. Adding sausage, such as merguez, makes the dish suitable for a light dinner or brunch.

1 tbsp	olive oil	15 mL
4	cloves garlic, minced	4
1 tbsp	ground cumin (see Tips, left)	15 mL
2 tsp	sweet paprika	10 mL
1	piece (about 2 inches/5 cm long) cinnamon stick	1
1	can (14 oz/398 mL) diced tomatoes, with juice	1
½ tsp	harissa paste (see Tips, left)	2 mL
	Salt and freshly ground black pepper	

1. In a large saucepan, heat oil over medium heat. Add garlic and cook, stirring, until fragrant, about 1 minute. Stir in cumin, paprika and cinnamon stick. Add tomatoes and juice, and harissa to taste. Season to taste with salt and black pepper. Bring to a boil. Reduce heat and simmer until flavors are melded, about 20 minutes.

Variations

Cauliflower in Dersa: Complete Step 1. Add 3 to 4 cups (750 mL to 1 L) cauliflower florets to pan. Bring to a boil. Cover, reduce heat and simmer until cauliflower is tender. Transfer to a serving bowl and garnish with parsley.

Legumes in Dersa: Complete Step 1. Add 3 cups (750 mL) drained cooked legumes, such as chickpeas or lentils, to pan. Heat through. Transfer to a bowl and garnish with parsley.

Potatoes and Merguez in Dersa: Complete Step 1. While sauce is simmering, in a skillet, heat 1 tbsp (15 mL) oil over medium heat. Add 1 lb (500 g) merguez sausage and cook, turning, until browned on all sides and cooked through. Transfer to a cutting board and cut into 2-inch (5 cm) pieces. Drain off all but 2 tbsp (30 mL) of the fat in skillet and return to medium heat. Add 2 cups (500 mL) diced cooked potatoes. Cook, turning, until browned on all sides. Transfer sausage and potatoes to a bowl. Add dersa and toss to coat. Garnish with parsley.

Thai-Style Red Curry Paste

Curry pastes are used throughout Southeast Asia to add delicious depth of flavor to dishes. Although recipes usually call for a specific type (red, green or yellow, to name just three), any Thai curry paste can be substituted for another, according to my friend Thai food expert Nancie McDermott, whom I respect. So feel free to use this fresh-tasting, pungent and flavorful version in any recipe that calls for curry paste.

MAKES ABOUT ⅓ CUP (75 ML)

VEGAN FRIENDLY

GLUTEN-FREE FRIENDLY

Tips

If you are not cooking for vegetarians, add the fish sauce. It adds desirable umami flavor to the paste. If you are avoiding gluten, be sure to use gluten-free fish sauce.

The seeds of the chiles will not pulverize in the blender, so you'll need to press the paste through a fine-mesh sieve to achieve the desired smooth texture and strain out the seeds.

- Spice grinder, or mortar and pestle
- Blender or mini food processor
- Fine-mesh sieve
- 8-oz (250 mL) preserving jar with lid, sterilized (see Tip, page 396)

1 tbsp	coriander seeds	15 mL
1 tsp	cumin seeds	5 mL
1 tsp	black peppercorns	5 mL
10	small dried red chiles, such as red Thai bird's-eye or chile de árbol	10
1	stalk lemongrass, trimmed and finely chopped	1
½ cup	chopped shallots	125 mL
2 tbsp	chopped garlic	30 mL
2 tbsp	chopped gingerroot	30 mL
2 tbsp	water	30 mL
2 tbsp	fish sauce (optional)	30 mL
½ tsp	salt	2 mL

1. In a dry small skillet over medium heat, toast coriander and cumin seeds and peppercorns until fragrant, about 4 minutes. Transfer to spice grinder and grind to a powder. Transfer to blender.

2. Add dried chiles, lemongrass, shallots, garlic, ginger, water, fish sauce (if using) and salt. Purée until almost smooth (see Tips, left). Using a spatula, press paste through fine-mesh sieve into a small bowl. Discard solids.

3. Spoon into prepared jar. Press a piece of plastic wrap directly onto the surface of the paste. Wipe rim and screw on lid. Store in the refrigerator for up to 1 month.

Sriracha Sauce

Fifty years ago, Sri Racha (or Si Racha), a coastal city in Thailand not far from Bangkok, was far from a household word in the West. It did, however, have one claim to local fame: *nam prik Sriracha*, a pungent red sauce made from chiles, garlic and vinegar with a touch of sugar and salt. Its moment as a culinary superstar began when a Vietnamese refugee named David Tran arrived in the United States. He eventually established a business making spicy Asian condiments, including his own version of sriracha sauce, which he first bottled in 1983.

Made from ripe red jalapeño peppers, the American version is not authentically Thai—but no matter. It has become ubiquitous in North America. It is a great addition to almost any dish that requires a flavor jolt, and there are myriad ways to use it in the kitchen. Add it to mayonnaise, ketchup and even cream cheese for an Asian-inspired version of pimento cream cheese. It makes a great chile butter (see page 406); you need about 2 tbsp/30 mL sriracha sauce per each ½ cup/125 mL of butter. And while you can make homemade sriracha (there are lots of recipes on the Internet, if you are so inclined), this is one situation in which I recommend purchasing the ready-made stuff. It's easy and much more economical.

XO Sauce

Although its history is disputed, this spicy sauce was likely invented in Hong Kong in the 1980s. It has a base of dried seafood (sometimes cured sausage or ham), but because it has become something of a darling among chefs, the ingredients added to it are becoming quite creative. XO Sauce is often served with grilled meat, such as steak, or robust fish; it is also stirred into cooked rice or noodles to provide what is often described as the ultimate hit of umami. You can buy prepared versions, but, in my opinion, it is better to make your own.

MAKES ABOUT ¾ CUP (175 ML)

GLUTEN-FREE FRIENDLY

Tips

Be sure to use gluten-free soy sauce or wheat-free tamari if you are making this sauce for someone who is sensitive to gluten. Check your cured meat to ensure it is gluten-free, too.

Dried shrimp are readily available in Asian markets. You will likely need to live in a city with a good Chinatown to find dried scallops, but I have seen them for sale online.

Shaoxing wine is a Chinese rice wine. Although I understand there are some elegant versions, the ones that are usually available outside China are unpleasantly salty. I prefer to use vodka in this recipe.

This quantity of hot pepper flakes produces a very spicy sauce. Feel free to adjust the amount to suit your heat tolerance.

Virtually any kind of cured meat will work in this sauce, from prosciutto to Chinese ham to other kinds of charcuterie. My preference is spicy salami, but the choice is yours.

- 8-oz (250 mL) preserving jar with lid, sterilized (see Tip, page 396)

3 tbsp	finely chopped dried scallops (see Tips, left)	45 mL
2 tbsp	finely chopped dried shrimp	30 mL
⅓ cup	vodka or Shaoxing wine (see Tips, left)	75 mL
2 tbsp	oil	30 mL
¼ cup	minced shallot	60 mL
1	whole star anise	1
2 tbsp	hot pepper flakes (see Tips, left)	30 mL
2 tbsp	minced garlic	30 mL
2 tbsp	minced gingerroot	30 mL
3 tbsp	minced cured meat, such as Chinese ham, finely chopped (see Tips, left)	45 mL
2 tbsp	soy sauce	30 mL

1. In a small bowl, combine dried scallops and shrimp. Add vodka and stir well to combine. Let stand at room temperature for 4 hours. Drain, reserving soaking liquid.

2. In a medium skillet, heat oil over medium heat. Add shallot and star anise and cook, stirring, until shallot is softened, about 2 minutes. Add hot pepper flakes, garlic and ginger and stir well to combine. Add cured meat, and reserved shrimp and scallops and cook, stirring, for 1 minute. Add reserved soaking liquid and soy sauce. Bring to a boil. Reduce heat and simmer until almost all of the liquid is evaporated, about 3 minutes. Remove from heat. Let cool.

3. Transfer sauce to prepared jar. Wipe rim and screw on lid. Store in the refrigerator for up to 1 month.

Korean Hot Pepper Sauce

This is a staple in the Korean cupboard. It is an all-purpose sauce, used as a marinade for barbecued meat or as a finishing sauce to drizzle over cooked foods, such as chicken. Try it with fried chicken; it's delicious.

MAKES ABOUT ½ CUP (125 ML)

VEGAN FRIENDLY

GLUTEN-FREE FRIENDLY

Tips

If you are making this sauce for vegans, be sure to use sugar that has not been filtered through bone char.

Look for gluten-free versions of Korean red pepper paste in well-stocked Korean markets. (Most brands are not gluten-free.) Also be sure to use gluten-free soy sauce or wheat-free tamari if you are serving this sauce to someone who is sensitive to gluten.

I like to add this sauce to mayonnaise to make a spicy mayo (see page 402); you need 1 tbsp (15 mL) of the sauce per each ¼ cup (60 mL) of mayonnaise. It's so tasty on hamburgers—and plenty of other things.

2 tbsp	unseasoned rice vinegar	30 mL
2 tsp	granulated sugar	10 mL
2 tbsp	Korean red pepper paste	30 mL
2 tbsp	soy sauce	30 mL
1 tbsp	toasted sesame oil	15 mL
2 tsp	Korean red pepper powder	10 mL

1. In a small bowl, combine vinegar and sugar, stirring until sugar is dissolved. Whisk in red pepper paste, soy sauce, sesame oil and red pepper powder until blended. Transfer to an airtight container and store in the refrigerator for up to 1 month.

TASTY TIDBIT

Many cultures have unique spice blends that contain varying amounts of pungent peppers and are used in different ways. One called *gulášové koření*—made with hot paprika, caraway seeds, salt and other spices—is used throughout Poland and the former Czechoslovakia. It is available in specialty markets or online, and is often labeled "goulash seasoning mix" because it is commonly used to flavor soups and stews, such as goulash (see page 222).

Chinese Salted Chiles

Salted chiles are in some ways the Chinese equivalent of Moroccan preserved lemons. They are just as easy to make and are ubiquitous in Hunan cooking, where they are added to stir-fries and other cooked dishes or simply used as a condiment. I've made them with a number of different chile varieties, from mild to hot. They are useful to have on hand because they add zest to many dishes; for instance, on their own they are a nice finish to a perfectly grilled steak.

Tip

To sterilize preserving jars and lids: Wash jars and lids thoroughly in hot soapy water and rinse well. In large saucepan of boiling water, immerse jar so it's completely covered with water and boil for 10 minutes. If you live in a location that is above 1,000 feet (305 m) in altitude, boil for 1 extra minute for each additional 1,000 feet (305 m) of elevation. Meanwhile, in a separate small saucepan of boiling water, immerse lids and boil for 5 minutes.

- 4-oz (125 mL) preserving jar with lid, sterilized (see Tip, left)

2 oz	red finger chiles (about 4), finely chopped	60 g
1 tbsp	coarse sea salt, divided	15 mL

1. In a small bowl, combine finger chiles and 2 tsp (10 mL) of the salt. Mix well. Spoon into prepared jar. Spoon remaining salt over top. Wipe rim and screw on lid. Let stand at room temperature for 24 hours.
2. Transfer to refrigerator and store for up to 6 months.

Chinese Quick-Pickled Chiles

These are a good alternative to the salted chiles above. Thanks to Jeffrey Alford and Naomi Duguid, who in their book *Beyond the Great Wall* suggested this technique for speeding up the chile-pickling process. It's helpful when I am making a dish such as Hunan-Style Pork with Peppers (page 280) because I can prepare the chiles at the outset and by the time the dish is cooked, they are ready to be added. I usually remove them from the vinegar with a slotted spoon before serving. Sichuan peppercorns are often included in pickled chiles to add an extra layer of flavor.

To quick-pickle chiles: In a small bowl, combine 1 red finger chile, minced; ¼ cup (60 mL) unseasoned rice vinegar; ¼ tsp (1 mL) salt; and a pinch of ground Sichuan peppercorns (optional). Stir well to combine. Let stand at room temperature for 30 minutes. Drain chiles before using. Transfer any leftovers (with the vinegar) to a sterilized jar and store in the refrigerator for up to 6 months.

Your Very Own Hot Sauce

If you don't want to use a prepared hot pepper sauce, such as Tabasco, this makes a fine substitute. It is very easy to make and you know exactly what it contains. Once you get the hang of it, you can vary the chiles, perhaps combining different varieties to create a result that is uniquely yours.

**MAKES ABOUT
¼ CUP (60 ML)**

VEGAN FRIENDLY

GLUTEN-FREE FRIENDLY

Tip

I usually make this sauce with smallish red chiles such as cayenne—that informs the quantity called for here. If you want to be creative, you can use larger dried chiles and vary the amount. You want this sauce to be hot, so some type of very pungent chile should always be included.

- Food processor or blender
- Fine-mesh sieve
- 4-oz (125 mL) preserving jar with lid, sterilized (see Tip, opposite)

15	dried red chiles, stems removed	15
	Boiling water	
¼ cup	white vinegar	60 mL
½ tsp	fine sea salt	2 mL

1. Place dried chiles in a medium heatproof bowl and cover generously with boiling water. Let stand until softened, about 30 minutes, weighing down with a cup to ensure they stay submerged. Drain. Transfer peppers to food processor fitted with the metal blade.

2. Add vinegar and salt and purée until smooth. Strain through fine-mesh sieve into prepared jar, pressing solids to extract as much liquid as possible. Discard solids. Wipe rim and screw on lid. Store in the refrigerator for up to 1 month.

Hot Pepper Vinegar

A cruet of chile-infused vinegar is an essential condiment in the Deep South, where it likely arrived via the Caribbean. It doubles as a mignonette sauce with fresh or fried oysters and can be substituted for regular vinegar whenever you feel a salad dressing needs a lift. In the South it is often added to mayonnaise—and it may be the secret ingredient in the region's classic deviled eggs.

Pepper vinegar is incredibly easy to make. Add white wine vinegar to a cruet, leaving room for the volume the added chiles (fresh or dried) will displace. If you're using large chiles, chop them coarsely. Small bird-type chiles can be added whole, although if they are fresh I recommend pricking them with the tines of a fork before adding them to the vinegar. Use a skewer or chopstick to push the chiles down into the vinegar, making sure they stay submerged. You will need about 4 hot chiles per each 1 cup (250 mL) of vinegar. Plug the top with the stopper and refrigerate the mixture until you are ready to use it, or for at least 24 hours to allow the flavor to infuse. Store in the refrigerator for up to 6 months.

Chile Oil

Chile-infused oil is offered as a condiment or table sauce in many different locales, where it's used in all sorts of ways: from sprinkling over cooked kabobs to drizzling over pizza. It is also good in salad dressings. Here is an all-purpose version that can be tweaked to suit your taste (see Variations, below).

MAKES ½ CUP (125 ML)

VEGAN FRIENDLY

GLUTEN-FREE FRIENDLY

Tip

To sterilize preserving jars and lids: Wash jars and lids thoroughly in hot soapy water and rinse well. In large saucepan of boiling water, immerse jar so it's completely covered with water and boil for 10 minutes. If you live in a location that is above 1,000 feet (305 m) in altitude, boil for 1 extra minute for each additional 1,000 feet (305 m) of elevation. Meanwhile, in a separate small saucepan of boiling water, immerse lids and boil for 5 minutes.

- Instant-read thermometer
- Fine-mesh sieve
- 4-oz (125 mL) preserving jar with lid, sterilized (see Tip, left)

⅔ cup	oil	150 mL
3 tbsp	crushed dried red chiles	45 mL

1. In a small saucepan, heat oil over medium heat just until thermometer registers 175°F (80°C).
2. Place dried chiles in a heatproof glass measuring cup. Pour in warm oil. Stir well to combine. Let cool for at least 8 hours or overnight.
3. Strain through fine-mesh sieve into prepared jar. Wipe rim and screw on lid. Store in the refrigerator for up to 1 month.

Variations

Chinese-Style Chile Oil: Add 1 tbsp (15 mL) Sichuan peppercorns to crushed chiles before adding the oil.

Italian-Style Chile Oil: Used dried *peperoncino* peppers. Add minced garlic and/or fresh thyme leaves to taste.

Portuguese-Style Chile Oil: Use dried piri-piri peppers.

Chile-Spiked Crema

In Latin America, some kind of cultured cream product is often part of the meal. Depending on your location, it may be used to finish a taco or an arepa, or as an accompaniment to grilled meat. Often it turns up in the form of crumbled fresh cheese. Stateside, crème fraîche seasoned with roasted chiles has become a popular finish for grilled fish and meats; this is due, I suspect, to the influence of chefs such as Bobby Flay, who have been experimenting with Southwest cuisine. These "cremas" also work well as a topping for Tex-Mex faves, such as fajitas. If you are coloring outside the lines, they're also delicious on baked potatoes.

To make chile-spiked crema: Start with about ½ cup (125 mL) of real Mexican crema (their version of crème fraîche), crème fraîche or sour cream (that's my order of preference). Add finely chopped roasted peppers to taste, such as poblanos, jalapeños, or even bell peppers. (I recommend about 2 poblanos for this quantity of crema.) Mix well, using a food processor, if you like, and season to taste with salt and freshly ground black pepper. If the result is not spicy enough for you, add a little ancho or New Mexico chile powder; hot paprika; or, if you are lucky enough to have it, merkén (see page 374) to taste. You can also mix up the peppers for a more complex taste—try a green bell pepper combined with a jalapeño. Refrigerate for at least 30 minutes or up to 1 day before serving.

Roasted Red Pepper Vinaigrette

A mixture of oil and vinegar (or lemon juice) seasoned with various types of capsicum is a popular condiment in many parts of the world. This version is probably Spanish in origin— it resembles the red pepper mojo I like to serve with wrinkled potatoes (see page 74). If you are tired of the same old salads, this dressing makes a refreshing change.

MAKES ABOUT ½ CUP (125 ML)

VEGAN FRIENDLY

GLUTEN-FREE FRIENDLY

Tip

To turn this dressing into a sauce for grilled fish, meat or vegetables, add 2 to 3 tbsp (30 to 45 mL) dry bread crumbs to the food processor along with the lemon juice.

- Food processor

1	red bell pepper, roasted (see Tips, page 384)	1
3 tbsp	freshly squeezed lemon juice or white wine vinegar	45 mL
⅓ cup	extra virgin olive oil	75 mL
	Salt and freshly ground black pepper	

1. Peel, seed and cut roasted red pepper into chunks. In food processor fitted with the metal blade, purée roasted pepper with lemon juice until smooth. With motor running, pour oil through the feed tube in a slow, steady stream until the mixture is emulsified. Season to taste with salt and black pepper.

2. Use immediately or transfer to a small bowl, cover and refrigerate for up to 1 week.

Variation

Jumped-Up Roasted Red Pepper Vinaigrette: This Spanish-inspired dressing makes a perfect finish for robust greens, such as arugula; garnish them with chopped nuts. It also makes a nice dressing for warm potato salad, and can do double duty as a marinade for shrimp or chicken kabobs. Substitute sherry vinegar for the lemon juice. Add 1 clove garlic, chopped; 2 tsp (10 mL) ground cumin; 1 tsp (5 mL) sweet paprika; and ¼ tsp (1 mL) smoked hot paprika along with the roasted red pepper. Don't substitute smoked paprika for the sweet paprika—the result will be unpleasantly smoky. Use immediately or refrigerate for up to 3 days.

Spicy Mayo

Mayonnaise is a classic French sauce: a simple emulsion of eggs, acid and oil. Even in France, where the cuisine is not typically associated with pungent spice, mayonnaise is frequently seasoned with a pinch of piment d'Espelette, cayenne and/or paprika. I have a 50-year-old book on preparing sauces by the late chef Raymond Oliver, who acquired and maintained the ultimate third Michelin star while at the helm of the majestic Paris restaurant Le Grand Véfour. Writing on mayonnaise, he daringly suggests the possibility of adding a range of unconventional ingredients, including sweet and hot peppers. I strongly believe he would be thrilled to see how far that idea has come in the new millennium.

Today, it would be impossible to count the number of iterations of spicy mayo that exist—and not only in countries whose culinary heritage owes a debt to France. Japanese mayonnaise is a favorite among chefs. Mixed with chile paste, such as *tobanjan* (spicy bean sauce), and finished with Japanese ground chile seasonings, such as *ichimi* or *shichimi*, this mayo is the ingredient that gives that sushi bar staple, the spicy tuna roll, its characteristic heat. These days, mayonnaise laced with any kind of Asian chile sauce—such as sriracha or Korean red pepper paste (*koch'ujang*, or *gochujang*)—has become something of a cliché. A note of caution: Kewpie, the most popular brand of Japanese mayonnaise, contains MSG; if you have problems with this additive, use another brand or make your own.

Spicy mayo, whatever the source of its heat, is popular because it is a very easy way of creating a great finish for a variety of dishes. You can slather it on burgers (see Grilled Turkey Burgers with Chipotle Mayo, page 209) or sandwiches, add it to salad dressings or deviled eggs, or pass a small bowl at the table to dab on simply grilled steak or to use as a dip for fries. If you are adding prepared chile paste, I recommend about a 4:1 ratio of mayo to chile paste. Simply whisk in until blended.

If you don't have chile paste on hand, it is almost as easy to spice up prepared mayo with your favorite preserved peppers. Try chipotle peppers with a bit of the accompanying adobo sauce, or pickled peppers, such as jalapeño, malagueta or piri-piri. Just pulse the mayo and peppers together in a food processor until the desired consistency is achieved.

Pepper pastes and/or pickled peppers are a simple way of adding pungency and other more complex flavors to mayo, but some recipes go further and include other ingredients—tomato paste and ketchup are two of the most common. Andalouse sauce, the traditional partner to Belgian double-fried *frites*, is a mixture of tomato paste and peppers, with whatever else the chef might want to throw in. Another variation is Cuban pimento mayonnaise (*mayonesa rosada*), which uses drained bottled pimentos to provide the capsicum hit. Marie Rose Sauce (below) is a British take, which can be used as a kind of template for other versions.

Marie Rose Sauce

This enhanced (and deliciously spicy) version of the British creation is often served with French fries for a decadent dipping experience, or instead of plain mayo on burgers. This version works beautifully in both those circumstances, but it really earns its stripes as an elegant finish for cold seafood, particularly shrimp. It makes about 1¼ cups (300 mL), is gluten-free and can be vegetarian (see Tip, right).

• Food processor

1 cup	mayonnaise	250 mL
4	green onions (white and a bit of the green parts), cut in chunks	4
½ cup	coarsely chopped red bell pepper	125 mL
1	long red chile	1
2 tbsp	tomato-based chili sauce	30 mL
1 tbsp	Worcestershire sauce	15 mL

1. In food processor fitted with the metal blade, combine mayonnaise, onions, bell pepper, red chile, chili sauce and Worcestershire sauce. Purée until blended.

2. Transfer to a serving bowl. Cover and refrigerate for at least 30 minutes before serving. Store in the refrigerator for up to 5 days.

Tip
If you're making this recipe for a vegetarian, be sure to use lemon juice (see Variations, below) or vegan Worcestershire sauce. Worcestershire usually contains anchovies.

Variations
You can substitute ¼ cup (60 mL) ketchup for the chili sauce; fresh lemon juice for the Worcestershire sauce; and hot or sweet ground pepper, such as paprika, smoked paprika, Aleppo pepper or cayenne, for the fresh chile. The possibilities are endless using this recipe template.

Kimchi

Kimchi is to Korea as the Big Mac is to the United States: iconic. In Korea, people make kimchi from a wide variety of vegetables, but napa cabbage is the most common.

Tips

When making fermented foods such as kimchi, use filtered water to avoid chemicals that will destroy the friendly bacteria.

If you're serving this kimchi to someone with gluten intolerance, use gluten-free soy sauce and gluten-free fish sauce.

This recipe produces a pleasantly spicy result.

Most kimchi features large pieces of cabbage. I prefer to cut mine into relatively thin strips because, in my opinion, it makes the kimchi much easier to eat.

Puréeing the ginger and garlic ensures that they will incorporate into the kimchi mixture more evenly. Use a sharp-toothed rasp grater, such as those made by Microplane.

The fish sauce provides umami; in Korea, dried shrimp are often used. If you are a vegan, substitute 1 tbsp (15 mL) unseasoned rice vinegar for the fish sauce.

- Large heatproof nonreactive bowl
- Four 8-oz (250 mL) preserving jars with lids, sterilized (see Tips, page 411)

10 cups	packed sliced napa cabbage (about 1-inch/2.5 cm wide strips), see Tips, left	2.5 L
¼ cup	coarse sea salt	60 mL
1 cup	boiling water, preferably filtered	250 mL
	Ice, preferably made from filtered water	
	Cold water, preferably filtered (see Tips, left)	
8	green onions (white and green parts), thinly sliced	8
1	carrot, finely shredded	1
3 tbsp	Korean red pepper flakes or coarse powder	45 mL
2 tbsp	each soy sauce, fish sauce and agave nectar	30 mL
1 tsp	each puréed gingerroot and garlic	5 mL

1. In bowl, combine salt with boiling water, stirring until salt is dissolved. Add ice and cold water until mixture is reduced to room temperature. Add cabbage and press down into liquid to immerse. Using your hands, slosh cabbage around to ensure every piece comes into contact with the salted water. Add cold water to cover. Let stand at room temperature for 3 hours.

2. Drain cabbage well. Rinse out bowl to remove any residual salt. Return cabbage to bowl.

3. Meanwhile, in a small bowl, toss together onions, carrot, red pepper flakes, soy sauce, fish sauce, agave nectar, ginger and garlic until well combined. Toss with cabbage until well combined.

4. Spoon kimchi into prepared jars, leaving 1-inch (2.5 cm) headspace (cabbage will expand during fermentation). Using your hands, pack down tightly. Wipe rims and screw on lids.

5. Refrigerate for at least 3 days before serving. Store in the refrigerator for up to 6 months.

Chile Butters

Chile butters are a type of compound butter. Called *beurre composé*, this is a French preparation that combines softened butter with seasonings, such as herbs, spices and aromatics. The closest I have come to a French chile-infused version is one that featured piment d'Espelette. A friend who grew up in France prepared it as an accompaniment for grilled fish, and it was the perfect light touch. Compound butters seasoned with various types of chile and, possibly, other herbs, make a great finish for many dishes, such as grilled fish, meat or vegetables. Use the following recipe and variations to get you started, then let your imagination take over.

Roasted Red Pepper Butter

If you are looking for an elegant presentation, this butter can be pressed into molds to create fancy shapes or rolled into logs and sliced. Usually, I just serve mine in a small ramekin because it's easy. It makes about ½ cup (125 mL).

½ cup	butter, at room temperature	125 mL
1	red bell pepper, roasted (see Tips, page 384), peeled, seeded and diced	1
1 tsp	grated lemon zest	5 mL
	Salt and freshly ground black pepper	
	Ground dried red pepper (optional)	

1. In a medium bowl, using a wooden spoon, beat butter until smooth and creamy. Add roasted pepper, lemon zest, and salt, black pepper and ground red pepper (if using) to taste. Stir until blended. (You can also do this in a mini food processor, if you prefer.) Spoon into a ramekin or small bowl, cover and chill for at least 2 hours before using.

Tip

If you are adding dried red pepper to this butter, you can vary the type to change the heat level. A mild chile, such as piment d'Espelette, will add just a hint of heat, Aleppo pepper will be slightly more intense, and hot paprika or cayenne have the potential to add serious spiciness, depending on the quantity you add.

Variations

Chipotle Butter: Omit red bell pepper and lemon zest. Stir in 2 chipotle peppers in adobo sauce, minced; ½ tsp (2 mL) grated lime zest; and 1 tsp (5 mL) lime juice.

Cilantro Chile Butter: This butter is particularly delicious with roasted salmon. Omit red bell pepper and lemon zest. Stir in 2 tbsp (30 mL) finely chopped fresh cilantro (leaves and tender stems); 1 red Thai bird's-eye chile, minced; 1 fresh makrut lime leaf, finely chopped, or 1 tsp (5 mL) grated lime zest. Season to taste with roasted chile powder (see Tips, page 131), if desired.

Pickled Sweet Red Peppers

These peppers are pickled in a typical Middle Eastern style, which means in a mild brine. They have a more pleasing flavor than North American pickled peppers, which go heavy on the acid to allow for room-temperature storage when sealed. Pickles are widely consumed in the Middle East, as a meze or an accompaniment to a main dish. They're particularly pleasing as a finish for *pide*, the pizza-like snack that is ubiquitous in Turkey.

MAKES ABOUT 5 CUPS (1.25 L)

VEGAN FRIENDLY

GLUTEN-FREE FRIENDLY

Tip

When preserving any vegetable or fruit, it is always important to use the freshest and most pristine produce you can buy. While blemished peppers may be fine for eating, their imperfections seem to magnify over time. Plus, since food safety is always paramount in preserved foods, visual flaws may put people off.

• Five 8-oz (250 mL) preserving jars with lids, sterilized (see Tips, page 411)

1½ lbs	red bell peppers	750 g
3 cups	water	750 mL
1 cup	white wine vinegar	250 mL
1	clove garlic, crushed	1
⅓ cup	coarse sea salt	75 mL
5	small dried red chiles (optional)	5

1. Cut bell peppers in half. Using a grapefruit spoon, scrape out seeds and membranes. Slice peppers thinly.

2. In a small saucepan, combine water, vinegar, garlic and salt. Bring to a boil. Reduce heat and simmer until salt is thoroughly dissolved and flavors are melded, about 5 minutes. Remove from heat and discard garlic.

3. Pack sliced peppers into prepared jars, burying a dried chile (if using) in the middle of each jar and leaving about ½-inch (1 cm) headspace. Add hot vinegar solution, leaving ½-inch (1 cm) headspace. Wipe rims and screw on lids. Let stand at room temperature until cool.

4. Refrigerate for 2 weeks before using to allow flavors to meld. Store in the refrigerator. Peppers may be kept refrigerated for up to 3 months after opening.

Focus on: Chiles in Japan

Although Japan is not noted for its love of spicy food, grilled shishito peppers are ubiquitous in season (see page 77). Year round, chiles are widely used in garnishes and seasoning blends. *Rayu,* or chile-infused sesame oil, is often used as a finishing touch on salads, ramen and dumplings.

Fiery dried red pepper flakes known as *ichimi togarashi* are sprinkled over many dishes at the table. Japanese seven-spice powder, or *shichimi togarashi*, comes in varying degrees of pungency (mild, medium or hot), depending on the quantity of *ichimi togarashi* it contains. It is widely available and is a pantry staple in most restaurants and homes; it is often served as a table seasoning, like salt, for diners to sprinkle over noodles, rice and grilled meats. Shichimi togarashi is also one of the spices used to flavor the mayo that gives spicy tuna rolls their kick. While red chiles provide most of the pungency, other spices—such as *sansho*, a non-capsicum relative of the Sichuan peppercorn—also add heat.

Yuzu kosho is a kind of Japanese pepper paste. According to Nancy Singleton Hachisu, who provides a recipe for it her book *Japanese Farm Food*, it is usually made from fresh green chiles, which are small and pungent (sometimes red chiles are used for a more rounded flavor), grated skin of the yuzu citrus fruit and sea salt—and sometimes whatever else strikes the chef's fancy. Long popular on the island of Kyushu, in southwestern Japan, it has recently gained considerable traction elsewhere. Yuzu kosho can be used to season rice, noodles, meats and fish, and it makes a nice addition to plain vinaigrettes. Singleton Hachisu points out that some types of chiles are widely used in Japanese country cooking.

Santaka chiles are small, red and pointed; they, along with hontaka chiles, may be identified as chile japones. They are quite pungent at 50,000 to 100,000 SHU. Often sold dried and ground, they may be added to daikon to make spicy grated radish (*momiji oroshi*), which sushi chefs often use as a garnish for sashimi. Tobanjan, a Japanese version of Korean spicy fermented bean paste, comes in plastic squeeze bottles and is used as a seasoning for a variety of dishes, from tofu to noodles.

Haitian-Style Pickled Cabbage (Pikliz)

This Haitian specialty of spicy, fresh-pickled cabbage is traditionally served with Haitian-Style Pork (*Griot*), page 268. It can add a spark to just about any dish you like and is lovely with grilled meats. Try drizzling the liquid over rice or beans to give them a flavor boost.

MAKES ABOUT 3 CUPS (750 ML)

VEGAN FRIENDLY

GLUTEN-FREE FRIENDLY

Tips

You want the slices of cabbage and onion to be very thin, so use a mandoline to cut them.

Mixing the vegetables in a bowl ensures they are well combined before you transfer them to the jar.

- 1-quart (1 L) preserving jar with lid, sterilized (see Tips, page 411)

3 cups	very thinly sliced green cabbage (see Tips, left)	750 mL
1	onion, halved vertically and very thinly sliced	1
¾ cup	shredded carrot	175 mL
1	green bell pepper, finely diced	1
2 tbsp	minced garlic	30 mL
2 to 4	habanero peppers, minced	2 to 4
1 tsp	salt	5 mL
4	whole cloves	4
4	whole allspice berries	4
1 cup	cider vinegar (approx.)	250 mL
2 tbsp	freshly squeezed lime juice	30 mL

1. In a large bowl, combine cabbage, onion, carrot, bell pepper, garlic, habanero peppers to taste, salt, cloves and allspice berries. Toss well to combine. Transfer mixture to prepared jar, packing tightly.

2. In a small saucepan, bring 1 cup (250 mL) vinegar to a boil. Stir in lime juice and pour over cabbage mixture in jar. Using the back of a large spoon, press vegetables down. Add additional vinegar if necessary to ensure vegetables are just covered with liquid. Screw on lid.

3. Refrigerate for at least 48 hours before serving. Store in the refrigerator for up to 6 months.

Three-Chile Tomato Jam

This combination of tomatoes, fresh jalapeño pepper, dried hot pepper flakes and sweet smoked paprika produces a mildly spicy, highly savory jam. The cinnamon and allspice add appealing sweetness to balance the heat. This is a great ingredient to keep on hand: it makes an instant appetizer served on crostini, is perfect alongside grilled meats or fish, and tastes great on burgers in place of ketchup. It's also lovely served with cheese instead of the usual quince paste. The opportunities are endless.

MAKES ABOUT 5 CUPS (1.25 L)

VEGAN FRIENDLY

GLUTEN-FREE FRIENDLY

Tips

If you are making this jam for vegans, be sure to use sugar that has not been filtered through bone char.

If you are a heat seeker, feel free to increase the quantity of jalapeño and/or hot pepper flakes to suit your taste.

- Five 8-oz (250 mL) preserving jars with lids, sterilized (see Tips, opposite)

5 lbs	Roma or plum tomatoes, peeled and chopped	2.5 kg
2 cups	granulated sugar	500 mL
½ cup	freshly squeezed lemon juice	125 mL
1	jalapeño pepper, peeled (see Tips, page 385) and minced	1
1	piece (about 2 inches/5 cm long) cinnamon stick	1
1 tsp	salt	5 mL
1 tsp	hot pepper flakes	5 mL
½ tsp	ground allspice	2 mL
½ tsp	smoked sweet paprika	2 mL

1. In a large saucepan over medium heat, combine tomatoes, sugar, lemon juice, jalapeño pepper, cinnamon stick, salt, hot pepper flakes, allspice and paprika. Stir well and bring to a boil. Reduce heat and simmer until mixture is thickened and jam-like, about $1\frac{1}{2}$ hours.

2. Spoon hot jam into prepared jars, leaving $\frac{1}{4}$-inch (0.5 cm) headspace. Wipe rims and screw on lids. Store in the refrigerator for up to 6 months. Once opened, use within 2 months.

Jalapeño Jam

This is another terrific condiment to keep on hand. It is delicious with grilled meats, and a generous dollop transforms even the most mundane slice of cheese on a cracker into something quite special.

MAKES ABOUT 2 CUPS (500 ML)

VEGAN FRIENDLY

GLUTEN-FREE FRIENDLY

Tips

To sterilize preserving jars and lids: Wash jars and lids thoroughly in hot soapy water and rinse well. In large saucepan of boiling water, immerse jar so it's completely covered with water and boil for 10 minutes. If you live in a location that is above 1,000 feet (305 m) in altitude, boil for 1 extra minute for each additional 1,000 feet (305 m) of elevation. Meanwhile, in a separate small saucepan of boiling water, immerse lids and boil for 5 minutes.

If you are making this jam for vegans, be sure to use sugar that has not been filtered through bone char.

- Food processor
- Four 4-oz (125 mL) preserving jars with lids, sterilized (see Tips, left)

4 oz	jalapeño peppers, stemmed and seeded	125 g
¾ cup	cider vinegar	175 mL
2 cups	granulated sugar	500 mL
Pinch	salt	Pinch
1	pouch (85 mL) liquid pectin	1

1. In food processor fitted with the metal blade, combine jalapeño peppers and vinegar. Purée until smooth. Transfer to a medium saucepan. Stir in sugar and salt and bring to a boil over medium heat, stirring constantly and skimming off foam. Boil for 10 minutes.

2. Increase heat to high. When mixture reaches a rolling boil (one that can not be stirred down), stir in pectin. Boil hard, stirring constantly, for 1 minute.

3. Spoon into prepared jars, leaving ¼-inch (0.5 cm) headspace. Wipe rims and screw on lids.

4. Immerse jars in a boiling water canner and boil for 10 minutes. Let cool. Store sealed jars in a cool dark place for up to 1 year. If jars do not seal, or if you prefer not to process them, store unopened unprocessed jars in the refrigerator for up to 6 months. Once opened, use within 2 months.

Variation

For a more intriguing and pungent flavor, add ⅛ tsp (0.5 mL) ground chipotle chile powder to the boiling mixture just before adding the pectin.

Drinks and Desserts

Indian-Spiced Roasted Tomato Juice

Deeply flavorful, this makes a very refreshing hot-weather shooter. The juice is good on its own, but if you're so inclined, you can increase the quantity, add a shot of vodka and some ice, and call it an Indian-inspired Bloody Mary. Roasting the tomatoes intensifies their flavor, while the cumin adds an intriguing hint of earthiness.

MAKES ABOUT 3 CUPS (750 ML)

VEGAN FRIENDLY

GLUTEN-FREE FRIENDLY

Tips

Because the cumin is not cooked in this recipe, it's particularly important to toast the seeds before grinding and adding them. Otherwise, their earthiness will overwhelm their lovely nutty flavor.

To toast cumin seeds: In a dry small skillet over medium heat, toast cumin seeds, stirring, until fragrant, about 3 minutes. Immediately transfer to a mortar or a spice grinder and grind to a powder.

If you have access to an authentic Indian chile, such as byadagi or kanthari, by all means substitute it for the finger chile in this recipe.

- Preheat oven to 425°F (220°C)
- Rimmed baking sheet
- Blender

4	medium tomatoes	4
½ cup	water	125 mL
½ tsp	ground cumin (see Tips, left)	2 mL
¼ to ½	red finger chile (see Tips, left)	¼ to ½
	Salt and freshly ground black pepper	

1. Cut tomatoes in half and place on baking sheet. Roast in preheated oven until wrinkled, about 45 minutes. Remove from oven and let cool.

2. Remove skins and transfer tomatoes to blender. Add water, cumin and finger chile to taste. Purée until smooth. Season generously to taste with salt and black pepper.

3. Cover and refrigerate until thoroughly chilled, at least 2 hours or up to 3 days. Serve chilled.

Cumin Mint Cooler

Spicy, tart and intriguingly flavored, this is a traditional cooler enjoyed in India, where people really understand how to beat the hot weather. This version is adapted from one that appears in Suneeta Vaswani's excellent *Complete Book of Indian Cooking*.

MAKES 4 CUPS (1 L)

VEGAN FRIENDLY

GLUTEN-FREE FRIENDLY

Tips

One chile produces a spicy result, which is very refreshing on a hot day. However, if you're heat-averse, you may want to reduce the quantity.

You can substitute a fresh green kanthari or jwala chile if you can find one.

- Spice grinder, or mortar and pestle
- Blender

2 tsp	cumin seeds	10 mL
1 cup	fresh mint leaves	250 mL
¼ cup	fresh cilantro leaves	60 mL
¼ cup	Thai tamarind purée, broken into pieces	60 mL
1	green finger chile, coarsely chopped (see Tips, left)	1
1 tbsp	coarsely chopped gingerroot	15 mL
4 cups	cold water	1 L

1. In a dry small skillet over medium heat, toast cumin seeds, stirring, until fragrant, about 3 minutes. Transfer to spice grinder and grind to a powder. Set aside.

2. In blender, combine mint, cilantro, tamarind, finger chile, ginger and reserved cumin. Add 1 cup (250 mL) of the cold water and blend until mixture is very smooth.

3. Transfer to a large pitcher. Stir in remaining cold water. Cover and refrigerate until thoroughly chilled, at least 3 hours or up to 3 days.

To Seed or Not to Seed

Whether you seed and remove the veins inside your peppers is a matter of preference. With the exception of bell peppers, I usually don't seed and devein because, in my opinion, it affects the taste and experience of the pepper. I like the texture the seeds add to a dish. The veins are the placental tissue inside the peppers, and they contain any spiciness, so removing them may be a good idea if you are heat-averse; you can also reduce the quantity of chile called for in a recipe or substitute a chile that ranks lower on the Scoville scale.

Mexican-Style Tomato Juice (*Sangrita*)

Whip up this Mexican-inspired spicy tomato-citrus juice during the dog days of summer, when tomatoes are abundant and in season. It's a delicious nonalcoholic refreshment, but if you want to liven up the experience, add a dash of vodka or (as they often do in Mexico) a splash of tequila.

**MAKES ABOUT
6 CUPS (1.5 L)**

VEGAN FRIENDLY

GLUTEN-FREE FRIENDLY

Tips

Use a whole jalapeño pepper only if you are a true heat seeker. It creates a very spicy result.

You can substitute another fresh Mexican pepper, such as serrano or habanero, for the jalapeño. If you are using a habanero, use only about one-quarter of a pepper.

- Large fine-mesh sieve
- Cheesecloth
- Blender

3 lbs	Roma or plum tomatoes (15 to 20), cut into chunks	1.5 kg
½ to 1	jalapeño pepper (see Tips, left)	½ to 1
1 cup	freshly squeezed orange juice	250 mL
½ cup	loosely packed fresh cilantro leaves and stems	125 mL
⅓ cup	freshly squeezed lime juice	75 mL
⅓ cup	freshly squeezed lemon juice	75 mL
2 tsp	fine sea salt, or to taste	10 mL
	Agave nectar (optional)	

1. Place sieve over a large bowl and line with 2 layers of dampened cheesecloth. In blender, in batches, purée tomatoes, jalapeño pepper to taste, orange juice, cilantro, lime juice and lemon juice until smooth. If necessary, add water, 1 tbsp (15 mL) at a time, to facilitate puréeing. Strain through sieve as completed and stir gently. When most of the liquid has passed through, lift the 4 corners of the cheesecloth and twist around tomato mixture to form a tight ball. Using your hands, squeeze remaining liquid into bowl. Discard solids.

2. Transfer liquid to a large pitcher. Season to taste with salt. Refrigerate until well chilled, about 3 hours. Taste the mixture; if it is not sweet enough for you, add agave nectar (if using) to taste. Serve very cold, over ice if desired.

Thai-Style Pineapple with Chile

A great deal of the food in Thailand is served on the streets and in its famous night markets. If you are feeling the heat in that country, a perfect solution is to indulge in coconut water (drunk through a straw inserted into a fresh coconut) and a cup of cut-up fruit (juicy pineapple is a perennial favorite). Here, lime, chile and cilantro complement the flavors of this luscious fruit to create an ideal hot-weather dessert.

MAKES 16 PIECES

VEGAN FRIENDLY

GLUTEN-FREE FRIENDLY

Moreover ...

One of my most amusing shopping experiences happened at the night market in Phuket town: a large crab escaped from its bucket and scurried at quite a surprising pace down the aisle.

3 tbsp	freshly squeezed lime juice	45 mL
2 tbsp	coconut sugar	30 mL
1	red Thai bird's-eye chile, minced	1
Pinch	salt	Pinch
1	pineapple (about 2½ lbs/1.25 kg)	1
	Finely chopped fresh cilantro (leaves and tender stems)	
	Roasted chile powder (optional), see Tips, page 131	

1. In a small bowl, combine lime juice and coconut sugar, stirring until sugar is dissolved. Stir in chile and salt. Set aside.

2. Place pineapple on a cutting board and cut off top and bottom to make two flat surfaces. Stand pineapple on cutting board and, using a sharp knife, cut downward along the side to remove the peel and "eyes." Turn pineapple on its side and cut lengthwise in half. Cut each half lengthwise in half. Cut core off side of each wedge and discard. Cut each wedge in half lengthwise and crosswise to produce 16 small wedges total.

3. Place pineapple wedges on a serving platter. Drizzle with sugar mixture and garnish to taste with cilantro. Season to taste with roasted chile powder (if using).

4. Refrigerate until well chilled, about 1 hour. Serve cold.

Variation

Barbecued Thai-Style Pineapple with Chile: Substitute ⅛ tsp (0.5 mL) cayenne pepper or ground dried red Thai bird's-eye chile for the fresh chile. Complete steps 1 through 3. Place pineapple wedges, seasoned side up, on preheated barbecue and cook, turning often to ensure even browning, until lightly browned, about 10 minutes. Transfer to a serving platter and serve immediately.

Melon in Spicy Syrup

This is another dessert that makes a perfect finish for a summertime meal. It is light and refreshing, but the spices add an interesting touch.

Tips

If you are making this recipe for vegans, be sure to use sugar that has not been filtered through bone char.

You can use any type of pungent fresh green chile in the syrup. Try serrano peppers or fresh jwala chiles if they are available.

To purée gingerroot quickly and easily, use a sharp-toothed rasp grater, such as those made by Microplane.

- Fine-mesh sieve

1	cantaloupe, seeded, peeled and cubed (about 1 inch/2.5 cm)	1
	Fresh mint sprigs	

Spicy Syrup

1¼ cups	granulated sugar	300 mL
1 cup	water	250 mL
1	jalapeño pepper (see Tips, left), minced	1
2 tbsp	finely grated lime zest	30 mL
1 tsp	puréed gingerroot (see Tips, left)	5 mL
6	green cardamom pods, crushed	6

1. *Spicy Syrup:* In a small saucepan, bring sugar, water, jalapeño pepper, lime zest, ginger and cardamom to a boil. Reduce heat and simmer for 1 minute. Remove from heat and let stand until flavors are infused, about 30 minutes. Strain through fine-mesh sieve into a small bowl. Cover and refrigerate until chilled, about 30 minutes.

2. Place cantaloupe in a serving bowl. Add spicy syrup and toss to coat. Cover and refrigerate until well chilled, about 2 hours or up to 4 hours. Just before serving, garnish to taste with mint sprigs.

Variation

This spicy syrup is tasty with many different fruits; berries, such as strawberries or raspberries, are particularly delicious partners. Other types of melon, such as honeydew or even watermelon, also work well.

Mexican-Style Strawberry Ice Pops (Paletas)

Paletas are Mexican ice pops. Usually made from fresh fruit, they are much healthier than traditional sugary, fruit-flavored frozen treats. With a pleasant hint of chile, these strawberry pops are quite delicious and wonderfully refreshing. They make a perfect dessert or snack on a hot, humid day.

MAKES 8 TO 10 POPS

VEGAN FRIENDLY

GLUTEN-FREE FRIENDLY

Tip

Piloncillo is Mexican brown raw cane sugar. It comes in solid cones, which need to be broken into pieces before use. For this quantity, you'll need one 4-oz (125 g) cone.

- Blender
- Ice pop molds (see Tips, opposite)

½ cup	brown raw cane sugar, such as piloncillo (see Tip, left)	125 mL
½ cup	water	125 mL
4 cups	halved hulled strawberries, thawed if frozen	1 L
¼ cup	freshly squeezed lime juice	60 mL
½ tsp	ancho chile powder	2 mL

1. In a small saucepan, combine sugar and water. Bring to a boil, stirring until sugar is dissolved. Remove from heat.
2. In blender, combine strawberries, lime juice and chile powder. Add sugar syrup and purée until smooth. Let cool completely.
3. Pour into molds and freeze according to the manufacturer's instructions until solid, about 4 hours.

Variation

Substitute another fairly mild chile powder, such as guajillo or New Mexico, for the ancho.

Coconut Ice Cream Pops (*Kulfi*)

Kulfi, or Indian ice cream, is richly flavored with a wide variety of spices and often studded with nuts. It is rich and dense enough to be frozen on a stick, which makes it a popular, enjoyable treat. In India, street vendors specializing in this creamy refreshment are known as *kulfi wallahs*. This version is very pleasantly spiced with cardamom, cloves and orange, with a gentle hint of chile.

MAKES ABOUT 8 POPS

VEGETARIAN FRIENDLY

GLUTEN-FREE FRIENDLY

Tips

You can substitute another type of dried red chile, such as cayenne, for the Kashmiri.

No ice pop molds? Substitute small disposable cups and wooden ice pop sticks. Insert the sticks once the mixture has frozen to a slushy consistency, then freeze until solid.

- Large wide, heavy-bottomed saucepan
- Fine-mesh sieve
- Ice pop molds (see Tips, left)

1	can (12 oz/354 mL) evaporated milk	1
1 cup	half-and-half (10%) cream	250 mL
2	dried Kashmiri chiles (see Tips, left), broken into pieces	2
8	green cardamom pods, crushed	8
2	whole cloves	2
2 tbsp	coconut sugar (optional)	30 mL
½ cup	sweetened condensed milk	125 mL
1 tbsp	finely grated orange zest	15 mL
1 tsp	orange extract	5 mL

1. In saucepan, combine evaporated milk, cream, dried chiles, cardamom and cloves. Bring to a boil. Reduce heat to medium-high and boil, stirring every few minutes and stirring in any skin that forms, until mixture is reduced by about one-quarter, about 7 minutes. (Reduce the heat a little if the mixture threatens to boil over.)

2. Place sieve over a large heatproof glass measuring cup and strain liquid into cup. Discard solids. Stir in coconut sugar (if using) until dissolved, then sweetened condensed milk, orange zest and orange extract. Let cool completely, stirring occasionally and making sure to stir in any skin that forms.

3. Pour into molds and freeze according to the manufacturer's instructions until solid, about 4 hours.

Frozen Yogurt with Chile and Orange

Slightly sour yogurt combined with spicy chile and sweet orange is a marriage made in heaven. This dessert is so easy to whip up, you can always have it on hand for a tasty snack. If you want to make a large batch, feel free to double the recipe.

MAKES ABOUT 2 CUPS (500 ML)

VEGETARIAN FRIENDLY

GLUTEN-FREE FRIENDLY

Tips

Orange blossom water is often available in well-stocked supermarkets. If you can't find it, look for it in Middle Eastern markets or online.

The chile flavor in this dessert is pleasantly mild. If you don't have Aleppo pepper, substitute another mild chile powder, such as piment d'Espelette or ancho.

- Ice cream maker

½ cup	granulated sugar	125 mL
¼ cup	water	60 mL
2 tsp	finely grated orange zest	10 mL
1 tsp	orange blossom water (see Tips, left)	5 mL
2 cups	plain full-fat yogurt	500 mL
1½ tsp	Aleppo pepper (see Tips, left)	7 mL

1. In a small saucepan over medium heat, stir sugar with water until dissolved. Remove from heat. Stir in orange zest and orange blossom water.

2. In a bowl, combine yogurt and Aleppo pepper. Stir well to combine. Add sugar syrup and stir well. Cover and refrigerate until well chilled, about 1 hour.

3. Transfer to ice cream maker and freeze according to manufacturer's instructions.

Watermelon Sorbet

Fruity and sweet, with just a hint of chile, this sorbet makes a very refreshing dessert. If you are enjoying a multicourse meal, it can be a fabulous palate cleanser between courses. It is lovely served in a cocktail glass, garnished with a sprig of fresh mint.

Tips

If you are making this recipe for vegans, be sure to use sugar that has not been filtered through bone char.

If you like, substitute ½ of a jalapeño or ¼ of a habanero for the serrano pepper.

- Food processor or blender
- Ice cream maker

¾ cup	granulated sugar	175 mL
¾ cup	water	175 mL
1	piece (about 2 inches/5 cm long) cinnamon stick	1
2 lbs	cubed seedless watermelon (approx.)	1 kg
	Juice and finely grated zest of 1 lime	
4	sprigs fresh cilantro	4
½	serrano pepper (see Tips, left), chopped	½

1. In a small saucepan over medium heat, stir together sugar, water and cinnamon until sugar is dissolved. Remove from heat. Let cool until flavors are infused, about 30 minutes. Discard cinnamon stick.

2. In food processor fitted with the metal blade, in batches, purée together sugar syrup, watermelon, lime juice, lime zest, cilantro and serrano pepper until smooth. Transfer to a large bowl. Cover and refrigerate until well chilled, about 2 hours.

3. Transfer to ice cream maker and freeze according to manufacturer's instructions.

Spicy Orange Coconut Cashew Ice Cream

This ice cream is not only delicious but also nutritious and suitable for vegans. I love the combination of cashew and orange, melded with creamy coconut milk and finished with a hit of mildly pungent Aleppo pepper. What's not to enjoy?

Tip

Aleppo pepper is mildly hot and has a deep, fruity flavor that complements the other ingredients in this ice cream. However, if you don't have it, substitute an equal quantity of piment d'Espelette or ½ tsp (2 mL) cayenne pepper.

- Preheat oven to 350°F (180°C)
- Rimmed baking sheet
- Blender
- Ice cream maker

2	cans (each 14 oz/400 mL) full-fat coconut milk	2
1½ cups	coconut sugar	375 mL
2 tsp	orange extract	10 mL
½ tsp	ground sumac	2 mL
	Finely grated zest of 1 orange	

Spicy Cashews

2 cups	raw cashews	500 mL
1 tbsp	oil	15 mL
1 to 2 tbsp	Aleppo pepper (see Tip, left)	15 to 30 mL
½ tsp	salt	2 mL

1. *Spicy Cashews:* In a bowl, combine cashews, oil, Aleppo pepper to taste and salt. Toss well to coat. Spread evenly on baking sheet and roast in preheated oven, tossing frequently, until nicely browned, about 10 minutes. Transfer to a bowl and let cool. (You can make the cashews ahead and store them in an airtight container at room temperature for up to 5 days.)

2. In a large saucepan, combine coconut milk and coconut sugar. Bring to a simmer over medium heat. Simmer, stirring occasionally, until sugar is dissolved, about 2 minutes. Remove from heat. Stir in orange extract, sumac and orange zest.

3. Transfer coconut milk mixture and spicy cashews to blender, in batches, and purée until smooth. Transfer to a medium bowl. Cover and refrigerate until well chilled, at least 4 hours or overnight.

4. Stir coconut milk mixture well. Transfer to ice cream maker and freeze according to manufacturer's instructions.

Bean and Sweet Potato Ice Cream with Chile

This is an offbeat dessert rooted in the cuisine of the Dominican Republic, where this combination is often served as a kind of pudding. If you are looking for something different, this is it. "Unusual but also delicious" is how one friend describes it.

**MAKES ABOUT
4 CUPS (1 L)**

VEGETARIAN FRIENDLY

GLUTEN-FREE FRIENDLY

Tips

To make 1½ cups (375 mL) of cooked red beans: Soak and cook ¾ cup (175 mL) dried red beans, or measure out this quantity of canned beans after draining and thoroughly rinsing them.

Feel free to substitute 1 jalapeño or ¼ of a habanero pepper for the serrano.

- Food processor
- Ice cream maker

1½ cups	drained cooked red beans (see Tips, left), such as kidney or small red beans	375 mL
1½ cups	full-fat coconut milk	375 mL
¾ cup	mashed cooked sweet potato	175 mL
¾ cup	sweetened condensed milk	175 mL
¼ cup	freshly squeezed lime juice	60 mL
¼ cup	agave nectar	60 mL
1	serrano pepper (see Tips, left), coarsely chopped	1
2 tsp	vanilla extract	10 mL
½ tsp	ground cinnamon	2 mL
Pinch	salt	Pinch
½ cup	Thompson raisins	125 mL
¼ cup	dark rum	60 mL

1. In food processor fitted with the metal blade, combine beans, coconut milk, sweet potato, condensed milk, lime juice, agave nectar, serrano pepper, vanilla, cinnamon and salt. Purée until smooth. Transfer to a large bowl, cover and refrigerate until well chilled, at least 4 hours or overnight.

2. Meanwhile, in a small saucepan over low heat, bring raisins and rum to a simmer. Remove from heat. Let cool until flavors are infused, about 30 minutes. (You can let them stand longer if you like. Just cover and refrigerate until ready to use.)

3. Stir coconut milk mixture well. Transfer to ice cream maker and freeze according to manufacturers instructions, adding raisin mixture during last 5 minutes of churning.

Indian-Spiced Coconut Rice Pudding

This pudding is like a sweet, more nutritious version of risotto. Sweet brown rice is glutinous, so it releases starch and thickens the liquid around it; look for it in the natural foods aisle of the grocery store. Garam masala, a blend of savory and sweet spices, adds the perfect finish. The pudding is lovely warm, but chilled leftovers are also delicious.

MAKES 4 TO 6 SERVINGS

VEGAN FRIENDLY

GLUTEN-FREE FRIENDLY

Tips

Kashmiri chile powder, which is a beautiful shade of red, is slightly milder than cayenne. Look for it in Indian markets. This quantity provides a very pleasant hit of heat, which will likely inspire your guests to ask about the seasoning.

Garam masala is a blend of Indian spices, generally balanced between savory and sweet, and is usually not pungent. However, since it is a blend, formulas vary greatly. Add ½ tsp (2 mL) to start, then taste the pudding before adding any more.

The pudding will thicken as it stands or after chilling.

1	can (14 oz/400 mL) full-fat coconut milk	1
1½ cups	water or coconut water	375 mL
½ cup	coconut sugar	125 mL
6	green cardamom pods, crushed	6
1	piece (2 inches/5 cm long) cinnamon stick	1
⅛ tsp	Kashmiri chile powder or cayenne pepper (see Tips, left)	0.5 mL
1 cup	sweet brown rice	250 mL
½ cup	chopped unsalted pistachios	125 mL
½ to 1 tsp	garam masala (see Tips, left)	2 to 5 mL

1. In a large saucepan, combine coconut milk, water, coconut sugar, cardamom, cinnamon stick and chile powder. Bring to a boil. Stir in rice until well combined and return to a boil. Reduce heat to low and simmer, stirring often, until rice is tender and mixture is thickened, about 40 minutes.

2. Remove from heat. Stir in pistachios, and garam masala to taste. Let stand at room temperature for at least 30 minutes before serving. Serve warm or chilled (see Tips, left).

Chocolate Cookies with Spicy Pecans

These cookies are not just delicious but also gluten-free and made from mostly whole grain flours. Be sure not to overcook them; like brownies, they are best slightly underdone. The hot smoked paprika adds a delightful, unexpected flavor note.

MAKES ABOUT THIRTY-SIX 3-INCH (7.5 CM) COOKIES

VEGETARIAN FRIENDLY

GLUTEN-FREE FRIENDLY

Tip

If you use real raw cane sugar, it is quite dry and the quantity called for should be fine. Some brown raw sugars labeled Demerara are wetter and more like regular brown sugar; you may need a bit more than called for to complete the task.

- Preheat oven to 300°F (150°C), with racks positioned in top and bottom thirds
- 3 large baking sheets, lined with parchment paper
- Hand mixer

1 cup	brown rice flour	250 mL
½ cup	buckwheat flour	125 mL
½ cup	potato starch	125 mL
½ cup	unsweetened cocoa powder, sifted	125 mL
1 tsp	salt	5 mL
¾ tsp	xanthan gum	3 mL
½ tsp	baking soda	2 mL
¼ tsp	hot smoked paprika	1 mL
1¼ cups	granulated sugar	300 mL
1 cup	unsalted butter, softened	250 mL
2	eggs	2
1 tsp	vanilla extract	5 mL
6 oz	bittersweet chocolate chunks	175 g
½ cup	brown raw cane sugar, such as Demerara or panela (approx.), see Tip, left	125 mL

Spicy Pecans

1 cup	chopped pecans	250 mL
1 tbsp	butter, melted	15 mL
½ tsp	hot smoked paprika	2 mL

1. *Spicy Pecans:* In a small bowl, combine pecans, butter and paprika. Toss to coat. Spread evenly on 1 of the prepared baking sheets and bake in preheated oven, stirring occasionally, until lightly browned, about 15 minutes. Remove from oven and let cool.

Tips

Panela is a Latin American version of brown raw cane sugar. Look for it in Latin American markets.

The dough is quite sticky; refrigerating it before baking firms it up.

FYI: I use the term "gluten-free friendly" whenever I include prepared ingredients in a recipe that would otherwise be gluten-free. Manufacturers often add wheat products to prepared foods, so you need to check the label to ensure these products are actually gluten-free.

2. In a large bowl, whisk together rice flour, buckwheat flour, potato starch, cocoa, salt, xanthan gum, baking soda and paprika. Set aside.

3. In another large bowl, using hand mixer, beat granulated sugar with butter at medium speed until light and creamy. Add eggs, 1 at a time, beating each until incorporated before adding the next. Beat in vanilla. Gradually add flour mixture, beating just until blended. Stir in reserved pecans and chocolate chunks. Place dough on a large piece of plastic wrap, press into a disc and wrap tightly. Refrigerate until firm, about $1^1/_2$ hours.

4. Preheat oven to 350°F (180°C). Shape dough into 36 balls, each about $1^1/_2$ inches (4 cm) in diameter. Spread raw cane sugar on a plate and roll balls in sugar to evenly coat. Place on prepared baking sheets as completed, leaving wide spaces between balls. Flatten with a spatula or the palm of your hand, ensuring there is about 2 inches (5 cm) of space between flattened cookies.

5. Bake in top and bottom thirds of preheated oven, switching top and bottom pans and rotating them from front to back halfway through baking, until almost firm in the center, about 15 minutes.

6. Let cool on pans on wire racks for 5 minutes. Transfer cookies to wire racks and let cool completely. Store in an airtight container for up to 5 days.

Peppery Pecan Pie

Spiced pecans are a specialty of the American South, where the nuts grew wild before they were identified and cultivated. Pecan pie, a Southern classic, is another delightful result of this bounty. Why not combine the two? Most pecan pies contain copious amounts of corn syrup, which make them overwhelmingly sweet; here, I've substituted a mix of nutritious maple syrup, raw cane sugar and agave syrup. The large proportion of spicy pecans also helps balance the sweetness of the syrupy base.

MAKES 8 SERVINGS

VEGETARIAN FRIENDLY

Tips

If you don't have an ovenproof skillet, make the coating in a small saucepan and toss it with the pecans in a bowl. Spread them on a rimmed baking sheet and bake as directed.

If you're making this pie for vegetarians and using a prepared pie crust, make sure it doesn't contain lard. Some commercial ones do.

Blind baking the crust before adding the filling helps it brown nicely and protects against sogginess.

This is dessert, after all, so add a dollop of whipped cream or vanilla ice cream for the perfect finish.

- Preheat oven to 325°F (160°C)
- Large ovenproof skillet (see Tips, left)
- 10-inch (25 cm) deep-dish pie plate
- One 15-inch (38 cm) square of foil, buttered on 1 side
- Pie weights or dried beans
- Food processor

1	unbaked pie crust	1

Spiced Pecans

¼ cup	butter	60 mL
¼ cup	raw cane sugar, such as turbinado or Demerara	60 mL
1 tsp	sweet paprika	5 mL
1 tsp	ground cinnamon	5 mL
½ tsp	ground ginger	2 mL
¼ tsp	freshly grated nutmeg	1 mL
¼ tsp	cayenne pepper	1 mL
2 cups	pecan halves	500 mL

Filling

3	eggs	3
½ cup	raw cane sugar, such as turbinado or Demerara	125 mL
½ cup	maple syrup	125 mL
¼ cup	agave nectar	60 mL
2 tbsp	butter, melted	30 mL
2 tbsp	whiskey, preferably bourbon	30 mL
1 tsp	vanilla extract	5 mL
½ tsp	salt	2 mL

1. *Spiced Pecans:* In ovenproof skillet over medium heat, melt butter. Add sugar, paprika, cinnamon, ginger, nutmeg and cayenne and stir until blended. Add pecans and toss to coat well. Transfer skillet to preheated oven. Bake, stirring occasionally, until nuts are nicely browned, about 25 minutes. Transfer to a bowl and let cool.

2. Meanwhile, fit crust into pie plate and freeze for 15 minutes. Using the tines of a fork, prick bottom 4 or 5 times. Place prepared foil over crust, buttered side down, ensuring rim is covered. Spread pie weights over bottom. Bake in preheated oven for 7 minutes. Remove from oven and carefully remove foil and weights. Discard foil. Let crust cool.

3. *Filling:* Increase oven temperature to 350°F (180°C). In food processor fitted with the metal blade, combine eggs, sugar, maple syrup, agave nectar, butter, whiskey, vanilla and salt. Purée until smooth. Add spiced pecans and pulse until coarsely chopped, about 4 times. Spoon into cooled crust.

4. Bake in preheated oven until filling is set but center is still a bit jiggly, about 45 minutes. Let cool in pan on a wire rack. Serve warm or at room temperature.

Chile-Spiked Chocolate Pots

This is an updated version of classic French *pots de crème*. You won't taste the chile, but it adds appealing depth to the flavor of the chocolate. Served with a big dollop of sweetened whipped cream, this dessert is a welcome indulgence.

MAKES 4 TO 6 SERVINGS

VEGETARIAN FRIENDLY

GLUTEN-FREE FRIENDLY

Tips

This makes four ½-cup (125 mL) servings. If you prefer, you can make 6 smaller servings, reducing the cooking time slightly.

To make these chocolate pots in your slow cooker: You may need to play with cups or ramekins to find 6 that will fit comfortably in your slow cooker. Demitasse cups make a spectacular presentation. I also use taller French porcelain ramekins, which fit nicely in my largest (7-quart/7 L) slow cooker. Place them in the stoneware insert and pour in hot water to come halfway up the side of the cups. Cook on High for 1 hour, then cool and chill as directed. If your slow cooker will only accommodate 4 ramekins, they will obviously be fuller, so expect the cooking time to be closer to 2 hours.

- Fine-mesh sieve
- 4-cup (1 L) heatproof glass measuring cup or heatproof bowl with spout
- 4 to 6 tall ramekins or demitasse cups (see Tips, left)
- Large roasting pan

3½ oz	bittersweet chocolate, coarsely chopped	105 g
¾ cup	heavy or whipping (35%) cream	175 mL
¾ cup	whole milk	175 mL
¼ cup	granulated sugar	60 mL
2	eggs	2
1	egg yolk	1
2 tbsp	unsweetened cocoa powder	30 mL
1 tsp	Aleppo pepper, divided	5 mL
½ tsp	vanilla extract	2 mL
Pinch	salt	Pinch
	Sweetened whipped cream	

1. In a medium saucepan, combine chocolate and cream. Cook over low heat, stirring, until chocolate is melted. Add milk and sugar, whisking well to combine, and bring to a simmer. Remove from heat.

2. In a medium bowl, beat together eggs, egg yolk, cocoa powder, ½ tsp (2 mL) of the Aleppo pepper, vanilla and salt. Whisk in ½ cup (125 mL) of the chocolate mixture until well combined. Gradually whisk in remaining chocolate mixture until blended.

3. Preheat oven to 350°F (180°C). Place fine-mesh sieve over measuring cup and strain chocolate mixture into cup. Pour into ramekins and sprinkle remaining Aleppo pepper over top. Cover ramekins tightly with foil. Set in roasting pan and pour in enough boiling water to come halfway up the sides of the ramekins.

4. Place pan in preheated oven and immediately reduce the temperature to 325°F (160°C). Bake just until the centers of the custards quiver, about 25 minutes.

5. Remove ramekins from pan and let cool completely. Refrigerate until well chilled, about 4 hours. Serve each with a dollop of whipped cream.

Chocolate Brownies with Chipotle Cream Cheese Icing

There is nothing like sweetness tempered by a bit of heat. This recipe takes the classic chocolate treat and updates it with just a hint of smoky chipotle pepper.

**MAKES
16 BROWNIES**

VEGETARIAN FRIENDLY

Tips

The brownies will continue to cook and firm up after they are removed from the oven, so be sure to take them out while they are still a bit spongy in the center.

To make these brownies gluten-free: Substitute an equal quantity of teff flour combined with ¼ tsp (1 mL) xanthan gum for the all-purpose flour.

- Preheat oven to 350°F (180°C)
- 8-inch (20 cm) square metal baking pan, greased

8 oz	bittersweet chocolate, chopped	250 g
¼ cup	butter	60 mL
3	eggs	3
1 cup	granulated sugar	250 mL
1 tsp	vanilla extract	5 mL
¾ cup	all-purpose flour	175 mL
1 tbsp	instant espresso powder	15 mL
1 tsp	baking powder	5 mL
1 cup	chopped pecans	250 mL

Icing

4 oz	cream cheese, softened	125 g
4 oz	bittersweet chocolate, melted	125 g
1 tsp	vanilla extract	5 mL
½ tsp	chipotle chile powder	2 mL
1½ cups	confectioner's (icing) sugar, sifted	375 mL
	Cream (optional)	

1. In a saucepan over very low heat, melt chocolate with butter, stirring constantly until smooth. Remove from heat.

2. In a large bowl, beat together eggs, sugar and vanilla just until blended. Stir in chocolate mixture. Gradually stir in flour, espresso powder and baking powder until well combined. Stir in pecans. Spread evenly in prepared pan.

3. Bake in preheated oven until almost set and still slightly spongy in center (see Tips, left), about 25 minutes. Let cool completely in pan on a wire rack. When cool, run a knife around the edge of the pan to release brownies, then invert onto a cake plate.

4. *Icing:* Meanwhile, in a medium bowl, beat together cream cheese, chocolate, vanilla and chile powder until smooth. Beat in sugar until smooth and spreadable. If icing is too stiff, add cream (if using), 1 tbsp (15 mL) at a time, until spreadable. Ice cooled brownies and cut into squares.

Coconut Macaroons with Spicy Toasted Almonds

The chile adds a very pleasant but mild hint of intriguing spice to these tasty fruit, nut and coconut cookies. They make a lovely after-dinner treat and an irresistible snack.

MAKES 16 COOKIES

VEGETARIAN FRIENDLY

Tip

If you prefer, substitute 2 tsp (10 mL) Aleppo pepper for the paprika and cayenne in the spicy toasted almonds.

- Preheat oven to 350°F (180°C), with racks positioned in top and bottom thirds
- 2 baking sheets, lined with parchment paper

3 cups	shredded or desiccated coconut	750 mL
¾ cup	granulated sugar	175 mL
¼ cup	all-purpose flour	60 mL
4	egg whites	4
1 tsp	almond extract	5 mL
½ cup	dried cherries, coarsely chopped	125 mL

Spicy Toasted Almonds

1 cup	raw almonds, coarsely chopped	250 mL
1 tsp	oil	5 mL
1 tbsp	granulated sugar	15 mL
2 tsp	sweet paprika	10 mL
⅛ tsp	cayenne pepper	0.5 mL
Pinch	salt	Pinch

1. *Spicy Toasted Almonds:* Spread almonds on a baking sheet. Toast in preheated oven until browned, about 8 minutes. Transfer to a bowl. Add oil and toss to coat.

2. Meanwhile, in a small bowl, stir together sugar, paprika, cayenne and salt. Add to toasted almonds and toss well to coat. Set aside.

3. In a medium bowl, stir together coconut, sugar and flour. Set aside.

4. In a large bowl, whisk egg whites with almond extract until foamy. Stir in coconut mixture, spiced almonds and cherries until dry ingredients are moistened.

5. Using about 2 tbsp (30 mL) per cookie, drop dough onto prepared baking sheets, ensuring there is about 2 inches (5 cm) of space between each cookie. Bake in top and bottom thirds of preheated oven, switching top and bottom pans and rotating them from front to back halfway through baking, until golden, about 20 minutes.

6. Let cool completely on pans on wire racks.

Spicy Peanut Brittle

I've always enjoyed peanut brittle, which I imagined originated in the Deep South. I was surprised to discover that at least two Asian countries—Korea and China—have their own versions, so I decided to create a "fusion" version of this treat.

MAKES 2 LBS (1 KG)

VEGETARIAN FRIENDLY

GLUTEN-FREE FRIENDLY

Tips

Roast the peanut mix on an unprepared baking sheet. Line the second baking sheet with parchment paper sprayed with cooking oil and use it for the sugary brittle mixture.

If you have two nonstick silicone mats (called Silpats), you can skip the prepared baking sheet. Place the mats, overlapping, on the counter to create a large nonstick surface and pour the sugar mixture onto it. Using silicone mats significantly reduces the challenges associated with making brittle because nothing sticks to them.

Making candy requires patience. Expect the entire process to take at least half an hour.

As soon as you pour the brittle mixture, as it begins to harden, use a spatula to lift and aerate it. This helps prevent sticking.

The candy hardens quickly and you want it to be as even as possible. To spread it out quickly, you can place a piece of parchment paper over top of the warm brittle and use a rolling pin to flatten it.

- Preheat oven to 400°F (200°C)
- Candy/deep-fry thermometer (see Tips, opposite)
- 2 large rimmed baking sheets (see Tips, left)

2 cups	granulated sugar	500 mL
1 cup	light corn syrup	250 mL
½ cup	water	125 mL
3 tbsp	butter	45 mL
2 tsp	baking soda	10 mL
¾ tsp	vanilla extract	3 mL
½ tsp	salt	2 mL

Spicy Nuts and Seeds

1 cup	unsalted raw peanuts	250 mL
1 cup	raw pumpkin seeds (pepitas)	250 mL
1 tbsp	olive oil	15 mL
1 tsp	salt	5 mL
1 tsp	Korean red pepper powder (or ½ tsp/2 mL cayenne pepper)	5 mL

1. *Spicy Nuts and Seeds:* In a bowl, combine peanuts, pumpkin seeds, oil, salt and red pepper powder. Toss well. Spread evenly on unprepared baking sheet and roast in preheated oven, tossing frequently, until nicely browned, about 8 minutes. Let cool.

2. Meanwhile, in a large saucepan over medium heat, bring sugar, corn syrup and water to a boil. Cook, stirring, until sugar is dissolved. Reduce heat to low and cook, without stirring, until mixture reaches the soft-crack stage, or when thermometer registers 280°F (138°C).

3. Stir in spicy nuts and seeds. Cook, stirring often, until mixture reaches the hard-crack stage, or when thermometer registers 300°F (149°C). Remove from heat. Stir in butter, baking soda, vanilla and salt until well combined.

4. Quickly pour mixture onto prepared baking sheet. Using a greased spatula, spread as thinly as possible. Once the brittle is cool enough to handle, using your hands, pull and stretch it so that it's as thin as possible. Let cool completely. Break into pieces.

Chile-Spiked Salted Chocolate Caramels

Soft, chewy caramels remind me of the simple pleasures of being a kid. This version—designed for grown-ups—includes bittersweet chocolate and just a hint of chile and sea salt. Yum!

MAKES ABOUT 2½ LBS (1.25 KG)

VEGETARIAN FRIENDLY

GLUTEN-FREE FRIENDLY

Tips

Use a candy/deep-fry thermometer or a high-performance instant-read thermometer, such as a Thermapen, to ensure the temperature of your sugar mixture is accurate.

Make sure you allow enough time for your caramels to cool completely before cutting them. Twenty-four hours is ideal.

Before cutting the caramels, wipe a paper towel soaked in cooking oil over the edge of your knife. This will keep them from sticking to the blade. Repeat as necessary between cuts.

- Candy/deep-fry thermometer (see Tips, left)
- 8-inch (20 cm) square glass baking dish, lined with parchment paper

¾ cup	butter	175 mL
1½ cups	dark brown raw cane sugar, such as turbinado	375 mL
¾ cup	light corn syrup	175 mL
1	can (14 oz or 300 mL) sweetened condensed milk	1
3 oz	bittersweet chocolate, broken into small pieces	90 g
¼ to ½ tsp	cayenne pepper	1 to 2 mL
1 tsp	vanilla extract	5 mL
½ tsp	chocolate extract	2 mL
2 tsp	coarse sea salt	10 mL

1. In a large saucepan over medium heat, melt butter. Add sugar and corn syrup and cook, stirring, until sugar is dissolved. Stir in condensed milk, chocolate, and cayenne to taste. Cook, stirring often, until mixture reaches the firm-ball stage, or when thermometer registers 246°F (119°C), about 40 minutes.

2. Remove from heat. Stir in vanilla and chocolate extracts. Pour into prepared baking dish. Let cool slightly, then sprinkle salt evenly over top.

3. Let cool completely, at least overnight or for up to 24 hours. Once cooled, using the parchment paper as handles, lift candy out of the pan. Cut into squares. Wrap individually in plastic wrap.

Selected Resources

Adams, Paul. "FYI: What is the Hottest Pepper in the World?" Popsci.com. Available online at www.popsci.com/science/article/2011-06/fyi-what-hottest-pepper-world.

Albala, Ken, ed. *Food Cultures of the World Encyclopedia.* 4 vols. Santa Barbara, CA: Greenwood, 2011.

Andrews, Colman. *The Country Cooking of Italy.* San Francisco: Chronicle Books, 2011.

Andrews, Jean. *Peppers: The Domesticated Capsicums.* Austin: University of Texas Press, 1984.

———. *The Pepper Trail: History & Recipes from Around the World.* Denton: University of North Texas Press, 1999.

Billing, Jennifer, and Paul W. Sherman. "Antimicrobial Functions of Spices: Why Some Like It Hot." *The Quarterly Review of Biology* 73 (March 1998): 3–49.

Bosland, Paul W. "Capsicums: Innovative Uses of an Ancient Crop." *Progress in New Crops, Proceedings of the Third National Symposium.* Available online at www.hort.purdue.edu/newcrop/proceedings1996/V3-479.html.

Brissenden, Rosemary. *South East Asian Food.* London: Penguin Books, 1972.

Capsicum Pepper Varieties and Classification. New Mexico State University Library: College of Agriculture and Home Economics, Circular 530 (1990). Available online at http://contentdm.nmsu.edu/cdm/ref/collection/AgCircs/id/12518.

Collins, Lauren. "Fire-Eaters: The Search for the Hottest Chili." *The New Yorker:* November 4, 2013. Available online at www.newyorker.com/magazine/2013/11/04/fire-eaters.

Cost, Bruce. *Asian Ingredients: A Guide to the Foodstuffs of China, Japan, Korea, Thailand and Vietnam.* New York: Quill, 2000.

David, Elizabeth. *Spices, Salt and Aromatics in the English Kitchen.* London: Penguin Books, 1971.

Davidson, Alan. *The Oxford Companion to Food.* Oxford: Oxford University Press, 1999.

der Haroutunian, Arto. *North African Cookery.* London: Grub Street, 2009.

DeWitt, Dave. *The Chile Pepper Encyclopedia: Everything You'll Ever Need to Know About Hot Peppers, with More than 100 Recipes.* New York: William Morrow, 1999.

DeWitt, Dave, and Paul W. Bosland. *The Complete Chile Pepper Book: A Gardener's Guide to Choosing, Growing, Preserving and Cooking.* Portland: Timber Press, 2009.

Dunlop, Fuchsia. *Land of Plenty: Authentic Sichuan Recipes Personally Gathered in the Chinese Province of Sichuan.* New York: W. W. Norton & Company, 2003.

———. *Revolutionary Chinese Cookbook: Recipes from Hunan Province.* New York: W. W. Norton & Company, 2007.

Erdmann, Jeanne. "Brendan Borrell Jets to Bolivia for a Hot Story on Chili Peppers." Theopennotebook.com. Available online at www.theopennotebook.com/2010/11/24/brendan-borrell-chili-peppers/#.

Ezekiel, Jolayemi Adebayo Taiwo, and Ojewole John Akanni Oluwole. "Effects of Capsaicin on Coagulation: Will This Be the New Blood Thinner." *Clinical Medicine Research* 3 (September 2014): 145–149.

Friese, Kurt Michael, Kraig Kraft and Gary Paul Nabhan. *Chasing Chiles: Hot Spots Along the Pepper Trail.* White River Junction, VT: Chelsea Green Publishing, 2011.

Hachisu, Nancy Singleton. *Japanese Farm Food.* Kansas City, MO: Andrews McMeel, 2012.

Hemphill, Ian, with recipes by Kate Hemphill. *The Spice & Herb Bible.* 3rd ed. Toronto: Robert Rose, 2014.

Hepinstall, Hi Soo Shin. *Growing Up in a Korean Kitchen: A Cookbook.* Berkeley, CA: Ten Speed Press, 2001.

Hess, John L., and Karen Hess. *The Taste of America.* New York: Viking Press, 1977.

Hess, Karen, and Robert M. Weir. *The Carolina Rice Kitchen: The African Connection.* Columbia, SC: University of South Carolina Press, 1998.

Kennedy, Diana. *The Cuisines of Mexico.* New York: Harper & Row, 1972.

———. *From My Mexican Kitchen: Techniques and Ingredients.* New York: Clarkson Potter, 2003.

Kochilas, Diane. *The Glorious Foods of Greece.* New York: William Morrow, 2001.

Kremer, William. "Is the Chilli Pepper Friend or Foe?" *BBC World Service Magazine:* October 5, 2015. Available online at www.bbc.com/news/magazine-34411492.

Lv, Jun, et al. "Consumption of Spicy Foods and Total and Cause Specific Mortality: Population Based Cohort Study." *The BMJ* 2015; 351: h3942.

McKendry, Maxime. *The Seven Centuries Cookbook: From Richard II to Elizabeth II.* New York: McGraw-Hill, 1973.

Miller, Mark, and John Harrisson. *The Great Chile Book.* Berkeley, CA: Ten Speed Press, 1991.

Naj, Amal. *Peppers: A Story of Hot Pursuits.* New York: Alfred A. Knopf, 1992.

"The Official State Food of Texas: Chili." Amaranthpublishing.com. Available online at www.amaranthpublishing.com/Chili.htm.

Omolo, Morrine A., et al. "Antimicrobial Properties of Chili Peppers." *Journal of Infectious Diseases and Therapy* 2 (June 2014): 145.

Oseland, James. *Cradle of Flavor: Home Cooking from the Spice Islands of Indonesia, Malaysia and Singapore.* New York: W.W. Norton, 2006.

Presilla, Maricel E. *Gran Cocina Latina: The Food of Latin America.* New York: W. W. Norton & Company, 2012.

Prudhomme, Paul. *The Prudhomme Family Cookbook: Old-Time Louisiana Recipes.* New York: William Morrow, 1987.

Roden, Claudia. *The New Book of Middle Eastern Food.* London: Penguin Books, 1985.

———. *The Book of Jewish Food: An Odyssey from Samarkand to New York.* New York: Alfred A. Knopf, 1997.

———. *The Food of Spain.* New York: Ecco, 2011.

Rolland, Jacques L., and Carol Sherman, with other contributors. *The Food Encyclopedia: Over 8,000 Ingredients, Tools, Techniques and People.* Toronto: Robert Rose, 2006.

Schweid, Richard. *Hot Peppers: Cajuns and Capsicum in New Iberia, Louisiana.* Berkeley, CA: Ten Speed Press, 1989.

Shaida, Margaret. *The Legendary Cuisine of Persia.* New York: Interlink Books, 2002.

Smith, Paul G., and Charles B. Heiser, Jr. "Taxonomic and Genetic Studies on the Cultivated Peppers, Capsicum annuum L. and C. frutescens L." *American Journal of Botany* 38, no. 5 (1951): 362–368.

Stradley, Linda. "History of Chili, Chili con Carne." Whatscookingamerica.net. Available online at http://whatscookingamerica.net/History/Chili/ChiliHistory.htm.

Tannahill, Reay. *Food in History.* London: Eyre Methuen, 1973.

Taylor, John Martin. *Hoppin' John's Lowcountry Cooking: Recipes and Ruminations from Charleston & the Carolina Coastal Plain.* New York: Bantam Books, 1992.

Thiam, Pierre, and Jennifer Sit. *Senegal: Modern Senegalese Recipes from the Source to the Bowl.* New York: Lake Isle Press, 2015.

Thompson, Andrea. "Self-Defense: Why Chili Peppers Pack Heat." Livescience.com. Available online at www.livescience.com/2774-defense-chili-peppers-pack-heat.html.

Thompson, David. *Thai Food.* Berkeley, CA: Ten Speed Press, 2002.

Villas, James. *The Glory of Southern Cooking: Recipes for the Best Beer-Battered Fried Chicken, Cracklin' Biscuits, Carolina Pulled Pork, Fried Okra, Kentucky Cheese Pudding, Hummingbird Cake and 375 Other Delectable Dishes.* Hoboken, NJ: John Wiley and Sons, 2007.

von Bremzen, Anya. *The New Spanish Table.* New York: Workman Publishing, 2005.

Wolfert, Paula. *Couscous and Other Good Food from Morocco.* New York: Quill, 2001.

Yong, Ed. Blog. "Why Aren't All Chillies Hot?" Discovermagazine.com. Available online at http://blogs.discovermagazine.com/notrocketscience/2011/12/20/why-arent-all-chillies-hot/#.VzDErdfbkgs.

Zivkovic, Bora. Blog. "Hot Peppers—Why Are They Hot?" Scientificamerican.com. Available online at http://blogs.scientificamerican.com/a-blog-around-the-clock/hot-peppers-why-are-they-hot/.

Library and Archives Canada Cataloguing in Publication

Finlayson, Judith, author
    The chile pepper bible : from sweet to fiery & everything in between / Judith Finlayson.

Includes index.
ISBN 978-0-7788-0550-2 (paperback)

    1. Hot peppers. 2. Peppers. 3. Cooking (Hot peppers). 4. Cooking (Peppers). 5. Cookbooks. I. Title.

TX803.P46F56 2016   641.6'384   C2016-904291-X

Index